CALIFORNIA CONDORS IN THE 21ST CENTURY

Frontispiece. Adult female condor 126 in flight over the Paria Plateau, Arizona (photo: Chris Parish). In 2005, this 12-year-old condor successfully reared one of only six wild-bred young to fledge by the end of 2006 in the U.S. Recovery Program.

SERIES IN ORNITHOLOGY, NO. 2

CALIFORNIA CONDORS IN THE 21ST CENTURY

EDITED BY

ALLAN MEE AND LINNEA S. HALL

PUBLISHED BY

AND

NUTTALL ORNITHOLOGICAL CLUB
CAMBRIDGE, MASSACHUSETTS

THE AMERICAN
ORNITHOLOGISTS' UNION
WASHINGTON, D.C.

2007

SERIES IN ORNITHOLOGY

Editor: Douglas Causey

Vice Provost for Research and Graduate Studies
University of Alaska Anchorage
3211 Providence Drive
Anchorage, Alaska 99508

Acquisitions Editor: John Faaborg

Project Manager: Mark C. Penrose
Managing Editor: Richard D. Earles

AOU Publications Office
622 Science Engineering
Department of Biological Sciences
University of Arkansas
Fayetteville, Arkansas 72701

The *Series in Ornithology* is published by the Nuttall Ornithological Club and the American Ornithologists' Union. All material in this monograph may be copied for noncommercial purposes of educational or scientific advancement without need to seek permission.

Editors of this book: Allan Mee and Linnea S. Hall

Library of Congress Control Number 2007928963

Printed by Cadmus Communications, Lancaster, PA 17601

Issued 30 June 2007

Series in Ornithology, No. 2, viii + 296 pp.

ISBN: 978-0-943610-71-1 (hard cover)
ISBN: 978-0-943610-74-0 (soft cover)

Table of Contents

From the Editors

This symposium volume, focused on current knowledge of California Condors, is the second in what we expect will be a long-running series presenting some of the best in ornithological literature by combining the resources of the Nuttall Ornithological Club (NOC) and the American Ornithologists' Union (AOU).

The NOC is the oldest of the existing bird clubs, having started in the Boston area in 1873. It published quarterly "Bulletins" from 1876 through 1883, then started a series of "Memoirs" in 1886, with the most recent of those released in 2000. The NOC's "Publications" series started in 1957, and since then it has produced 28 book-length treatments of a variety of ornithological topics, most of which are still available from its website (www.mcz.harvard.edu/Publications/nuttall.htm).

Although it did not begin until 1883, the AOU has grown to become the largest ornithological society in the world, with over 3,500 members. It has produced a variety of publications during its history, with the most important being its quarterly journal *The Auk*. During the period 1964 through 2003, the AOU's series entitled *Ornithological Monographs* produced book-length treatments on varied ornithological topics, many of which are still available on the AOU website (www.aou.org). Starting in 2004, the *Ornithological Monographs* series shifted to smaller (usually less than 100 printed pages) but more regular (3 or 4 times a year) coverage of ornithological research and conservation. As such, the development of this cooperative *Series in Ornithology* provides AOU members an outlet for ornithological research too large to fit into the new version of the monographs series.

Authors with manuscripts that they would like to have us consider for this new series are encouraged to contact the AOU editor, John Faaborg, at faaborgj@missouri.edu or the NOC editor, Douglas Causey, at dcausey@uaa.alaska.edu. We can discuss the possibilities with regard to having your work published as part of this series and describe the process involved in getting from first draft to final product. We hope you enjoy this in-depth review of condor biology and we hope you find the *Series in Ornithology* a regular part of your reading future.

John Faaborg
Douglas Causey

INTRODUCTION

California Condors in the 21st Century

Linnea S. Hall[1] and Allan Mee[2]

ABSTRACT.—The collection of papers in this volume resulted from a symposium entitled "Endangered species recovery: The California Condor as a model," held at the American Ornithologists' Union Annual Meeting in 2005. The primary aim of the symposium was to provide a forum for California Condor (*Gymnogyps californianus*) biologists and researchers to exchange ideas, present up-to-date research results on condor populations, and review the status of the recovery program in captivity and in the wild. The papers presented here represent most (12 of 16) of those presented at the symposium plus an additional paper on the Big Sur, California, population, and another on recommendations for the future. The volume is divided into five sections providing (i) a historical overview, (ii) the current status of populations in Arizona, (iii) the status of populations in California, (iv) an evaluation of captive rearing methods, and (v) recommendations for future research and recovery. A primary focus of much of the research summarized in this volume is the extent of lead toxicity in condor populations and its deleterious effects on current survivorship and chances for recovery. The recommendations chapter provides strong suggestions for improving the future success of the recovery program, and we hope that these can be implemented immediately to help prevent further losses of California Condors in the wild.

> But for me the heart of California lies in the Condor country. And for me the heart of mystery, of wonder, and of desire lies with the California Condor, that majestic and almost legendary figure, which still haunts the fastnesses of our lessening wilderness. (Dawson 1923)

The California Condor (*Gymnogyps californianus*), one of only two extant New World condor species, is the largest avian scavenger in North

[1]*Western Foundation of Vertebrate Zoology, 439 Calle San Pablo, Camarillo, California 93012, USA. E-mail: linnea@wfvz.org*
[2]*CRES, Zoological Society of San Diego, 15600 San Pasqual Valley Road, Escondido, California 92027, USA.*

America and the focus of intensive recovery efforts. Although being formally protected by law in California since 1885 (Wilbur 1978) and one of the first species to be listed under the U.S. Endangered Species Act, California Condors declined precipitously during the 20th century, necessitating efforts to save the species from extinction. In 1987, with the capture of the last wild individual and its removal to captivity to join an expanding captive-breeding program, the California Condor gained the dubious distinction of being extinct in the wild. For the first time in millennia the skies of western North America were completely devoid of condors, a group of scavengers once represented by at least three *Gymnogyps* species and the even larger *Teratornis* species in prehistoric times (Miller 1911, Emslie 1988).

Condor recovery efforts in the 1980s were often mired in controversy (see for example Phillips 1983, Snyder and Snyder 2000). More recent recovery efforts aimed at reintroduction of the species into its former range have similarly been attended by frequent controversy as populations have expanded and encountered the same mortality factors responsible for the decline of the historical population, or new problems have emerged to threaten the success of the recovery (see Meretsky et al. 2000, Snyder and Snyder 2000). However, although research results from studies of the captive population have been published (e.g., Kuehler and Witman 1988, Cox et al. 1993, Geyer et al. 1993, Hartt et al. 1994, Harvey et al. 1996), for the most part few data or results from the managed condor populations in Arizona, California, and Mexico have been presented recently by biologists within the recovery program (but see Cade 2004, Mee 2004). Thus, it has been difficult to evaluate the effects of current recovery efforts. Although previous research has given us valuable insights into the biology of condors in the wild (e.g., Finley 1908; Koford 1953; Snyder and Snyder 1989, 2000), and popular science books and articles have brought condors into the public eye (e.g., Smith and Easton 1964, Meyer 1983, Kiff 1990, Arnold 1993), questions about the management and scientific direction of the condor recovery program persist.

With this in mind, on 27 August 2005, a symposium on "Endangered Species Recovery: the California Condor as a Model" was held at the Annual Meeting of the American Ornithologists' Union on the campus of the University of California at Santa Barbara, organized and chaired by AM. The symposium consisted of 16 oral papers presented on the history and current status of the recovery effort for California Condors. The present volume represents the majority of the papers presented at August's symposium (12 of the original 16 papers), plus two additional papers—one on the Big Sur, California, population, and one on recommendations for the future. All of the manuscripts include updated statistics on wild and zoo populations of condors through the end of the year 2005.

OVERVIEW OF CHAPTERS

This volume is divided into five sections:
I. Historical overview of condor declines and genetics (2 papers)
II. Current status of the population in Arizona (4 papers)
III. Current status of the population in California (4 papers)
IV. Evaluations of modifications to captive rearing practices (3 papers)
V. Recommendations for the future (1 paper)

The authors of the papers included in this volume have many years of collective experience working with California Condors in the wild and in captivity. In the first section, for example, N. F. R. Snyder (Chapter 1) summarizes the history of limiting factors affecting condor populations, and concludes that although a great variety of negative factors have impacted condors over the years, the most important current problem for the species is mortality due to lead poisoning from the ingestion of lead bullet fragments in hunter-killed carcasses and their remains.

M. S. Adams and F. X. Villablanca (Chapter 2) provide an updated analysis of condor genetics. They confirm low levels of genetic diversity in the captive population, but question whether the reduced diversity is a consequence of the 20th century bottleneck—when the entire population crashed to a low of 22 individuals in 1982—or if diversity has been historically low.

In Section II (Current status of the population in Arizona), C. P. Woods et al. (Chapter 3) report that from 1996 to 2005, condor survival rates in the Arizona population were only ~80% for birds newly released into the wild, but were 98% for those surviving five years or longer. Lead poisoning from ingested shotgun pellets and bullet fragments was the greatest cause of condor fatalities for birds after their first 90 days free-flying, although many surviving condors were also treated with chelation therapy at least once to reduce elevated blood-lead levels. They recommend that successful stability of the Arizona population will require the reduction or elimination of lead in the condors' food supply. These authors also summarize condor breeding attempts in Arizona since 2001 and conclude that breeding success to date (45%) was similar to the recent wild historical population and that the success of pairs has tended to improve over time.

Another research team in Arizona, headed by W. G. Hunt et al. (Chapter 4), analyzed the movements of condors and other observations, and similarly conclude that the hypothesis of bullet fragments in hunter-killed deer carrion as the primary cause of elevated blood-lead levels in condors is supported by several different lines of evidence, including a recent study showing that the remains of most rifle-killed deer contain numerous lead fragments, that condor blood-lead levels increase with the increased use of deer hunting areas on the Kaibab Plateau, and that blood-lead levels and condor visitation to the Kaibab Plateau spike during and just after deer hunting season. C. N. Parish et al. (Chapter 5) also present blood-lead evidence demonstrating that lead poisoning was the most frequently diagnosed cause of death among free-flying California Condors in Arizona during 1996–2005 and that lead may also have caused additional undiagnosed fatalities. Overall findings indicate that condors in northern Arizona frequently ingest lead, and suggest that rifle- and shotgun-killed animals are an important source of toxic exposure for condors.

To address the impacts of lead ammunition on condors, K. Sullivan et al. (Chapter 6) present an overview of a program started in Arizona to reduce lead exposure from spent lead ammunition in animal carcasses and gut piles. Using public education about condor foraging ecology and conservation efforts, and encouraging voluntary use of non-lead ammunition—which has been supported by sportsmen's groups and government agencies—they report encouraging results showing that 93% of survey respondents who harvested deer in Arizona in 2005 said that non-lead ammunition provided by the Arizona Game and Fish Department performed the same as, or better than, lead ammunition. In addition, 97% of the respondents who tested the non-lead ammunition stated its accuracy was average to excellent, and 72% of the respondents said they would recommend non-lead ammunition to other hunters.

In Section III (Current status of the population in California) J. Grantham (Chapter 7) overviews the successes and failures in the reintroduced southern California condor population, identifying shooting, ingestion of trash by young birds, food contaminants, poor nest success and breeding effort, nutritional issues resulting from a single food provisioning source, and innate tameness as the serious issues needing to be addressed for this population. M. Hall et al. (Chapter 8) analyzed data from 44 individual condors in the southern California population which were regularly assessed for blood-lead levels. From 1992 to 2005, 52% of the released condors (primarily sub-adults) were exposed to lead on multiple occasions, with the highest blood-lead levels seen during deer hunting seasons. The authors conclude that in the southern California population, lead poisoning is the most significant limiting factor for free-flying condors.

A. Mee et al. (Chapter 9) report on their study of condors breeding in southern California from 2002–2005. Overall, they observed extremely low fledging success (8%), with nest failure primarily due to the ingestion of trash and other items. In addition, they observed lower feeding rates of nestlings by adult condors and more prolonged periods of food deprivation than at historical nests. They suggest that the provisioning of food at a single site—implemented primarily to keep condors from foraging on hunter-killed carcasses in the wild—is likely having deleterious effects on chick mortality. They recommend strategies including the closing and cleaning up of trash sites, and altering current management to reduce the dependence of condors on a single provisioning site. However, without the removal of the threat of lead poisoning from hunter-killed carcasses, they caution that this strategy may result in increased exposure of condors to lead as individuals forage more widely and encounter contaminated food. K. J. Sorenson and L. J. Burnett (Chapter 10) summarize the results from blood tests of 33 free-flying condors in Big Sur, California, between 1998 and 2006. Similar to the findings of M. Hall et al. in this volume, 64% of condors tested were exposed at least once to lead, and 27% were exposed on two or more occasions. Most notably, exposures were highest during the months of September and October, again during the fall deer-hunting season.

In Section IV (Evaluations of modifications to captive rearing practices), the zoo programs report on their recent activities. A. T. Bukowinski et al. (Chapter 11) summarize their preliminary assessment of a mentoring program that was implemented at the San Diego Wild Animal Park, in California, to address concerns that young, puppet-reared condors exhibited unacceptable levels of maladaptive behavior when released to the wild. They report that a condor cohort observed pre- and post-release exhibited a consistent dominance hierarchy before and after release, and that the lowest ranking bird remained solitary even after release. Their findings indicate that assessment of social behavior prior to release can serve as a good predictor of initial post-release activity.

M. Clark et al. (Chapter 12) report on modifications made to the condor chick-rearing program at the Los Angeles Zoo, in California. Initiated in 2000, the modifications were implemented to more closely mimic the social experience of parent-reared chicks. Modifications included rearing nestlings singly instead of in cohorts, using less traumatic handling, using rearing puppets more assertively and realistically, using mentors in fledging pens, and using greater isolation from humans throughout the captive phase. Observations indicated that chicks reared with the modified methods behaved more similarly to captive, parent-reared young than did chicks produced using original methods. One consistent difference exhibited by young condors was their intense negative reaction to the presence of people in their pens, representing a distinct behavioral improvement over previous captive-reared condors.

M. P. Wallace et al. (Chapter 13) report on a preliminary evaluation of the effects of the modifications to the puppet rearing technique discussed in Chapter 11, by monitoring the post-release behavior of California Condors in the Sierra San Pedro Mártir region of Northern Baja California, Mexico. Preliminary results with condors over a three-year period indicate that the rearing modifications may have had a positive effect on the behavior of released condors, based on observations that condors in Baja exhibited activities more restricted to remote areas and also showed an increased wariness of humans.

Finally, in Section V (Recommendations for the future), A. Mee and N. F. R. Snyder (Chapter 14) present a synopsis of the major conservation problems currently facing condor populations in the wild, namely, achieving adequate survival rates, adequate reproduction, and normal behavior. In this highly useful paper, they not only present the conservation dilemmas, but also propose multiple solutions to these problems. The authors also provide a list of seven major recommendations that should steer the course of condor research and management over the next decade. The highest priority item is the need for the removal of the lead threat from the range of the California Condor, since adequate survival rates and the achievement of species-typical behaviors in wild condors are ultimately dependent on this. Thus, they advocate the immediate and complete replacement of lead ammunitions with non-toxic ammunition alternatives. Fortunately, efforts in Arizona to test the effectiveness of non-lead ammunition for hunting and the attractiveness of non-lead ammunition to hunters seem to indicate that it might be possible to enact such policies in Arizona and California.

SUMMARY

Based on the findings presented in these manuscripts, one can summarize the current status of California Condors as follows: wild and zoo population numbers are increasing annually, but the prognosis currently is not good for attaining population viability in the wild. The southern California population is experiencing a crisis in reproduction, and the population may never be viable given the tremendous hurdles of overcoming lead-poisoning within its foraging range, and the ingestion of trash by young condors. The central California population has yet to produce any young in the wild, but human pressures are fewer than in southern California, so the population's viability is as yet impossible to assess. The Arizona population continues to produce young, but lead poisoning from hunter-killed carcasses on the Kaibab Plateau presents a serious challenge to the long-term viability of the population. The Baja, Mexico, population's success remains to be seen: observations indicate that low human presence, coupled with changes in the rearing techniques of released birds and relatively minor use of lead ammunition in the population's range, may be a recipe for long-term success.

Although the challenges still facing the restoration of the California Condor to the wild are serious and difficult to surmount, we remain hopeful that a coordinated effort can eventually work to achieve full recovery of this magnificent species. This present volume, representing the current state of our knowledge about the California Condor in the first years of the

21st century, should help with that endeavor, as it represents the majority of the projects being conducted on condors in their historic range. The authors have identified many critical areas for research, management, and public policy to make an impact on the recovery of the species. We hope that this publication will catalyze the implementation of the many recommendations presented by the authors, because the ultimate viability of condor populations depends on the immediate initiation of such recommendations.

LITERATURE CITED

ARNOLD, C. 1993. On the Brink of Extinction: The California Condor. Gulliver Books, Harcourt Brace Jovanovich, San Diego, CA.

CADE, T. J., S. A. H. OSBORN, W. G. HUNT, AND C. P. WOODS. 2004. Commentary on released California Condors *Gymnogyps californianus* in Arizona. Pages 11–25 *in* Raptors Worldwide: Proceedings of VI World Conference on Birds of Prey and Owls (R. D. Chancellor and B.-U. Meyburg, Eds.). World Working Group on Birds of Prey and Owls/MME-Birdlife, Hungary.

COX, C. R., V. I. GOLDSMITH, AND H. R. ENGELHARDT. 1993. Pair formation in California Condors. American Zoologist 33:126–138.

DAWSON, W. L. 1923. The Birds of California. South Moulton Company, San Diego, CA.

EMSLIE, S. D. 1988. The fossil history and phylogenetic relationships of condors (Ciconiiformes: Vulturidae) in the New World. Journal of Vertebrate Paleontology 8:212–228.

FINLEY, W. L. 1908. Life history of the California Condor III: home life of the condor. Condor 10:59–65.

GEYER, C. J., O. A. RYDER, L. G. CHEMNICK, AND E. A. THOMPSON. 1993. Analysis of relatedness in the California Condor from DNA fingerprints. Molecular Biology and Evolution 10:571–589.

HARTT, E. W., N. C. HARVEY, A. J. LEETE, AND K. PRESTON. 1994. Effects of age at pairing on reproduction in captive California Condors (*Gymnogyps californianus*). Zoo Biology 13:3–11.

HARVEY, N. C., K. PRESTON, AND A. J. LEETE. 1996. Reproductive behavior in captive California Condors (*Gymnogyps californianus*). Zoo Biology 15:115–125.

KIFF, L. 1990. To the brink and back: the battle to save the California Condor. Terra 28:7–18.

KOFORD, C. B. 1953. The California Condor. National Audubon Research Report 4:1–154.

KUEHLER, C. M., AND P. N. WITMAN. 1988. Artificial incubation of California Condor *Gymnogyps californianus* eggs removed from the wild. Zoo Biology 7:123–132.

MEE, A., G. AUSTIN, M. BARTH, C. BEESTMAN, T. SMITH, AND M. WALLACE. 2004. Courtship behaviour in reintroduced California Condors: evidence for extra-pair copulations and female mate guarding. Pages 75–82 *in* Raptors Worldwide: Proceedings of VI World Conference on Birds of Prey and Owls

(R. D. Chancellor and B.-U. Meyburg, Eds.). World Working Group on Birds of Prey and Owls/MME-Birdlife, Hungary.

MERETSKY, V. J., N. F. R. SNYDER, S. R. BEISSINGER, D. A. CLENDENEN, AND J. W. WILEY. 2000. Demography of the California Condor: implications for reestablishment. Conservation Biology 14:957–967.

MEYER, J. 1983. To save the condor. Outdoor California 44:1–33.

MILLER, L. H. 1911. Avifauna of the Pleistocene cave deposits of California. University of California Publications, Bulletin of the Department of Geology 6:385–400.

PHILLIPS, D. 1983. Shedding light on the controversy. Outdoor California 44: 20–33.

SMITH, D., AND R. EASTON. 1964. California Condor, Vanishing American. McNally and Loftin, Charlotte/Santa Barbara.

SNYDER, N. F. R., AND H. SNYDER. 1989. Biology and conservation of the California Condor. Current Ornithology 6:175–267.

SNYDER, N. F. R., AND H. SNYDER. 2000. The California Condor, A Saga of Natural History and Conservation. Academic Press, London, U.K.

WILBUR, S. R. 1978. The California Condor, 1966-1976: a look at its past and future. U.S. Fish and Wildlife Service. North American Fauna 72:1–136.

1

Limiting Factors for
Wild California Condors

Noel F. R. Snyder

ABSTRACT.—Recovery of endangered species normally entails identification and correction of crucial limiting factors causing population declines. The search for primary causes of the California Condor's (*Gymnogyps californianus*) endangerment has continued over a century, and a great variety of negative factors have been identified. However, by far the most important problem for the species, at least in recent decades, has been excessive mortality due in large measure to pervasive lead poisoning resulting from ingestion of lead bullet fragments and shot in hunter-killed carcasses and carcass remains. This problem still exists, and although its impacts have been reduced by subsidies of clean food offered to birds in the wild and by emergency chelation treatment of birds found heavily contaminated, the only satisfactory long-term solution to the problem appears to be removal of the lead threat from the wild. Nevertheless, whether correction of the lead problem may be enough to produce viable wild populations remains to be seen, as other significant mortality and reproductive stresses have also been documented in recent years.

Considered threatened with imminent extinction since the late 19th century (Cooper 1890), the California Condor (*Gymnogyps californianus*) has shown a surprisingly stubborn capacity to endure, even though clearly viable wild populations of the species have never been documented in historical or more recent decades. At the time of the first western explorers in the late 18th century, the condor could still be found along the Pacific Coast of North America from southern Canada to northern Baja California, but by the late 1930s this range had shrunk to a horseshoe-shaped region surrounding the San Joaquin Valley of southern California (Koford 1953). Undoubtedly, the total population of condors had also declined enormously over the same period of time, although this contraction in numbers was not quantified by any credible estimates of population sizes.

P.O. Box 16426, Portal, Arizona 85632, USA. E-mail: nfrs16426@vtc.net

Intensive research and conservation efforts for the condor were begun in the 1930s (Koford 1953). But despite these efforts, the historic wild population exhibited a continuing decline in numbers until the mid 1980s, when captive breeding became the only viable option left to prevent the species' extinction. A low point of just 22 individuals in existence was reached in 1982, and the last wild individual was trapped into captivity in 1987 (see Snyder and Snyder 2000). First breeding in captivity occurred in 1988, and since then, the captive population has shown a rapid increase (Kuehler et al. 1991, Snyder and Snyder 2000). By the end of the 20th century, the total numbers of condors had once again reached a level roughly equal to the wild population of 1950 (approximately 150 individuals), and the totals continue to increase today (273 individuals, with 146 in captivity and 127 in the wild, as of 30 November 2005).

Efforts to reestablish the species in the wild began in 1992, but although increasing numbers of condors are again flying free, reestablishment efforts have yet to achieve either self-sustaining wild populations or populations with fully species-typical behavior (Meretsky et al. 2000). Many of the problems encountered center around difficulties with an important limiting factor known since the mid 1980s—lead poisoning (see Hall et al., Hunt et al., Parish et al., Woods et al., this volume). However, lead poisoning is not the only remaining threat to the species in the wild, and ultimate success in achieving viable wild populations with proper behavior also depends on solving a number of other problems, including those that have so far led to relatively low breeding effort and success in some reintroduced populations.

To gain an understanding of the importance of adequately addressing lead poisoning and other threats, it is valuable to briefly review the history of research efforts to identify and evaluate important limiting factors for the species. Primary source materials for this review are the detailed general accounts of the species' history and biology provided by several of the biologists involved in intensive studies of the species (Koford 1953; Miller et al. 1965; Wilbur 1978b; Snyder and Snyder 2000, 2005). The process of elucidating the major causes of the species' decline has been slow and meandering, with many false leads and misunderstandings. The condor has not been easy to study, and for many years insufficient manpower and inadequate research methods greatly hampered progress. Nevertheless, enough has been learned that the major threats to the species are now known with considerable confidence.

Historical Hypotheses and Research Regarding Limiting Factors

The first suggestions regarding important threats to the condor were those of Taylor (1859), Henshaw (1876), and Streator (1888), who emphasized widespread incidental losses of the species resulting from poisoning efforts conducted by ranchers to reduce losses of cattle (*Bos taurus*) and sheep (*Ovis aries*) to grizzly bears (*Ursus horribilis*) and wolves (*Canis lupus*). Reputedly, the poisoned carcasses used to kill these predators were often fed upon by condors, and early commentators claimed that in addition to grizzlies and wolves, large numbers of condors were lost during such poisoning campaigns. Cooper (1890) and Bendire (1892) likewise considered predator poisoning to be the primary threat to the condor, but as an additionally important threat, Cooper also called attention to a general decline in food supplies (cattle and sheep carcasses) resulting from changing land-use patterns. A third stress mentioned by Cooper was direct losses to shooting.

The main toxin used to poison grizzlies and wolves was strychnine, but there was some early use of cyanide as well, and although early condor-poisoning events were not well documented by first-hand reports, it appears likely that both poisons may have killed many condors up until the 1920s, when both wolves and grizzlies were completely exterminated from California. However, both strychnine and cyanide continued to be employed in control of coyotes (*Canis latrans*) through much of the 20th century, and the threats these toxins posed to condors did not cease completely in the 1920s (Snyder and Snyder 2000).

Shooting of condors was a relatively well-documented historical threat because many of the birds killed by shooting wound up as museum specimens, whether they were deliberately shot for that purpose or not. In addition to museum collecting, there was considerable shooting for curiosity and sport, and a certain amount to obtain large hollow flight feathers to serve as gold dust containers for early prospectors (Harris 1941, Snyder and Snyder 2000). Museum collecting also reduced the numbers of wild condors through the taking of eggs from nesting pairs. The numbers of birds known to be lost historically to these and other stresses were summarized by Wilbur (1978b), and shooting was by far the most frequently documented cause of loss.

Declines in food supplies have been a continuing concern into more modern times, although whether the condors of recent centuries have ever been significantly stressed by food scarcity has never been clear. Early concerns over food supplies were not based on the finding of starving condors or any clear documentation of failures of birds to breed successfully, but depended mainly on the observation that livestock abundance was clearly declining and fears that this could represent problems for the condors (see Cooper 1890, Wilbur 1978a). Livestock carcasses had become a principal food supply for the species by the 19th century, but crop farming was rapidly replacing grazing as the predominant land use in many regions during the late 19th century, and reductions in grazing lands have continued more recently.

Studies of Carl Koford.—Additional real and potential threats to the condor emerged once intensive research on the species began in the late 1930s, primarily conducted by Carl Koford (1953). This research, supported by the University of California and the National Audubon Society, was focused on breeding populations in Ventura and Santa Barbara counties, although additional observations of foraging and roosting birds were made in other nearby regions, mainly in San Luis Obispo, Kern, Los Angeles, and Tulare counties. Koford expressed concerns about a great variety of stresses additional to predator poisoning, food supplies, and shooting. These included potential problems due to ingestion of 1080-poisoned California ground squirrels (*Spermophilus beecheyi*), potential problems with desertion of nests caused by human disturbance, problems with collisions of birds with above-ground wires and poles, problems with miring of birds in oil ponds and drowning of birds in cattle tanks, and problems with fires sweeping through nesting areas. Without presenting any quantitative data to substantiate his assessment, Koford considered food supplies to be the most important factor determining condor numbers in the long run, and considered wanton shooting, collecting, poisoning of various sorts, trapping, accidents, starvation, fires, and disturbance from roads, trails, photographers, and oil development to be other major stresses. Sickness and disease, ingestion of foreign objects, storms, killing for quills, and historical capture for ceremonial and spectacle purposes were in his view minor factors.

Koford presented no data or analyses to clarify whether primary problems for the species lay in reproduction or mortality, or just which specific factors were of major importance. In fact, Koford considered the condor population to have been close to stable for many years and believed that long-term conservation of the species might be ensured by providing full federal protection to the species, by the creation of sanctuaries protecting the most important nesting and roosting habitats from disturbance, by effective warden activity, and by proper education efforts. Koford's recommendations led to the creation of the Sespe Condor Sanctuary in Los Padres National Forest lands of Ventura County in 1947. Maintained closed to human access, this large sanctuary, together with the earlier-established and much smaller Sisquoc Condor Sanctuary in Santa Barbara County, protected a major fraction of the nest sites and roosts known for the species at that time.

In hindsight, it is highly unlikely that Koford was dealing with a stable condor population in the early to mid-20th century, and despite creation of the Sespe and Sisquoc sanctuaries, it became apparent soon after the publication of his monograph (Koford 1953) that condor numbers were still progressively declining. The most important continuing causes of decline remained highly speculative.

Studies of Alden Miller and Ian and Eben McMillan.—In response to the continuing decline of the condor, a follow-up study to Koford's was conducted in the early 1960s by Alden Miller in collaboration with Ian and Eben McMillan (Miller et al. 1965), a study supported by the National Audubon Society and the National Geographic Society. By comparing flock sizes seen in the early 1960s with flock sizes seen by Koford in the late 1930s and 1940s, these workers estimated that the condor population had declined by about 30% since Koford's study, and because Koford had estimated a population of about 60 birds, a 30% decline translated into an estimate of about 40 to 42 birds left in the early 1960s (see Fig. 1).

In retrospect, more recent counts and population determinations extrapolated into the past by comparisons of flock sizes in various regions through time strongly suggest that the population estimates of both Koford and Miller et al. were much too low. Koford probably had about 150 birds in the population in the 1940s, while Miller and the McMillans were probably dealing with about 100 birds in the early 1960s (see discussion in Snyder and Snyder 2000, 2005). Regardless of disagreements over the size of the wild population, however, all researchers after Koford agreed that the population was in continuing steep decline.

With respect to the evaluation of limiting factors, Miller et al. (1965) concluded that reproduction of the species appeared to be healthy, judging from the ratios of immatures to adults they observed in some flocks and

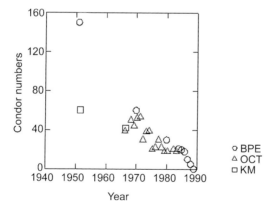

Fig. 1. Principal condor population estimates and counts from 1950 through the 1980s. The estimates of Koford, Miller, and the McMillans (KM values on legend) were much lower than those of Sibley, Wilbur, and the 1980s photo census (the Best Population Estimates; BPE on legend), but both lineages of estimates indicated rapidly approaching extinction. The October Survey counts (OCT on legend) paralleled the best estimates, but were consistently lower, suggesting that none of the October Survey Counts accounted for all birds in the population.

their estimates of total numbers of immatures and adults. But because of
a desire to avoid any disturbance to nesting pairs, they made no direct
evaluation of breeding effort and success to fully confirm this judgment.
In addition, they carried out a gross survey of the availability of various
kinds of foods taken by the species, and concluded that the species was not
likely suffering from any significant food shortage, either in a seasonal or
overall sense.

With no clear evidence for reproductive or food supply problems,
Miller et al. (1965) concluded that the primary problems faced by the species must instead be ones of excessive mortality, and in this sphere their
concerns were focused heavily on the potential impacts of wanton shooting
and poisoning resulting from ingestion of 1080-killed ground squirrels.
In documenting the shooting threat, they provided a substantial amount
of anecdotal evidence of shooting events involving condors, although they
were not able to evaluate what fraction of total mortality these events
might represent and how the shooting threat might compare to other mortality threats in severity. Their evidence for potential problems with 1080
poisoning was limited to observations of the condors feeding on 1080-
poisoned squirrels and kangaroo rats (*Dipodomys* spp.) and to the finding
of several dead condors in regions where squirrel poisoning had been carried out. However, they lacked any evidence of 1080 residues in the dead
condors that were located, leaving the actual causes of death of these birds
quite speculative. Later evidence was to indicate that 1080 poisoning was
unlikely as a major threat to the species (Snyder and Snyder 2000).

Although the study of Miller et al. (1965) represented a significant
advance over the study of Koford in recognizing that the species was in
steep decline and in attempting to determine the most important causal
factors, the conservation recommendations of these researchers were very
similar to those of Koford (1953) and emphasized protecting the birds
from shooting and poisoning threats and from disturbance in their nesting
areas. However, neither Miller et al., nor Koford, recommended any sweeping restrictions on hunting or 1080-poisoning activities in the range of the
species, possibly because of the potential for major backlash from hunters and ranchers and major problems with enforcement of such restrictions. Instead they emphasized the need for further research on 1080, for
increased warden and education activities, and for the closure of very specific high-risk regions from shooting.

Development of the October Survey.—Crucial to the evaluation of limiting factors and effectiveness of countermeasures was the development of
improved censusing techniques. Shortly after the completion of the study
of Miller et al. (1965), a large-scale two-day simultaneous count of condors was organized, utilizing observers stationed at prominent viewpoints
throughout the known range of the species. This count became the annual

October Survey and continued until 1981 (see Mallette and Borneman 1966, Verner 1978, Wilbur 1978b).

The October Survey provided a much better basis for estimating condor numbers than was available previously, but it had some significant weaknesses. Without individually marked birds, it was often impossible to rigorously differentiate condors seen at one station from condors seen at another station at a non-overlapping time. There also was no guarantee that all condors in the population would be visible during the count period. The final total for each survey was based on a consensus analysis of participants.

Overall, the first October Surveys in the mid-late 1960s yielded several totals of more than 50 birds, and since it was reasonable to believe that some birds may have been missed, the actual population size might well have been close to 60 birds at that time, a total that receives support from backward extrapolations of firm counts of the 1980s via comparisons of high flock counts in various regions through time (see Snyder and Snyder 2000). The estimate of 60 birds for the late 1960s was much higher than the previous population estimate of Miller et al. (1965) and equal to Koford's (1953) early estimate, but although this provided some initial encouragement about the plight of the species, counts on the October Surveys progressively declined over the years, and by the late 1970s, it appeared that the population might have diminished by something like 50% from the late 1960s (Fig.1).

Studies of Fred Sibley and Sanford Wilbur.—A principal leader of the October Survey in its first years was Fred Sibley, who began studies as the first U.S. Fish and Wildlife Service (USFWS) condor biologist, following the passage of the first federal Endangered Species Act in 1966. This act provided full federal protection to the condor, as one of the first endangered birds listed, and also provided funding for continuing field studies of the species. During the four years he spent in the condor program, Sibley made a major effort to evaluate breeding activity in the population, principally in connection with evaluating potential impacts of a proposed project to dam the Sespe River (Sibley 1969). With intensive efforts, Sibley, aided by John Borneman of the National Audubon Society (NAS), found a number of active and formerly active nests, many of them outside the Sespe Sanctuary, and determined that nest success, at about 45%, still appeared to be reasonably strong in the species.

Even so, Sibley had worries that the number of nesting pairs might not be as strong as needed for population viability, especially in the Sespe Sanctuary, and indeed, even though the ratios of immatures to adults on the October Surveys were strong through 1966, this ratio dropped substantially in 1967 and especially in 1968 (see Verner 1978). Sibley was convinced of the existence of a major continuing decline in the wild population that was evident in steadily declining flock sizes seen in various regions. With good reason he also believed that the number of condors left, about 60 judging from the October Surveys, was actually far fewer than the numbers present during the studies of Koford and Miller et al., despite the low estimates of numbers of condors given in those earlier studies.

Toward the end of his years in the USFWS condor program, Sibley began an effort to provide a supplemental food supply for the condors in the Sespe Sanctuary region to see if this might bolster breeding activity in the region, an effort that was continued and expanded by his successor in the program, Sanford Wilbur, who began studies in 1969. Wilbur (1978b) documented continuing declines in potential livestock food supplies for the condor and questioned the validity of the conclusion of Miller et al. (1965) that food supplies were more than adequate. He was convinced that the wild population had largely stopped breeding and believed that this might trace to food shortages that were especially acute during the summer.

Nevertheless, Wilbur's attempts to find condor nests were much less comprehensive than those of Sibley, especially outside the Sespe Sanctuary, and left open the possibility that he might be missing much of the breeding activity occurring in the population. While ratios of immatures to adults on the October Survey remained low through 1974, it was unclear if this was a valid result (see Snyder and Snyder 2000). And even if valid, immature-adult ratios on the survey could as easily have reflected fluctuations in mortality of juveniles as fluctuations in reproduction, so these ratios did not clearly point toward reproductive problems.

The supplemental feeding program carried on through the 1970s under Wilbur's supervision attracted only relatively small numbers of condors, and their use of provided carcasses was highly sporadic (Wilbur 1978a). Further, Wilbur failed to obtain any convincing evidence of increased reproduction in the Sespe Sanctuary, and indeed the condor population exhibited a continuing major decline through the 1970s. By 1978, Wilbur (1980) estimated only about 30 individuals left in the wild. These results were not highly supportive of food supplies being a major problem for the species, but for various reasons did not rule out this possibility completely. In particular, some of the carcasses used in the feeding program were evidently animals killed with lead ammunition (J. Grantham pers. comm.) and were potentially lethal for condors, thus confounding interpretation of results.

Like Koford and Miller et al., neither Sibley nor Wilbur was able to conduct any comprehensive studies of mortality rates in the wild population, as all these researchers lacked capacities to reliably identify individuals or accurately monitor population sizes or reproduction totals in the population. Neither were any of these workers able to conduct comprehensive studies of the specific mortality factors affecting condors, as none had the technology to routinely recover dead birds for analysis of causes of mortality. And although Wilbur (1978b) completed a major review of the causes of condor mortality documented in museum records and in the literature, the biases in this data set were likely large because of the non-systematic way in which data were collected over the centuries. As just one indication of the problems with this data set, shooting mortality was likely greatly overrepresented because shot birds are relatively likely to be recovered and their causes of death established. Such mortalities were surely much better documented than deaths to many other causes where dead birds were unlikely to be discovered or their causes of death determined. Diagnostic methods were simply unavailable in early times to confirm deaths from many causes (e.g., lead poisoning or various diseases), so it is not surprising that known mortalities from these causes are missing from the historical record, regardless of how common such mortalities may have been.

The Expanded Condor Program of the 1980s

In response to a continuing decline of the wild population and to pessimistic outside reviews of the condor program provided by Verner (1978) and Ricklefs (1978), Congress approved the development of an intensified research and conservation program for the species in 1979. This was a cooperative program involving many agencies and individuals (see Snyder and Snyder 2000 for details), and research activities were led by the U.S. Fish and Wildlife Service and National Audubon Society.

By 1980, it was still unclear whether the decline of the condor was due more to reproductive or to mortality factors, and which specific stress factors might be most important was unknown. A number of hypotheses were on the table, but none had been adequately tested. Perhaps the most plausible suggestions were those of Miller et al. (1965), Wilbur (1978b), and Kiff et al. (1979). Miller et al. saw the condor's decline as primarily a result of excessive mortality caused by shooting and various sorts of poisoning, and they believed there was no good evidence of reproductive deficiency. Wilbur, in contrast, felt that recent problems lay mostly in a failure of most adults to attempt breeding, potentially caused by food scarcity or perhaps by long distances between available nest sites and currently available food supplies. Kiff et al. called attention to the possibility that the recent decline was in large part due to DDE contamination, a stress that generally operates through eggshell thinning, increased egg breakage, and reduced nesting success (see Newton 1979). In particular, a small number of eggshell fragments collected from active nests by Fred Sibley in the 1960s were found to be extremely thin and heavily contaminated with DDE. By comparison with eggshell thinning and DDE contamination levels in other bird species, it appeared that the condor might be one of the species most severely stressed by this pesticide.

To evaluate these and other hypotheses, the program of the 1980s was conceived as a major effort to (1) improve censusing of the population, (2) document reproductive effort and success and the factors affecting reproduction in detail, and (3) determine mortality rates and the important factors affecting mortality in detail. These were interrelated goals, as for example, accurate documentation of mortality rates would likely be possible only with accurate censusing of the population.

Improved censusing.—Accurate censusing of the wild population, although originally envisioned as something to be achieved mainly through radio-telemetry and/or marking birds with visually detectable wing tags, came to depend primarily on the development of photo-census efforts across the range of the species (Snyder and Johnson 1985). The photo-census efforts were a major cooperative program of many parties and revealed that all condors were already individually marked by distinctive natural flight feather patterns (i.e., molt and feather damage patterns) that could be reliably followed by continuous efforts to photograph all flying condors encountered in the wild. With powerful telephoto equipment it was possible to get diagnostic photographs from distances as far away as several hundred meters, and so long as enough photographs were taken through time and the geographic distribution of photographs included all major parts of the species' range, it proved possible to continuously monitor the size of the population, determine ranges of individual birds, determine quite accurately when birds were lost from the population, and determine mortality rates with considerable precision (Snyder and Johnson 1985, Snyder et al. 1987, Meretsky and Snyder 1992, Meretsky et al. 2000).

The photographic censusing efforts confirmed a precipitously declining wild population, starting with an apparent 23 birds in early 1982, dropping to 21 birds in late 1982, to 19 birds in late 1983, 15 birds in late 1984, and just 9 birds by mid 1985 (Fig. 1). Three birds were trapped into captivity in mid-1985, and after another bird died in early 1986, most of the remaining birds were taken captive in the same year. The last wild bird was captured in the spring of 1987.

Mortality rates were very high. Between early 1982 and early 1986, when the population dropped from a probable 23 birds to 5 birds, the average annual mortality rate was 26.6%, or 18.9%, 16.7%, 43.2%, and 27.5% for the four years respectively. As Meretsky et al. (2000) calculated, expanding on earlier demographic analyses by Mertz (1971) and Verner (1978), these mortality rates were far in excess of what a stable population of normally reproducing condors might tolerate. Specifically, under conditions of normal reproduction, the population could be expected to absorb no more than about 9.9% annual mortality and still remain stable. Thus the condor population of the mid-1980s exhibited a mortality rate more than two and a half times as great as was apparently sustainable. Clearly a major cause of decline in this period was excessive mortality. But whether the population was also suffering significant reproductive problems depended on an accurate determination of breeding activity in the population.

Reproductive studies.—Reproduction was evaluated by a massive labor-intensive effort to locate the remaining breeding pairs and study their success directly in continuous distant observations of active nests. To this end, many of the increased numbers of personnel of the 1980s were allocated initially to checking historically known nest sites for activity, and then increasingly to following condors in the field to find new nest sites. Only 2 of the 25 nest sites found to be active with eggs or young in the 1980s turned out to be previously known sites, although evidence such as layers of internal excrement clearly showed that most active sites had also been active in earlier years. Thus, the efforts to follow condors to their nests, although requiring a much larger field staff than earlier available, proved far more productive than efforts to check historically known sites and revealed that most of the nesting activity in the population was likely missed in previous studies, in part because it was occurring in locations far from the Sespe Sanctuary that were virtually unstudied in earlier efforts.

With several years of effort, the nesting areas of all breeding pairs were located and it became apparent that the majority of adults were breeding and breeding with rates of success that matched those seen in earlier studies of Koford and Sibley, rates that were evidently within the general range to be expected for solitary nesting vultures (for details see Snyder 1983; Snyder and Snyder 2000, 2005). There were no signs of major deficiencies either in breeding effort or breeding success, although a moderate number of nests were lost to predation on eggs by Common Ravens (*Corvus corax*). However, the wild pairs exhibited a strong tendency to lay replacement eggs after egg losses, and the impacts of egg losses were considerably less than might otherwise have been calculated.

Significantly, no cases of egg breakage were documented in the 1980s that could not conclusively or potentially be attributed to predation by Common Ravens, and broken eggs were no thinner in shell thickness than eggs that hatched normally, either in the 1980s or 1960s, strongly suggesting that shell thinning was not a primary cause of breakage. Coupled with data indicating normal nest success in the species, both in the 1980s and in the 1960s, these results gave no evidence of significant problems with DDE contamination even though substantial levels of DDE were continuing to be found in condor eggs. No strong inverse correlation of shell thickness with DDE was confirmed, and it appeared that the exceptionally thin-shelled eggshell fragments collected in the 1960s and analyzed by Kiff et al. 1979 might simply have come from relatively small eggs, because a strong correlation of eggshell thickness with egg size was documented in eggs of the 1980s and in historical museum eggs (Snyder and Meretsky 2003).

The lack of evidence for significant problems with breeding effort and success was also basically inconsistent with Wilbur's concerns that the population might be suffering from food availability problems. Indeed, detailed studies of feeding rates at nests strongly suggested that the breeding population was obtaining adequate food supplies (Snyder and Snyder 2000). Thus, by 1984 it had become apparent that the historical hypothesis that was closest to correct in explaining the decline of the condor was the excessive mortality hypothesis of Miller et al. (1965). However, it was not yet clear that the specific mortality factors emphasized by these authors were in fact the factors of most importance.

Causes of mortality.—Unfortunately, the efforts to determine specific causes of mortality in the 1980s were hampered by delays in implementation of radio telemetry and by apparent bad luck in the allocation of radio transmitters. For unknown reasons (it may just have been chance) survival rates proved to be much higher in birds fitted with transmitters than in those left without transmitters. Consequently, relatively few dead birds were recovered for necropsy. This bias was especially marked in the winter of 1984–1985 when five of seven birds without transmitters perished, while only one of eight birds carrying transmitters died. In sum, 11 of 15 condors dying between 1982 and 1986 were never recovered and their causes of death remain unknown.

Nevertheless, four birds dying during the 1980s were recovered, two by radiotelemetry and two by fortuitous discovery, and causes of death were determined for all four. Further, despite the small sample size, the specific causes of mortality determined for these birds gave such a compelling picture of the nature of mortality threats faced by the species that the conservation program was obliged to completely reorient its priorities and strategies (Plates 1 and 2).

Three of the four condors recovered dead in the 1980s were victims of apparently independent lead-poisoning events (Janssen et al. 1986, Wiemeyer et al. 1988). Two of the three lead-poisoned birds still had apparent ammunition fragments in their digestive tracts (Plate 2), and all had potentially been poisoned by ingestion of lead ammunition fragments in carcasses. These were the first wild condors ever diagnosed as dying of lead poisoning, but there was no reason to believe that this was a new problem, considering the apparent source of the contamination. Further, because the three cases appeared to be independent events, it quickly became plausible to hypothesize that lead poisoning might be and might have been the most important factor in causing the decline of the condor (see Snyder and Snyder 2000). Lead poisoning had not been recognized as a significant potential problem by any historic researcher on the species, despite the fact that it was well known that condors often fed on the carcasses of animals shot by hunters. In fact, prior to the program of the

1980s, only two dead condors had ever been tested for lead contamination and neither was clearly a victim of lead poisoning, so it is really no surprise that the problem was not recognized earlier.

In addition to the three condors found dead from lead poisoning, there were several other pieces of information available in the 1980s that supported a prominent role for this mortality factor: (1) the absence of a significant difference in mortality rates in juvenile and adult condors, as documented by photo-census efforts; (2) the seasonal timing of losses of birds, as documented by photo-census efforts; (3) the documentation of frequent lead contamination in other scavenging birds of California (Wiemeyer et al. 1986); and (4) the existence of significant lead contamination in living condors trapped in the 1980s (Wiemeyer et al. 1988).

The mean annual mortality rates for juvenile and adult condors documented in the mid 1980s were 22.2% and 26.8%, respectively, strongly suggesting that the main mortality factors affecting the population were not highly age dependent. In most avian studies overall mortality rates of juveniles are much greater than rates for adults, because of higher susceptibility of juveniles to factors such as shooting, accidents, predation, and starvation. Few mortality stresses can be expected to affect all ages relatively equally in any species, but among such stresses are poisons, such as lead ingested in food. In a study of a sympatric scavenger, the Golden Eagle (*Aquila chrysaetos*), Pattee et al. (1990) found high levels of lead contamination but no differences in lead contamination between age classes. These findings strongly supported the potential for similar results in condors and for lead poisoning being a major cause of the mortality documented in condors in the same region.

The eagle study of Pattee et al. (1990) also documented a seasonal pattern of lead contamination very similar to the seasonal timing of losses of condors. Contamination of Golden Eagles was greatest in the fall through winter to early spring period, exactly the season when most condor mortalities of the 1980s had occurred, and the time of year that included the main hunting seasons in the region, when lead was presumably most prevalent in carcasses; a seasonal pattern of contamination that has since been confirmed for condors in California (Hall et al. this volume) and Arizona (Hunt et al., Parish et al. this volume).

Also supporting lead as an important cause of mortality was the finding of frequent lead contamination in still another scavenger in the region, the Turkey Vulture (*Cathartes aura*). Wiemeyer et al. (1986) found elevated lead in the bones of 10 of 16 Turkey Vultures collected. Evidently, the lead threat was both geographically and taxonomically widespread for scavengers of the region.

Finally, 5 of 14 wild condors trapped alive and sampled for their blood-lead concentrations between 1982 and 1986 had elevated lead levels

(Wiemeyer et al. 1988). Two of the five condors subsequently died due to lead poisoning and a third disappeared without being recovered.

Together, the various lines of evidence gathered in the 1980s were strongly supportive of a major threat from lead contamination. The discovery of the lead-poisoning problem, evidence for its severity, and the lack of a practical means for quickly solving this problem, coupled with the severe losses of condors (40% of the population) over the winter of 1984–1985, caused at least in part by this problem, were the principal reasons leading to 1985 decisions by the California Fish and Game Commission and the USFWS to capture all the last wild condors for captive breeding.

SUBSEQUENT EVIDENCE FOR LEAD AND OTHER THREATS

Evidence implicating lead contamination has only increased in recent years, and as reviewed by Fry and Maurer (2003), the primary source of lead contamination for condors indeed appears to be carcasses of animals shot with lead ammunitions. Perhaps the most convincing support for the importance of the problem to condors has come from the numerous cases of severe lead poisoning occurring in releases of captive condors into the wild in the 1990s and 2000s, despite continuing provision of a food subsidy of lead-free carcasses in all release efforts (see Fry and Maurer 2003, Hall et al., Parish et al. this volume). Because released birds have routinely carried radio transmitters, it has been possible to get much more information on mortality threats in releases than was obtained for the historic wild population of the 1980s. But even so, causes of death have not been determined for about a third of the birds dying in the release program, mostly because of a failure to recover the carcasses of these birds (see Fry and Maurer 2003).

Provision of clean carcasses was a primary justification presented for conducting releases without actually removing the threat of lead poisoning in release regions, but it has proved only partly successful in preventing such contamination (see Hall et al., Hunt et al., Parish et al. this volume). By 2000, six released condors had died of apparent lead poisoning and another 16 had been saved from severe poisoning by recapture and emergency chelation therapy, a treatment that removes lead from a bird's bloodstream and allows it to be excreted. Quite clearly, the birds were taking some contaminated foods in addition to the clean carcasses provided in the subsidy program.

Cases of lead toxicity have increased substantially in released condors since 2000, and as of October 2005, the mortalities attributable to lead have increased to nine while the number of emergency chelations of heavily contaminated birds has risen to an astonishing 77 for all releases combined (see Hall et al., Parish et al., Hunt et al. this volume). Data summarized by Fry and Maurer (2003) indicated that over 60% of the released birds tested in California exhibited elevated blood lead levels (>20 µg dL^{-1}), while 15% were classifiable as clinically affected by lead contamination (>60 µg dL^{-1}). It simply can no longer be doubted that lead contamination is truly a widespread, common, chronic, and serious threat. Further, it deserves emphasis that the documented incidence of lead-killed birds and birds heavily contaminated with lead would presumably have been much greater if there had not been efforts to provide clean food supplies to the birds during the period of releases.

What fraction of the birds detoxified by chelation would otherwise have died from their contamination is unknown, but these birds were chelated only because of veterinary judgment that their very high lead levels indicated they were in jeopardy, so it is only prudent to consider these birds as additional potential mortalities averted. Further, there is evidence from numerous studies of human health that at least some of the sub-lethal effects of lead poisoning to the nervous system and other physiological systems are long-lasting and highly detrimental (e.g., Otto and Fox 1993, Rosen 1995, Brewster and Perazella 2004). Consequently, birds whose lives are spared from severe lead contamination by chelation may well be permanently compromised in their future prospects for survival and reproduction (see Burger and Gochfeld 2000). Studies in the United Kingdom have revealed elevated lead levels in Mute Swans (*Cygnus olor*) dying from collisions with powerlines, suggesting that risks of collisions are increased by sub-lethal levels of exposure (O'Halloran et al. 1989, Kelly and Kelly 2005).

Thus, it is invalid and misleading to consider the extent of the lead problem to be limited to the body count of birds dying immediately from acute lead toxicity. When a full accounting of the lead threat is made, including recognition of the substantial numbers of deaths likely averted by chelations and clean food subsidy, the likelihood that a sizeable proportion of dead birds that were not recovered were also lead mortalities, and the likelihood that lead may have been a contributing cause to other deaths, lead poisoning has evidently been by far the single most important mortality threat for birds in the release program (see tabulations through 2002 in Fry and Maurer 2003). More recent research using stable isotope analyses has additionally implicated lead poisoning as the cause of death in two condors previously unknown to have succumbed to lead poisoning (Church 2005), and it is likely this technique will soon reveal other previously unsuspected lead mortalities. It is very difficult to view the data accumulated so far as indicating anything less than a massive lead problem, very likely adequate in of itself to ensure failure of release efforts to achieve viable populations unless effectively countered (see also Woods et al. this volume).

The incidence of severe lead poisoning has been most frequent (with some 66 chelations in total) in the Arizona releases, in which the birds have been relatively, but not completely, independent of clean food subsidy (Parish et al. this volume). This high frequency is not surprising in the light of frequent feeding of these birds on deer carcasses, and the fact that 94% of hunter-shot deer carcasses and 90% of deer gutpiles examined by Hunt et al. (2006) were found to contain ammunition fragments. However, in southern California, where condors have tended to be much more highly dependent on clean food at provisioned sites, the incidence of lead poisonings has dropped strongly in the most recent years. This apparent local improvement cannot be taken as a demonstration that the prevalence of contaminated carcasses has declined in southern California, only that the threat is much less obvious now than earlier, likely because of a recent low frequency of foraging away from feeding stations (see Hall et al. this volume). Unfortunately, the strong focus of the southern California birds on feeding stations appears to be coming at a considerable cost in terms of other goals of the reestablishment program (see Mee et al. this volume).

Other mortality threats.—As quantitatively dominant as the lead-poisoning problem has come to be recognized, it is not, and has not been the only mortality threat of significance to the historical and released populations. As tabulated by Fry and Maurer (2003) two other sources of mortality have affected substantial numbers of released birds: (1) collisions with overhead wires, often associated with electrocution, and (2) predation by eagles and coyotes. No losses to these causes were documented in the 1980s.

Ten released birds have been lost to collisions and/or electrocutions to date, and four of these incidents came very early in the release program (in 1993–1994) when problems were especially severe with birds landing on phone poles and human structures. Aversion training of birds with electrified dummy phone poles was started in the mid 1990s and this appears to have had some beneficial effect, although collision deaths still continue to occur (six deaths between 1997 and 2004). As long as released birds continue to frequent civilized areas it appears that collisions are likely to remain a significant, although moderate, mortality factor.

Collisions have been especially problematic in California releases, where overhead wires are particularly abundant, although relatively few collision-related deaths were documented in the historic California population (only three), possibly because that population generally avoided developed areas. Only a single collision death has been documented in the Arizona releases, where overhead wires are relatively scarce.

Losses of released condors to apparent Golden Eagle and coyote predation have also been substantial (nine cases in U.S., see Woods et al. this volume). Such losses were not observed with the historic wild population, although two cases were witnessed in the 1980s of attempted predation on nestling condors by Golden Eagles (Snyder and Snyder 2000). To some extent the losses in releases may have represented an absence of parental guardians for released birds, but it is also possible that some of the condors killed by predators might have been birds compromised by starvation and other maladies. In addition, some cases may actually have been condors scavenged by eagles or coyotes after death from other causes. Because of these and other uncertainties, the extent to which such losses may continue to threaten release efforts is very difficult to project, although it seems plausible that their incidence may decline as larger fractions of birds coming into released populations are fledged naturally by parent birds in the wild.

Surely one of the most intriguing sources of mortality from a historical standpoint is shooting, as many early researchers identified this threat as probably the most important threat to the species (especially Miller et al. 1965). Yet with only five shooting deaths of released condors between 1992 and late 2005, the shooting threat appears to be of much less relative importance than it was rated in earlier accounts. Conceivably this could represent a recent decline in shooting threats, but it could as easily represent the very poor historical documentation of non-shooting threats. Regardless, the number of recent shootings still remains a significant source of mortality, and a source that can be expected to remain significant in the future, even if it does not loom as the major threat it was once considered to be.

One other source of mortality that does not appear in Fry and Maurer's (2003) tabulation is the death and/or near death of several very recent nestlings due to impactions of their crops with trash such as metal, plastic, and glass objects evidently provided as "food" by their parents (Mee et al. this volume). Although this stress could alternatively be considered a reproductive stress—since only nestlings have been known to be affected, not free-flying birds—it has become a repetitive pattern in the releases in southern California that may well trace in large part to the limited foraging movements of parent birds and their frequenting of civilized areas. Trash ingestion is evidently not something new, as a low incidence of trash was found in nests in studies of the 1980s (see Snyder and Snyder 2000, 2005), but it was not identified as a source of any condor mortalities historically.

Nevertheless, this stress, in conjunction with an apparent stress from low bone supplies, was identified as a major mortality problem for Cape Vulture (*Gyps coprotheres*) nestlings of South Africa in the 1970s (Mundy and Ledger 1976, Mundy et al. 1992). In South Africa, chick survival was greatly increased after nesting colonies were provided with nearby "vulture restaurants" providing abundant sources of carcasses and bone, in part on the assumption that trash ingestion was largely a result of low bone supplies. However, Benson et al. (2004) have suggested that trash ingestion in Cape Vultures may alternatively be produced mainly by low food supplies rather than low bone supplies. Additions of bone supplies to carcass provisioning sites have been attempted in southern California (albeit sporadically and at low levels), but have not as yet produced any obvious amelioration of the trash impaction problem (Mee et al. this volume). Other more "miscellaneous" sources of mortality documented in the program of the 1980s and in more recent efforts have included two drownings, a poisoning by ethylene glycol, a cancer victim, and a case of cyanide poisoning in 1983, but none of these threats appears to have been a major source of mortality in recent years.

Overall, it is remarkable how different the list of mortality threats considered above is from the lists presented by Koford and Miller et al., a difference strongly indicating the importance of continuing research on such matters. Surely, to achieve an adequately low mortality rate in the reestablishment program, efforts should be made to reduce all known mortality factors that can be countered in any practical way. However, efforts to solve the lead contamination threat appear to be by far the most crucial priority and are likely essential for success.

DISCUSSION

Although the death toll of released condors to lead poisoning has likely been greatly reduced by clean food subsidy and emergency chelations, both techniques are viable only as short-term solutions. Both these solutions are demanding, expensive, and only partly effective, and neither, either alone or in combination, represents a desirable long-term answer to the lead problem. The chelation strategy for reducing mortalities entails repeated trapping of all birds to monitor their blood lead levels (see Hall et al., Parish et al. this volume) and poses unknown long-term risks to the birds derived from the chelation process itself and unavoidable risks involved in repeated trapping of condors, including behavioral changes inherent in repeated contact with humans (see Jones and Waddington 1992). Over the long run it entails prodigious costs in management, and since some birds die of lead poisoning in spite of all efforts to detect and reduce their contamination, it is not clear that stable or increasing wild populations are possible even with major efforts to resuscitate poisoned birds. In fact, the term "self-sustaining" is indeed an oxymoron when applied to populations maintained either by chelation therapy or food subsidy.

The recent history of events in the southern California releases suggests that intensive clean food subsidy can lead to a much reduced incidence of lead poisoning, but at the substantial costs of condors largely abandoning or never developing natural wide-ranging foraging behavior and chronic difficulties with ingestion of trash, not to mention other problems, such as collisions, resulting from frequent interactions with humans and human structures. Breeding success of released birds in southern California has been very poor, in significant measure associated with chronic feeding of trash to nestlings (Mee et al. this volume). In Arizona, breeding has been more successful and apparently largely free of problems with trash ingestion, while foraging behavior has been much more typical of historic wild condors. But the price paid has been a very high incidence of lead poisoning countered only by endless desperate rounds of chelation therapy (see Parish et al. this volume).

Thus, at least for the two release populations that have been in existence long enough to allow much in the way of evaluation, the short-term subsidy and chelation solutions to lead contamination implemented so far offer little long-term hope of achieving fully self-sustaining populations, naturally behaving populations, or acceptable levels of expenditures in sustaining wild populations.

A better solution.—Probably the most desirable solution to the lead-contamination problem for condors is to replace the lead in all ammunitions with safe alternatives, much as has been done with the lead in gasoline, paint, waterfowl ammunitions, plumbing, and fishing sinkers in many regions of the United States. If lead-based ammunitions can be eliminated, there presumably will be no need for perpetual food subsidy, continual trapping of birds to monitor lead levels, or frequent emergency chelation therapy. With these constraints removed, the chances for achieving truly naturally-behaving and self-sufficient wild populations will presumably be greatly enhanced. The contamination problem for condors stemming from lead ammunitions has now been known for decades and was the overwhelming reason why the USFWS and the California Fish and Game Commission decided to bring all wild condors into captivity in 1985. Solving the lead problem appears to be essential to achieving viable wild condor populations, and a practical solution to the problem apparently exists in the form of alternative non-toxic ammunitions now available for hunting that are practical, affordable, and effective (see Sullivan et al. this volume). So why has a conversion to these ammunitions not taken place?

The answer appears to lie in a combination of factors, not the least of which have been a long-standing denial of the problem in some quarters and a lack of courage to propose changes that might offend some special interests. Many senior officials remember the political difficulties of achieving a switch from lead shot to steel shot for waterfowl hunting in the 1980s, and evidently want no part of another similar controversy. Yet the conversion to steel shot did take place successfully even though steel shot was an inferior type of ammunition in ballistic characteristics. The same problem of inferior hunting characteristics is not posed by various alternative non-toxic ammunitions available today, both shot and bullets, so one would think a conversion to fully non-toxic ammunitions could be a much easier process than the earlier steel-shot conversion in terms of overcoming hunter reluctance and misunderstandings. In interview studies, the responses of hunters to the prospect of using non-toxic ammunitions have been quite positive (Sullivan et al. this volume), so there does not appear to be any need for pessimism about hunter acceptance of well-conceived efforts to substitute non-toxics for lead in all ammunitions.

But significantly, instead of recommending that lead ammunitions be fully replaced by non-toxic varieties, most parties involved in the condor program have been willing to go only as far as to recommend education of the public about the lead problem and to encourage hunters to voluntarily adopt nontoxic ammunitions (see Sullivan et al. this volume). Such an approach, although surely highly beneficial in and of itself and probably essential as a first step, nevertheless falls far short of what is truly needed, a full phase-out of a very dangerous and insidious toxin that poses many risks beyond those to condors, especially the health risks faced by those who consume wild game shot with lead ammunitions. The data and photographs of the prevalence of lead ammunition particles in deer carcasses presented by Hunt et al. (2006), combined with information on the detrimental effects on human health of low lead concentrations (e.g., Otto and Fox 1993, Rosen 1995, Brewster and Perazella 2004), should be enough to convince the great majority of hunters of the advisability of switching to safe alternatives for personal health reasons alone.

Policies limited to voluntary use of non-toxic ammunitions do not preclude the continued legal use of lead ammunitions indefinitely and provide no clear incentives for ammunition makers to phase out lead ammunitions or to develop and promote only safe alternatives. Costs of non-toxic alternatives are likely to remain relatively high and their availability will likely remain limited so long as they remain specialty, rather than standard, ammunitions. Thus, "voluntary-only" policies may well represent still more unnecessary delay in achieving effective and highly beneficial goals. No serious consideration was ever given to voluntary or partial reductions of the lead in gasoline or paint as a solution to the poisoning threats resulting from these sources. Clearly just as lead was not essential for gasoline or paints, lead ammunitions are not essential for hunting activities, and because of the toxic properties of lead ammunitions and the potential they have for contaminating not just condors, but many other species, they should be fully removed from the market as rapidly as possible. If only partial reductions are achieved, condor lead poisonings will presumably continue, and together with other sources of continuing mortality may still remain too frequent to permit viable condor populations, while continuing to be detrimental for other wildlife and humans.

Publicizing the expected benefits to human health may well be the most powerful way to gain public support for needed full conversion to non-toxic ammunitions, yet this approach has not been emphasized in hunter education efforts so far. The literature on detrimental health effects of lead on humans is vast and indicates that even extremely low concentrations are harmful and that there is probably no safe threshold for contamination with this material. For hunters using lead ammunitions there does not appear to be any practical way to avoid contamination, especially with lead particles in the flesh of game consumed, but also resulting from inadvertent exposure in handling and firing of lead ammunitions. Hunters face real health risks in continuing to use lead ammunitions (see Tsuji et al. 1999; Nieboer 2001a, b).

SUMMARY AND FINAL REMARKS

It is a well-established principle that reintroductions of extirpated species into their former ranges need to be preceded by the correction of major limiting factors causing prior extirpation. The last wild condors in the historic population were taken captive in the mid 1980s primarily because of a lead-poisoning threat, and evidence since that time has confirmed the overwhelming importance of lead contamination in the endangerment of the species. Nevertheless, reestablishment efforts for the condor have been proceeding in the absence of any real progress in removing this threat. The problem has been partially obscured from view by the practices of clean food subsidy and chelation of severely contaminated birds, but these practices have had many detrimental side effects, and have amounted to little more than expensive and demoralizing scotch tape and safety pins in the efforts to achieve truly self-sustaining wild populations behaving in a species-typical way.

What is clearly needed is complete removal of the primary source of contamination, lead ammunitions, and in practical terms the most promising means to achieve full removal appears to be through substitution of non-toxic ammunitions for lead ammunitions in hunting and other shooting activities. At the very least, this removal should occur throughout the present and anticipated range of the condor, but much more beneficial would be nationwide or universal removal, because of (1) widespread contamination threats posed to species other than condors, including humans, and (2) enforcement problems in ensuring compliance with geographically limited removal regulations.

The removal of lead from gasoline, paint, and plumbing, has taken place on a nationwide basis, not on a limited geographic basis, and has been successful largely because it has rested on well-documented general threats to human health. Such an emphasis may well prove to be the most successful approach with lead ammunitions as well. In particular, if hunters could be made fully aware of the human health risks from lead contamination intrinsic to eating game killed with lead ammunitions, there would likely be relatively little resistance to achieving a full nationwide conversion to non-toxic ammunitions. Limiting the issue to condor conservation alone risks making the condor an enemy among ammunition users and provides no impetus for changes outside condor range, leaving other wildlife species and our own species deprived of the benefits of widespread lead removal. Further delay in achieving a full solution to the problem serves no one's best interests.

Finally, as important as the lead issue is, and as unlikely as it is that the condor reestablishment program can succeed without its correction, it is well to realize that its correction may still leave reestablishment efforts shy of full success. Losses of condors to shooting, collisions, and ingestion of trash continue to occur, and together, these and other losses apart from lead poisoning may also prove too frequent to allow fully self-sustaining populations. What is more, both breeding effort and success have remained below historical levels, especially in southern California, and diverse problems resulting from excessive attraction of condors to humans and human structures continue to be widespread. Many of these problems are surely solvable, but will require well-designed research and experimentation for resolution. Research has had a low priority in the condor program in the past 15 years, but the needs for high quality research remain as cogent today as in early decades of the program.

Acknowledgments

The number of people and organizations that have contributed significantly to condor research and conservation efforts over the years is huge, and no attempt will be made to enumerate these many contributors here, as it would take many pages. Needless to say, the conservation program is much farther along now than before because of these many contributions. But it is also important to remember that the goal of real success in recovery of the California Condor still lies ahead, and much still remains to be accomplished before this goal is reached.

Literature Cited

Bendire, C. 1892. Life histories of North American birds. Smithsonian Institution Special Bulletin, no. 1

Benson, P. C., I. Plug, and J. C. Dobbs. 2004. An analysis of bones and other materials collected by Cape Vultures at the Kransberg and Blouberg colonies, Limpopo Province, South Africa. Ostrich 75:118–132.

Brewster, U. C., and M. A. Perazella. 2004. A review of chronic lead intoxication: an unrecognized cause of chronic kidney disease. American Journal of the Medical Sciences 327:341–347.

BURGER, J., AND M. GOCHFELD. 2000. Effects of lead on birds (Laridae): a review of laboratory and field studies. Journal of Toxicology and Environmental Health Part B: Critical Reviews 3:59–78.

CHURCH, M. 2005. Sources of lead exposure in California Condors. M.S. thesis, University of California, Santa Cruz, CA.

COOPER, J. G. 1890. A doomed bird. Zoe 1:248–249.

FRY, D. M., AND J. R. MAURER. 2003. Assessment of lead contamination sources exposing California Condors. Final Report to California Department of Fish and Game, Sacramento.

HALL, M., J. GRANTHAM, R. POSEY, AND A. MEE. 2007. Lead exposure among reintroduced California Condors in southern California. Pages 139–162 in California Condors in the 21st Century (A. Mee and L. S. Hall, Eds.). Series in Ornithology, no. 2.

HARRIS, H. 1941. The annals of Gymnogyps to 1900. Condor 43:3–55.

HENSHAW, H. W. 1876. Report on the ornithology of the portions of California visited during ....1875. In Annual report upon the geographical surveys..., by G.M. Wheeler, pp 224–278. Washington, D.C., Government Printing Office.

HUNT, W. G., W. BURNHAM, C. N. PARISH, K. BURNHAM, B. MUTCH, AND J. L. OAKS. 2006. Bullet fragments in deer remains: implications for lead exposure in avian species. Wildlife Society Bulletin 34:168–171.

HUNT, W. G., C. N. PARISH, S. C. FARRY, T. G. LORD, AND R. SIEG. 2007. Movements of introduced California Condors in Arizona in relation to lead exposure. Pages 79–96 in California Condors in the 21st Century (A. Mee and L. S. Hall, Eds.). Series in Ornithology, no. 2.

JANSSEN, D. L., J. E. OOSTERHUIS, J. L. ALLEN, M. P. ANDERSON, D. G. KELTS, AND S. N. WIEMEYER. 1986. Lead poisoning in free-ranging California Condors. Journal of the American Veterinary Medical Association 189:1115–1117.

JONES, R. B., and D. WADDINGTON. 1992. Modification of fear in domestic chicks, Gallus gallus domesticus, via regular handling and early environmental enrichment. Animal Behaviour 43:1021–1033.

KELLY, A., AND S. KELLY. 2005. Are Mute Swans with elevated blood lead levels more likely to collide with overhead power lines? Waterbirds 28:331–334.

KIFF, L. F., D. B. PEAKALL, AND S. R. WILBUR. 1979. Recent changes in California Condor eggshells. Condor 81:166–172.

KOFORD, C. B. 1953. The California Condor. National Audubon Research Report 4: 1–154.

KUEHLER, C. M., D. J. STERNER. D. S. JONES, R. L. USNIK, AND S. KASIELKE. 1991. Report on captive hatches of California Condors (Gymnogyps californianus): 1983–1990. Zoo Biology 10:65–68.

MALLETTE, R. D., AND J. C. BORNEMAN. 1966. First cooperative survey of the California Condor. California Fish and Game 52:185–203.

MEE, A. J., J. A. HAMBER, AND J. SINCLAIR. 2007. Low nest success in a reintroduced population of California Condors. Pages 163–184 in California Condors in the 21st Century (A. Mee and L. S. Hall, Eds.). Series in Ornithology, no. 2.

MERETSKY, V. J., AND N. F. R. SNYDER. 1992. Range use and movements of California Condors. Condor 94:313–335.

MERETSKY, V. J., N. F. R. SNYDER, S. R. BEISSINGER, D. A. CLENDENEN, AND J. W. WILEY. 2000. Demography of the California Condor: implications for reestablishment. Conservation Biology 14:957–967.

MERTZ, D. B. 1971. The mathematical demography of the California Condor population. American Naturalist 105:437–453.

MILLER, A. H., I. McMILLAN, AND E. McMILLAN. 1965. The current status and welfare of the California Condor. National Audubon Society Research Report 6:1–61.

MUNDY, P., D. BUTCHART, J. LEDGER, AND S. PIPER. 1992. The Vultures of Africa. Academic Press, London, U.K.

MUNDY, P. J., AND J. A. LEDGER. 1976. Griffon vultures, carnivores and bones. South African Journal of Science 72:106–110.

NEWTON, I. 1979. Population Ecology of Raptors. T. & A.D. Poyser, Berkhampstead, England.

NIEBOER, E. 2001a. The definitive identification of lead shotshell as a major source of lead exposure in native communities. Health Canada and Environment Canada, Toxic Substances Research Initiative #287.

NIEBOER, E. 2001b. Toxicological profile and related health issues: inorganic lead. Regional Niagara Public Health Department.

O'HALLORAN, J., A. A. MYERS, AND P. F. DUGGAN. 1989. Some sub-lethal effects of lead on Mute Swans Cygnus olor. Journal of Zoology (London) 218:627–632.

OTTO, D. A., AND D. A. FOX. 1993. Auditory and visual dysfunction following lead exposure. Neurotoxicology 14:191–207.

PARISH, C. N., W. R. HEINRICH, AND W. G. HUNT. 2007. Lead exposure, diagnosis, and treatment in California Condors released in Arizona. Pages 97–108 in California Condors in the 21st Century (A. Mee and L. S. Hall, Eds.). Series in Ornithology, no. 2.

PATTEE, O. H., P. H. BLOOM, J. M. SCOTT, AND M. R. SMITH. 1990. Lead hazard within the range of the California Condor. Condor 92:931–937.

RICKLEFS, R. E. (ED.). 1978. Report of the advisory panel on the California Condor. National Audubon Society Conservation Report 6:1–27.

ROSEN, J. F. 1995. Adverse health effects of lead at low exposure levels: trends in the management of childhood lead poisoning. Toxicology 97:11–17.

SIBLEY, F. C. 1969. Effects of the Sespe Creek Project on the California Condor. U.S. Fish and Wildlife Service, Laurel, Maryland.

SNYDER, N. F. R. 1983. California Condor reproduction, past and present. Bird Conservation 1:67-86.

SNYDER, N. F. R., AND E. V. JOHNSON. 1985. Photographic censusing of the 1982–1983 California Condor population. Condor 87:1–13.

SNYDER, N. F. R., E. V. JOHNSON, AND D. A. CLENDENEN. 1987. Primary molt of California Condors. Condor 89:468–485.

SNYDER, N. F. R., AND V. J. MERETSKY. 2003. California Condors and DDE: a re-evaluation. Ibis 145:136–151.

SNYDER, N. F. R., AND H. A. SNYDER. 2000. The California Condor: A Saga of Natural History and Conservation. Academic Press, San Diego, CA.

SNYDER, N. F. R., AND H. A. SNYDER. 2005. Introduction to the California Condor. California Natural History Guides, University of California Press, Berkeley.

STREATOR, C. P. 1888. Notes on the California Condor. Oologist 13(2):30.

SULLIVAN, K., R. C. SIEG, AND C. PARISH. 2007. Arizona's efforts to reduce lead exposure in California Condors. Pages 109–122 *in* California Condors in the 21st
Century (A. Mee and L. S. Hall, Eds.). Series in Ornithology, no. 2.

TAYLOR, A. S. 1859. The great condor of California. Hutching's California Magazine
3(12):540–543, 4(1):17–22, 4(2):61–64.

TSUJI, L. J. S., E. NIEBOER, J. D. KARAGATZIDES, R. M. HANNING, AND B. KATAPATUK.
1999. Lead shot contamination in edible portions of game birds and its dietary
implications. Ecosystem Health 5:183–192.

VERNER, J. 1978. California Condors: status of the recovery effort. General Technical
Report PSW-28, U.S. Forest Service, Washington, D.C.

WIEMEYER, S. N., R. M. JUREK, AND J. R. MOORE. 1986. Environmental contaminants
in surrogates, foods, and feathers of California Condors (*Gymnogyps californianus*). Environmental Monitoring and Assessment 6:91–111.

WIEMEYER, S. N., J. M. SCOTT, M. P. ANDERSON, P. H. BLOOM, AND C. J. STAFFORD.
1988. Environmental contaminants in California Condors. Journal of Wildlife
Management 52:238–247.

WILBUR, S. R. 1978a. Supplemental feeding of California Condors. Pages 135–140
in Endangered Birds, Management Techniques for Preserving Threatened
Species (S. A. Temple, Ed.). University of Wisconsin Press, Madison.

WILBUR, S. R. 1978b. The California Condor, 1966–1976: a look at its past and future.
U.S. Department of the Interior, Fish and Wildlife Service, Washington, D.C.

WILBUR, S. R. 1980. Estimating the size and trend of the California Condor population, 1965–1978. California Fish and Game 66:40–48.

WOODS, C. P., W. R. HEINRICH, S. C. FARRY, C. N. PARISH, S. A. H. OSBORN, AND T. J. CADE.
2007. Survival and reproduction of California Condors released in Arizona.
Pages 57–78 *in* California Condors in the 21st Century (A. Mee and L. S. Hall,
Eds.). Series in Ornithology, no. 2.

2

Consequences of a Genetic Bottleneck in California Condors: A Mitochondrial DNA Perspective

Mary S. Adams and Francis X. Villablanca[1]

ABSTRACT.—The California Condor (*Gymnogyps californianus*) has recently survived a severe population bottleneck. The entire population was reduced to 27 individuals in 1982. The number of genetic founders was even smaller. We obtained 482 base pairs of DNA sequence from the mitochondrial control region (CR) of all founder individuals that potentially represented unique maternal haplotypes. Four unique haplotypes were present in the genetic founders. One of these haplotypes is unique to Topatopa, a male brought into captivity in 1967, whose haplotype will not persist in the future population. Haplotype diversity (h) was reduced by 25% between the founder population and our census of the 2002 population. Nucleotide diversity (θ) did not vary significantly between the founders and the current population. Our results provide insights into condor genetics. First, where recessive deleterious alleles have been expressed in progeny (e.g., chondrodystrophy) the breeding pair shares the same mitochondrial haplotype. Second, we identified the presence of a nuclear copy of the mitochondrial control region and provide condor specific primer sequences to preferentially amplify DNA of mitochondrial origin. Third, we confirm low levels of genetic diversity in the captive population as suggested by previous research. Forth, we question whether the low level of diversity is a consequence of the 20th century bottleneck, or if diversity has been historically low over a much longer time scale.

California Condors (*Gymnogyps californianus*) are North America's largest soaring birds. Condors inhabited much of the continental United States prior to European settlement (Simons 1983, Steadman and Miller 1986, Wilbur 1978). However, the range of the species had contracted to

Biological Sciences Department, California Polytechnic State University, San Luis Obispo, California 93407, USA.
[1]*Address correspondence to this author. E-mail: fvillabl@calpoly.edu*

its final remnant distribution by at least the 1970s (Fig. 1). By 1987 the
entire species was represented by only 27 individuals and that year the last
wild Condor was brought into captivity (Snyder and Snyder 2000). All living California Condors are descended from that single population, which
occupied southern California prior to its captivity.

The rapid decline of the California Condor population during the
second half of the 20th century raised concerns about genetic inbreeding. Population genetics theory predicts that severe population bottlenecks
result in a loss of genetic variation (Nei et al. 1975, Lacy 1997, Frankham
1995). This loss of genetic variation increases the likelihood of inbreeding,
reducing individual fitness and overall population viability (Lande 1988).
Inbreeding can reduce fitness through the production of homozygotes.
Homozygotes result in reduced fitness when (1) heterozygotes for rare lethal
or nearly lethal alleles interbreed (Lande 1988), or (2) when homozygotes

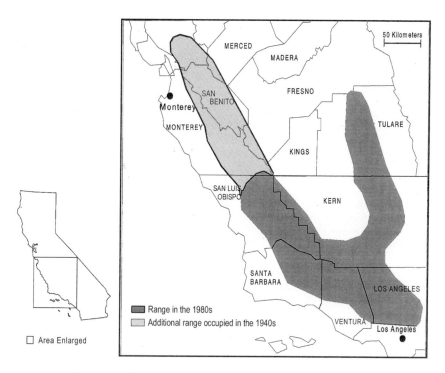

Fig. 1. Range of the recent historical California Condor population, as summarized by Snyder and Snyder (2000). The 1940s distribution (gray plus black) as
proposed by Koford (1953) and Robinson (1940). The 1980 distribution (black) is
based on intensive observations of marked and unmarked but individually identifiable birds (Snyder and Johnson 1985, Meretsky and Snyder 1992). County names
and delineations are included.

are produced at loci where overdominace (heterozygote advantage) is acting. In addition to these well known inbreeding effects, theory also predicts
that smaller populations are more likely to respond to genetic drift than
to selection even when selection is acting (Barton and Charlesworth 1984,
Ohta 1995). Overall, a loss of genetic diversity reduces individual fitness
and mean population fitness, and results in less evolution through natural
selection and more evolution via genetic drift.

The empirical effects of a genetic bottleneck include a loss of heterozygosity (Nei 1987, Frankham et al. 1999), a decrease in allele frequency,
a loss of alleles (Bouzat et al. 1998, Glenn et al. 1999), and an increase in
frequency or fixation of alleles that may be deleterious (Lacy 1997, Ralls et
al. 2000). However since these measures are only meaningful if they can be
used to demonstrate a loss or change, they are best interpreted through comparisons with a pre-bottleneck sample from the same population (Bouzat
et al. 1998, Matocq and Villablanca 2000). Otherwise, we may erroneously
attribute low genetic diversity to a demographic bottleneck (change) when
in fact it reflects historically low levels of diversity (no change).

Review of condor genetics.—Of the 169 fertile California Condor eggs
laid in captivity through 1998, five resulted in severely deformed embryos.
These birth defects were diagnosed as chondrodystrophy, a lethal form of
dwarfism (Ralls et al. 2000). On review of the expression of chondrodystrophy in condors, Ralls et al. (2000) concluded that chondrodystrophy is
likely inherited as an autosomal recessive allele, which is the same mode
of inheritance as in chickens, turkeys and quail. Ralls et al. estimated the
frequency of the chondrodystrophy allele at 0.09 based on the observed
expression of lethality and attributed this high frequency to a founder
event. Since a founder event, or more specifically, the associated increase in
inbreeding, is a requisite of the Ralls et al. hypothesis, their hypothesis is
testable. One could determine if the demographic founders are more inbred
relative to a pre-bottleneck population of California Condors. If there is no
increase in inbreeding, then the chondrodystrophy allele would have been
present at roughly the same frequency over the last 100+ years. In other
words, there is an untested null hypothesis: the frequency of chondrodystrophy alleles may not have changed from the historic frequency.

Several studies have been conducted to evaluate relatedness and
genetic diversity in California Condors. Corbin and Nice (1988) assessed
genetic diversity using blood enzymes and found the population to be
monomorphic or invariant at 24 of 31 loci surveyed. This is a relatively low
level of polymorphism in comparison to other avian species (Corbin and
Nice 1988). Geyer et al. (1993) employed minisatellite DNA fingerprints
to characterize relatedness of 28 captive founders and 4 deceased founders for which tissues were available (Fig. 2). Fingerprint data were used to
identify three distinct clans, where condors within a clan were more closely

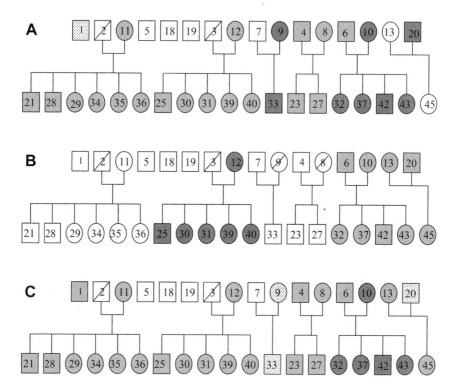

Fig. 2. Genealogical relationships between founding members of the captive flock and results from three different analyses of California Condor genetic variation. Numbers are the studbook (SB) numbers (Mace 2002). Circles represent females and squares represent males. Slashes indicate individuals for which data were not obtained, or were obtained indirectly. Individuals SB #2, and #3 represent two males that died in the wild and whose genotypes have not been recovered. Haplotypes for females SB #8 and #9 were obtained indirectly from offspring (A and C). Maternal genetic founders are the four individual females (SB #10, #11, #12, and #13) that produced female offspring (A and C). (A) Haplotypes identified using mtDNA sequence data. The un-shaded individuals represent haplotype 1, individuals shaded with light gray represent haplotype 2, spotted shading represents Topatopa (SB #3), an individual having a unique haplotype, and individuals shaded in dark gray represent haplotype 4. (B) Clans identified by Geyer et al. (1993) using nuclear DNA fingerprinting. No shading, light shading and dark shading identify individuals grouped into each of three clans. (C) Maternal haplotypes identified from mtDNA RFLP analyses (Chemnick et al. 1999). Unique haplotypes are identified by no shading, light shading, dark shading and spotted shading.

related to each other than to condors in any other clan. When compared to Andean Condors (*Vultur gryphus*), California Condors showed much less diversity and a higher degree of relatedness (Geyer et al. 1993). This is interesting given that Andean Condors themselves have very low genetic diversity (Hendrickson et al. 2003). Finally, Chemnick et al. (2000) used mitochondrial restriction fragment length polymorphism (RFLP) analysis to assess the genetic diversity of 14 potentially unrelated maternal lineages in the founding population (Fig. 2). This study identified four unique maternal lineages and showed that only two of these lineages persisted in the extant population.

The studies of Corbin and Nice (1988), Geyer et al. (1993), and Chemnick et al. (2000) have provided information on the relatedness of founder birds, and were instrumental in developing the initial captive breeding strategy. However, these studies do not provide information regarding the magnitude or rate of loss of genetic diversity in the extant population. Nor are the methods used applicable to the study of preserved (archived museum) specimens. Therefore, they cannot yield an assessment of change in genetic diversity. In other words, using these methods, we could never ask the larger question—has there been a reduction in genetic diversity over the last 100+ years?

Here, we consider the genetic effects of the California Condor population bottleneck. For several reasons, the California Condor offers an important opportunity to measure the genetic effects of a severe demographic bottleneck. First, the condor's decline has been well documented over the past 50 years, and the number of survivors is known (Wilbur 1978, Snyder and Snyder 2000). Second, the pedigree of over 90% of the surviving condors is known (Mace 2002). Third, there is no evidence of historic or recent population subdivision (N. Clipperton unpubl. data, N. Snyder pers. comm.) meaning that all individuals should represent a single breeding population (but *contra* Wilbur [1978] who contended that there were two breeding populations). We provide an assessment of changes in genetic diversity associated with the founding of a captive population. It is our intent that ultimately, data from archival museum specimens will be compared with our data, to determine patterns of genetic variation over a longer time scale.

Demographic and genetic founders.—The global population of wild California Condors was ultimately reduced to 27 individuals by 1987 (Snyder and Snyder 2000). We term these birds the demographic founders. Eleven of the demographic founders never bred in captivity, while sixteen of the demographic founders did breed or had offspring raised in captivity. We term these 16 the genetic founders (Fig. 2A, B, C). These 16 represent those individuals that are hypothetically unrelated and thus potentially represent unique lineages. Our objective was to determine the level of genetic diversity in these 27 (demographic) and subsequently the 16 (genetic) founders. Four of the 16 genetic founders, two males and two females, died in the wild. Therefore, no genetic material was directly available from which to genotype these individuals. However, the mtDNA haplotype was obtained for the two deceased founder females (Table 1 and Fig. 2, studbook [SB] #8 and SB #9) by determining the haplotype of an offspring. Thus, DNA sources were available for 14 of the 16 genetic founders (lacking two males). Ralls and Ballou (2004) state that the genetic founders were 14 individuals. These authors do not consider the two males that were never captured, but which are known to have left progeny (Fig. 2, SB #2 and #3).

Importantly, the maternal inheritance of mitochondrial DNA reduces the genetic founders to only the *maternal* genetic founders. In the genetic founder population only four individual females, SB #10, #11, #12, and #13, produced female offspring who have since reproduced to maintain these maternal haplotype lineages (Fig. 2A, B, C).

In this study we explored mtDNA genetic diversity in three subpopulations of California Condors. Throughout we will refer to the 27 demographic founders (founders of the captive flock), the 16 genetic founders (of which 14 are potentially unrelated), and the 4 maternal genetic

Table 1. Identity of the 14 California Condors genotyped in this study (studbook numbers from Mace 2002), and respective sequence at all variable sites. Base 1 is at the 5' end of the Control Region's Region I and Base 482 is the base at the 5' end of the TDKD primer in CR Region II. Nucleotide positions that are not shown were not variable. Haplotypes are numbered sequentially in order of discovery within the founder California Condor population.

California Condor (Studbook #)	Haplo-type	Base 163	Base 170	Base 237	Base 318	Base 321
AC1 (19)	1	C	A	C	C	T
AC5 (7)	1	C	A	C	C	T
AC6 (5)	1	C	A	C	C	T
BFE (18)	1	C	A	C	C	T
UN1 (13)	1	C	A	C	C	T
AC2 (6)	2	C	A	T	C	T
AC7 (4)	2	C	A	T	C	T
AC8 (12)	2	C	A	T	C	T
Paxa (23)[a]	2	C	A	T	C	T
Tama (11)	2	C	A	T	C	T
Topa (1)	3	C	A	T	C	C
AC3 (10)	4	T	G	T	T	T
AC4 (20)	4	T	G	T	T	T
Sequoia (33)[a]	4	T	G	T	T	T

[a] Progeny used to identify the haplotype of a female genetic founder that was not captured from the wild.

founders (female founders that produce female offspring). Using data from the genetic founders and the pedigree, we extrapolate maternal haplotypes through the population bottleneck (as of 30 June 2002). The current population includes: all living demographic founders, and all living captive born birds (both captive and released).

Measures of genetic diversity.—The amount of genetic variation in a population is a function of the effective population size (N_e) (Wright 1938, Nei 1987, Frankham 1995, Crandall et al. 1999). When there is a rapid reduction in N_e, theory predicts that rare alleles are lost first (Allendorf 1986, Tajima 1989, Matocq and Villablanca 2000). Thus, the first detectable change should be a reduction in the *number* of haplotypes, due to a loss of rare or infrequent sequences, as measured by haplotype diversity. As more and more time accumulates, changes in haplotype *frequencies* can also be used to study loss of genetic diversity. Rare haplotypes, which are lost first, have a small effect on overall haplotype frequency. Significant changes in the frequency of the more common haplotypes are required before shifts in haplotype frequency are detectable. Nucleotide diversity (Nei 1987) reflects frequency differences, but is a measure that is slow to change compared to haplotype diversity.

Mitochondrial DNA.—Our study makes use of DNA sequences from the highly variable mitochondrial control region (CR). The avian CR is subdivided into three regions or domains (Fig. 3A) based on the relative rate of evolution within each region. Region II, the central conserved region (Clayton 1991), is flanked by two variable regions (Tarr 1995, Baker and Marshall 1997, Zink and Blackwell 1998, Saunders and Edwards 2000). Region I contains the most variation, and therefore is the most informative for studies of genetic diversity at the population level (Wenink et al. 1994, Baker and Marshall 1997, Glenn et al. 1999).

Mitochondrial DNA sequence data are a powerful tool for quantifying population level genetic variation (Wilson et al. 1985, Avise et al. 1987, Hillis and Moritz 1990, Geyer et al. 1993, Baker and Marshall 1997). The mitochondrial genome (haploid and maternally inherited) responds more quickly to drift than does the nuclear (diploid) genome (Birky et al. 1989, Palumbi et al. 2001), the mutation rate is up to 10 times faster than in nuclear loci, and there is no recombination (Hillis and Moritz 1990, Baker and Marshall 1997, Futuyma 1998, Palumbi et al. 2001).

Statistical power is greatest when numerous loci are used to make estimates of genetic diversity because of the inclusion of stochastic, or random, variance in genetic drift between loci (Lynch and Crease 1990). This is a compelling reason for using sequences from multiple nuclear loci. However, due to the rapid rate of evolution in the mitochondrial genome relative to the nuclear genome, and the rapid rate of lineage sorting (drift) relative to nuclear genes (Palumbi et al. 2001), our use of mtDNA maximizes

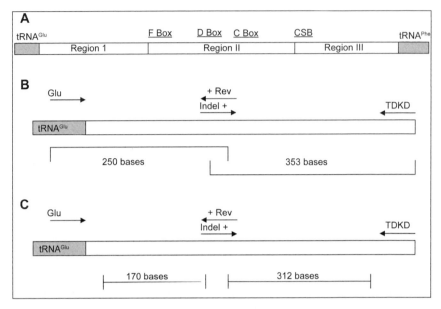

Fig. 3. Schematic representation of the mtDNA locus (Control Region [CR]) under investigation, and the primers used to amplify mitochondrial specific copies of the CR. (A) The three regions of the mitochondrial CR and the location of the conserved sequence blocks (F Box, D Box, C Box and CSB-1), shown on the L strand in 5'–3' orientation. Shaded portions flanking the control region represent tRNA's. (B) Primers shown amplify from tRNA^{Glu} (Glu) to the D Box (TDKD) in two mitochondrial DNA specific fragments (250 and 353 nucleotides in length). (C) Data presented here are from the two fragments (170 and 312 nucleotides) without primers or overlap.

the power available from a single locus (Bouzat et al. 1998, Matocq and Villablanca 2000).

Nuclear copies of mtDNA.—Nuclear copies of mitochondrial sequences (numts) are known to exist. Nuclear paralogs (duplicated sequences) of avian mitochondrial sequences have been observed by several researchers (Quinn and White 1987, Quinn 1992, Kidd and Friesen 1998, Tiedemann and Kistowski 1998, Zhang and Hewitt 1996). Care must be taken to ensure that sequences used for analysis are orthologous (derived by mutation and not gene duplication). If undetected or misidentified, nuclear paralogs can confound phylogenetic and population genetic analysis as they are diploid, bi-parentally inherited (Bensasson et al. 2001), and would erroneously inflate estimates of genetic diversity.

During this study we identified a nuclear copy of our target mitochondrial DNA sequence (for details see Adams 2002). Thus, polymerase chain reaction (PCR) primers were designed to preferentially amplify each of the two (mt and numt) sequences following the methods of Quinn and White (1987) and Sorenson and Fleischer (1996). Condor specific *and* mitochondria control region specific primers were used to preferentially amplify sequences presented herein.

In this study, we used DNA sequences from California Condors to quantify mitochondrial control region genetic diversity using 482 nucleotides of Region I and part of Region II. We evaluated the number of haplotypes, haplotype frequency, haplotype diversity (h), and nucleotide diversity (θ). These measures were then used to determine if there was a significant difference in genetic diversity between the genetic founders, the maternal genetic founders, and the current extant population (as of 30 June 2002), thereby directly assessing changes in genetic diversity over the last 25 years.

METHODS

Samples.—DNA samples for all captive founders were provided by O. Ryder, Conservation and Research for Endangered Species (CRES). Whole genomic DNA was extracted from blood at CRES under sterile laboratory conditions. We obtained mtDNA sequence data from all genetic founders that were brought into captivity (Fig. 2 and Table 1). In addition, in order to confirm our methods, we obtained and compared data from several dam-offspring lineages (SB #12 [AC8] and offspring, $n = 5$; SB #11 [Tama] and offspring, $n = 1$; SB #10 [AC3] and offspring, $n = 1$). Finally, because we inferred the sequence of the CV female (SB #8) from her offspring, we sequenced both offspring (SB #23 and SB #27).

Amplification and sequencing.—Polymerase chain reactions were performed with the avian universal primer L16758 which is complementary to the tRNA^{Glu} adjacent to the control region (Sorenson et al. 1999), and TDKD, a vertebrate universal primer, that binds the conserved D Box sequence (Quinn and Wilson 1993) (Fig. 3A). Each of these was paired with a Condor specific primer, Indel+ (5'-CAAGAACACTACCATCAGACC-3') or +Reverse (5'-GGTCTGATGGTAGTGTTCTTG-3') to amplify mitochondrial specific copied of California Condor control regions. A schematic of these amplicons is shown in Figure 3B, C.

Polymerase chain reactions were performed using ready-to-go PCR beads following the manufacturer's specifications (Amersham Pharmacia Biotech Inc. 2000). The 25 μl reactions included 2.2 μl of each 10 μM primer, 1.0 μl template, 1.5 μl ampliTaq DNA Polymerase, 10mM Tris HCl, 50mM KCL, 1.0mM MgCl$_2$, 200 μM each dNTP and BSA. Polymerase chain reactions were subjected to 30 cycles at 94°F for 30 s, 52–58°F for 30 s, and 72°F for 30 s in a PTC-100 Programmable Thermocycler (MJ Research, Inc. 1991). The PCR fragments (L16758/+reverse, and indel+ /TDKD) were sequenced in both directions. Prior to cycle sequencing, the PCR products were cleaned using QIAquick PCR Purification Kit following the manufactures specifications (QIAGEN, 1999, QIAquick PCR purification kit, Valencia, California).

Cycle sequencing reactions were performed using cycle sequencing (Perkin-Elmer Corp., 1995, Big Dye Terminator Cycle Sequencing version 2.0., California) following manufacturer's specifications (PE Biosystems, 1999, ABI prism big dye terminator cycle sequencing ready reaction kit protocol, California). Cycle sequencing products were purified using ethanol precipitation methods modified from Promega Corp. (1996) and run on an ABI 377 DNA Sequencer.

Chromatograms were visualized, edited, and manually aligned using Sequencher 4.1 (Gene Codes Corporation, Inc. 1999). The composite fragment used in this study extended 482 bases, from Base 1 of the control region (Glenn et al. 1999) to the 5' end of the TDKD primer in the D box, and excluded the 21 base pair sequence of the Indel + and +Reverse primers (Fig. 3C).

Phylogenetics.—MODELTEST, version 3.0 was used to determine the most appropriate model of molecular evolution and to calculate the average nucleotide frequency among all sequences (Posada and Crandall 1998). MODELTEST sequentially compares nested models of DNA substitution using a hierarchical likelihood ratio test. The following parameters (null hypotheses) are tested: equal base frequencies, equal transition and transversion rate, equal rate among sites, and no invariant sites (Posada and Crandall 1998). The most likely model was the HKY model (Hasegawa et al. 1985). The parameters of this model are unequal nucleotide base frequencies (estimated at A = 0.3322, C = 0.2970, G = 0.1215 and T = 0.2493) and a transition bias (transition/transversion ratio) of 5:0. A weighted parsimony model (PAUP*) was used to generate a phylogeny of the haplotypes (Fig. 4). The HKY model was also used in analyses conducted using the FLUCTUATE program (LAMARC, Kuhner et al. 1997).

Haplotype and nucleotide diversity.—Pairwise sequence comparisons were conducted using PAUP (V 4.0b, Swofford 1998) to identify unique haplotypes, calculate number of polymorphic sites, and calculate haplotype frequencies in the genetic and maternal genetic founders. The haplotype frequency was tabulated as a function of the number of individuals in each group (genetic founders $n = 14$; maternal genetic founders $n = 4$; and the extant population as of June 2002, $n = 207$) having each of the possible haplotypes.

Haplotype diversity (h) was calculated for the demographic and maternal genetic founders, and for the current population (following Nei 1987, equation 8.1). Haplotype diversity ranges from 0 to 1 (Nei 1987). If all individuals in a large sample have a unique haplotype, the haplotype

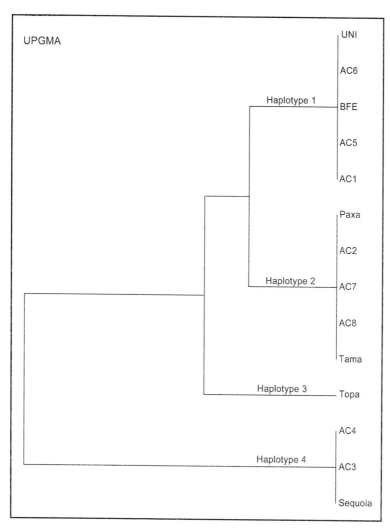

Fig. 4. Neighbor joining UPGMA phylogeny for all 14 genetic founders of the California Condor captive flock. These 14 founders processed 4 haplotypes.

diversity of the population will approach 1.0. If all individuals in a large sample have the same haplotype the haplotype diversity of the population is 0.

Nucleotide diversity, or the average sequence diversity at the nucleotide level (θ), was calculated for each of the three groups following Watterson (1975) and using the FLUCTUATE program, version 1.1 (Kuhner et al. 1997). Theta (θ) is a population parameter that is a function of effective population size (N_e) and the mutation rate (μ), ($\theta = N_e\mu$). Theta is estimated from samples of sequences using nucleotide diversity (π) which is a function of the haplotype frequencies and the number of nucleotide differences (distance) between haplotypes (Nei 1987). The FLUCTUATE program uses Metropolis-Hastings Markov Chain Monte Carlo genealogy sampling to make a maximum likelihood estimate of the population parameters θ and g (growth rate) assuming the loci sampled are not affected by selection or recombination. This method for estimating θ is preferred since FLUCTUATE does not require an assumption of a stable population size. This is an assumption we were not willing to make since population size is a parameter we predict is changing. The accuracy of the θ estimate was determined using the likelihood curve or the graph of the log likelihood values associated with each estimate of theta. This curve is used to visualize an estimated 95% confidence interval of θ (Kuhner et al. 1998). We used a short chain length of 100 times the number of sequences and a long chain length of 1000 times the number of sequences, with 10 and 2 chains respectively per run. FLUCTUATE analyses for each of the three groups were replicated 500 times and the average θ was calculated for each set of replicates. Some replicates produced estimates of θ that were near infinity or negative infinity. These replicates were discarded and re-run. We used the data from the FLUCTUATE run that was nearest to the global average θ for further analysis.

Herein we have quantified the actual number of maternal lineages in the entire population and the fraction of those that are still extant in the breeding population. We have genotyped all female individuals that were brought into captivity or produced offspring that were brought into captivity. Consequently, we are not evaluating sample statistics, but are looking at the actual population parameter.

Results

Haplotype frequency and diversity.—The genetic founders revealed four haplotypes or unique sequences (Table 1 and Fig. 4). The four haplotypes are defined by five polymorphic sites (Table 1). The distribution of these haplotypes on the pedigree is shown in Figure 2A. One of these haplotypes is unique to Topatopa, the first male brought into captivity in 1967. Since males do not genetically transmit mtDNA to their offspring and Topatopa is the only living representative of this maternal lineage, only three of the four haplotypes will persist in the future California Condor population.

The frequencies of haplotypes have shifted over time (Table 2). Haplotype 1 has become progressively more rare and haplotype 2 progressively more common. Haplotype 4 was relatively uncommon in the genetic founders compared to haplotypes 1 and 2 but has increased its frequency relative to haplotype 1. As noted above, haplotype 3 will not survive into the

Table 2. Haplotype count (frequency) in genetic founders, maternal genetic founders, and the current California Condor population (as of 30 June 2002). Haplotype diversity (h) where $h = 1 - \sum x^2_i$, and x is the frequency of each haplotype.

Group name and population size	Haplotype 1	Haplotype 2	Haplotype 3	Haplotype 4	h
Genetic Founders					
$n = 14$	5 (0.357)	5 (0.357)	1 (0.071)	3 (0.214)	0.694
Maternal Founders					
$n = 4$	1 (0.25)	2 (0.50)	0 (0.00)	1 (0.25)	0.625
2002 Population					
$n = 207$	30 (0.145)	128 (0.618)	1 (0.005)	48 (0.232)	0.543

future. Assuming no mutation in the mitochondrial CR, and using the pedigree (Mace 2002) to extrapolate haplotypes, we predicted haplotypes for the entire extant California Condor population ($n = 207$). Haplotype diversity (h) for genetic founders was 0.694. In the extant population h was 0.524. The changes in h reflected a 25% decrease in haplotype diversity (Table 2).

Nucleotide diversity.—There was no shift in nucleotide diversity (Table 3). The mean nucleotide diversity (± standard error) in the maternal genetic founders overlaps with that of genetic founders in the 2002 population (Table 3).

Discussion

We examined mitochondrial control region sequences from genetic founders of the captive California Condor population. The nucleotide sequences of the entire Region I and part of Region II in the mitochondrial CR were determined by direct sequencing of 2 PCR products for 14 individuals (12 founders for which samples were available and 2 founder females for whom samples were only available through offspring; see Fig. 2). We detected a reduction in haplotype diversity and little or no change in nucleotide diversity. Thus, some diversity was lost in the population that was brought into captivity. Whether this population was genetically impoverished relative to pre-1900s California Condors remains unknown.

Table 3. Nucleotide diversity (θ) in Region I plus part of Region II of the mt Control Region in California Condors. None of the differences between founding groups are statistically significantly (standard errors [SE] overlap with mean values between comparisons).

Group name and population size (n)	θ	SE
Genetic founders (14)	0.00300	0.00027
Maternal genetic founders (4)	0.00470	0.00113
2002 population (207)	0.00333	0.00003

Inheritance patterns for haplotypes.—When tested, sequences of mitochondrial origin were identical between female parents and their offspring. This allowed us to verify that sequences within a maternal line were identical. In addition, because we inferred the sequence of the CV (SB #8) female from her offspring, we sequenced both Cuyama (SB #27) and Paxa (SB #23). As expected the two female offspring sequences were identical.

Haplotype frequencies.—Haplotype frequencies in the California Condor population have changed. Genetic drift theory predicts that in a randomly mating population haplotype frequencies would change due to chance alone, with some frequencies increasing, moving toward fixation, and some declining (Table 2). An alternative hypothesis is that natural selection on mtDNA haplotypes has shifted. With condors, this alternative hypothesis is unlikely. First, artificial selection has occurred since pairings were made at the captive breeding facilities according to the genetic desirability criteria (e.g., forced pairing with non-clan members following Geyer et al. 1993). Second, even if natural selection is acting on this small population, chance is more likely to effect genotype frequencies than selection simply because of the populations' small size (Barton and Charlesworth 1984, Ohta 1995).

Haplotye diversity.—We observed a 25% decrease in haplotype diversity (Table 2). This is a direct result of the recent increase in population size of condors in captivity, and the associated shifts in haplotype frequency. For example Topatopa's haplotype "fell" from a frequency of about 1 in 20 to about 1 in 200 simply as a result of population growth. Baker and Marshall (1997) compiled data from several avian species and assessed the haplotype diversity in Region I of the CR, finding that values of Nei's (1987) h ranged from 0.449 to 0.982. In their study, values for non-bottlenecked species ranged from 0.827 to 0.982. One species (the Knot, *Calidris canutus*) with known low genetic diversity for nuclear markers (allozymes) was the low value of 0.449. Indeed, when compared to Baker and Marshall's non-bottlenecked avian species, the haplotype diversity in the genetic founder ($h = 0.694$) and current California Condor population ($h = 0.524$) were both low enough to be outliers. Haplotype diversity in California Condors is lower than in the wide-ranging and apparently non-bottlenecked Andean Condor (Hendrickson et al. 2003). Thus, it is possible that the low values we observe are consistent with the low values expected for megafauna with a restricted range (Hendrickson et al. 2003), or it is possible that diversity has been lost during a bottleneck. A historic, pre-bottleneck population sample of the California Condor is necessary to correctly determine whether the starting value of haplotype diversity we observe ($h = 0.694$) represents a historical value or recent reduction.

Nucleotide diversity.—The nucleotide diversity estimate for the genetic founders reflects the remnant genetic diversity of the wild California Condor population prior to its captivity. The nucleotide diversity estimate for the 2002 population reflects the demographic history of the California Condor since its captivity and growth from the four maternal genetic founders. These two populations showed no significant difference in nucleotide diversity. Populations that have the same demographic history should have statistically indistinguishable values of theta (θ) (Slatkin 1987). Therefore, we expected that the log likelihood estimates of theta would not be significantly different under three possible scenarios: the population size reduction was not significant compared to past reductions; the population size reduction was too brief to have an evolutionary consequence; and/or the California Condor has already been through such demographic–genetic bottlenecks during its history. From the results of our study, it might be concluded that the population size reduction has not lasted long enough to have any effect on haplotype diversity. Most likely, if more time had passed, there would have been a greater (significant) reduction in nucleotide diversity. That no difference was observed implies that this measure of genetic diversity is insensitive to very large but temporary changes in population size. Or, alternatively, that this demographic crash (including its duration) is not too distinct from other naturally occurring crashes experienced by this species. Again, we would like to point out that a historic population sample of the California Condor is necessary to correctly discriminate between these alternative hypotheses.

Comparison with other genetic studies of California Condors.—The DNA fingerprint analysis of Geyer et al. (1993) was based on nuclear DNA digested with three restriction endonucleases. Their study revealed three clans. Their resulting groupings differed from the four haplotype groupings identified in this study. This difference might be expected when comparing mitochondrial sequence data to nuclear minisatellite data (see Fig. 2A, B, respectively). It is of note that in our study Topatopa was identified as having a unique mitochondrial haplotype, yet based on Geyer et al.'s nuclear analysis, Topatopa was placed into the largest clan.

The mitochondrial genome of California Condors has been studied previously through an RFLP analysis. Using five restriction enzymes, Chemnick et al. (2000) identified four haplotypes, but found only two persisting in the extant population. Our results were generally concordant with the results of the mtDNA RFLP analysis, with the exception that Topatopa has a unique mitochondrial haplotype in our analysis. It is important to note that none of the restriction enzymes used in the RFLP analysis would have detected the DNA sequence variation identified herein, because the recognition sequences of those enzymes are not contained in the fragment that we sequenced.

In summary, we corroborate the loss of genetic (mtDNA) diversity associated with the founding of the captive population. The number of haplotypes has been reduced as has haplotype diversity. Although our results do show a 25% decrease in the haplotype diversity between the genetic founders and the current population, our results did not show an apparent change in the average nucleotide diversity (θ). Haplotype diversity is more sensitive to changes in population size and the frequency of haplotypes within the population. In contrast nucleotide diversity is an estimate of heterozygosity at the nucleotide level. It is known that heterozygosity is slower to change than allele frequencies since rare alleles are the ones lost first and these contribute little to heterozygosity (Nei et al. 1975, Watterson 1975, Hartl and Clark 1989).

The genetic founders have only four unique mitochondrial CR haplotypes, defined by five polymorphic sites. Interestingly, haplotype 3 is unique to Topatopa, the oldest living California Condor brought into captivity as a chick in 1967. Due to the maternal inheritance of mitochondrial DNA this haplotype will not persist in the population, as Topatopa cannot pass it on to his offspring. Topatopa may be part of the largest nuclear clan, yet the unique mtDNA haplotype suggests that he also carries some additional nuclear genetic variance not found in other founders. Importantly, he has bred very successfully in the captive breeding program.

Inbreeding.—The entire captive flock was founded by six breeding pairs (Fig. 2). Males from two of these pairs were never genotyped. The dam and sire in three of the four genotyped pairs had different mitochondrial haplotypes from each other. Our DNA sequence result corroborates the same finding as the mitochondrial RFLP analysis (Chemnick et al. 2000; see our Fig. 2C). The CV pair (SB #4 and #8) is the only pair to share the same maternal haplotype. This is of interest because (1) it may indicate a higher level of relatedness within this pair; (2) these are the parents of the only known wild hatched chick that died with abnormal limb and skull development which are symptomatic of the lethal recessive chondrodystrophy gene (Snyder and Snyder 2000); and (3) they are also the parents of a male, Cuyama (SB #27), which fathered chicks expressing chondrodystrophy in captivity (Ralls et al. 2000).

Although a behavioral component has not yet been linked to chondrodystrophy or any another genetically based condition, behavior may affect fitness. Both Paxa and Cuyama exhibited abnormal behavior as chicks. Observed behaviors included excessive gaping and wing drooping, respectively (Snyder and Snyder 2000). Field observations in the early 1980s resulted in the documentation of several abnormal reproductive behaviors among wild pairs. These included poor coordination of egg incubation resulting in egg neglect and nest failure, aggressive interaction at the nest site and attempted homosexual copulation between two birds (Snyder and Snyder 2000).

Future implications.—In the captive California Condor population, the expression of deleterious alleles is concordant with the mating of individuals sharing the same haplotype (i.e., the CV pair [SB #4 and #8] and offspring). If we assume that individuals sharing a haplotype are more closely related than individuals with different haplotypes then we could use haplotypes to infer inbreeding. We suggest our results be used in exactly that manner.

Because mtDNA is passed along from a female to all her offspring without recombination, the techniques developed in this study can be used to identify maternal parents. For example, if maternity of a wild born condor is unknown and the potential female parents are from different maternal lineages (have different haplotypes) the maternal parent can be identified by sequencing a small fragment of mitochondrial DNA. A possible source of DNA that could be used includes feathers or egg shell fragments from the nest site.

Until recently, genetic diversity could only be assessed in extant populations. In addition, the amount of diversity was usually evaluated in comparison to some closely related species or population. However, this approach has the potential to lead to erroneous conclusions (see Bouzat et al. 1998, Matocq and Villablanca 2000). With current molecular methods and the primers developed in this study, it is possible to directly quantify the genetic variability of the California Condor both before and after the bottleneck of 1987. Such an analysis would allow us to fully understand the impact of this bottleneck and determine if and how much genetic diversity has been lost. Moreover, such an analysis would allow us to determine if the California Condor is one of a small number of species that show historically low levels of genetic diversity (Matocq and Villablanca 2000, Pertoldi et al. 2001).

ACKNOWLEDGMENTS

Scholarship funds to M.A.S. were provided by the Los Angeles County Audubon Society. Support and training were provided through NSF DBI #9510822 to F.X.V.

LITERATURE CITED

ADAMS, M. S. 2002. Genetic Variation in the Captive Population of the California Condor (*Gymnogyps californianus*). Masters Thesis. California Polytechnic State University, San Luis Obispo, CA.

ALLENDORF, F. W. 1986. Genetic drift and the loss of alleles versus heterozygosity. Zoo Biology 5:181–190.

AMERSHAM PHARMACIA BIOTECH, INC. 2000. Ready to go PCR beads. Instruction manual. New Jersey, USA.

AVISE, J. C., J. ARNOLD, R. M. BALL, E. BERMINGHAM, T. LAMB, J. E. NEIGEL, C. A. REEB, AND N. C. SAUNDERS. 1987. Intraspecific phylogeography: the mitochondrial

DNA bridge between population genetics and systematics. Annual Review of Ecology and Systematics 18:489–522.

BAKER, A. J., AND H. D. MARSHALL. 1997. Mitochondrial control region sequences as tools for understanding evolution. Pages 30–50 *in* Avian Molecular Evolution and Systematics (D. P. Mindell, Ed.). Academic Press, San Diego.

BARTON, N. H., AND B. CHARLESWORTH. 1984. Genetic revolutions, founder effects, and speciation. Annual Review of Ecology and Systematics 15:133–164.

BENSASSON, D., D. X. ZHANG, D. L. HARTL, AND G. M. HEWITT. 2001. Mitochondrial pseudogenes: evolution's misplaced witnesses. Trends in Ecology and Evolution 16:314–321.

BIRKY, C. W., P. FUERST, AND T. MARUYAMA. 1989. Organelle gene diversity under migration, mutation and drift: equilibrium expectations, approach to equilibrium, effects of heteroplasmic cells, and comparison to nuclear genes. Genetics 121:613–628.

BOUZAT, J. L., H. A. LEWIN, AND K. N. PAIGE. 1998. The ghost of genetic diversity past: Historical DNA analysis of the greater prairie chicken. American Naturalist 229:1–6.

CHEMNICK, L. G., A. T. KUMAMOTO, AND O. A. RYDER. 2000. Genetic analyses in support of conservation efforts for the California Condor. International Zoo Yearbook 37:330–339.

CLAYTON, D. A. 1991. Replication and transcription of vertebrate mitochondrial DNA. Annual Review of Cell Biology 7:453–478.

CORBIN, K., AND C. C. NICE. 1988. Genetic variation of California Condors. Journal of Minnesota Academy of Science 53:27.

CRANDALL, K. A., D. POSADA, AND D. VASCO. 1999. Effective population sizes: missing measures and missing concepts. Animal Conservation 2:317–319.

FRANKHAM, R. 1995. Effective population size/adult population size ratios in wildlife: a review. Genetical Research 66:95–107.

FRANKHAM, R., K. LEES, M. E. MONTGOMERY, P. R. ENGLAND, E. H. LOWE, AND D. A. BRISCOE. 1999. Do population size bottlenecks reduce evolutionary potential? Animal Conservation 2:255–260.

FUTUYMA, D. J. 1998. Evolutionary Biology, 3rd edition. Sinauer Associates, Sunderland Massachusetts.

GENE CODES CORPORATION, INC. 1999. Sequencher 4.1 user manual. Michigan, USA.

GEYER, J. C., O. A. RYDER, L. G. CHEMNICK, AND E. A. THOMPSON. 1993. Analysis of relatedness in the California Condors from DNA fingerprints. Molecular Biology and Evolution 10:571–589.

GLENN, T. C., W. STEPHAN, AND M. J. BRAUN. 1999. Effects of a population bottleneck on whooping crane mitochondrial DNA variation. Conservation Biology 13:1097–1107.

HARTL, D. L., AND A. G. CLARK. 1989. Principles of Population Genetics, 2nd edition. Sinauer Associates, Sunderland Massachusetts.

HASEGAWA, M., H. KISHINO, AND T. YANO. 1985. Dating the human-ape splitting by molecular clock of mitochondrial DNA. Journal of Molecular Evolution 21:485–501.

HENDRICKSON, S. L., R. BLEIWEISS, J. C. MATHEUS, L. S. DE MATHEUS, N. L. JACOME, AND E. PAVEZ. 2003. Low genetic variability in the geographically widespread Andean Condor. Condor 105:1–12.

HILLIS, D. M., AND C. G. MORITZ. 1990. Molecular Systematics. Sinauer Associates, Sunderland, Massachusetts.

KIDD, M. G., AND V. L. FRIESEN. 1998. Sequence variation in the guillemot (Alcidae: *Cepphus*) mitochondrial control region and its nuclear homolog. Molecular Biology and Evolution 15:61–70.

KOFORD, C. B. 1953. The California Condor. National Audubon Research Report 4: 1–154.

KUHNER, M. P., P. BEERLI, AND J. YAMAMOTO. 1997. LAMARK software package. [Online.] Available at http:// evolution. genetics. washington. edu/ lamarc/ fluctuate.html.

KUHNER, M. K., J. YAMATO, AND J. FELSENSTEIN. 1998. Maximum likelihood estimation of population growth rates based on the coalescent. Genetics 149:429–434.

LACY, R. C. 1997. Importance of genetic variation to the viability of mammalian populations. Journal of Mammalogy 78:320–335.

LANDE, R. 1988. Genetics and demography in biological conservation. Science 241: 1455–1460.

LYNCH, M., AND T. CREASE. 1990. The analysis of population survey data on DNA sequence variation. Molecular Biology and Evolution 7:377–394.

MACE, M. 2002. California Condor Studbook 2002. Zoological Society of San Diego.

MATOCQ, M. D., AND F. X. VILLABLANCA. 2000. Low genetic diversity in an endangered species: Recent or historic pattern? Biological Conservation 98:61–68.

MERETSKY, V. J., AND N. F. R. SNYDER. 1992. Range use and movements of California condors. Condor 94:313–335.

MJ RESEARCH, INC. 1991. The PTC-100 Programmable thermal controller operations manual. Massachusetts, USA.

NEI, M. 1987. Molecular Population Genetics and Evolution. New York.

NEI, M., T. MARUYAMA, AND R. CHAKRABORTY. 1975. The bottleneck effect and genetic variability in populations. Evolution 29:1–10.

OHTA, T. 1995. Synonymous and nonsynonomous substitutions in mammalian genes and the nearly neutral theory. Journal of Molecular Evolution 40:56–63.

PALUMBI, S. R., F. CIPRIANO, AND M. P. HARE. 2001. Predicting nuclear gene coalescence from mitochondrial data: the three-times rule. Evolution 55:859–868.

PERTOLDI, C., M. M. HANSEN, V. LOESCHCKE, A. B. MADSEN, L. JACOBSEN, AND H. BAAGOE. 2001. Genetic consequences of population decline in the European Otter: an assessment of microsatellite DNA variation in Danish otters from 1883–1993. Proceedings of the Royal Society of London, Series B 268:1775–1781.

POSADA, D., AND K. A. CRANDALL. 1998. MODELTEST: testing the model of DNA substitution. Bioinformatics 14:817–818.

PROMEGA CORP. 1996. Protocols and Application Guide (K. Dole, Ed.). Promega Corporation, Madison, Wisconsin.

QUINN, T. W. 1992. The genetic legacy of mother goose—phylogenetic patterns of lesser snow geese *Chen caerulescens caerulescens* maternal lineages. Molecular Ecology 1:105–117.

QUINN, T. W., AND A. C. WILSON. 1993. Sequence evolution in and around the mitochondrial control region in birds. Journal of Molecular Evolution 37:417–25.

QUINN, T. W., AND B. N. WHITE. 1987. Analysis of DNA sequence variation. Pages 163–198 *in* Avian Genetics: A Population and Ecological Approach (F. Cooke and P. A. Buckley, Eds.). Academic Press, London.

Ralls, K., and J. D. Ballou. 2004. Genetic status and management of California Condors. Condor 106:215–228.

Ralls, K., J. D. Ballou, B. A. Rideout, and R. Frankham. 2000. Genetic management of chondrodystrophy in California Condors. Animal Conservation 3:145–153.

Robinson, C. S. 1939. Observations and notes on the California Condor from data collected on Los Padres National Forest. U.S. Forest Service, Santa Barbara, California.

Saunders, M. A., and S. V. Edwards. 2000. Dynamics and phylogenetic implications of mtDNA control region sequences in New World jays (Aves: Corvidae). Journal of Molecular Evolution 51:97–109.

Simons, D. D. 1983. Interactions between California Condors and humans in prehistoric far west North America. Pages 470–494 in Vulture Biology and Management (S. R. Wilbur and J. A. Jackson, Eds.). U.C. Berkley Press.

Slatkin, M. 1987. The average number of sites separating DNA sequences drawn from a subdivided population. Theoretical Population Biology 32:42–49.

Snyder, N. F. R., and E. V. Johnson. 1985. Photographic censusing of the 1982–1983 California Condor population. Condor 97:1–13.

Snyder, N. F. R., and H. A. Snyder. 2000. The California Condor: A Saga of Natural History and Conservation. Academic Press, San Diego, CA.

Sorenson, M. D., J. C. Ast, D. E. Dimcheff, T. Yuri, and D. P. Mindell. 1999. Primers for a PCR-based approach to mitochondrial genome sequencing in birds and other vertebrates. Molecular Phylogenetics and Evolution 12:105–114.

Sorenson, M. D., and R. C. Fleischer. 1996. Multiple independent transpositions of mitochondrial DNA control region sequences to the nucleus. Proceedings of the National Academy of Sciences USA. 93:15239–15243.

Steadman, D. W., and N. G. Miller. 1986. California Condors associated with spruce-Jack pine woodlands in the late Pleistocene of New York. Quatenary Research 28:415–426.

Swofford, D. L. 1998. PAUP*. Phylogenetic Analysis Using Parsimony, version 4b. Sinauer Associates, Sunderland Massachusetts.

Tajima, F. 1989. The effect of change in population size on DNA polymorphism. Genetics 123:597–601.

Tarr, C. L. 1995. Primers for amplification and determination of mitochondrial control region sequences in oscine passerines. Molecular Ecology 4:527–529.

Tiedemann, R., and K. G. von Kistowski. 1998. Novel primers for the mitochondrial control region and its homologous nuclear pseudogene in the Eider Duck Somateria mollissima. Animal Genetics 29:468.

Watterson, G. A. 1975. On the number of segregating sites in genetical models without recombination. Theoretical Population Biology 7:256–276.

Wenink, P. W., A. J. Baker, and M. G. J. Tilanus. 1994. Mitochondrial control-region sequences in two shorebird species, the Turnstone and the Dunlin, and their utility in population genetic studies. Molecular Biology and Evolution 11:22–31.

Wilbur, S. R. 1978. The California Condor, 1966–1976: a look at its past and future. U.S. Department of the Interior, Fish and Wildlife Service, Washington, D.C.

Wilson, A. C., R. L. Cann, S. M. Car, M. George, U. B. Gyllensten, K. M. Bychowski, R. G. Higuchi, S. R. Palumbi, E. M. Prager, R. D. Sage, and M. Stoneking. 1985.

Mitochondria DNA and two perspectives on evolutionary genetics. Biological Journal of the Linnean Society 26:375–400.

WRIGHT, S. 1938. Size of population and breeding structure in relation to evolution. Science 87:430–431.

ZHANG, D. X., AND G. M. HEWITT. 1996. Nuclear interactions: Challenges for mitochondrial DNA markers. Trends in Ecology and Evolution 11:247–251.

ZINK, R. M., AND R. C. BLACKWELL. 1998. Molecular systematics and biogeography of aridland gnatcatchers (genus *Polioptila*) and evidence supporting species status of the California gnatcatcher (*Polioptila californica*). Molecular Phylogenetics and Evolution 9:26–32.

3

Survival and Reproduction of California Condors Released in Arizona

*Christopher P. Woods, William R. Heinrich,
Shawn C. Farry, Chris N. Parish,
Sophie A. H. Osborn, and Tom J. Cade* [1]

ABSTRACT.—A drastic decline in California Condors (*Gymnogyps californianus*) resulted in their complete removal from the wild in the 1980s and subsequent establishment of captive populations to propagate offspring for reintroductions. In 1996 The Peregrine Fund began releasing captive-raised condors in the Grand Canyon region of northern Arizona. By July 2005, 77 juvenile or immature condors had been released, 26 (34%) of which had died. Eight condors perished in their first 90 days following release and 14 in total during their first year in the wild (survival rate of 79.6% as determined by days of exposure). Survivorship increased to 89.5% for condors in the second through fourth years following release, and to 97.8% from the fifth year onward. Lead poisoning from ingested shotgun pellets and bullet fragments was the greatest cause of fatalities for birds after their first 90 days free-flying, with six birds known and two suspected to have died from lead toxicity. Many surviving condors were also treated with chelation therapy at least once to reduce high blood lead levels. Under a program of intensive management, survival rates were in the range expected for wild condors, and as of December 2005 the released population had aged to include 14 adults which had laid 11 eggs and fledged 5 young. Self-sustainability, however, will require that lead in the condors' food supply be greatly reduced or eliminated.

The Peregrine Fund, 5668 Flying Hawk Lane, Boise, Idaho 83709, USA.
[1]*Address correspondence to this author. E-mail: tcade@peregrinefund.org*

The ranges of the two largest extant cathartids, the Andean Condor (*Vultur gryphus*) and the slightly smaller California Condor (*Gymnogyps californianus*), have contracted greatly in historical times, and the California Condor is critically endangered (BirdLife International 2000). Few California Condors remained by the time Koford (1953) undertook the first concerted effort to study them and little is known conclusively regarding their natural mortality, whether they ever occurred at high densities, or what factors limited their numbers in the past. It is certain, however, that human-related factors, including shooting, poisoning, and encroachment into breeding and foraging areas were associated with a precipitous population decline in the last two centuries (Koford 1953; Wilbur 1973, 1978; Kiff 2000; Snyder and Snyder 2000; Fry and Maurer 2003; Snyder this volume).

In the 1980s all remaining condors were brought into captivity, and captive breeding populations were established, with the ultimate goal of restoring wild populations (see Kiff 2000, Snyder and Snyder 2000). Reintroductions began in 1992, when two condors were released at the Sespe Condor Sanctuary in southern California. Since then the magnitude of the release program has grown, and more than 100 condors now fly freely in southern and central California, northern Arizona and southern Utah, and Baja California, Mexico.

Condors seem always to have occurred in landscapes that included rugged or otherwise inaccessible terrain for nesting, open areas that allowed for extended soaring flight, and an adequate supply of medium and large mammalian carcasses. California Condors ranged across North America in prehistoric times, and formerly bred in northern Arizona along the Colorado River in what is now Grand Canyon National Park (Miller 1960, Emslie 1987). Big birds require big country, and habitat in the canyonlands of northern Arizona and southern Utah appears suitable for condor recovery because it contains extensive rugged terrain with abundant potential nesting cliffs, open areas, strong updrafts, large ungulate populations, and relatively limited human disturbance (Rea 1981).

Since 1996, condors have been released in northern Arizona along escarpments 85 to 150 km north of Grand Canyon National Park as a "nonessential experimental" population under provisions of Section 10(j) of the Endangered Species Act. As of July 2005, 50 juvenile (less than one year of age) and 27 immature (one to six years of age) condors have been released, 26 of which have died. Now, as birds from the earliest-released cohorts have begun to breed and eventual population sustainability can be contemplated, a review of mortality factors for the released birds is timely. Meretsky et al. (2000) summarized early, unpublished reports on mortality for condors in both Arizona and California; here we update and examine the factors that have led to condor deaths specifically in Arizona and Utah, and provide estimates of survival for different age groups.

METHODS

California Condors were released in groups of two to eight individuals (three birds were also released singly) at two sites in northern Arizona: a primary site at Vermilion Cliffs, Coconino Co., (release years: 1996, 1997, 2000 onward; Fig. 1) and an alternate one at Hurricane Cliffs, Mohave Co., (release years: 1998, 1999; see Harting et al. [1995] and Johnson and Garrison [1996] for site description and release protocol). Condors to be released were always first maintained together at the site. Prior to 2000, condors were generally held for four to six weeks in a release pen at the cliff edge before release (Plate 7). From 2000 onward, pre-release birds were usually held in a large flight pen set back from the cliff for weeks to months before being moved to the release pen, from which they were released after a week or so. After the first release, free-flying condors had access to the exterior of the pen(s) and sometimes interacted with the pre-release birds. Interactions with humans were kept to a minimum. Nearly half (49%) of all condors were released in November or December, and 65% were less than one year old when released, having hatched the previous March, April, or May (Table 1). Four captive-reared adult condors were released experimentally in December 2000, but two quickly perished and the remaining two were consequently retrapped (see Results for further details). Owing to the unique nature and short duration of those releases, data from those birds were not included in any analyses in this paper except where stated explicitly. The earliest releases typically consisted of cohorts of six or more condors released together, although this protocol was replaced in 2002 by successive releases of birds in smaller cohorts. Condors released in Arizona were captive-reared at three facilities: 53 birds were reared at The Peregrine Fund's World Center for Birds of Prey in Boise, Idaho; 12 at the Los Angeles Zoo; and 12 at the San Diego Wild Animal Park. Five wild-reared young

Fig. 1. Condor release site at the Vermilion Cliffs, Arizona, as seen from the southwest. (Photo by C. N. Parish.)

Table 1. Release dates and numbers of California Condors released in northern Arizona between December 1996 and July 2005. All releases except those in 1998 and 1999 were at the Vermilion Cliff release site in Coconino County.

Release date	Condors released (n)	Mean age at release (days ± SD)	No. free-flying in July 2005
12 Dec 1996	6	205 ± 9	3
14 May 1997	4	771 ± 13	2
26 May 1997	5	760 ± 19	4
20 Nov 1997	4	211 ± 16	2
18 Nov 1998	9 [a]	215 ± 22	3
6 Dec 1999	7 [b]	246 ± 26	3
29 Dec 2000	8 [c]	243 ± 10 [d]	6 [e]
16 Feb 2002	6	289 ± 14	3
25 Sep 2002	3	500 ± 4	2
9 Dec 2002	2	592 ± 13	2
3 Mar 2003	3	315 ± 9	3
4 Oct 2003	2	532 ± 2	2
29 Nov 2003	2	580 ± 5	2
9 Jan 2004	1	614	1
20 Mar 2004	4	338 ± 5	3
16 Oct 2004	3	559 ± 10	3
4 Feb 2005	3	651 ± 15	3
1 Mar 2005	5	298 ± 20	4
Overall	77	394 ± 205	50

[a] One bird was released singly on 23 Nov 1998. That bird was 965 days old, and is not included in average age calculation for this release.

[b] One bird was released singly on 23 Dec 1999.

[c] Four adults were also released about this time: one pair on 7 Dec 2000 and the second pair on 19 Dec 2000. These were not included in average age calculation for this release (see text for details).

[d] Not included in average age calculation for this release is one 586-day-old condor.

[e] One bird from this cohort was permanently removed from the free-flying population.

also fledged in Arizona; data from those condors, one of which later died, were not included in analyses in this paper.

All released condors were fitted with a redundant system of two radio transmitters, usually consisting of paired patagial transmitters although for a few the second transmitter was tail-mounted (Wallace et al. 1980, Meretsky and Snyder 1992). All transmitters are presently equipped with a fatality sensor, although this was not the case for birds from the earliest releases, for which death was initially inferred from lack of variation in signal strength or direction. More recently some condors have also carried GPS satellite transmitters. All birds were given large numbered patagial tags for visual identification. Condors have been monitored continually since the initial release in 1996 using radio telemetry and visual confirmation of individual identity. Whenever possible, birds have been located daily and, consequently, field data have confirmed to within a day or so the date of most deaths. For four birds that disappeared and were presumed to have perished, however, the last day of radio contact was used as the day of death, although those birds could conceivably have lived for weeks or months thereafter.

Carcasses of dead condors were removed from the field and chilled as quickly as conditions permitted, and then shipped to the San Diego Zoo, in California, where necropsies were performed. Two exceptions occurred in which law enforcement agencies were involved and took possession of the carcasses. Diagnosis of lead poisoning was based on toxicological analyses routinely performed for each fatality at the San Diego Zoo and by the presence of lead bullet fragments or shotgun pellets in some poisoned birds (determined by radiograph and/or necropsy). One condor whose carcass was unrecoverable but whose death coincided with a widespread lead-poisoning event was assumed to have succumbed to lead toxicity (see Results). Fatalities ascribed to Golden Eagles (*Aquila chrysaetos*), whether resulting from aggressive interactions or predation, were characterized by partially plucked carcasses, puncture wounds about the head consistent with large talons, and field observations of eagles in the vicinity. Deaths attributed to coyote (*Canis latrans*) predation were characterized by partially consumed carcasses, chewed feathers, fresh coyote tracks, and scat in the immediate area. Signs of struggle distinguished predation by coyotes from scavenging.

Because the daily fates of all members of the population were almost always known, survivorship of released birds could be determined precisely using days of exposure. For each bird, the day of first release was considered exposure day 1, and each subsequent day during which the bird was free-flying for any part of the day was considered an exposure day. All birds were periodically captured and re-released owing to concerns about transmitters, health, behavior, or to test for lead exposure. Complete days during which an individual was in captivity were not counted as exposure, although days of exposure were otherwise cumulative in regard to the time a condor was free-flying following its initial release. Nearly two-thirds (64%) of the birds were captive for less than 100 days in total following their release. Twenty-eight individuals, however, were held for longer than 100 days, and seven of those were held for one to three years and are thus substantially older than the number of days free-flying suggests.

To evaluate survivorship, we partitioned the number of exposure days into five stages based on annual benchmarks and our observations of apparent differences in survival rates. The stages were: initial release (the first 90 exposure days following release); remainder of the first year (91 to 365 exposure days post-release); second year (366 to 730 exposure days post-release); third through fourth years (731 to 1,460 exposure days post-release); and the fifth year onward (1,461+ exposure days post-release). We determined daily, exposure stage, and annual survivorship based on Trent and Rongstad (1974), where daily survival rate ($\hat{S}$) was calculated as the total number of exposure days within any stage, minus the number of days in the stage during which a death occurred, divided by the total number of exposure days in the stage. Survivorship throughout specific stages was $\hat{S}^n$, where n was the number of calendar days in each particular stage.

To gain an indication of what survival in the released population might have been without intensive management and chelation treatments to reduce acute blood lead levels (see Parish et al. this volume for methods), we also recalculated survival under two hypothetical scenarios: (1) all birds that were found to have blood levels of lead greater than 250 µg dL^{-1} died on the date of detection, and (2) all those with lead levels above 100 µg dL^{-1} died. For each situation, we used a standard growth rate calculation developed by Hunt (2002) to determine lambda (λ) values, which depict the direction and strength of population trajectories. For growth rate calculations, we used our calculated survival in the first year following release as a substitute for juvenile (first year) survival, our calculated survival in the second through fourth years free-flying as a substitute for immature survival, and our calculated survival from the fifth year free-flying onward to represent adult survival. We used hypothetical reproductive parameters determined by Meretsky et al. (2000).

We used chi-square analyses to evaluate differences in the number of condors that survived based on sex, rearing method (parent- vs. puppet-reared), and age when released (more or less than one year old at release). Because many condors died in the first year following their release (see Results), we also repeated those analyses but tested specifically for differences in the number of condors that survived their first year free-flying. Data for all chi-square analyses included only condors released before July 2004 (65 in total), as the more recently released birds had not yet spent a full year free-flying. Also excluded was a single bird permanently removed from the free-flying population, since it was removed less than one year after its release.

For condors that bred, the date at which egg-laying occurred was determined by changes in behavior of the adult birds, including periodic incubation exchanges at nest sites. Behavioral changes that characterized hatching, including the sudden onset of daily nest exchanges by the adults, were also used to determine laying dates, assuming an average incubation period of 57 days (Snyder and Snyder 2000). Nest sites with young were monitored carefully as the date of fledging approached, and the date and time of fledging were determined by direct observation. Where possible, nest sites were entered for close examination after the breeding effort ended.

Unless otherwise noted, all statistics are in the form of mean ± SD. The levels of lead in condors are frequently expressed in µg dL^{-1} when measured in blood and ppm when measured in the liver, and we follow those conventions here. The two measurements are easily converted, however, since 1 ppm equals 100 µg dL^{-1}.

RESULTS

Survivorship overview.—As of July 2005, 77 young condors (43 males and 34 females) had been released in northern Arizona: 61 at the Vermilion Cliffs site and 16 at the Hurricane Cliffs site (Table 1). Of the released birds, 50 (65%) were released when less than one year of age (average age = 255 ± 46 days; range = 172–345) and 27 (35%) were released at ages ranging from 494 to 965 days (average age = 651 ± 116 days). The average age at release for all 77 birds was 394 ± 205 days. Twenty-six of the released birds died, one was removed from the free-flying population, and 50 remained in the wild in July 2005. Not included in the number of released birds or deaths are four adult birds (two breeding pairs eight to nine years old) that were released as an experimental effort to include breeders with other released birds. Coyotes killed two of the adults shortly after release (19 and 22 days), probably as a result of unsafe roosting behavior, and the other two were recaptured and permanently removed

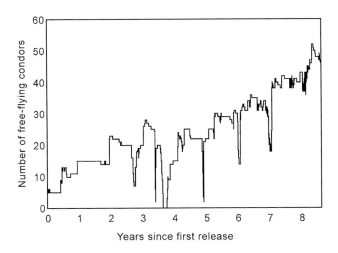

FIG. 2. Number of free-flying California Condors in northern Arizona since the first cohort was released in December 1996. Reductions in the population occurred when birds were captured and held temporarily for behavioral or health reasons. The population went to zero from mid-July through mid-August 2000 when all birds were held during a lead poisoning incident (see text).

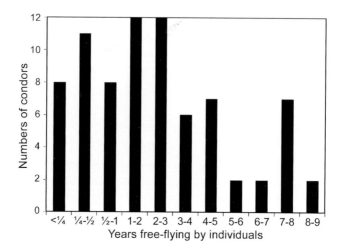

Fɪɢ. 3. Years free-flying by 77 California Condors released in northern Arizona between December 1996 and July 2005.

from the free-flying population. Since the first release in 1996, the number of birds in the wild generally increased over time, to a temporary maximum of 52 in March 2005 (Fig. 2). As of July 2005, 42 (55%) of the released birds were free-flying for 1.5 years or longer (Fig. 3), and individuals averaged 2.7 ± 2.5 years ($n = 77$; range = 4 days–8.2 years) in the wild.

The likelihood of survival did not differ significantly based on sex of the released birds, whether considering survival through the first year free-flying or overall ($\chi^2 = 0.84$, df = 1, $P = 0.526$; $\chi^2 = 0.06$, df = 1, $P = 0.802$, respectively). Survival also did not differ significantly based on rearing method (first year free-flying: $\chi^2 = 0.08$, df = 1, $P = 0.772$; overall: $\chi^2 = 0.15$, df = 1, $P = 0.694$). In contrast, individuals that were greater than one year of age when released were significantly more likely to survive than individuals that were released when less than one year old. Of 21 birds released when more than one year old, one (5%) perished in its first year free-flying, compared to 12 of 44 birds (27%) released when younger than one year of age ($\chi^2 = 4.94$, df = 1, $P = 0.026$). Overall, four of 21 birds (19%) released when greater than one year of age died, compared to 21 of 44 birds (48%) released when less than one year old ($\chi^2 = 4.50$, df = 1, $P = 0.034$).

We documented 75,053 exposure days in total, including 22,391 (77 birds) in the first year and 16,640 (20 birds) from the fifth year onward (Table 2). Annual survival through the first year, 79.6%, was heavily influenced by relatively high mortality of recently released birds; of the 14 that perished during their first year, eight died within the first three months. The likelihood of survival increased to 89.3% in the second year and 89.6% in the third and fourth years combined (89.5% for the second through fourth

Table 2. Survivorship based on exposure days for 77 California Condors released in northern Arizona, December 1996 through July 2005.

Stage[a]	Condors (n)	Exposure days	No. of deaths	Survivorship (%) Daily	Survivorship (%) Stage	Survivorship (%) Annual
Initial release[a]	77	6,519	8	99.877	89.5	–
Remain. 1st year[b]	69	15,872	6	99.962	90.1	–
Combined 1st year	77	22,391	14	99.937	–	79.6
2nd year	50	16,069	5	99.969	–	89.3
3rd and 4th year	38	19,953	6	99.970	–	89.6
5th year onwards	20	16,640	1	99.994	–	97.8
Overall	77	75,053	26	99.965	–	88.1

[a] Initial release is the first 90 days following release.

[b] Remain. 1st year is the remainder of first year following release (see text for further details).

years). Survival from the fifth year onward was 97.8%. Fatalities occurred sporadically throughout the release program, with the exception of four deaths in June 2000, but condor deaths were rare following four years in the wild, and by July 2005 only one bird that had been free-flying for longer than four years had perished.

Given the rates of survival found in our study, and assuming a population with a stable age distribution and a conservative reproductive rate of 0.25 for breeding age females (e.g., 50% of females breed per year with 50% breeding success), the Arizona population would be expected to grow at the rate of 2.6% per year (i.e., $\lambda = 1.026$). If the reproductive rate increased to 0.33 per year, the annual growth rate would rise to 3.7%. If, on the other hand, there were no management for lead exposure, and one assumed that all condors with acute blood levels of lead above 250 µg dL^{-1} died, resulting in an additional nine deaths, immature and adult survival would have been 81.7% and 90.9% respectively (juvenile survival would have been unaffected), and the population would have declined at 2.8% per year. With the more stringent assumption that lead levels in blood greater than 100 µg dL^{-1} were always lethal, resulting in seven deaths in addition to the nine previously mentioned, immature and adult survival would have been 72.4% and 76.9% respectively (again, there would have been no affect on juvenile survival), and the population would have declined at the greater rate of 18.6% per year.

Sources of mortality:—Fourteen condors perished in the first year following their release, mainly from predation or other experience-related factors (Table 3). Amongst those 14 deaths, predators (coyotes and Golden Eagles) killed four and possibly five condors, three birds disappeared and are

Table 3. Causes of death for 26 California condors released in northern Arizona between December 1996 and July 2005. Birds are ranked by the number of days free-flying prior to death.

Source of mortality	Sex free-flying	Days	Age at death (days)	Month/year of death
Deaths during first year free-flying				
Coyote	M	4	284	02/2002
Eagle	M	24	225	01/1997
Coyote	M	37	271	12/1998
Poor Condition[a]	M	39	326	04/2005
Septicemia[b]	M	40	256	01/2000
Poor Condition[a]	F	43	287	02/2001
Eagle	F	60	317	02/2000
Unknown–lost	F	62	817	07/1997
Unknown–lost	F	120	333	04/2000
Powerline	F	158	350	05/1997
Unknown–lost	F	173	509	09/2004
Lead	M	177	487	08/2002
Shot	M	242	508	10/2002
Coyote suspected	M	318	501	10/1998
Deaths after first year free-flying				
Lead	F	522	768	06/2000
Lead suspected	M	524	810	06/2000
Eagle	F	537	880	09/2000
Shot	M	542	1,599	08/2002
Shot	F	609	1,436	03/1999
Lead	M	816	1,355	01/2005
Lead	M	932	1,149	06/2000
Unknown[c]	M	1,021	1,634	09/2003
Lead	M	1,024	1,785	03/2000
Lead suspected	F	1,263	1,491	06/2000
Lead	F	1,345	1,700	01/2005
Unknown–lost	F	1,696	2,155	02/2004

[a] Poor body condition of unknown cause led to starvation-like deaths in these birds (see text for further details).

[b] Septicemia resulted from airsacculitis owing to aspiration.

[c] Cause of death undetermined by necropsy.

presumed to have perished, and two succumbed to starvation-like poor body condition resulting from an unknown cause or causes. In each case where coyotes appeared to kill a condor, the bird had roosted in a location that was accessible to coyotes. It is unknown whether poor body condition or other factors increased the susceptibility to predation of birds whose deaths were attributed to coyotes, but one bird appeared healthy and vigorous when captured by field personnel eight days prior to its death and another was killed after only four days in the wild. Necropsy could not determine or explain what led to the poor body condition apparent in the birds that died with starvation-like symptoms, especially considering that each had been in the wild for only a few weeks and had been seen feeding at the release site during that time (lead poisoning was not implicated in either death).

Twelve condors that had been free-flying for more than one year died, and the single greatest contributor to mortality was lead toxicity, to which seven of those birds were known (5) or suspected (2) to have succumbed. Two of the other five condors that died were shot, one by a hiker who killed the condor with a small caliber handgun in Grand Canyon National Park, and another that was shot with an arrow in the Kaibab National Forest.

At least four confirmed or suspected lead toxicity deaths and many chelations were associated with episodes characterized by multiple poisonings, but two or three birds that died of lead poisoning did so in what appeared to be isolated events. The source of lead was identified in four deaths: three involved shotgun pellets and the fourth followed the ingestion of bullet fragments. Additionally, 10 non-lethal exposures occurred in which the source of lead was identified: six involved bullet fragments and four involved shotgun pellets.

The first lead poisoning death occurred in March 2000, and the first known multiple poisoning occurred in June of that year. Within a four week period beginning in June 2000, at least two and as many as four birds perished from lead toxicity, and nine others with high lead levels received chelation therapy. The first of those fatalities occurred early in June, but the carcass had deteriorated by the time of recovery and necropsy was inconclusive. The second death occurred on 12 June and followed the ingestion of at least 17 lead shotgun pellets of two or more different sizes (as determined by radiograph). A third condor died on 16 June and had a lead level in the liver after death (17 ppm) that strongly suggested the bird succumbed to lead poisoning. In contrast to the other poisoned birds, however, it was also severely emaciated when captured on the day prior to its death and had a high copper level in the liver after death (181 ppm); these factors, as well as a lack of lead shot visible on radiographs, suggest that it may have been poisoned in an unrelated incident. The cause of the fourth fatality on 25 June was unknown because the carcass was unrecoverable, but the timing of this bird's death suggested lead poisoning. Evidence indicates that most if not all of the lethal and non-lethal poisonings were associated with shotgun pellets, owing to both the temporal proximity of the poisonings and the fact that shot of three different sizes was found in five of the poisoned birds. It is unlikely that groups of condors would encounter and consume enough carcasses of the smaller animals usually hunted with shotguns to explain the number of poisoned birds. Consequently, we suspect that the exposure occurred at a single large carcass or many closely-spaced smaller ones, which were loaded with shot of varying sizes.

Large-scale lead exposure episodes also occurred during and just after the local November hunting seasons in 2002 and 2004 (Parish et al. this volume). During November many mule deer (*Odocoileus hemionus*) are killed by hunters on the Kaibab Plateau, which is heavily used by condors for foraging during fall (Hunt et al. this volume; Plate 7). No birds died, and bullet fragments appeared on radiographs of only two poisoned birds during the two episodes combined, but in each episode approximately 35 to 40% of the free-flying population (2002: 11 birds; 2004: 17 birds) received chelation therapy in response to blood lead levels that ranged from 50 to 900 µg dL^{-1}.

The episodic pattern of wide-scale poisonings, as well as the seemingly sudden onset of lead exposures within the population, was highlighted by the fact that no bird perished or required chelation in the first 18,000 exposure days of the release program, and only a single chelation treatment was necessary in over 15,500 exposure days between August 2000 and August 2002. In the years following the first poisoning episode, however, blood lead levels determined during semi-annual and opportunistic test-ing frequently were above the expected background levels of 20 µg dL^{-1}. Furthermore, nearly all the older birds in the population have been exposed to high lead levels since 2002, and most have received chelation therapy at least once (Parish et al. this volume).

Reproduction.—The first breeding attempt in the new Arizona popula-tion occurred in 2001, when a six-year-old male courted two six-year-old females, one of which laid an egg that was broken shortly afterward. In the years since, at least nine adults (five females, four males) attempted to breed (including courtship, nest selection, and egg laying), and all six ten-year-olds—the oldest cohort in the population—had produced one or more fledglings by the end of 2005. The average age at which the nine confirmed breeders first attempted to breed (i.e., the first time an egg was laid by the female in a pair) was 7.6 ± 1.3 years, but two birds attempted to breed at six years of age and another did not breed until its tenth year.

The population in July 2005 included 14 condors seven years of age or older, five of which were not confirmed breeders. Four of those five were males, however, and thus three lacked available mates (Fig. 4). Breeding pairs nested at seven different sites: four in Grand Canyon National Park (e.g., Fig. 5), two in Vermilion Cliffs National Monument, and one in the Kaibab National Forest. One site was used three times, two sites twice, and four sites were used only once. Early pair formation was sometimes equivo-cal—three or more birds were associated with two nesting attempts, and one male bred with at least two females in successive years. Two established pairs, however, have not switched mates in three breeding attempts each over four years and as of December 2005 remain paired.

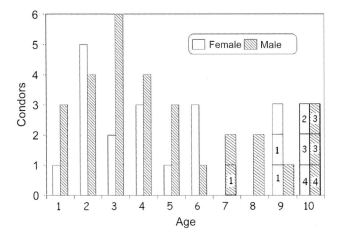

FIG. 4. Age structure of free-flying released condors in northern Arizona as of July 2005. Numerals within bars indicate the number of times an individual bred or attempted to breed between 2001 and 2005.

FIG. 5. Nest cave on the west face of The Battleship, Grand Canyon National Park, Arizona. An established condor pair bred at the site in 2002, 2003, and 2004, successfully producing one fledgling condor in 2004. (Photo by C. N. Parish.)

Overall, at least 11 eggs were laid, five of which were known to hatch, and five condors fledged successfully. Success for nesting attempts from 2001 through 2005 was thus 45% (5 fledglings produced from 11 eggs laid), but pairs typically failed in their first breeding attempts, and consequently success generally improved over time. Nesting success in

2001 through 2003 was 17% (one of six nests), but was 80% (four of five nests) for 2004 and 2005. The dates at which eggs were laid varied widely, the earliest being 21–22 February and the latest 7–10 April, but at least six and as many as eight eggs were laid in March. All eggs that hatched did so between 3–5 May and 4–5 June. The earliest bird to leave the nest site fledged on 5 November (at 184–186 days of age) and the latest on 23 December (at 202–203 days of age); the others fledged on 23 November (at 195–196 days of age), 25 November (at 186–187 days of age), and 30 November (at 185–187 days of age).

Discussion

Impact of natural predators.—The natural predation rate on wild condors is unknown, but as for most vultures it was probably always very low, especially for adults (for example, see Mundy et al. 1992). Few predators have been identified that prey on free-flying condors, and although harassment and/or predation by Golden Eagles and Common Ravens (*Corvus corax*) may impact egg and nestling survival, condor mortality has been mostly attributed to human-induced causes (Koford 1953, Snyder and Snyder 2000). Our data support the notion that immature and adult condors are rarely killed by predators other than humans, since only a single fatality was attributed to predation in more than 52,000 exposure days for birds that have been in the wild longer than 1 year, and moreover that death was of a two-year-old condor.

The same was not true for newly-released birds, however, as predation by coyotes or Golden Eagles accounted for the deaths of four or more birds in their first year free-flying. Black-backed jackals (*Canis mesomelas*), which compete for food with vultures, are known to kill juvenile African White-backed Vultures (*Gyps africanus*), and red foxes (*Vulpes vulpes*) sometimes kill recently fledged Egyptian Vultures (*Neophron percnopterus*; Mundy et al. 1992). Coyotes specifically appeared responsible for half or more of the eight actual predator-caused deaths (including the two adults released and killed in 2000), suggesting that in Arizona coyote predation could become a significant contributor to mortality of newly-released condors that do not roost in appropriate locations. There is no historical evidence to indicate that coyotes were a cause of condor fatalities in the past, but young condors in historical populations presumably benefited by observing the behavior of adult birds, an opportunity that was lacking early in the Arizona release program. Moreover, the coyote population may be artificially increased in the vicinity of the release site as a result of readily available carcasses placed for the condors, thus exacerbating the potential for predation. No newly-released condors have been preyed upon, however, since March 2002 when a program of hazing new birds to safe roost spots was instituted.

Human causes of condor deaths.—In modern times, condors and vultures must contend with hazards for which they are perhaps ill-equipped through their evolution (Mendelssohn and Leshem 1983). Collision with power transmission lines and electrocution, for example, have emerged as global threats to vultures (e.g., Mundy et al. 1992, Sarrazin et al. 1994, van Rooyen 2000), and at least nine condors have perished in California as a result of power line collisions. Only one condor died in a similar collision in Arizona during our study, and the lower frequency is probably related to the scarcity of power lines in the vicinity of the release sites (Harting et al. 1995). Releases in Arizona, however, also followed the onset of aversion training to utility poles in 1995. Shooting was also a prominent source of mortality for condors in the past (Wilbur 1978, Snyder and Snyder 2000, Snyder this volume), and the fact that at least three condors were shot in Arizona during our study reflects the continuation of this unfortunate human habit.

Factors influencing survival of newly-released condors.—The success of any species reintroduction is dependent in part on survival of the young animals that are produced or released. In Arizona, the increased vulnerability of some newly-released condors could be due to differences between birds captive-reared by different methods and released at different ages. Puppet-rearing, for example, is an efficient technique used in the captive breeding of many rare birds slated for future release, because excess young can be produced in the absence of adults to rear them (Cade and Fyfe 1978, Wallace 1994). The technique can be counter-productive, however, if puppet-reared birds die at a substantially higher rate than parent-reared or wild-reared offspring. Superficially, puppet-reared birds may be assumed to be less behaviorally adept than those reared by parents, especially for social birds that are slow to mature, but our data do not support that assumption, at least for condors reared in captivity, since there was no apparent difference in mortality between those that were puppet-reared and those that were parent-reared.

The advantages and disadvantages of releasing birds at an early age are also equivocal for long-lived birds that require an extended period of maturation. Increased maturity during additional time spent in captivity prior to release could result, for example, in acclimation to captivity and a reduction in age-appropriate behavior on release. On the other hand, young birds released prematurely might lack wariness or other behavioral attributes necessary for survival, some of which may be innate and slow to develop. In Arizona, 95% first-year survival of birds released when greater than one year of age, compared to 73% for birds released at less than one year old, strongly indicates that older birds benefited from increased maturity prior to release, even in the absence of free-ranging experience in the wild. This finding has important implications for managing the release of young condors and perhaps other species with life histories that include long periods of juvenile dependence and maturation.

Adult survival.—For long-lived animals with low reproductive rates and few natural predators, breeding success or the survival of young birds are not as critical to the stability of populations as adult survival, since even in the best of times slow breeding rates place a higher premium on longevity than fecundity (cf. Mertz 1971). Thus, populations of long-lived birds are generally characterized by both low adult mortality and a relatively small proportion of immatures (e.g., Houston 1974, Weimerskirch et al. 1987), although not necessarily in newly reestablished populations (Blanco and Martínez 1996, Blanco et al. 1997). Verner (1978) and Meretsky et al. (2000) modeled hypothetical cases of condor mortality, and both generally concluded that annual survival for adults and immatures must exceed 90% to maintain population stability (Verner: 91% adult and 89% immature; Meretsky et al.: 90.1% for both adult and immature), and that adult survival should approach 95% annually to compensate for immature survival of about 85%. In Arizona, where immature condors currently outnumber adults, survival of 89.5% for birds in their second through fourth years free-flying has thus met those immature survival requirements. Because there are still relatively few adults in the population, the long-term adult survival rate remains speculative, but it is promising that none of the 14 condors to reach adulthood has perished, and that survival has approached 98% for all birds free-flying for more than four years.

Reproduction and population growth.—Given the current rates of survival and reproduction, can this population become self-sustaining or grow without supplementation as long as management of the lead exposure problem continues? A near-term increase in the number of breeding pairs is complicated by the shortage of unpaired adult females (Fig. 4). Two or three additional females should, however, become potential breeders in 2006 or 2007, and barring unanticipated catastrophes there could be at least 15 adult females and 20 or more adult males in the population within five years due to natural aging of individuals. Not all adults in the Arizona population will necessarily breed, but so far most with the opportunity to breed have done so. Moreover, nesting success improved as pairs became established, and success for established pairs presently lies in the range proposed for wild condors historically (estimates range from 22 to 56% prior to 1980, and 41 to 47% in the 1980s; Snyder and Snyder 2000). It remains speculative whether these rates are adequate for population stability or growth, but they appear to be when compared to hypothetical models of California Condor demography (Meretsky et al. 2000), as well as data on colonial Griffon Vultures (*Gyps fulvus*) in France (Sarrazin et al. 1994), and several solitary-breeding Old World vultures (Mundy 1982).

Lead poisoning and its consequences.—Poisoning by various means is a ubiquitous contemporary threat to adult vultures and condors (e.g., Mendelssohn and Leshem 1983, Janssen et al. 1986, Mundy et al. 1992, Mundy 2000), and lead contamination is the primary concern for long-term viability of modern California Condor populations (Wiemeyer et al. 1988, Pattee et al. 1990, Kiff 2000, Meretsky et al. 2000, Snyder and Snyder 2000, Fry and Maurer 2003, Cade et al. 2004). Because condors are gregarious and efficient scavengers that feed principally, although not exclusively, on medium and large mammalian carcasses, they are particularly vulnerable to lead poisoning when animals are shot and carcasses are not recovered or viscera are left. Lack of recovery may arise from unintended hunter loss or shooting activities that place little emphasis on carcass recovery, including poaching big game for trophy mounts, shooting coyotes and other predators, and killing jackrabbits (*Lepus* spp.), ground squirrels (*Spermophilus* spp.), and other small animals. Consequently, as long as lead ammunition is used by hunters and shooters in regions where condors and other scavenging animals live, wildlife will continue to be inadvertently killed by lead poisoning.

Meretsky et al. (2000) suggested that lead in general, and lead bullets in particular, are a pervasive component of the contemporary environment, with patterns of contamination and rates of exposure that make the reintroduction of condors untenable at present. We agree that lead contamination has hindered and will continue to hinder condor restoration, especially considering that lead poisoning was the only verified cause of mortality for adult or immature birds after their first two years in the wild. Moreover, although annual survival was nearly 98% for condors that had been free-flying for more than four years, that value does not represent expected survival of those condors in the absence of management for lead poisoning, as all of them received chelation therapy one or more times, and some might have perished otherwise. How many might have died? Acute lead levels greater than 100 μg dL^{-1} in blood indicate that a condor's physiology has been compromised, but they are not necessarily lethal. Crop stasis and other complications resulting in death can, however, occur at blood lead levels in the range of 250 μg dL^{-1} or more (Fry and Maurer 2003). Without intervention, adult survival might therefore have been 90% or less during our study, and perhaps one third or more of the current adult population could have been lost. Thus, although our data suggest that lead poisoning should not prevent the establishment of a condor population in Arizona that is stable or able to grow in numbers, the population will require continued monitoring of lead levels in blood and chelation therapy when lead poisonings occur.

Conclusions.—For long-term survival and self-sufficiency of condors in Arizona, the lead that they encounter must be reduced or eliminated, because as the population grows and expands its range, intensive management of individual birds will become increasingly difficult and costly. To that end, several factors critical in understanding the risks of lead require further study. The pattern of lead encounters that has so far emerged in Arizona includes intermittent but widespread episodes that have resulted in the poisoning of multiple birds, superimposed on a persistent background of individual poisonings. Identifying the sources of lead that have caused those poisonings is essential to safeguard Arizona's condors. The shotgun pellet-related poisonings in June 2000 were enigmatic, and it is possible that an inadvertent or unique shooting event led to the exposure. Lead shot is, however, an environmental hazard that killed many North American water birds until its use for waterfowl hunting in the United States was banned in 1991, and two additional condor deaths attributed to shotgun pellets in 2005 suggest that ingestion of lead shot may be more onerous to condors than had been presumed. Poisoning of birds during autumn is more troubling still, since exposures in our study during 2002 and 2004 were likely associated with the annual hunting season on the Kaibab Plateau, where condors fed on the carcasses of deer and coyotes that had been shot (Hunt et al. this volume). The magnitude of future poisonings associated with lead-based bullets is uncertain, but lead fragments extensively contaminate the wound channel and offal of hunter-killed deer (Hunt et al. 2006) and lead bullet-induced poisonings may threaten populations of Steller's and White-tailed Sea Eagles (*Haliaeetus pelagicus* and *H. albicilla*, respectively) in Japan (Iwata et al. 2000, Kurosawa 2000, Ueta and Masterov 2000). Finally, subclinical lead levels in condors throughout the year often exceed anticipated background levels, and although the cumulative effects of chronic sublethal exposure on reproduction and survival are unknown, there are likely dysgenic effects on condors of continued, long-term exposure to lead (Cade et al. 2004).

Successful breeding by released birds in the wild nevertheless portends the coming of a new period in condor reestablishment. Given the production of wild-reared condors, as well as the high survival of birds after their first year free-flying, we are optimistic about the long-term prospects of establishing a self-sustaining condor population in Arizona, even considering significant problems associated with lead exposure. The fact that an experimental population of this, or any, endangered species is not yet adequately protected from humans and their environmental contaminants does not in itself argue for the suspension of restoration efforts, as some have maintained (e.g., Meretsky et al. 2000, Snyder and Snyder 2000). Small populations will always be vulnerable to stochastic and catastrophic events (Pimm 1991), and removal of condors from Arizona would substantially hinder our ability to identify sources of lead contamination and other biological hazards. We must instead maintain the effort to build a condor population in Arizona large enough to sustain losses while continuing to identify the sources of lead in the environment, inform the public of the threat of lead to condors and other wildlife, and promote the adoption of environmentally safe alternatives to lead ammunition.

ACKNOWLEDGMENTS

Comments by Bill Burnham, Linnea Hall, Grainger Hunt, Lloyd Kiff, and Allan Mee greatly improved earlier versions of this manuscript. Over the years, many individuals have been important to the success of the Arizona condor project, and we are grateful for the field assistance of Jill Adams, Stephen Agius, Jody Bartz, Roger Benefield, Tim Bischof, Jason Blackburn, Kristy Bly, Brandon Breen, Jessi Brown, Ann Burke, Daniel Burnetti, Gant Charping, James Christian, Joseph Crapanzano, Chris Crowe, Janelle Cuddeford, Marta Curti, Ann Marie DiLorenzo, Tyrone Donnelly, Gretchen Druliner, Sam Elizondo, Beau Fairchild, Kevin Fairhurst, Edward Feltes, Chadd Fitzpatrick, Paul Flournoy, Lisa Fosco, Vincent Frary, Erin Gott, Melissa Gray, Sean Grimland, Courtney Harris, Adam Hutchins, Helen Johnson, Paul Juergens, Jeffrey Kingscott, Karen Leavelle, Kristine Lightner, Amy Lindsley, David Loomis, Thomas Lord, Megan Lout, Tyana Maddock, Michael Maglione, Blake Massey, Kristine McConnell, David McGraw, Phil McKenna, Grant Merrill, Christopher Michaud, Angel Montoya, Betty Moore, Dennis Mott, Paul Mueller, Nichole Munkwitz, Brian Mutch, Curt Mykut, Frank Nebengurgh, Amy Nicholas, Hannah Ogden, Chad Olson, Kathryn Parmentier, Mary Schwartz, Molly Severson, Elise Snyder, Melanie Spies, Kirk Stodola, Molly Thomas, Mark Vekasy, Jonna Wiedmaier, Eric Weis, Anne Welch, and Jim Willmarth. Cooperators in the recovery effort include the US Fish and Wildlife Service, Los Angeles Zoo, Zoological Society of San Diego, Arizona Game and Fish Department, Bureau of Land Management, National Park Service, Utah Division of Wildlife, Southern Utah's Coalition of Resources Economics, and the Ventana Wildlife Society. Assisting with transportation of the condors and crew has been the Bureau of Land Management's Boise Smoke Jumpers, the Idaho National Guard, Norm Freeman, and the Salt River Project. Dr. Kathy Orr at the Phoenix Zoo and Dr Bruce Rideout and his staff at the San Diego Zoo have been especially helpful with ailing condors and necropsies, respectively. We extend special thanks to Norm Freeman and Maggie Sacher, as well as the local communities, ranchers and land owners, and lodge owners, all of whom have been crucial to the success of the project.

Recovery efforts of this magnitude cannot be conducted without significant financial resources, and we gratefully acknowledge the assistance of the U.S. Fish and Wildlife Service, Peter Pfendler, Connie Pfendler, the Geraldine R. Dodge Foundation, the Turner Foundation, Inc., Ron and Linda Yanke, the Wells Family Charitable Foundation, the Bureau of

Land Management-Idaho, the ARCO Foundation, the Wallace Research Foundation, Yvon and Malinda Chouinard/Patagonia, the Jane Smith Turner Foundation, the Burns Family Foundation, the Globe Foundation, Merle and Miriam Hinrichs, the Del Webb Corporation, the Offield Family Foundation, the Norcross Wildlife Foundation, Inc., Bank One Arizona, N.A., the Nina Mason Pulliam Charitable Trust, the Chichester duPont Foundation, the Charles Engelhard Foundation, Natural Encounters Conservation Fund, the Philadelphia Foundation, Earth Friends Wildlife Foundation, the Philanthropic Collaborative, Grand Canyon Conservation Fund, Earthquest, the Disney Wildlife Conservation Fund, the Phelps Dodge Corporation, the Arizona Public Service Foundation, Inc., Jim and Karin Nelson, the William H. Gates Foundation, Harry Bettis, Conni Williams, the Sidney S. Byers Charitable Trust, The Kearny Alliance, the Ten Times Ten Foundation, the Evan Frankel Foundation, Tejon Ranch, the Steele Reese Foundation, and the Ledder Family Charitable Trust.

Literature Cited

BirdLife International. 2000. Threatened Birds of the World. Birdlife International, Cambridge, United Kingdom.

Blanco, G., and F. Martínez. 1996. Sex differences in breeding age of Griffon Vultures (*Gyps fulvus*). Auk 113:247–248.

Blanco, G., F. Martínez, and J. M. Traverso. 1997. Pair bond and age distribution of breeding Griffon Vultures *Gyps fulvus* in relation to reproductive status and geographic area in Spain. Ibis 139:180–183.

Cade, T. J., and R. W. Fyfe. 1978. What makes Peregrine Falcons breed in captivity? Pages 251–262 *in* Endangered Birds: Management Techniques for Preserving Threatened Species (S. A. Temple, Ed.). University of Wisconsin Press, Madison.

Cade, T. J., S. A. H. Osborn, W. G. Hunt, and C. P. Woods. 2004. Commentary on released California Condors *Gymnogyps californianus* in Arizona. Pages 11–25 *in* Raptors Worldwide: Proceedings of VI World Conference on Birds of Prey and Owls (R. D. Chancellor and B.-U. Meyburg, Eds.). World Working Group on Birds of Prey and Owls/MME-Birdlife, Hungary.

Emslie, S. D. 1987. Age and diet of fossil California Condors in Grand Canyon, Arizona. Science 237:768–770.

Fry, D. M., and J. R. Maurer. 2003. Assessment of lead contamination sources exposing California Condors. Final report to the California Department of Fish and Game, Sacramento.

Harting, A., L. Kiff, and R. Mesta. 1995. Final environmental assessment: release of California Condors at the Vermilion Cliffs (Coconino County, Arizona). The Peregrine Fund, Boise, Idaho.

Houston, D. C. 1974. Mortality of the Cape Vulture. Ostrich 45:57–62.

Hunt, W. G. 2002. Golden Eagles in a perilous landscape: predicting the effects of mitigation for wind turbine blade-strike mortality. California Energy Commission Report P500-02-043F.

HUNT, W. G., W. BURNHAM, C. N. PARISH, K. BURNHAM, B. MUTCH, AND J. L. OAKS. 2006. Bullet fragments in deer remains: implications for lead exposure in scavengers. Wildlife Society Bulletin 34:168–171.

HUNT, W. G., C. N. PARISH, S. C. FARRY, T. G. LORD, AND R. SIEG. 2007. Movements of introduced California Condors in Arizona in relation to lead exposure. Pages 79–96 in California Condors in the 21st Century (A. Mee and L. S. Hall, Eds.). Series in Ornithology, no. 2.

IWATA, H., M. WATANABE, E.-Y. KIM, R. GOTOH, G. YASUNAGA, S. TANABE, Y. MASUDA, AND S. JUJITA. 2000. Contamination by chlorinated hydrocarbons and lead in Steller's Sea Eagle and White-tailed Sea Eagle from Hokkaido, Japan. Pages 91–106 in First Symposium on Steller's and White-tailed Sea Eagles in East Asia (M. Ueta and M. J. McGrady, Eds.). Wild Bird Society of Japan, Tokyo.

JANSSEN, D. L., J. E. OOSTERHUIS, J. L. ALLEN, M. P. ANDERSON, D. G. KELTS, AND S. N. WIEMEYER. 1986. Lead poisoning in free-ranging California Condors. Journal of the American Veterinary Medical Association 189:1115–1117.

JOHNSON, T. B., AND B. A. GARRISON. 1996. California Condor reintroduction proposal for the Vermillion Cliffs, northern Arizona. Nongame and Endangered Wildlife Program Technical Report 86. Arizona Game and Fish, Phoenix.

KIFF, L. 2000. The California Condor recovery programme. Pages 307–319 in Raptors at Risk: Proceedings of the 5th World Conference on Birds of Prey and Owls (R. D. Chancellor and B.-U. Meyburg, Eds.). Hancock House Publishers and the World Working Group on Birds of Prey and Owls, Blaine, Washington.

KOFORD, C. B. 1953. The California Condor. National Audubon Research Report 4: 1–154.

KUROSAWA, N. 2000. Lead poisoning in Steller's Sea Eagles and White-tailed Sea Eagles. Pages 107–109 in First Symposium on Steller's and White-tailed Sea Eagles in East Asia (M. Ueta and M. J. McGrady, Eds.). Wild Bird Society of Japan, Tokyo.

MENDELSSOHN, H., AND Y. LESHEM. 1983. The status and conservation of vultures in Israel. Pages 86–98 in Vulture Biology and Management (S. R. Wilbur and J. A. Jackson, Eds.). University of California Press, Berkeley.

MERETSKY, V. J., AND N. F. R. SNYDER. 1992. Range use and movements of California Condors. Condor 94:313–335.

MERETSKY, V. J., N. F. R. SNYDER, S. R. BEISSINGER, D. A. CLENDENEN, AND J. W. WILEY. 2000. Demography of the California Condor: implications for reestablishment. Conservation Biology 14:957–967.

MERTZ, D. B. 1971. The mathematical demography of the California Condor population. American Naturalist 105:437–453.

MILLER, L. 1960. Condor remains from Rampart Cave, Arizona. Condor 62:70.

MUNDY, P. J. 1982. The Comparative Biology of Southern African Vultures. Academic Press, London, U.K.

MUNDY, P. J. 2000. The status of vultures in Africa during the 1990s. Pages 151–164 in Raptors at Risk: Proceedings of the 5th World Conference on Birds of Prey and Owls (R. D. Chancellor and B.-U. Meyburg, Eds.). Hancock House Publishers and the World Working Group on Birds of Prey and Owls, Blaine, Washington.

MUNDY, P., D. BUTCHART, J. LEDGER, AND S. PIPER. 1992. The Vultures of Africa. Academic Press, London, U.K.

PARISH, C. N., W. R. HEINRICH, AND W. G. HUNT. 2007. Lead exposure, diagnosis, and treatment in California Condors released in Arizona. Pages 97–108 *in* California Condors in the 21st Century (A. Mee and L. S. Hall, Eds.). Series in Ornithology, no. 2.

PATTEE, O. H., P. H. BLOOM, J. M. SCOTT, AND M. R. SMITH. 1990. Lead hazards within the range of the California Condor. Condor 92:931–937.

PIMM, S. L. 1991. The Balance of Nature?: Ecological Issues in the Conservation of Species and Communities. University of Chicago Press, Chicago.

REA, A. M. 1981. California Condor captive breeding: a recovery proposal. Environment Southwest 492:8–12.

SARRAZIN, F., C. BAGNOLINI, J. L. PINNA, E. DANCHIN, AND J. CLOBERT. 1994. High survival estimates of Griffon Vultures (*Gyps fulvus fulvus*) in a reintroduced population. Auk 111:853–862.

SNYDER, N. F. R. 2007. Limiting factors for wild California Condors. Pages 9–34 *in* California Condors in the 21st Century (A. Mee and L. S. Hall, Eds.). Series in Ornithology, no. 2.

SNYDER, N. F. R., AND H. A. SNYDER. 2000. The California Condor: A Saga of Natural History and Conservation. Academic Press, San Diego, CA.

TRENT, T. T., AND O. J. RONGSTAD. 1974. Home range and survival of cottontail rabbits in southwestern Wisconsin. Journal of Wildlife Management 38:459–472.

UETA, M., AND V. MASTEROV. 2000. Estimation by a computer simulation of population trend of Steller's Sea Eagles. Pages 111–116 *in* First Symposium on Steller's and White-tailed Sea Eagles in East Asia (M. Ueta and M. J. McGrady, Eds.). Wild Bird Society of Japan, Tokyo.

VAN ROOYEN, C. S. 2000. Raptor mortality on powerlines in South Africa. Pages 739–750 *in* Raptors at Risk: Proceedings of the 5th World Conference on Birds of Prey and Owls (R. D. Chancellor and B.-U. Meyburg, Eds.). Hancock House Publishers and the World Working Group on Birds of Prey and Owls, Blaine, Washington.

VERNER, J. 1978. California Condor: status of the recovery effort. General Technical Report PSW-28. U.S. Forest Service, Washington, D.C.

WALLACE, M. P. 1994. Control of behavioral development in the context of reintroduction programs for birds. Zoo Biology 13:491–499.

WALLACE, M. P., P. G. PARKER, AND S. A. TEMPLE. 1980. An evaluation of patagial markers for cathartid vultures. Journal of Field Ornithology 51:309–314.

WEIMERSKIRCH, H., J. CLOBERT, AND P. JOUVENTIN. 1987. Survival in five southern albatrosses and its relationship with their life history. Journal of Animal Ecology 56:1043–1055.

WIEMEYER, S. N., J. M. SCOTT, M. P. ANDERSON, P. H. BLOOM, AND C. J. STAFFORD. 1988. Environmental contaminants in California Condors. Journal of Wildlife Management 52:238–247.

WILBUR, S. R. 1973. The California Condor in the Pacific northwest. Auk 90: 196–198.

WILBUR, S. R. 1978. The California Condor, 1966–1976: a look at its past and future. U.S. Department of the Interior, Fish and Wildlife Service, Washington, D.C.

4

Movements of Introduced California Condors in Arizona in Relation to Lead Exposure

W. Grainger Hunt,[1,3] *Chris N. Parish,*[1]
Shawn C. Farry,[1] *Thom G. Lord,*[1] *and Ron Sieg*[2]

ABSTRACT.—The California Condor (*Gymnogyps californianus*) restoration program in Arizona has benefited by the close monitoring of movements of condors with respect to food acquisition, mortality factors, and encounters with humans and artifacts. All 69 individuals released during 1996–2004 were equipped with VHF transmitters, and 18 carried satellite-reporting GPS transmitters for varying periods since fall 2003. Tracking data revealed an evolving cycle of annual movement, with increasing predictability overall as flock members gained experience and guided the behavior of newly-released birds. Condors generally remained near the site of initial release during winter and then traveled in spring and summer to the Colorado River corridor and the Grand Canyon. Summer and fall use of the Kaibab Plateau increased each year, as did the contingent of birds summering in the Kolob region of southern Utah. Movement was more expansive in winter 2004–2005 than in previous winters, in part reflecting an increasing number of pairs establishing breeding territories. We obtained circumstantial evidence of lead sources by examining itineraries of condors on a case-by-case basis during the weeks prior to lead testing. Information supporting the hypothesis of bullet fragments in hunter-killed deer carrion as the primary cause of elevated blood lead levels in condors included (1) a recent study showing that the remains of most rifle-killed deer contain numerous lead fragments; (2) observations of condors in association with deer remains ($n = 78$ cases); (3) an increase of blood lead levels with increased condor use of deer hunting areas of the Kaibab Plateau in 2002; (4) spikes in blood lead levels and condor visitation to the Kaibab Plateau during and just after the 2002, 2003, and 2004 deer hunting seasons; and (5) significantly higher lead levels among condors visiting the Kaibab Plateau in the weeks prior to testing.

[1]*The Peregrine Fund, 5668 West Flying Hawk Lane, Boise, Idaho 83709, USA.*
[2]*Arizona Game and Fish Department, 3500 South Lake Mary Road, Flagstaff, Arizona 86004, USA.*
[3]*Present address: Grainger Hunt, 552-205 James Drive, McArthur, California 96056, USA. E-mail grainger@peregrinefund.org*

Condors (*Gymnogyps* and *Vultur*), like tropical oceanic birds, are known for their longevity, delayed onset of breeding, and for the extraordinary distances they travel to forage. Wallace and Temple (1987) found breeding Andean Condors (*V. gryphus*) foraging as far as 200 km from their nests, with an overall range of up to 1,300 km^2. Meretsky and Snyder (1992) reported typical foraging distances of 50–70 km for nesting California Condors (*G. californianus*), and extremes of 180 km; the foraging range of the nonbreeders covered about 7,000 km^2.

Foraging widely means that condors visit a variety of environments, some anthropogenic, and some exposing them to mortality risks. The most prevalent of these risks has been lead (Pb) poisoning, a factor that some have invoked as a primary cause for the decline of the wild population (Meretsky et al. 2000). In California, prior to the mid-1980s when all wild condors were brought into captivity, lead ingestion was the principal recorded mortality agent based on a sample of five necropsies (Janssen et al. 1986, Wiemeyer et al. 1988). Likewise, Woods et al. (this volume) found lead poisoning the most frequently diagnosed cause of death of captive-bred condors outside their release site in northern Arizona.

The remains of animals killed by rifles and shotguns appear the most logical source of condor lead ingestion in Arizona, as suggested by the occurrence of lead shot and apparent bullet fragments in radiographs of 14 lead-poisoned condors (Parish et al. this volume). The hypothesis of rifle bullets as a principal source of lead in condors in Arizona is parsimonious because mule deer (*Odocoileus hemionus*), elk (*Cervus elaphus*), and other large animals known to be eaten by condors are typically killed by rifles. Because rifle bullets may pass completely through deer-sized animals, however, there was uncertainty about the extent to which bullet fragments remain in gut piles or carcasses lost to wounding. Hunt et al. (2006) addressed this question by radiographing the remains of 38 deer (*Odocoileus hemionus and O. virginianus*) killed with a variety of standard centerfire hunting bullets. Metal fragments were present in 18 of 20 offal piles (range = 2–521 fragments); five contained 0–9 fragments, five had 10–100, five had 100–199, and five showed more than 200 fragments. Five whole deer carcasses showed 416–783 fragments (mean = 551, SD ± 139). These results, together with the large amount of offal present in some regions, suggest a high potential incidence of lead exposure for scavengers. Fry and Maurer (2003) summarized, from game management statistics, the availability of shot animals to condors within the eight California counties comprising the former condor range; they reported that shooters annually left over 8,000 deer gut piles, offal from some 17,000 feral pigs (*Sus scrofa*), and carcasses of about 11,000 coyotes (*Canis latrans*).

The Peregrine Fund began its condor restoration program in the Grand Canyon region of northern Arizona (36°N, 112°W) in 1996, and continued releases brought the number of free-flying birds to about 50 by spring 2005, including two fledged from wild pairs. Frequent testing of blood lead levels of condors returning to the release site, particularly after 2002, revealed a large number of lead exposures, many at levels regarded as clinically significant and some as acutely toxic (Eisler 1988, Kramer and Redig 1997, Parish et al. this volume). The number of fatalities prevented by chelation treatment and removal of lead bodies by purging or surgery is likely substantial (Parish et al. this volume). Considering the necessity of high adult survival for population viability in this slowly reproducing species, the high incidence of lead exposure in Arizona and its potential to kill condors casts doubt upon the eventual success of establishing a self-sustaining population without the necessity of continual hands-on management (Cade et al. 2004; Mee et al., Woods et al. this volume). In this paper, we present evidence from radio-tracking and other avenues of study that pertain to sources of lead ingestion within the range of the free-flying condor population in Arizona.

Study Area

The terrain now frequented by condors in northern Arizona and southern Utah is a spectacularly rugged mix of canyons and plateaus, with elevations varying from about 600 m on the Colorado River in the Grand Canyon to about 2,800 m on the Kaibab Plateau where snow accumulates in winter (Fig. 1). Plant communities vary with elevation, from desert scrub in the lowland canyons, to semi-arid grasslands, to pinyon-juniper woodlands (1,500–2,100 m), to coniferous forests above 2,100 m. Abundant cliffs, winds, and warm summer temperatures provide updrafts upon which condors travel throughout the region. Ungulates providing carrion include mule deer, elk, big-horned sheep (*Ovis canadensis*), domestic sheep (*O. aries*), pronghorn (*Antilocapra americana*), American bison (*Bison bison*), range cattle (*Bos taurus*), and horses (*Equus caballus*) (Hoffmeister 1986).

We partitioned the general range of condor movement in northern Arizona and southern Utah into six zones (see Fig. 1). The Paria Zone contains the current release site, situated on top of the Vermilion Cliffs at the southwestern edge of a woodland plateau overlooking House Rock Canyon and the eastern slope of the Kaibab Plateau (Fig. 2). Food is continually provided at the release site in the form of dairy calf carcasses. The Colorado River Corridor Zone south of the Paria includes Marble Canyon and extends downstream from Powell Reservoir near Page, Arizona, to the confluence of the Little Colorado River in Grand Canyon National Park. The forested North Kaibab Plateau (Kaibab Zone) lies just to the west of the Paria, its western slopes becoming a juniper woodland dropping steeply into Kanab Creek where prevailing southwest winds provide updrafts for traveling

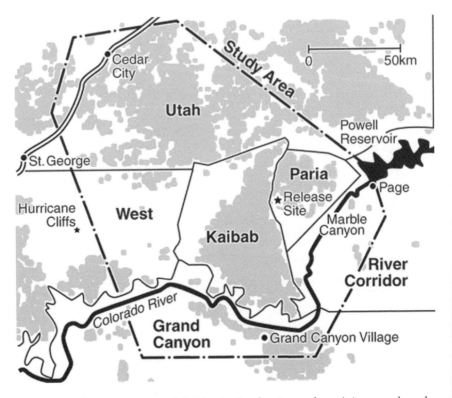

Fig. 1. The current range of California Condors in northern Arizona and southern Utah (forested areas in gray). The study area is divided into six zones of condor occurrence.

condors. Beyond Kanab Creek is the West Zone, an area of hilly woodland, with drier, open landscape to the north. The Grand Canyon National Park, south of the Kaibab Zone, comprises most of the Grand Canyon Zone, its forested rim dropping over 1,300 m through sparse woodland and desert scrub to the Colorado River (Plate 8). Grand Canyon Village on the South Rim is an area of intense human activity. The Utah Zone, to the north of the Kaibab, extends through the Kolob region northward to Cedar City, Utah; the area frequented by condors is generally composed of rugged, higher elevation coniferous forest with large, open meadows.

TRACKING AND MAPPING

Condors released in Arizona from 1966 to 2004 were equipped with radio transmitters (≤65 g) mounted on the patagium of each wing (or occasionally on the tail), along with numbered vinyl tags for visual identification

Fig. 2. The Peregrine Fund's condor release site at the Vermilion Cliffs in northern Arizona. (Photo by C. N. Parish.)

of individuals (see Wallace et al. 1994). VHF transmitters were detectable at line-of-sight distances of 100 km or more and contained "mortality sensors" designed to increase the pulse rate when the instrument was motionless for more than four hours. We captured condors in "walk-in" traps at the release site to replace failing transmitters and for other purposes, including lead testing (see Parish et al. this volume). Field crews of up to 11 individuals on foot or in road vehicles tracked VHF signals throughout the day by first situating themselves at vantage points, then following condors and maintaining visual contact when possible. A hierarchy of location codes facilitated records of sequential movement, and the last position fix of the day ("roost location") for each condor guided the next day's tracking strategy. Missing condors were occasionally sought by means of fixed-wing aircraft. Beginning in October 2003, we fitted 18 condors for various periods with GPS-equipped, satellite-reporting transmitters designed to yield hourly position fixes to within 50 m during daylight. We used ARCVIEW software to display and analyze data on topographical maps. The precise fixes provided by these transmitters together with results obtained from VFH radio-tracking led to the discovery of 196 dead animals that condors had either fed upon or closely attended. We attempted in all cases to ascertain the cause of death of these animals.

We examined seasonal changes in condor flock movements by tabulating 45,243 roost locations obtained by conventional telemetry and observation during July 2001 through June 2005, and then calculating the percentage of roost sites recorded in each zone. We tested the reliability of roost locations in predicting habitat selection by chronologically sorting the 29,756 satellite-reported GPS position fixes of individual condors (November 2003–June 2005), and randomly selecting 100 midday positions (~1,200 h) to compare with those of the last fixes of the day (~2,000 h). Condors stayed at the release site (Paria Zone) in 42 cases, moving 0–4 km during the afternoon. In the remaining 58 cases, condors traveled 0 to 65 km (mean = 18, SD ± 16), changing zones in 47% of cases. The latter outcome is consistent with ground tracking data in showing that condors visit a far greater number of locations than is apparent in the roost data alone.

MOVEMENTS IN THE EARLY YEARS

Unpredictability characterized the initial years of the release program in northern Arizona, as there were no condors with prior experience to guide the movements and behavior of the newly-released birds. In late winter 1997, soon after the first release of six captive-bred individuals, The Peregrine Fund began placing supplemental food at several locations within about 8 km of the Vermilion Cliffs (i.e., Paria Zone) release site. These distributions were intended to encourage expansion of movement patterns in accordance with the goal of a self-sustaining population. During the first six months after release, condors ventured as far as 70 km where they found their first nonproffered carcass in the vicinity of the town of LeChee on the Navajo Reservation. The greatest distance traveled in the first year was 301 km when a female went to Arches National Park, Utah, in July 1997.

The incipient flock remained sedentary at the release site throughout the following winter, but as the weather warmed in spring 1998, condors began traveling to the river corridor (Fig. 1). Excursions that year included a 387-km trip by three condors to Grand Mesa, Colorado, and a 516-km journey by one to Flaming Gorge, Wyoming; the bird returned to the release site six days later. With fall cooling, flock movement again contracted to within the 8–15 km radius of food provisioning around the release site. The birds found several cow (*Bovus*) carcasses in the River Corridor Zone in spring 1999, and that summer, a group of condors released at Hurricane Cliffs, a second site 112 km to the east of Vermilion Cliffs, traveled 548 km to visit Mesa Verde, Colorado, briefly.

By August 1999, the birds from both the Hurricane and Vermilion Cliffs release sites had joined at the South Rim of the Grand Canyon. Inappropriate behavior involving humans and human-related structures prompted a trapping effort to remove the instigators. We held problem birds at Vermilion Cliffs to encourage remaining flock members to abandon their focus on peopled areas along the South Rim, and it was during those trappings that we began sampling blood lead levels. Two of 13 initial samples taken in July and August 1999 indicated exposure to lead. South Rim condor visitation decreased as expected that fall, and the now coalesced flock displayed its usual winter sedentary behavior at Vermilion Cliffs. We continued feeding there and along the river corridor in an attempt to retain condors within areas comparatively devoid of humans; however, a large proportion of the flock returned to the South Rim in the spring of 2000. In early summer, ingestion of shotgun pellets killed 2–4 condors and required others to be treated with chelation therapy (Woods et al. this volume), an episode that brought about the current intensive program of blood lead testing (Parish et al. this volume).

MOVEMENT PATTERNS 2001–2004

Condor movements became more conservative as time progressed and the succession of newly-released condors joined older, more experienced flock members. We observed very few long range movements after 1999, and none beyond 220 km from the release site. Data on the movements of condors with VHF transmitters after June 2001 showed that condors released at Vermilion Cliffs tended to remain in that vicinity for several months before venturing out to other areas: 27 young condors stayed in the area of the release site (Paria Zone) for an average of 102 days (median = 82 days, range = 25–200) before roosting in another zone for the first time. The initial zone of visitation was usually that of the river corridor in Marble Canyon, a first destination for many condors in the early months of the year.

GPS-equipped condors moved widely within the study area, with concentrations on the Kaibab Plateau, the south rim of the Grand Canyon, and in the Kolob region of southern Utah (Fig. 3). A greater tendency to travel in the warmer months was likely related to the availability of thermal updrafts, but the increase in late-winter and spring traveling apparent in 2004 may predict a trend of diminishing reliance on food subsidy at the release site (Fig. 4). Further, movements of breeders to and from their Grand Canyon nest sites in 2003 and 2004 may have encouraged the movement of other condors.

The first general flock movements outside the release area and the Marble Canyon river corridor were to the South Rim of Grand Canyon National Park (Fig. 1), an area containing numerous tourists and buildings (Plate 9). The reasons why condors continued to frequent this area in spring and summer likely relates to human-induced concentrations of Common Ravens (*Corvus corax*) and Turkey Vultures (*Cathartes aura*), both species acting as indicators of food availability. Further, condors located carrion within the canyon itself and as vehicular kills on roads into

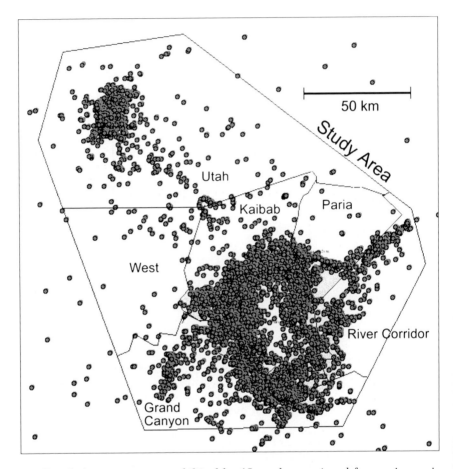

Fig. 3. Area use-pattern exhibited by 18 condors equipped for varying periods with satellite-reporting GPS transmitters during November 2003–June 2005, Arizona. Dots represent hourly GPS position fixes of individual condors during daylight (n = ~29,000 fixes).

and within the Park. These visits, particularly in the early years, resulted in encounters between condors and humans or their artifacts and prompted the development of a successful hazing program that has, together with the influence of older flock members upon the development of younger birds, tended to reduce the rate of undesirable behavior (Cade et al. 2004).

The extended use of the River Corridor Zone diminished after spring 2002 with the development of greater interest by condors in the Kaibab Plateau that summer and fall (Plate 9). Condors began visiting the Kolob region of southern Utah in the summer and fall of 2004, a pastoral area offering yet another opportunity for independent foraging.

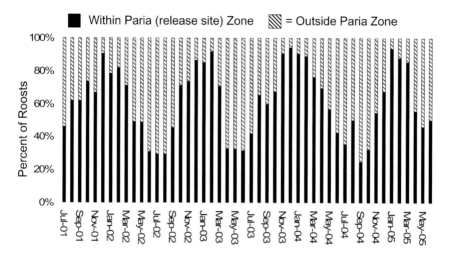

Fig. 4. Monthly roosting patterns of free-ranging condors within and outside the Paria (release site) Zone during July 2001–June 2005 (from VHF ground tracking data).

Movements in Relation to Lead Exposure

The moderately reduced numbers of condors using the Kaibab area in 2003 (Plate 9) in part reflected the longer holding of birds after testing in October and November in response to rising lead levels and those of the previous fall (Fig. 5). The many exposures recorded in November 2002 corresponded to the centerfire rifle deer seasons that extended intermittently from 18 October to 1 December on the nearby Kaibab Plateau. A total of 1,982 deer permits were issued that year compared to 975 in 2003, and 1,450 in 2004. Reported hunter success rates varied from 32–84%, meaning that an average of about 700 deer offal piles remained in the landscape each year. Data reported by Hunt et al. (2006) suggest that the majority of these would have contained bullet fragments (Fig. 6), as would an unknown number of deer carcasses lost to wounding. Observations by Peregrine Fund staff confirmed that condors fed upon deer offal and carcasses on the Kaibab Plateau and elsewhere, and suggested that ravens, which themselves may be drawn to carrion by gunshots (White 2005), attracted condors to deer carrion even in forest and woodland where visibility was restricted (see Koford 1953).

The temporal connection between lead exposure and the period of the Kaibab deer seasons (Fig. 7) led us to hypothesize that hunter-killed deer on the Kaibab Plateau could alone account for the high degree of lead exposure apparent in the fall. In a further attempt to find clarifying

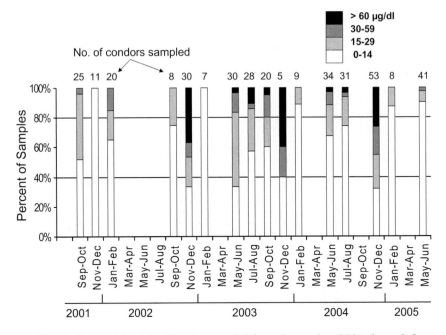

Fig. 5. Condor blood lead levels recorded from September 2001 through June 2005, Arizona.

evidence, and in consideration of the 7- to 20-day half-life of blood lead levels as reviewed by Fry and Maurer (2003), we ordered the data on movements to reflect condor roost zones during the 28 days prior to each blood lead sampling performed at the release site during July 2001–June 2005 (Parish et al. this volume). We calculated the percentage of roosting in each of the four zones, excluding the four Grand Canyon breeders and one wild-produced juvenile because of their association with active nests. We did not consider the West Zone in the analysis because condors visited it so rarely; only once was a condor detected in the West Zone during the 28-day period prior to testing.

Of 37 blood lead samplings of condors that roosted continually at the release site during the 28 days prior to sampling, none showed lead levels higher than 12 µg dL^{-1} (mean = 5.4, SD ± 3.3, see Parish et al. this volume). Among 11 additional lead samplings for which no data were available to indicate movement outside the release site, three condors showed exposures ranging from 20–26 µg dL^{-1}, and one indicated a high lead level of 81 µg dL^{-1}. However, its whereabouts outside the release site and those of the three with moderate exposure were unknown during most of the previous 28 days.

Two condors that died of ingesting shotgun pellets on 12 and 23 January 2005 were assumed to have obtained them from the same location

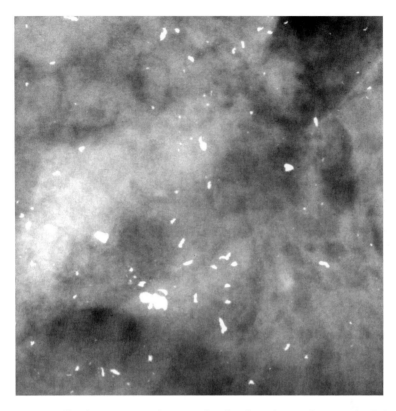

Fig. 6. Bullet fragments in the gut pile of a deer shot with a standard, lead-based, soft point hunting bullet as revealed by radiography.

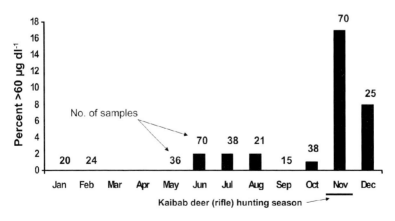

Fig. 7. Monthly differences in the percent of condor blood samples showing lead levels greater than 60 μg dL^{-1}. Monthly data are pooled from July 2001 to June 2005.

in the River Corridor Zone where they were observed together until 21 and 38 days prior to death. They both returned to the release site where they remained for 19 and 26 days before dying. The delay between exposure and death may have resulted from the retention of shotgun pellets in the stomach, evident in radiographs obtained at necropsy, a tendency also noted in an earlier episode involving ingestion of shotgun pellets by multiple condors in the summer of 2000 (Woods et al. this volume). The infrequent documentation of bullet fragments relative to the large number of putative exposures to rifle-killed animals in the region may result from the very small mass of most bullet fragments, allowing their complete absorption prior to radiography (Hunt et al. 2006). Additionally, their irregular shapes may adhere to food passing from the stomach into the intestine, whereas spherical shotgun pellets may be less likely to adhere, resulting in a protracted period of absorption.

The Kaibab Plateau showed a clear positive relationship between condor visitation and lead exposure ($\chi^2 = 24.4$, df = 3, $P < 0.001$, $n = 283$ samples), and the relationship remained pronounced when the analysis was shortened to 14 days prior to sampling ($\chi^2 = 22.0$, df = 3, $P < 0.001$) and even to seven days ($\chi^2 = 13.8$, df = 3, $P < 0.005$) (Table 1). This result is consistent with the hypothesis of hunter-killed deer on the Kaibab Plateau as a principal source of lead to condors tested in November and December. As a notable example, a 3.5-year-old condor tested on 26 November 2004 showed blood lead levels approaching 700 µg dL^{-1} and numerous metal fragments in radiographs of the stomach (Parish et al. this volume). Tracking data indicated that this condor had spent at least 21 of the previous 28 days on the Kaibab Plateau where the deer (centerfire rifle) season occurred within the period of 22 October to 28 November. In November 2004, 12 condors showing <30 µg dL^{-1} had an average of 3.7 recorded roosts in the Kaibab Zone during the previous 28 days, whereas 11 individuals showing >30 µg dL^{-1} averaged 8.1 roosts in that zone ($t = 1.9$, $P = 0.04$).

Table 1. Percentage of blood samples (n = 283) in which tested condors were detected in each zone at least once during the 28-day period prior to testing (see Parish et al. this volume for discussion of blood-lead levels); the period of study extended from September 2001 through June 2005.

Blood-lead level (µg dL^{-1})	No. of blood samples	Kaibab Zone (%)	Grand Canyon Zone (%)	River Corridor Zone (%)	Utah Zone (%)
0–14	141	76 (54)	110 (78)	40 (28)	19 (13)
15–29	63	33 (52)	49 (78)	8 (13)	8 (13)
30–59	40	30 (75)	30 (75)	8 (20)	3 (8)
>60	39	36 (92)	23 (59)	4 (10)	5 (13)

The other three zones showed no increasing trend of lead levels with condor visitation (Table 1). The River Corridor Zone had relatively few deer, and that portion of the Grand Canyon Zone most frequented by condors was national park land, an area where hunting was prohibited. The Utah Zone showed no relationship even though it had fall deer and elk hunting seasons and one condor died there of lead ingestion in August 2002. However, condors only recently began frequenting the region in numbers, and the sample of blood-assays of condors visiting that zone was relatively small ($n = 35$, compared with 175, 212, and 60 for the Kaibab, Grand Canyon, and River Corridor zones, respectively).

Condors were also exposed to lead in summer, albeit in lower proportion than fall (Fig. 7). Unlike the predictable annual production of rifle-killed deer carrion, however, we have no clear hypothesis regarding the sources of summer lead exposure. There were no summer firearms seasons for ungulates anywhere within the condor range in Arizona or Utah. The episode of multiple condor poisonings by shotgun pellets in June 2000 was therefore unexpected, like the similar poisonings in January 2005 (Woods et al. this volume). However, the chance discovery of a condor feeding upon a rifle-killed coyote in summer 2003 in a roadside meadow on the Kaibab Plateau suggested the possibility that predator shooting might be a significant factor in condor lead exposure (Parish et al. this volume). Radiographs of the partial remains of that coyote showed rifle bullet fragments, and radiographs of two condors associated with it showed bullet fragments in their stomachs. Subsequent inquiries suggested that coyote shooters travel to the Kaibab Plateau soon after snowmelt in mid-May when the roads open for travel. Predator shooting occurs throughout the condor range, but our data on movements indicated no principal area of summer exposure to lead.

CONDOR USE OF DEER REMAINS

Monitoring of condor movements from January 2002 through September 2005 led to the discovery of 196 dead animals within the study area. We found condors in association with the remains of 78 (40%) deer, 42 (21%) elk, 10 (5%) coyotes, 51 (26%) domestic livestock (cattle, horses, mules, and sheep), and 16 (8%) miscellaneous animals (Table 2). Carcasses in the Grand Canyon Zone, mainly elk, were primarily victims of road-vehicle collisions and falls from cliffs within the Grand Canyon National Park. In the Kaibab Zone, at least 15 of the 55 deer had been killed by hunters (six were gut piles); the remaining fatalities included 9 from road vehicle collisions and 32 from unknown causes. Twenty-five (78%) of the latter were found during fall deer hunting periods (50%) or in the weeks between them (28%). At least two of the nine coyotes on the

Table 2. Animal remains recorded in association with condors from 2002 through September 2005 in three zones in Arizona. We also found condors at two additional carcasses in other zones (a coyote and a horse).

	Deer	Elk	Coyote	Livestock	Miscellaneous	Total
Kaibab Zone	55	0	9	37	4	107
Grand Canyon Zone	21	41	0	6	9	77
Utah Zone	2	1	0	7	3	13

Kaibab Plateau had been shot (both contained bullet fragments), two were killed by road vehicles, and the remainder died of unknown causes.

DISCUSSION

The several lines of evidence presented in this report support the hypothesis that deer killed with lead-based rifle bullets on the Kaibab Plateau during the November hunting season were the primary source of elevated blood lead levels measured in condors in northern Arizona during 2002–2004. First, there is the known history of exposure. Although our data on blood lead levels were relatively sparse in the early years, the incidence and predictability of exposure increased dramatically in fall 2002 when condors began frequenting the Kaibab Zone in numbers (e.g., Plate 9, see also Parish et al. this volume). Second, the sharp annual peaks of exposure in November and December 2002–2004 were synchronous with the November deer hunting season in the Kaibab Zone (Fig. 7). Third, the exposure peak was also synchronous with the peak of condor occurrence there (Plate 9). Fourth, blood lead levels of condors visiting the Kabaib Zone within 7–28 days of testing were significantly higher than those of condors undetected in the zone during those periods; the other zones showed no trend of increase of lead exposure with visitation. These results were expected because the Kaibab Zone, an area of close proximity to the release site and of frequent use by condors, is one where many deer are annually killed by rifles. Hunters necessarily leave the offal of each harvested deer in the field, and most rifle-killed deer gut piles and whole deer lost to wounding are now known to contain numerous lead bullet fragments (Hunt et al. 2006).

As a result of these findings, the schedule of lead testing in Arizona is now geared in part to the regularity of the fall deer seasons so that the majority of condors can be screened. Lead exposures outside the time frame of the deer hunting seasons are more difficult to detect because of the evident scattering of exposures in time and space. Of the two other known avenues of lead exposure—shotgun pellets in the carcasses of unknown species and lead bullet fragments in coyote carcasses—neither can yet be anticipated or connected with specific condor-use areas. Data on movements suggest that the pellet episode exposing 12 or more condors in June

2000 derived from the western portion of the Grand Canyon Zone, and the two pellet ingestion fatalities in January 2005 appear to have been come from the River Corridor Zone. However, neither supposition can be corroborated with available evidence.

We believe that rifle-killed coyotes may be a frequent source of lead exposure in summer because there is widespread interest in coyote hunting in the region, and rifle-killed coyotes are likely to contain lead. Polymer-tipped bullets made specifically for coyote hunting are designed to explode into tiny fragments upon impact and remain entirely within the animal (Fig. 8). There is, however, little direct evidence to suggest that condors encounter rifle-killed coyotes in numbers sufficient to account for the rate of lead exposure recorded in summer (Fig. 7). Much, therefore, remains unknown about the geography of lead exposure among condors in Arizona and Utah and its implications for the welfare of the population. Although the evidence for lead-based projectiles as the main pathway of lead ingestion by condors released in Arizona is now unequivocal, we will continue to explore the possibility of other sources as the population expands.

Of particular interest is the demographic question of what proportion of condors showing high blood lead levels or lead bodies in radiographs

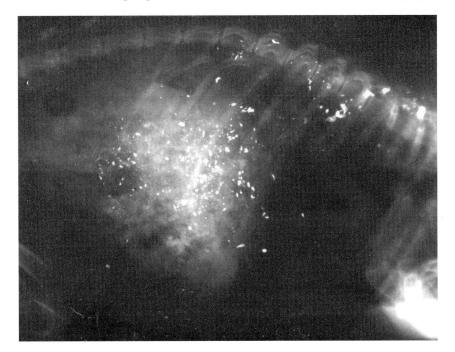

Fig. 8. A profusion of metal fragments is visible in this radiograph of a coyote shot with a standard, lead-based, polymer-tipped "varmint bullet." (Photo by Erin Gott.)

would die without the mitigating effects of monitoring and treatment. Computations by Woods et al. (this volume) suggest that an increase in the adult mortality rate arising from lack of such intervention would likely tip the demographic balance toward decline. Our data and those of Parish et al. (this volume) suggest that virtually all free-ranging condors in Arizona have been exposed to lead, and there is likely a proportion of the population that has survived high, undetected exposures. Whereas all exposed condors have ingested lead, removal of lead bodies by purging or surgery has occurred in only nine cases (Parish et al. this volume), implying that the majority of lead bodies are either passed into the intestine, expelled in castings, or completely absorbed. It is thus worth considering the possible long-term sub-lethal effects of repeated exposure, chelation, and radiography on condor health and fecundity. There is good evidence for other species of birds that lead exposure during development may permanently impair brain function (see Burger and Gochfeld 2005), an important issue considering the long developmental period in nestling condors and the likelihood of exposure during this period. In light of all these considerations, our findings suggest that a reduction in the use of lead-based ammunition within the condor range could well enable the existence of a self-sustaining condor population. Nontoxic bullets of proven high efficacy in deer hunting are readily available to hunters (McMurchy 2003, Towsley 2005, Sullivan et al. this volume), and shooters could easily remove coyotes, hares, and other species killed with lead-based bullets from the field.

Acknowledgments

Funding was provided by The Peregrine Fund, the U.S. Fish and Wildlife Service, and the Arizona Game and Fish Department. We thank Bill Burnham, Tom Cade, Bill Heinrich, Pat Hughes, Lloyd Kiff, Brian Mutch, Angel Montoya, Kurt Burnham, Pete Weidner, Chad Olson, Erin Gott, Kathy Orr, Sophie Osborn, Andi Rogers, Travis Rosenberry, Maggie Sacher, Duane Shroufe, Kathy Sullivan, Bruce Talbert, Paul Juergens, and Randy Townsend. Telemetry trackers included Jill Adams, Brandon Breen, Jessi Brown, Ann Burke, Daniel Burnetti, Gant Charping, James Christian, Joseph Crapanzano, Chris Crowe, Janelle Cuddeford, Marta Curti, Ann Marie DiLorenzo, Stephen Agius, Tyrone Donnelly, Gretchen Druliner, Sam Elizondo, Beau Fairchild, Kevin Fairhurst, Edward Feltes, Chadd Fitzpatrick, Paul Flournoy, Lisa Fosco, Vincent Frary, Jody Bartz, Melissa Gray, Sean Grimland, Courtney Harris, Adam Hutchins, Helen Johnson, Jeffrey Kingscott, Karen Leavelle, Kristine Lightner, Roger Benefield, Amy Lindsley, David Loomis, Megan Lout, Tanya Maddock, Michael Maglione, Frank Nebenburgh, Blake Massey, Khris McConnell, David McGraw, Phil McKenna, Grant Merrill, Tim Bischof, Christopher

Michaud, Betty Moore, Dennis Mott, Paul Mueller, Nichole Munkwitz, Curt Mykut, Frank Nebengurgh, Amy Nicholas, Jason Blackburn, Hannah Ogden, Kathryn Parmentier, Michael Maglione, Mary Schwartz, Molly Severson, Kirk Stodola, Elise Snyder, Melanie Spies, Molly Thomas, Mark Vekasy, Kristy Bly, Jonna Weidmaier, Eric Weis, Anne Welch, and Jim Wilmarth. Tom Cade, Allan Mee, and Linnea Hall provided critical reviews of the manuscript.

Literature Cited

Burger, J., and M. Gochfeld. 2005. Effects of lead on learning in Herring Gulls: an avian wildlife model for neurobehavioral deficits. Neurotoxicology 26:615–624.

Cade, T. J., S. A. H. Osborn, W. G. Hunt, and C. P. Woods. 2004. Commentary on released California Condors *Gymnogyps californianus* in Arizona. Pages 11–25 *in* Raptors Worldwide: Proceedings of VI World Conference on Birds of Prey and Owls (R. D. Chancellor and B.-U. Meyburg, Eds.). World Working Group on Birds of Prey and Owls/MME-Birdlife, Hungary.

Eisler, R. 1988. Lead hazards to fish, wildlife, and invertebrates: a synoptic review. U.S. Fish and Wildlife Service Biological Report 85 (1.14). Patuxent Wildlife Research Center, Laurel, Maryland.

Fry, D. M., and J. R. Maurer. 2003. Assessment of lead contamination sources exposing California Condors. Final report to the California Department of Fish and Game, Sacramento.

Hoffmeister, D. M. 1986. The Mammals of Arizona. University of Arizona Press, Tucson.

Hunt, W. G., W. Burnham, C. N. Parish, K. Burnham, B. Mutch, and J. L. Oaks. 2006. Bullet fragments in deer remains: implications for lead exposure in scavengers. Wildlife Society Bulletin 34:168–171.

Janssen, D. L., J. E. Oosterhuis, J. L. Allen, M. P. Anderson, D. G. Kelts, and S. N. Wiemeyer. 1986. Lead poisoning in free-ranging California Condors. Journal of the American Veterinary Medical Association 189:1115–1117.

Koford, C. B. 1953. The California Condor. National Audubon Research Report 4: 1–154.

Kramer, J. L., and P. T. Redig. 1997. Sixteen years of lead poisoning in eagles, 1980–95: an epizootiologic view. Journal of Raptor Research 31:327–332.

McMurchy, I. 2003. Barnes XLC bullets. American Hunter 31 (January):70–71.

Mee, A., J. A. Hamber, and J. Sinclair. 2007. Low nest success in a reintroduced population of California Condors. Pages 163–184 *in* California Condors in the 21st Century (A. Mee and L. S. Hall, Eds.). Series in Ornithology, no. 2.

Meretsky, V. J., and N. F. R. Snyder. 1992. Range use and movements of California Condors. Condor 94:313–335.

Meretsky, V. J., N. F. R. Snyder, S. R. Beissinger, D. A. Clendenen, and J. W. Wiley. 2000. Demography of the California Condor: implications for reestablishment. Conservation Biology 14:957–967.

Parish, C. N., W. R. Heinrich, and W. G. Hunt. 2007. Lead exposure, diagnosis, and treatment in California Condors released in Arizona. Pages 97–108 *in*

California Condors in the 21st Century (A. Mee and L. S. Hall, Eds.). Series in Ornithology, no. 2.

SULLIVAN, K., R. SIEG, AND C. PARISH. 2007. Arizona's efforts to reduce lead exposure in California Condors. Pages 109–122 in California Condors in the 21st Century (A. Mee and L. S. Hall, Eds.). Series in Ornithology, no. 2.

TOWSLEY, B. M. 2005. The hunting bullet redefined. American Rifleman 153 (December):34–43.

WALLACE, M. P., M. FULLER, AND J. WILEY. 1994. Patagial transmitters for large vultures and condors. Pages 381–387 in Raptor Conservation Today: Proceedings of the IV World Conference on Birds of Prey and Owls (B.-U. Meyburg and R. D. Chancellor, Eds.). World Working Group for Birds of Prey. Pica Press, Shipman, VA.

WALLACE, M. P., AND S. A. TEMPLE. 1987. Competitive interactions with and between species in a guild of avian scavengers. Auk 104:290–295.

WHITE, C. 2005. Hunters ring dinner bell for ravens: experimental evidence of a unique foraging strategy. Ecology 86:1057–1060.

WIEMEYER, S. N., J. M. SCOTT, M. P. ANDERSON, P. H. BLOOM, AND C. J. STAFFORD. 1988. Environmental contaminants in California Condors. Journal of Wildlife Management 52:238–247.

WOODS, C. P., W. R. HEINRICH, S. C. FARRY, C. N. PARISH, S. A. H. OSBORNE, AND T. J. CADE. 2007. Survival and reproduction of California Condors released in Arizona. Pages 57–78 in California Condors in the 21st Century (A. Mee and L. S. Hall, Eds.). Series in Ornithology, no. 2.

5

Lead Exposure, Diagnosis, and Treatment in California Condors Released in Arizona

Chris N. Parish,[1] *William R. Heinrich, and W. Grainger Hunt*

ABSTRACT.—Lead poisoning was the most frequently diagnosed cause of death among free-ranging California Condors (*Gymnogyps californianus*) released by The Peregrine Fund in Arizona during 1996–2005 and may have caused additional undiagnosed fatalities. We tested condors at least twice per year, and among 437 blood samples analyzed from March 2000 through December 2004 (excluding retests of exposed individuals), 137 showed above-background lead exposure levels of between 15 and 59 µg dL^{-1}, and 39 exceeded 60 µg dL^{-1}, elsewhere defined as the threshold of clinical affect. Laboratory tests showed that 25 samples among the latter group were above 100 µg dL^{-1}, 10 exceeded 200 µg dL^{-1}, and 5 were greater than 400 µg dL^{-1}. Chelation therapy was administered in 66 cases (28 individuals); all treated individuals survived. Condors showing moderate degrees of exposure were held for retesting to detect trends of blood lead depuration or increase, the latter indicating the need for radiography. Radiographs of seven condors (three alive, four dead) revealed shotgun pellets in their stomachs, and seven more (six alive, one dead) showed ingested lead fragments consistent with those of spent rifle bullets. Surgery or oral doses of psyllium fiber were used to purge lead from the stomachs of surviving individuals. Overall findings indicated that condors in northern Arizona frequently ingest lead and suggest that rifle- and shotgun-killed animals are an important source of toxic exposure for condors.

The endangered California Condor (*Gymnogyps californianus*) is among the most sensitive of all U.S. birds to changes in survival rates. The species defers breeding until six or more years of age and incubates a single egg (Koford 1953). Past data suggest that about one-half of nesting

The Peregrine Fund, 5668 West Flying Hawk Lane, Boise, Idaho 83709, USA.
[1]*E-mail cparish@perergrinefund.org*

attempts succeed, and successful pairs may not renest for 16–18 months after fledging young (Snyder and Snyder 2000). Such low reproductive potential necessitates high individual survival, particularly among the older age categories. Population viability models call for minimum annual adult survival rates in the range of 90–95% (Verner 1978, Meretsky et al. 2000), values that most certainly were not obtained in the wild during the 1970s and 1980s, when the number of individuals counted in surveys declined by about 40 percent (Snyder and Snyder 2000). Known mortality agents at the time included lead poisoning (Janssen et al. 1986, Weimeyer et al. 1988), shooting (Wilbur 1978), powerline collisions (Koford 1953, Brunetti 1965), drowning (Koford 1953), and predator control poisoning (Miller et al. 1965, Borneman 1966, Weimeyer et al. 1988). However, dead condors were usually not recovered, so the relative importance of mortality factors in the condor population could not be accurately determined.

To counter the continuing population decline, the U.S. Fish and Wildlife Service began in 1982 to capture condors for long-term captive propagation. A decision to leave even a few pairs in the wild was thwarted within a six-month period (October 1984–April 1985) when six of the remaining 15 wild condors perished; five of these went unrecovered, and the sixth was found to have died of lead poisoning (Snyder and Snyder 2000). These events prompted the removal of all remaining condors to breeding facilities where success in propagation from the remaining 27 individuals (14 females and 13 males) swelled the population to over 250 birds by 2005, almost half of which have been released to the wilds of California, Arizona, and Baja California, Mexico.

In 1996, The Peregrine Fund began releasing captive-bred condors in northern Arizona (36°N, 112°W) with the goal of establishing a self-sustaining population disjunct from other reintroduced condor populations. The current release site, situated atop Vermillion Cliffs and in view of the Kaibab Plateau to the west, lies approximately 80 km north of the south rim of the Grand Canyon (see Hunt et al. this volume for a description of the northern Arizona environs). Continuing releases brought the number of free-flying birds to about 50 by spring 2005, including three fledged from wild pairs (Woods et al. this volume). Daily monitoring by means of conventional and satellite-based GPS telemetry offered an opportunity to recover condor carcasses and assess proportional impact among the various mortality agents existing outside the immediate areas of release. Lead poisoning was principal among them, accounting for at least six of the 12 condor deaths unrelated to recency of release (Woods et al. this volume).

The first indication that lead would be a problem for condors in Arizona came in 2000 when at least two died from ingesting shotgun pellets from an unknown source. Thirteen others showed elevated blood lead levels, and were likely exposed during that same poisoning event (Cade et al. 2004). This episode, followed by a general expansion of condor movement and foraging in the region (Hunt et al. this volume), prompted the development of a regular program of blood lead testing, evaluation, and treatment. Here we report the results of the lead-testing program in Arizona.

METHODS

Lead monitoring.—We began capturing and testing condors for lead exposure during 1999–2001, and have since attempted to test all free-ranging birds at least twice per year. Each condor was identified by a studbook (SB) number assigned at fledging (Mace 2005). We captured condors in a "walk-in" chain-link trap measuring approximately 3.7 m × 3.7 m × 1.6 m in height. Pre-baiting with calf carcasses encouraged condors to enter and exit the trap freely. We observed from a blind and closed the door to the trap by means of a hand-operated cable and pulley system. We then entered the trap, caught each target condor with a hand net, and transported it to a nearby processing area. From one to three people held the condor while a fourth withdrew 1–3 mL of blood from the medial-tarsal vein using a 22-gauge needle and heparinized tubes for sample storage. Using standard techniques for blood collection and lead analysis in the field, we transferred 50 µg of whole blood from each sample to a vial containing 250 µl of 0.35 molar HCl, thence to a sensor strip inserted into a portable blood lead analyzer (LeadCare Blood Lead Testing System, ESA Inc., Chelmsford, Massachusetts) (Fry and Maurer 2003). This instrument determines and displays lead values between 0–65 µg dL^{-1}. We also submitted samples ($n = 163$) for testing to commercial laboratories, some for the purpose of comparison with field-instrument values, but in most cases to accurately determine lead values when they exceeded the field analyzer's limit of 65 µg dL^{-1}.

Except for occasional aberrations, consistency within samples of blood tested with the field analyzer ($n = 113$) were within the ±4.6 µg dL^{-1} standards reported by the manufacturer (Fig. 1A). Laboratory analyses of samples ($n = 56$) were also fairly consistent with duplicate samples sent to the same or different laboratories (Fig. 1B). However, in comparisons of field-vs. laboratory-tested values ($n = 99$), the latter showed higher levels in all but three cases (Fig. 2). For field values of greater than 30 µg dL^{-1} ($n = 17$ comparisons), the laboratory values averaged 1.8 times higher. By necessity, we made management and treatment decisions primarily in response to the field-tester, but in this report, where both field-tester and laboratory values were available, we list the laboratory values on the assumption of their greater accuracy.

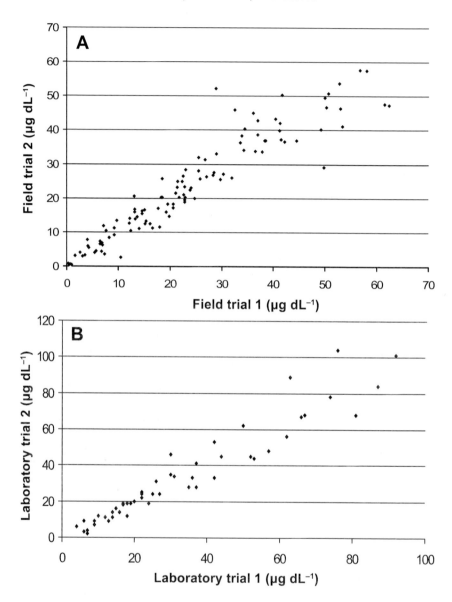

Fig. 1. (A) Comparisons within 113 duplicate sets of condor blood samples from Arizona, 1999–2004, tested with a portable field analyzer. (B) Comparisons within 56 duplicate sets of condor blood samples tested by commercial laboratories. The figure excludes three outliers: (1) 136 µg dL⁻¹:189 µg dL⁻¹, (2) 199 µg dL⁻¹: 415 µg dL⁻¹, and (3) 539 µg dL⁻¹:570 µg dL⁻¹.

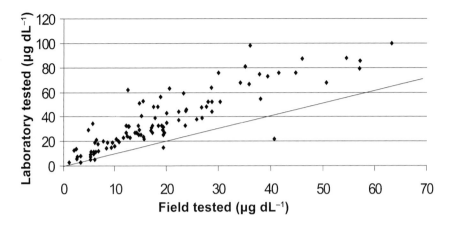

Fig. 2. Comparison of field and laboratory test results of duplicate condor blood samples (n =99), excluding a single outlier (ESA field tester = 35 µg dL⁻¹, Lab = 212 µg dL⁻¹). The line depicts the ideal parity of duplicates.

RESULTS

Lead exposure.—We annually tested condors for lead contamination during 1999–2004 (Fig. 3). We analyzed 437 samples during the period, of which 261 (60%) showed "background" lead concentrations of 0–14 µg dL⁻¹. Eighty-two samples (18.7%) yielded levels of 15–29 µg dL⁻¹ (indicating lead exposure), 55 (12.6%) showed 31–59 µg dL⁻¹, and 39 (9%) were over 60 µg dL⁻¹, the threshold at which the term "clinically affected" has been applied (Fry and Maurer 2003). Laboratory tests showed that 25 of the latter group were above 100 µg dL⁻¹ (termed "acutely toxic" by Kramer and Redig 1997); 10 of those exceeded 200 µg dL⁻¹, and 5 showed greater than 400 µg dL⁻¹. It is important to note that these reported lead levels do not preclude higher degrees of original exposure, as levels are subject to peaking and depuration between lead ingestion and testing (see Fry and Maurer 2003).

    Condors feeding primarily on proffered carcasses (dairy calves) at the release site showed blood lead levels in the range of 0–12 µg dL⁻¹. Aside from a shotgun pellet episode in summer 2000 that resulted in the deaths of at least two condors (see Woods et al. this volume), exposure levels did not increase until 2002 when condors began frequenting the Kaibab Plateau during the fall deer seasons (see Hunt et al. 2006). The apparent rise in the overall proportion of exposures during 2002–2004 (Fig. 3) was consistent with this increasing use of the Kaibab Plateau, and the period of highest exposure in each of those three years was during and just after the deer season (Hunt et al. this volume). The difference between the two

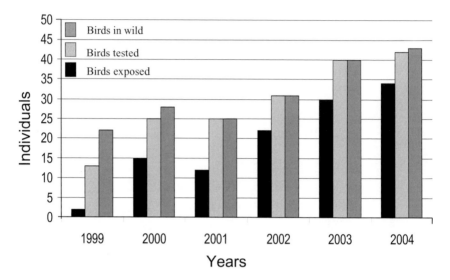

Fig. 3. Trend in lead testing and exposure of California Condors in Arizona during 1999–2004.

three-year periods—1999–2001 and 2002–2004—in the ratio of condors showing background levels (0–14 µg dL^{-1}) to those indicating exposure was highly significant ($\chi^2 = 15.4$, df = 1, $P < 0.001$).

Radiography.—We searched for radio-dense particles in condor radiographs produced by local veterinarians using standard diagnostic radiological equipment usually within 48 hours of blood assays in the field. In 2000, the first year of known exposure, radiographs of eight birds showed five with shotgun pellets in the digestive system; four of these birds were alive and one was dead (Woods et al. this volume). This incident prompted us over the next several years to x-ray all condors showing high lead levels (>60 µg dL^{-1}). However, results showed that of 13 lead-exposed condors radiographed during 2001–2002, only two (one alive, one dead) contained radio-dense fragments; in 2003, three of eight radiographed birds showed fragments. In an effort to reduce unnecessary overall exposure of condors to x-rays, we began radiographing only those retested birds showing increasing blood lead levels or those showing lack of immediate response to chelation therapy. In 2004, a year of many exposures, two condors showed trends of lead increase after capture, and both revealed fragments in radiographs.

Treatment.—Chelation therapy of condors showing high lead levels involved standard intramuscular (pectoral) injections of calcium edatate (or Ca EDTA) twice daily for five days (see Murase et al. 1992). Lethargic birds and those showing signs of dehydration were given oral and/or subcutaneous fluid (i.e., standard lactated Ringer's solution). Chelation usually resulted in rapid depuration of blood lead levels. For example, condor SB #133 on the first day of testing showed a field-test lead value of >65 µg dL^{-1}, and laboratory analysis of the same sample revealed a lead value of 162 µg dL^{-1}. We began chelation that day. On day three, the level had dropped to 42 µg dL^{-1} on the field-tester (lab value = 73 µg dL^{-1}), and by day five, the field-tester yielded 24 µg dL^{-1} (lab value = 39 µg dL^{-1}). After five days post-treatment, the field-tester showed a lead value of 11 µg dL^{-1}, and the bird was released. Retesting of this bird three and four months later showed no increase in lead levels.

In some cases, however, a second five-day round of chelation was needed. For example, condor SB #235 showed a field-test lead value of 36 µg dL^{-1} on the initial day of testing. We retained this bird to determine whether lead levels were increasing or decreasing. Five days later, the field-tester indicated a blood lead value of >65 µg dL^{-1}, and we began chelation. On the fourth and sixth day after treatment began, the lead levels remained at >65 µg dL^{-1}. No lead bodies were apparent in a radiograph taken on the eighth day of treatment, but lead levels had by then dropped to 46 µg dL^{-1}. We stopped treatment, and three days later, lead levels had fallen to 23 µg dL^{-1}. Differences between these two case histories suggest a difference in the chronology of exposure. Exposure of condor SB #235 was likely more recent than that of condor SB #133 at the time of testing, and lead levels may have been rising as a result of lead bodies remaining in the stomach.

Condors with detectable radio-dense particles were transported to the Phoenix Zoo Hospital for treatment. Shotgun pellets were surgically extracted in two cases. Condors with fragments were treated with fluids, chelation, and oral doses of psyllium fiber to purge lead from the digestive system. For example, 1.5 days after condor SB #235 was observed in the vicinity of a heavily scavenged coyote (*Canis latrans*) carcass, the remains of which were found to contain bullet fragments, the field-tester indicated a lead value of more than 65 µg dL^{-1}. A laboratory assay of the same blood sample showed a value of 555 µg dL^{-1}. Radiography revealed fragments in the stomach, and chelation and psyllium purging began within 48 hours of exposure detection. Two days later, laboratory testing showed a level of 489 µg dL^{-1}. Fecal materials were collected and radiographed to provide an indication of lead fragment passage, and all fragments had passed by the ninth day after their first detection in condor SB #235's stomach. Thirteen and 21 days after exposure detection, under continued treatment, laboratory lead values had declined to 37 and 28 µg dL^{-1}, respectively.

Although no treated condor died, one poisoning was too far advanced to begin chelation, and the bird died while being transported to the Phoenix Zoo for treatment. In all, 28 of the 50 condors in the Arizona flock received at least one chelation series during the reporting period, 17 received two chelations (20 injections), 5 were chelated four times, and 2 had six chelations (60 injections each). One of the latter two condors subsequently died of lead poisoning in January 2005, one month after successful treatment of a previous exposure. Eleven of the fourteen condors showing lead-shot (Fig. 4A) or fragments in radiographs (Fig. 4B) were found alive, and three were discovered post-mortem; all of the latter were diagnosed as having died of lead poisoning.

Discussion

Lead toxicity in birds appears to vary broadly among species and even among individuals (Carpenter et al. 2003); for example, Red-tailed Hawks (*Buteo jamaicensis*) and Turkey Vultures (*Cathartes aura*) show greater tolerance than Bald Eagles (*Haliaeetus leucocephalus*) (Reiser and Temple 1981, Carpenter et al. 2003). Clinical signs of lead toxicity, such as depression, lethargy, vomiting, diarrhea, nonregenerative anemia, anorexia, blindness, and seizures, have been observed in waterfowl and raptors with blood concentrations exceeding 100 µg dL^{-1} (Locke and Tomas 1996, Kramer and Redig 1997). However, threshold blood lead levels at which such manifestations appear in condors are still poorly known, and may remain undetected until just prior to death (Fry and Maurer 2003). Overt signs of lead poisoning may not be apparent in free-flying condors without close observations, and these are often difficult to make. It is therefore important to obtain a laboratory value as soon as possible when an exposure is detected at the upper limit of a field analyzer (i.e., >65 µg dL^{-1}).

In our study, laboratory results almost invariably exceeded those reported by the field-tester. However, the economics, portability, and speed of assay of the field instrument made it essential for classifying exposure levels for management decisions, for example, whether or not to hold a condor for further testing or for the return of laboratory results. Accordingly, we used the field tester's indicated value of about 60 µg dL^{-1} as the treatment threshold for condors, whereas laboratory comparisons suggested that, on average, the true value was nearly double (180%) that concentration, or about 108 µg dL^{-1} (Fig. 2).

Unfortunately, the lag in timing between field and laboratory testing, coupled with the logistical challenge of transporting condors for radiography, can hinder the process of evaluation and decision-making regarding treatment. Accurate assessment is further confounded by the question of when the condor was exposed versus when it was tested. Lead half-life in avian blood is estimated at 7–20 days, whereas lead in other tissues and bone may persist for many months (Reiser and Temple 1981, Eisler 1988, Fry and Maurer 2003). A high value may indicate recent exposure, but it may also reflect a

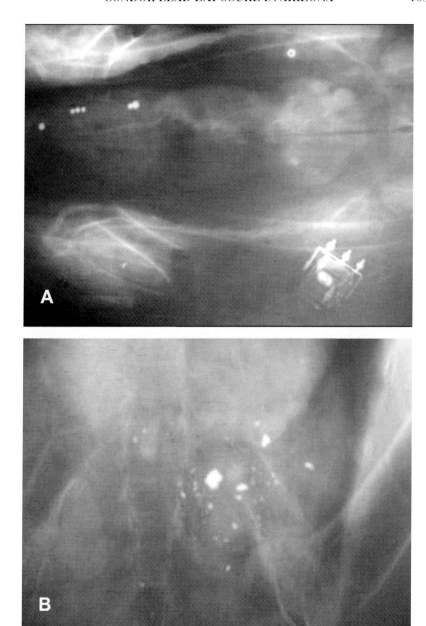

Fig. 4. (A) Radiograph of the digestive tract of condor SB #165 containing lead shotgun pellets of two sizes. Lead poisoning was the diagnosed cause of death (VHF transmitter visible). (B) Radiograph of condor SB #243's stomach containing lead bullet fragments; its blood lead level four days later showed 691 µg dL^{-1}.

point along a trend of depuration from an even higher level, or the continued presence within the stomach of lead bodies that may cause levels to rise after testing. It is thus important to consider that a measurement of moderate blood lead concentration at the time a free-ranging condor is captured for sampling may not reflect the degree of exposure. Thus, deciding whether to begin chelation is based on (1) an in-the-field detection of a high lead level (~60 µg dL^{-1}), (2) a clear trend of increase toward a higher level over several days, or (3) the continuance of a moderately high level over time (Fig. 5). Whereas the interval between lead ingestion and testing will usually remain unknown, as will the form and severity of exposure, retaining a condor and monitoring the trend of blood lead concentration over several days may shed light on the question of continued mobilization of lead into the bloodstream that may suggest the presence of lead in the condor's stomach (Fig. 4). This procedure minimizes the necessity of routine radiography and its potential for damaging DNA, particularly germ line DNA.

In conclusion, The Peregrine Fund has settled on a management program based upon the periodic testing of blood lead concentrations at a minimum of twice per year and concentrating effort at times of expected contamination based on exposure histories and seasonal events, particularly the fall deer hunting seasons when condors encounter lead in the form of spent bullet fragments (Hunt et al. 2006, this volume). Anomalous episodes, like those of shotgun pellet ingestion, are more difficult to anticipate, although close monitoring of condor movements and behavior have occasionally allowed us to identify exposed birds. By examining data on

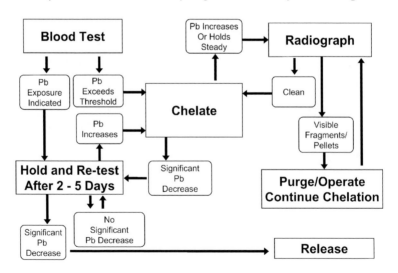

Fig. 5. Flow diagram representing The Peregrine Fund's protocol for evaluating and treating condors exposed to lead in Arizona.

the movements of condors associated with the affected individual(s) in the weeks prior to presumed exposure, we are able to identify and target those additional birds in need of testing (see Hunt et al. this volume). Among the many unknowns is whether or not the current blood lead thresholds (field-test value of ~60 µg dL^{-1}) are the appropriate levels at which treatment should commence. There are also the uncertain effects of multiple exposures within a short time span or the long term effects of more widely-spaced, multiple, subclinical exposures. As of September 2005, every condor in Arizona that is two years old or older has been exposed to lead, and eight of ten condors nine years old or older have shown lead levels exceeding 100 µg dL^{-1}. Whether such frequent and long-term exposure to lead will affect future reproductive capacity and survival is as yet unknown.

Acknowledgments

We thank Tom Cade, Shawn Farry, Sophie Osborn, Thom Lord, Eddie Feltes, Jonna Weidmaier, Frank Nebenberg, Chad Olson, Eric Weis, Vincent Frary, Michael Maglione, Jim Wilmarth, Roger Benefield, Beau Fairchild, Ron Sieg, Kathy Sullivan, Andi Rogers, Arizona Game and Fish Department, John and Karen Goodwin, Jerry Roundtree, and Christie VanCleve. We are grateful to Dr. Kathy Orr of The Phoenix Zoo and Dr. Cynthia Stringfield of Los Angeles Zoo for administering veterinary treatment and sharing their expertise. For extended acknowledgments, please refer to Woods et. al. this volume. Tom Cade, Allan Mee, and Linnea Hall provided critical reviews of the manuscript.

Literature Cited

Borneman, J. 1966. Return of a condor. Audubon Magazine 68:154–157.

Brunetti, O. 1965. Report on the cause of death of a California Condor. Unpublished report, California Department of Fish and Game, Sacramento, California.

Cade, T. J., S. A. H. Osborn, W. G. Hunt, and C. P. Woods. 2004. Commentary on released California Condors *Gymnogyps californianus* in Arizona. Pages 11–25 *in* Raptors Worldwide: Proceedings of VI World Conference on Birds of Prey and Owls (R. D. Chancellor and B.-U. Meyburg, Eds.). World Working Group on Birds of Prey and Owls/MME-Birdlife, Hungary.

Carpenter, J. A., O. H. Pattee, S. H. Fritts, B. A. Rattner, S. N. Wiemeyer, J. A. Royle, and M. R. Smith. 2003. Experimental lead poisoning in Turkey Vultures (*Cathartes aura*). Journal of Wildlife Diseases 39:96–104.

Eisler, R. 1988. Lead hazards to fish, wildlife, and invertebrates: a synoptic review. U.S. Fish and Wildlife Service Biological Report 85 (1.14). Patuxent Wildlife Research Center, Laurel, Maryland.

Fry, D. M., and J. R. Maurer. 2003. Assessment of lead contamination sources exposing California Condors. Final report to the California Department of Fish and Game, Sacramento.

HUNT, W. G., W. BURNHAM, C. N. PARISH, K. BURNHAM, B. MUTCH, AND J. L OAKS. 2006. Bullet fragments in deer remains: implications for lead exposure in scavengers. Wildlife Society Bulletin 34:168–171.

HUNT, W. G., C. N. PARISH, S. C. FARRY, T. G. LORD, AND R. SEIG. 2007. Movements of introduced California Condors in Arizona in relation to lead exposure. Pages 79–96 in California Condors in the 21st Century (A. Mee and L. S. Hall, Eds.). Series in Ornithology, no. 2.

JANSSEN, D. L., J. E. OOSTERHUIS, J. L. ALLEN, M. P. ANDERSON, D. G. KELTS, AND S. N. WEIMEYER. 1986. Lead poisoning in free-ranging California Condors. Journal of the American Veterinary Medical Association 189:1115–1117.

KOFORD, C. B. 1953. The California Condor. National Audubon Research Report 4: 1–154.

KRAMER, J. L., AND P. T. REDIG. 1997. Sixteen years of lead poisoning in eagles, 1980–95: an epizootiologic view. Journal of Raptor Research 31:327–332.

LOCKE, L. N., AND N. J. THOMAS. 1996. Lead poisoning of waterfowl and raptors. Pages 108–117 in Noninfectious Diseases of Wildlife, 2nd edition (A. Fairbrother, L. N. Locke and G. L. Huff, Eds.). Iowa State University Press, Ames, Iowa.

MACE, M. E. 2005. California Condor (*Gymnogyps californianus*) International Studbook. Zoological Society of San Diego, San Diego Wild Animal Park, Escondido, California.

MERETSKY, V. J., N. F. R. SNYDER, S. R. BEISSINGER, D. A. CLENDENEN, AND J. W. WILEY. 2000. Demography of the California Condor: implications for reestablishment. Conservation Biology 14:957–967.

MILLER, A. H., I. MCMILLAN, AND E. MCMILLAN. 1965. The current status and welfare of the California Condor. National Audubon Research Report 6:1–61.

MURASE, T., T. IKEDA, I. GOTO, O. YAMATO, K. JIN, AND Y. MAEDE. 1992. Treatment of lead poisoning in wild geese. Journal American Veterinary Medical Association 200:1726–1729.

REISER, M. H., AND S. A. TEMPLE. 1981. Effects of chronic lead ingestion on birds of prey. Pages 21–25 in Recent Advances in the Study of Raptor Diseases (J. E. Cooper and A. G. Greenwood, Eds.). Chiron Publications, Keighley, West Yorkshire, England.

SNYDER, N. F. R., AND H. A. SNYDER. 2000. The California Condor: A Saga of Natural History and Conservation. Academic Press, San Diego, CA.

VERNER, J. 1978. California Condors: status of the recovery effort. U.S. Forest Service General Technical Report PSW-28. U.S. Forest Service, Washington, D.C.

WEIMEYER, S. N., J. M. SCOTT, M. P. ANDERSON, P. H. BLOOM, AND C. J. STAFFORD. 1988. Environmental contaminants in California Condors. Journal of Wildlife Management 52:238–247.

WILBUR, S. R. 1978. The California Condor, 1966–1976: a look at its past and future. U.S. Department of the Interior, Fish and Wildlife Service, Washington, D.C.

WOODS, C. P., W. R. HEINRICH, S. C. FARRY, C. N. PARISH, S. A. H. OSBORN, AND T. J. CADE. 2007. Survival and reproduction of California Condors released in Arizona. Pages 57–78 in California Condors in the 21st Century (A. Mee and L. S. Hall, Eds.). Series in Ornithology, no. 2.

6

Arizona's Efforts to Reduce Lead Exposure in California Condors

Kathy Sullivan,[1,3] *Ron Sieg,*[1] *and Chris Parish*[2]

ABSTRACT.—Exposure to lead is one factor affecting the success of the California condor (*Gymnogyps californianus*) reintroduction program in Arizona. There have been 176 documented cases of lead exposure and 66 chelation treatments administered since 1999. Six condor deaths have been attributed by necropsy to lead poisoning. To address this, the Arizona Game and Fish Department (AGFD) and its partners are working to reduce lead exposure due to spent lead ammunition found in animal carcasses and gut piles. We have focused on public education, scientific research, and voluntary use of non-lead ammunition. In 2003, 205 Arizona hunters were interviewed by phone. Only 23% of the hunters were aware that lead poisoning was a problem faced by condors, but 83–97% were willing to take some action to help condors if credible lead exposure data were made available. Focus groups then rated condor conservation and lead reduction messages. As a result, condor lead data and conservation messages have been provided to the public since 2003. The AGFD and The Peregrine Fund are also funding research to investigate the link between lead ammunition and condor lead exposure. Preliminary results confirm lead from ammunition is a major source of lead exposure in condors. Other efforts include the formation of a voluntary lead reduction coalition consisting of sportsmen's groups and government agencies. The AGFD also funded a pilot program for the fall 2005 hunting season, providing free non-lead ammunition to deer hunters within the condor range. We hope the combination of these efforts will decrease the number of condor lead exposures in the future.

For several years, biologists have linked lead poisoning in wild California Condors (*Gymnogyps californianus*) to the ingestion of spent lead ammunition in animal carcasses (Janssen et al.1986; Weimeyer et al.1988; Snyder and Snyder 1989, 2000; Pattee et al.1990). More recently, lead from spent ammunition has been linked to lead exposure and lead

[1]*Arizona Game and Fish Department, 3500 South Lake Mary Road, Flagstaff, Arizona 86001, USA.*
[2]*The Peregrine Fund, HC 31 Box 22, Mormon Lake, Arizona 86038, USA.*
[3]*E-mail: ksullivan@azgfd.gov*

toxicity in reintroduced, captive-reared condors in both California and
Arizona (Meretsky et al. 2000, Snyder and Snyder 2000, Fry and Maurer
2003, Cade et al. 2004). In Arizona, significant efforts to verify the association between spent lead ammunition and condor lead exposure, as well
as to educate the public and engage hunters in voluntary lead reduction
efforts, began in 2003.

   The first release of California Condors in Arizona occurred on 12
December 1996. As of 30 September 2005, 84 condors have been released
in northern Arizona. Fifty-seven condors, including four wild-hatched
chicks, inhabit northern Arizona and southern Utah. Although the project
is making progress, 29 condors have died since 1996. The leading cause of
death is lead toxicity, with six confirmed cases. The first major condor lead
exposure event in Arizona occurred in June 2000, resulting in the death of
three condors (Woods et al. this volume). Since that time extensive trapping
and testing of condors for lead exposure has occurred in Arizona. Condor
blood tests have identified 176 cases of lead levels indicative of lead exposure, while in sixty-six cases, condors required chelation therapy to treat
dangerously high lead levels. Further, ingested lead pellets or bullet fragments have been recovered from 14 individual condors (Parish et al. this
volume). Without the intervention of chelation therapy and other measures,
additional condors would have succumbed to lead poisoning.

   As elsewhere in their current range, the condors are supplied with a
clean, lead-free supplemental food source of calf carcasses at the release
site in Arizona. As condors disperse from the release site, they forage on
carcasses of wild animals, such as mule deer (*Odocoileus hemionus*), elk
(*Cervus elaphus*), and coyotes (*Canis lantrans*). Since 2000, the highest
frequency of lead exposure in condors has been associated with increased
condor movements away from the release site, and the consumption of non-
proffered carcasses potentially containing lead (Hunt et al. this volume).
Moreover, the highest numbers of lead exposure events have repeatedly
occurred during the fall hunting season (Hunt et al. this volume). Although
field biologists have managed to reduce the number of condor deaths due
to lead toxicity by pursuing a rigorous monitoring and treatment protocol
(Parish et al. this volume), these efforts are highly invasive, labor intensive,
and costly. Moreover, the long-term sub-lethal effects of lead exposure in
condors are unknown (but see Snyder this volume). Thus, it is unlikely that
condors in Arizona will achieve a self-sustaining population at the current
lead exposure rates.

   While research into the prevalence and effects of lead on condors (e.g.,
Fry and Maurer 2003, Fry 2004, Church 2005) and lead reduction efforts
(see www.projectgutpile.org/) have also occurred in California, efforts in
Arizona have focused on voluntary measures to reduce the amount of lead
available to condors in the wild. This is due to a consensus among project

cooperators that voluntary measures are the best course of action to take in Arizona. Further, unlike releases in California, condors in Arizona are released under the 10(j) rule of the Endangered Species Act, which limits laws altering current land management practices (U.S. Fish and Wildlife Service [USFWS] 1996).

LEAD REDUCTION EFFORTS

Surveys and focus groups.—In May 2003, the lead mitigation subcommittee of the California Condor Recovery Team compiled a report on condor-lead issues (Redig et al. 2003). As part of the effort to reduce lead exposure in condors, USFWS contracted the Wildlife Management Institute (WMI) to determine hunter knowledge of and attitudes towards lead poisoning in condors. Responsive Management and D. J. Case and Associates (D. J. Case) were contracted by WMI to carry this out.

During the fall of 2003, Responsive Management conducted phone surveys of 205 Arizona hunters (Responsive Management 2003). Among other questions, hunters were asked if they were aware that lead poisoning was a problem faced by condors; if they were aware of any educational efforts to try to reduce lead poisoning in condors; and what actions they would be willing to take to help reduce lead exposure in condors (Responsive Management 2003). Key findings from the surveys included that only 23% of Arizona hunters were aware that lead poisoning was a problem faced by California Condors, and only 9% were aware of any educational efforts to reduce condor deaths from lead poisoning (Responsive Management 2003). However, 83–97% stated they would be somewhat to very willing to take some action to help condors (Responsive Management 2003). The actions hunters would be willing to take included: removing all carcasses from the field; burying or hiding all gut piles; removing bullets and surrounding affected flesh; and using non-lead ammunition (Responsive Management 2003). These data established a baseline to measure subsequent changes in hunter knowledge and opinions.

D. J. Case incorporated the data from these phone surveys with information from interviews of condor professionals and literature searches to develop condor conservation and lead reduction test messages. Test messages were discussed and rated on a scale of 1–5 during three focus group meetings of Arizona hunters and ranchers held in December 2003 (D. J. Case and Associates 2005). The best scoring (1.89) communication message from the focus groups was:

> Hunters and ranchers have a long history of caring for the land and conserving all kinds of wildlife. They can continue this tradition and help prevent lead poisoning in California condors by taking

one or more of the following actions in condor range: use non-lead
ammunition; retrieve all animal carcasses; hide carcasses or gut
piles to make them inaccessible to condors; and/or remove bullet
and affected flesh from animal carcasses left in the field. (D. J. Case
and Associates 2005)

Focus groups also revealed that hunters and ranchers were not convinced
that spent lead ammunition was a major cause of condor lead poisoning
(D. J. Case and Associates 2005). They requested credible data linking lead
ammunition to condor lead poisoning (D. J. Case and Associates 2005).
They also expressed a greater willingness to help condors if asked by a
credible source (D. J. Case and Associates 2005). In Arizona, hunters and
ranchers considered sportsmen's groups and the state wildlife agency to be
the most credible sources (D. J. Case and Associates 2005).

Focus group results were then utilized to develop a communication strategy. The strategy included actions such as increased education, communication and cooperation between condor project cooperators and the hunting
community, continued condor lead exposure research, and the implementation of a non-lead ammunition program (D. J. Case and Associates 2005).

Education and communication.—Data obtained from the phone surveys and focus groups were utilized to create an education and communication strategy (D. J. Case and Associates 2005) to gain support for voluntary
lead reduction efforts in Arizona's condor range. In 2003, the AGFD began
hunter education and communication efforts and have expanded these
efforts each subsequent year. Each year from 2003–2005, condor lead
exposure data, accompanied by a request for voluntary lead reduction
actions were mailed to 2,000–7,500 hunters drawn for hunts within the
condor range in northern Arizona (Fig. 1). In addition, a full page in the
Arizona hunting regulations has been devoted to the condor conservation
and lead reduction message since 2003.

The AGFD encouraged local sportsmen's groups to join a Condor
Coalition consisting of sportsmen's groups and government agencies sup-
porting voluntary efforts to reduce the amount of lead available to con-
dors. As of 31 December 2005, Condor Coalition members included the
Arizona Antelope Foundation, Arizona Deer Association, Arizona Desert
Bighorn Sheep Society, AGFD, Boone & Crockett Club, California Chapter
of the Foundation of North American Wild Sheep, California Deer Hunters
Association, California Department of Fish and Game, International
Hunter Education Association, National Shooting Sports Foundation,
North American Grouse Partnership, Sporting Arms and Ammunition
Manufacturers' Institute, USFWS, and Wildlife Management Institute.
Coalition members support voluntary lead reduction efforts within the
condor range, as well as fund condor conservation and lead reduction

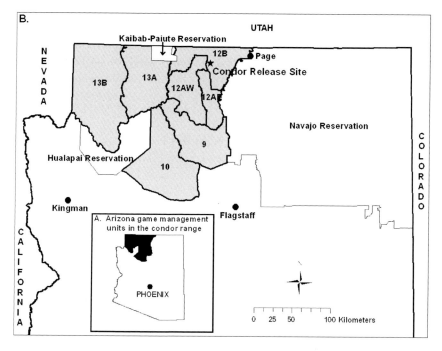

Fig. 1. Game Management Units (B) within the condor range in Arizona (A). Hunters drawn for rifle deer and big horn sheep hunts in Units 12AE, 12AW, and 12B qualified for the 2005 free non-lead ammunition program. Hunters drawn for big game rifle hunts in Units 9, 10, 13A, and 13B were mailed letters asking them to take voluntarily lead reduction actions.

educational efforts. The Coalition is currently funding an educational web page (see www.condorinfo.org/). Personnel from cooperating agencies of the Arizona condor project, including AGFD, The Peregrine Fund (TPF), National Park Service, USFWS, U.S. Forest Service, and Bureau of Land Management attended "one-voice" condor training on 5 August 2005. Project cooperators were trained to communicate a consistent and effective message regarding voluntary lead reduction efforts in the condor range. Personnel also continued to disseminate the condor lead exposure reduction message within their agencies and to the public. Representatives from Arizona sportsmen's groups also attended "one-voice" condor training on 6 August 2005 in order to disseminate accurate and consistent information to their members.

The general public has received the condor conservation and lead reduction message through educational presentations, wildlife fair displays, the Internet, and media outlets. Forty to seventy condor educational programs have been presented each year between 2003 and 2005. AGFD's web page (www.azgfd.gov/) first carried the condor lead reduction message in 2003, and has expanded and updated this site each year to incorporate ongoing research and new information on condors and lead. Media coverage has included magazine and newspaper articles in local publications, as well as a condor segment on AGFD's "Wildlife Views" television program.

    Lead research.—Arizona hunters and ranchers indicated they needed more data linking lead ammunition to condor lead poisonings to increase their support for voluntary lead reduction efforts (D. J. Case and Associates 2005). The AGFD and TPF responded by conducting and funding five research projects related to condor lead exposure and lead ammunition. Firstly, TPF condor project biologists recorded condor lead exposure and lead ammunition ingestion by condors starting in 1999 and have summarized the data through June 2005 (Parish et al. this volume). Secondly, lead toxicity mortality rates were recorded by TPF and summarized through January 2005 (Woods et al. this volume). Data from these two studies verify that lead exposure is a critical management issue in Arizona. Starting in 2004, condor lead exposure, lead ingestion, and lead toxicity data have been reported to hunters in the annual AGFD hunting regulations and reported to the public through educational programs.

    Thirdly, since 2003, AGFD has purchased 21 GPS satellite transmitters to track condor movements. Transmitters were mounted on the patagia of individual condors and TPF used data from these transmitters along with data from conventional VHF transmitters to compare condor movements between July 2001 and June 2005 in relation to lead exposure rates (Hunt et al. this volume). An association between high lead exposure rates and increased use of the Kaibab Plateau in northern Arizona during deer hunting season was confirmed (Hunt et al. this volume). Starting in 2005, data from this study have been shared with hunters and the public.

    Fourthly, TPF conducted research from 2002 to 2004 to determine the extent of lead bullet fragmentation in rifle-killed deer (Hunt et al. 2006). This study demonstrated that standard lead bullets typically fragment into hundreds of pieces before exiting a target such as a deer, and that these fragments remain in the deer carcasses as well as the gut piles. The study also confirmed that the fragmentation rate of pure copper bullets is minimal compared to that of lead bullets (Hunt et al. 2006).

    The fifth study is an ongoing lead isotope study funded by the AGFD and conducted by the University of Arizona, Tucson, using biological samples provided by TPF condor biologists. This study aims to conclusively determine the pathway for lead exposure in condors. Lead isotope ratios of condor blood and lead removed from condor digestive tracts are being compared to lead isotope ratios of lead retrieved from carcasses on which condors feed, lead ammunition, and other possible lead sources (J. Chesley et al. 2006). Preliminary results have established a direct match between lead ammunition and lead found in condor blood and digestive tracts (J. Chesley pers. comm.). As they become available, data from this study are incorporated into the communication strategy and shared with the public.

Non-lead ammunition program.—The AGFD, using money from the Heritage Fund (i.e., Arizona state lottery revenue), administered a free non-lead ammunition program for the fall 2005 hunting season. AGFD partnered with Cabela's, Sportsman's Warehouse, and Federal Ammunition to offer two free boxes of non-lead ammunition (Table 1) to 2,393 deer and bighorn sheep rifle hunters drawn for hunts in Game Management Units 12A and 12B (areas located within the core condor foraging range) (Fig. 1). Coupons to obtain the free ammunition accompanied a letter outlining condor lead poisoning issues and asking for hunters' help in reducing the amount of lead available to condors. Coupons were mailed at the beginning of August 2005. The 2005 rifle-hunting season began in late October and continued through December. Coupons were redeemable through 15 November 2005. Sixty-five percent ($n = 1,551$) of eligible hunters participated in the program by redeeming their coupon for non-lead ammunition.

To evaluate the success of this program, AGFD worked with D. J. Case to develop two post-hunt surveys, one for non-lead ammunition program participants and one for non-participants. Surveys were mailed in November to all 2,393 eligible hunters. A total of 1,105 surveys (46%), including 943 participant (61%) and 162 non-participant (19%) surveys

Table 1. Non-lead ammunition offered during Arizona Game and Fish Department's 2005 free non-lead ammunition program. Sixty-five percent (1,551) of the 2,393 eligible hunters drawn for big game rifle hunts within the primary condor range of Arizona redeemed a coupon to receive two free boxes of their choice of this rifle ammunition. One thousand six hundred fifty-eight coupons were redeemed (107 participants redeemed 2 coupons). The ammunition brand was Federal Premium Vital Shok, loaded with Barnes 100% copper Triple Shock X-bullets.

Caliber	Bullet grain weight	Number of coupons redeemed
.25-06 Remington	100	44
.270 Winchester	130	343
.270 Winchester Short Magnum	130	21
7MM Winchester Short Magnum	160	14
7MM Remington Magnum	160	291
.308 Winchester	150	130
.30-06 Springfield	180	534
.300 Winchester Short Magnum	180	47
.300 Winchester Magnum	180	182
.338 Winchester Magnum	225	52

were completed and returned by 15 December 2005. D.J. Case will submit a final report to AGFD in the spring of 2006.

Preliminary findings suggest the main reasons why hunters participated in the non-lead ammunition program were: they were asked to participate by AGFD (95%); they wanted to help condors (92%); and the ammunition was free (87%). Survey results indicate that 81% of all participants used the free non-lead ammunition during their hunts. Ninety-three percent of the respondents who harvested a deer ($n = 380$) said the non-lead ammunition performed the same as, or better than, lead ammunition. In addition, 97% of the respondents who tested the non-lead ammunition ($n = 796$) stated its accuracy was average to excellent. Eighty-nine percent of the respondents said they would use non-lead ammunition again if it was provided for free, and 56% indicated that they would purchase it on their own in the future. Lastly, 72% of the respondents said they would recommend non-lead ammunition to other hunters.

Non-participant survey results indicated several reasons why hunters did not participate in the free non-lead ammunition program. Twenty-five percent of respondents listed their main reason as the program failing to offer their desired caliber of non-lead ammunition, and 15% indicated that the program was too complicated or a hassle. Forty-three percent stated their reason for non-participation as "other." "Other" reasons included: coupon was lost ($n = 18$); forgot to participate ($n = 9$); already using non-lead ammunition ($n = 6$); did not hunt ($n = 3$); and do not support this program ($n = 3$). Non-participants suggested that offering more calibers of non-lead ammunition (64%) and providing more information on condor lead poisoning (38%) would have encouraged more hunters to participate in the free non-lead ammunition program.

Concurrent with our lead reduction efforts, TPF continued to track condor movements and foraging locations, as well as to collect lead exposure, treatment, and poisoning data in 2005 through periodic sampling of trapped birds consistent with approximate timing and methods used in previous years. The observed results from 2005 indicated a 40% reduction in samples indicating exposure from the previous year (Parish unpubl. data). Preliminary data also revealed a 29% decrease in the proportion of birds exposed from 2004 to 2005 (Parish unpubl. data). This appears to represent the first annual decrease in the proportion of tested condors with levels indicating exposure to lead since 2002, when birds first started using the Kaibab Plateau during the fall hunting season (Parish et al. this volume). Although these changes in indicated exposure may in part relate to differences in condor movement patterns between 2004 and 2005 (Hunt et. al. this volume), the reasonable assumption is that fewer lead-laden carcasses on the Kaibab Plateau in 2005 played a significant role in the decrease of condor lead exposures.

DISCUSSION

Although studies have identified lead from spent ammunition as a source of lead poisoning in condors (see Janssen et al.1986; Weimeyer et al. 1988; Snyder and Snyder 1989, 2000; Pattee et al.1990; Fry and Maurer 2003; Cade et al. 2004), phone surveys and focus groups revealed that the majority of hunters in Arizona were either unaware that lead was a problem for condors, or were not convinced that the use of lead ammunition contributed to lead toxicity in condors (Responsive Management 2003, D. J. Case and Associates 2005). Since hunter cooperation is crucial to reducing the amount of lead available to condors, we are providing hunters with the requested evidence linking condor lead poisoning to spent lead ammunition. In addition, efforts are being made to communicate the lead reduction message in the most effective manner by focusing on the proud tradition of hunter wildlife conservation. We believe this combined approach has resulted in a greater awareness of condor-lead issues among hunters in Arizona. It has also resulted in increased support from sportsmen's groups. We acknowledge that changing human behavior can be a cumbersome process, but we believe that by continuing to expand our efforts, we could see a significant effect of such changes on condor lead exposure rates, thus providing the opportunity for a self-sustaining condor population in Arizona. The apparent sizable reduction in condor lead exposures experienced in 2005 is hopefully the first step towards this goal.

It is important to note that while the current free non-lead ammunition program is focusing on reducing the use of lead bullets in condor range, reducing the use of lead shot in condor range is also important. In Arizona, lead shot has been removed from the digestive tract of condors as frequently as lead bullet fragments (Parish et al. this volume). Condor ingestion of lead bullet fragments has been associated with the fall hunting season (Hunt et al. this volume), while condor ingestion of lead shot has been less predictable, and is not associated with a well-defined hunting season. Therefore, a free non-lead shot program would be logistically complex and probably much less effective than a free non-lead bullet program. Future lead reduction efforts will include increased attempts to reduce the use of lead shot within the condor range. We do acknowledge, however, that these efforts may be less productive than lead bullet reduction efforts. We still remain hopeful that the voluntary use of non-lead shot will increase due to our communication efforts.

A significant factor in the success of voluntary lead reduction efforts is the availability and affordability of non-lead ammunition. Although non-lead shotgun pellets are commonly available, only a few bullet manufacturers offer non-lead rifle ammunition alternatives (Table 2), with a selection that is far less complete than that of lead ammunition. And although the

Table 2. A sample of ammunition manufacturers that offered non-lead ammunition in 2005. Non-lead rifle ammunition is loaded with 100% copper Barnes X, Barnes XLC, Barnes Triple Shock X, and Barnes Solid bullets. Non-lead shot is composed of steel, tungsten, and bismuth. For a more complete list, including available calibers and shot sizes, go to the California condor web page at www.azgfd.gov/condor.

Non-lead rifle ammunition manufacturers	Non-lead shot-gun ammunition manufacturers
Black Hills Gold	Bismuth Cartridge
Conley Precision Cartridge	Federal Premium Ultra Shok
Federal Premium Vital Shok	Hevi-shot
PMC Gold Line	Kent Cartridge
PMP Super Rifle Ammunition	Remington Premier
Safari Arms Ammunition	Sellier and Bellot
Superior Ammunition	Winchester
Weatherby Premium	Wolf Ammunition

recent increase in availability of non-lead ammunition gives cause for optimism, we encourage ammunition manufacturers to further expand the production of non-lead alternatives. We also request that ammunition retailers offer more non-lead ammunition for their customers. Our free non-lead ammunition program will not continue indefinitely, so it is crucial that sportsmen in the condors' range are able to procure a wide variety of non-lead ammunition at reasonable prices.

Future work to reduce condor lead exposure will include expanding education and communication efforts by increasing the number of educational presentations, while specifically targeting hunters and sportsmen. Future education and communication efforts will attempt to include the state of Utah, the Navajo Nation, the Kaibab-Paiute Reservation, as well as other American Indian Reservations within the condor range. We also plan to incorporate strategic use of the media. Attempts will be made to place the condor conservation and voluntary lead reduction message in popular literature as well as in sportsmen and hunter publications. Messages will focus on the conservation history of hunters and commend those hunters and sportsmen's groups who support lead reduction efforts within the condor range. The success of these efforts will therefore be dependent upon the cooperation of media organizations.

Future efforts to expand the Condor Coalition will focus on recruiting influential local and national sportsmen's groups. Since hunters consider sportsmen's groups the most credible source for information, the use of Coalition members' names in hunter correspondence will be a valuable communication tool. Coalition members will also be asked to contribute to educational efforts and possibly assist in funding the voluntary lead reduction program. Relevant lead research will also continue. Results from the University of Arizona's lead isotope study will be published and shared with the public, as will results from the free non-lead ammunition program. Future lead research will be considered and could include lead isotope studies of feathers to determine lead exposure levels and sources (Fry 2004).

It is essential to assess whether voluntary lead reduction efforts in Arizona are effective in reducing the amount of lead available to condors. To accomplish this, we will combine sustained condor lead exposure monitoring with hunter surveys. TPF will continue condor lead exposure testing to determine if lead exposure rates decrease. Contingent upon AGFD securing funding, a follow-up survey is proposed for 2007 (D. J. Case and Associates 2005) to determine if education and communication efforts have resulted in an increased awareness of condor issues and a decreased use of lead ammunition in the condor range.

Voluntary efforts to reduce lead in the condor range have been criticized as likely to be ineffectual in reducing the threat of lead to condors and hence the long-term success of condor populations. However, our results to date suggest that the voluntary program of non-lead ammunition use by hunters within the condor range of Arizona has the potential of being highly effective. We believe our efforts demonstrate the merits of communicating and collaborating with sportsmen on this issue. Since the opinions of surveyed hunters on the efficacy of non-lead ammunition have been consistent with widespread reports of its excellent ballistic qualities, we expect the use of non-lead ammunition to increase as it becomes more available and affordable, and hence benefit condor recovery efforts.

ACKNOWLEDGMENTS

We would like to thank all of the dedicated Peregrine Fund condor project field biologists for their invaluable work, as well as Bill Heinrich and Bill Burnham of TPF. We would also like to thank all the AGFD personnel who helped make this project possible, including Bruce Taubert, Andi Rogers, and Duane Shroufe. Susi MacVean of AGFD, as well as Grainger Hunt and Tom Cade of The Peregrine Fund offered valuable comments on drafts of this manuscript. Thanks to Allan Mee and Linnea Hall for editing this manuscript and providing their professional suggestions. A special thanks goes to Dr. Kathy Orr of the Phoenix Zoo, Dr. Roundtree of the Page Animal Hospital, and Christie Van Cleve for their assistance in treating lead-exposed condors. Funding was provided by the Heritage Fund of Arizona and private donations to The Peregrine Fund. We would also like to thank condor recovery program cooperators: U.S. Fish and Wildlife Service, Bureau of Land Management, National Park Service, U.S. Forest Service, and Utah Division of Wildlife Resources.

LITERATURE CITED

CADE, T. J., S. A. H. OSBORN, W. G. HUNT, AND C. P. WOODS. 2004. Commentary on released California Condors *Gymnogyps californianus* in Arizona. Pages 11–25 *in* Raptors Worldwide: Proceedings of VI World Conference on Birds of Prey and Owls (R. D. Chancellor and B.-U. Meyburg, Eds.). World Working Group on Birds of Prey and Owls/MME-Birdlife, Hungary.

CHESLEY, J., P. N. REINTHAL, T. CORLEY, C. PARISH, AND J. RUIZ. 2006. Radioisotopic analyzes of potential sources of lead contamination in California Condors. Invited Symposium on Applications of Stable and Radiogenic Isotopes in Wildlife and Fisheries. Joint Annual Meeting of the Arizona/New Mexico chapters of the Wildlife Society and the American Fisheries Society, February 2–4, 2006.

CHURCH, M. 2005. Sources of lead exposure in California Condors. M.S. thesis, University of California, Santa Cruz, CA.

D. J. CASE, AND ASSOCIATES. 2005. Communicating with hunters and ranchers to reduce lead available to California condors. Unpublished report, Wildlife Management Institute, Washington D.C. and U.S. Fish and Wildlife Service, Sacramento, California.

FRY, D. M. 2004. Analysis of lead in California condor feathers: Determination of exposure and depuration during feather growth. Unpublished report, California Department of Fish and Game.

FRY, D. M., AND J. R. MAURER. 2003. Assessment of lead contamination sources exposing California condors. Final report to the California Department of Fish and Game, Sacramento.

HUNT, W. G., W. BURNHAM, C. N. PARISH, K. BURNHAM, B. MUTCH, AND J. L. OAKS. 2006. Bullet fragments in deer remains: implications for lead exposure in avian species. Wildlife Society Bulletin 34:168–171.

HUNT, W. G., C. N. PARISH, S. G. FARRY, T. G. LORD, AND R. SIEG. 2007. Movements of introduced California condors in Arizona in relation to lead exposure. Pages 79–96 *in* California Condors in the 21st Century (A. Mee and L. S. Hall, Eds.). Series in Ornithology, no. 2.

JANSSEN, D. L., J. E. OOSTERHUIS, J. L. ALLEN, M. P. ANDERSON, D. G. KELTS, AND S. N. WIEMEYER. 1986. Lead poisoning in free ranging California condors. Journal of the American Veterinary Medical Association 189:1115–1117.

MERETSKY, V. J., N. F. R. SNYDER, S. R. BEISSINGER, D. A. CLENDENEN, AND J. W. WILEY. 2000. Demography of the California Condor: implications for reestablishment. Conservation Biology 14:957–967.

PARISH, C. N., W. R. HEINRICH, AND W. G. HUNT. 2007. Lead exposure, diagnosis, and treatment in California Condors released in Arizona. Pages 97–108 *in* California Condors in the 21st Century (A. Mee and L. S. Hall, Eds.). Series in Ornithology, no. 2.

PATTEE, O. H., P. H. BLOOM, J. M. SCOTT, AND M. R. SMITH. 1990. Lead hazards within the range of the California Condor. Condor 92:931–937.

REDIG, P., N. ARTZ, R. BYRNE, B. HEINRICH, F. GILL, J. GRANTHAM, R. JUREK, S. LAMSON, B. PALMER, R. PATTERSON, W. SANBORN, S, SEYMOUR, R. SIEG, AND M. WALLACE. 2003. A report from the California condor lead exposure reduction steering

Plate 1. The first condor documented dying of lead poisoning was recovered through radio-telemetry in the Sierra Nevada foothills in March 1984. John Schmitt examines the body of the bird under an apparent roost perch in a tall pine from which the bird had evidently fallen.

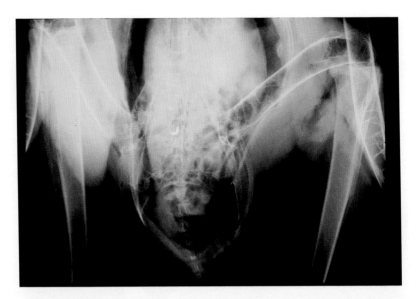

Plate 2. An X-ray of the lead-poisoned bird of 1984 revealed a small bullet fragment in its digestive system. A liver sample contained 35 parts per million lead, wet weight, a concentration high in the toxic range.

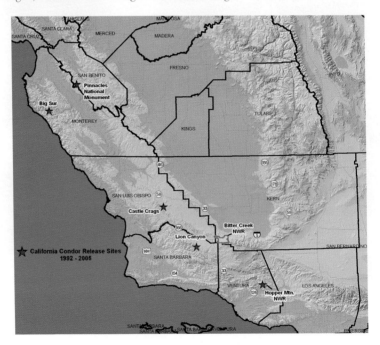

Plate 3. California Condor release sites in California.

Plate 4. California Condors perched on communication towers in Los Angeles County, July 2005 (U.S. Fish and Wildlife Service).

Plate 5. California Condors at trap site at Hopper Mountain National Wildlife Refuge, Ventura Co., California (U.S. Fish and Wildlife Service).

Plate 6. Release of founder male AC2 at Bittercreek National Wildlife Refuge in June 2005 after 19 years in captivity (U.S. Fish and Wildlife Service). AC2 was trapped at this same location and removed from the remnant wild population in 1986 to join the captive breeding program at the San Diego Wild Animal Park.

Plate 7. Condor release pen at the Vermilion Cliffs release site, Arizona. Northeastern foothills of the Kaibab Plateau are visible in the background. (Photo by C. Parish, The Peregrine Fund.)

Plate 8. The Grand Canyon of the Colorado River as viewed from the South Rim. (Photo by C. Parish.)

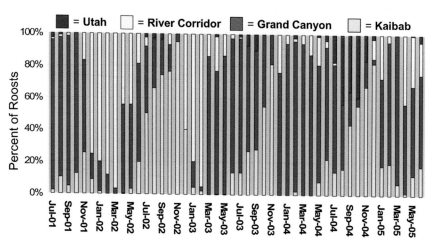

Plate 9. Monthly roost allocation by free-ranging condors (excluding breeders and wild-produced young) among four zones outside the Paria (release site) Zone from July 2001 through June 2005 ($n = 34,018$ relocations). The number of free-ranging condors represented in the graph increased each year, as follows: 23 individuals in 2001, 29 in 2002, 37 in 2003, 37 in 2004, and 42 in 2005.

Plate 10. Condor SB #149, an adult breeding female that successfully nested on Vermilion Cliffs in northern Arizona in 2004. (Photo by C. Parish.)

Plate 11. Adult male condor SB #123 with wild hatched offspring in the Grand Canyon, 2004. (Photo by C. Parish.)

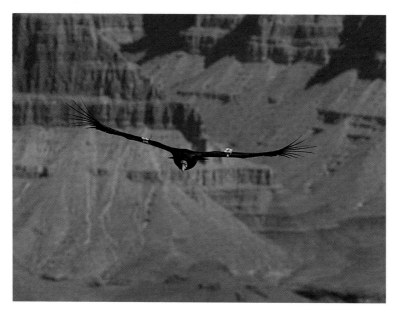

Plate 12. Condor SB #122, an adult breeding male in the Grand Canyon. (Photo by C. Parish.)

Plate 13. California Condors captured in a walk-in trap at Hopper Mountain National Wildlife Refuge (U.S. Fish and Wildlife Service).

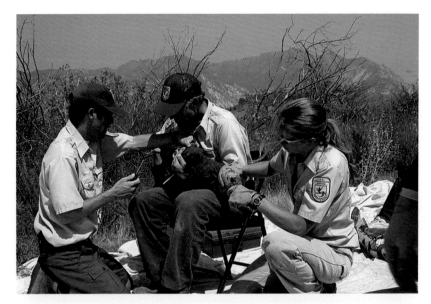

Plate 14. Transmitter replacement and blood-sampling of California Condor female SB #156 at Hopper Mountain National Wildlife Refuge. Refuge staff pictured (lt. to rt) are M. Barth, M. Hall, and G. Druliner (U.S. Fish and Wildlife Service).

Plate 15. Nesting habitat of California Condors in southern California. This cliff was the location of the first successful hatching of a wild-laid condor egg in 2002. (Photo by A. Mee.)

Plate 16. Four-month old condor nestling (SB #370) prior to removal from a nest in the Sespe Wilderness in August 2005. This nestling was found to have a large quantity of trash in its crop and gut and was subsequently transported to the Los Angeles Zoo for surgery. (Photo by A. Mee.)

Plate 17. Trash items removed from condor nestling (SB #370) by surgery at the Los Angeles Zoo in August 2005. This nestling held 168 items weighing 204.5 g in its crop and gut including plastic ($n = 82$), glass ($n = 54$) and metallic ($n = 30$) objects such as washers, bottle-tops, and bullet shells. (Photo by A. Mee.)

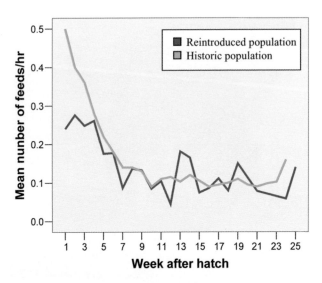

Plate 18. California Condor chick feeding rates at reintroduced ($n = 7$) and historical ($n = 5$) condor nests in southern California (2002–2005).

Plate 19. Condor nestling mortality at the SC2 nest in 2002. Male parent (SB# 107) attempted to defend the nestling despite it being dead for at least 1–3 days. This nestling was 149 days old when recovered on 22 October 2002. (Photo by A. Mee.)

Plate 20. California Condors at an established provisioning site at Hopper Mountain National Wildlife Refuge, Ventura County, in 2005. This location was also used as a trap site for transmitter replacement and blood-lead monitoring. (Photo by A. Mee.)

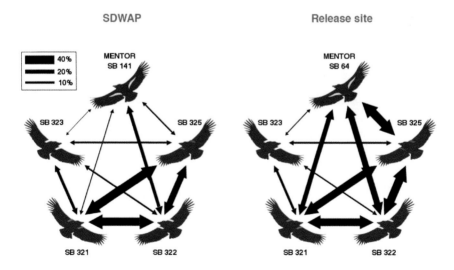

Plate 21. Sociogram of proximity of pre-release California Condors. Lines represent relative proportion of time each dyad spent in proximity (<4.6 m). Scale indicated in upper left.

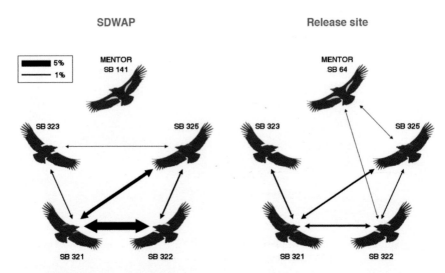

Plate 22. Sociogram of affiliative interactions of pre-release California Condors. Lines represent relative proportion of intervals in which each dyad engaged in any affiliative interaction. Scale indicated in upper left.

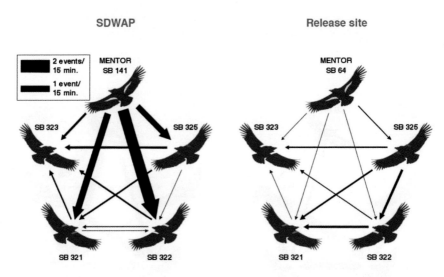

Plate 23. Sociogram of dominance interactions of pre-release California Condors. Lines represent relative rates (per 15 min) of dominance-related interactions for each dyad. The rate of interactions in which a bird was dominant is indicated by an arrow pointing away from that bird; the rate of interactions in which a bird was subordinate is indicated by an arrow pointing toward that bird. Scale indicated in upper left.

Plate 24. Five-month-old condor chick temporarily hooded during handing to reduce stress at the Los Angeles Zoo. (Photo courtesy of Los Angeles Zoo.)

Plate 25. Release of condor SB #261 at the Sierra San Pedro Mártir release site, Baja California, Mexico, in October 2002. In the background is the blind with one-way glass windows allowing concealed, close-up observation. The smaller enclosure used for isolating birds before release is visible on the left.

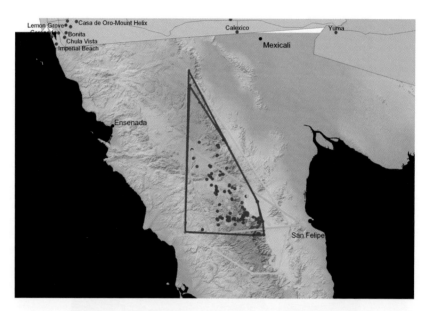

Plate 26. Movements of four condors tracked by GPS satellite telemetry in Baja California, Mexico, in June 2005. Polygons depict the maximum range of individual birds. The large black dot shows the location of the release site.

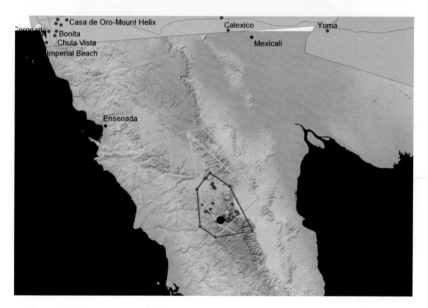

Plate 27. Movements of three condors tracked by GPS satellite telemetry in Baja California, Mexico, in August 2005. Polygons depict the maximum range of individual birds. The large black dot shows the location of the release site.

Plate 28. Adult male California Condor (SB #107) at a roost site in the Sespe Condor Sanctuary, Ventura Co., California. This 10-year-old male was one of the first condors to breed in the wild in 2001 and successfully reared the only condor juvenile to fledge in the wild in California to date. (Photo by A. Mee.)

Plate 29. Immature California Condor in flight over Hopper Mountain National Wildlife Refuge, Ventura Co., California. In recent years individuals in the southern California release population have exhibited much reduced foraging ranges compared to condors in the historical population. (Photo by A. Mee.)

Plate 30. Oil spillage into a tributary of Hopper Creek, Ventura Co., California in 2002. Hopper Creek is the principal drainage forming the eastern boundary of the Sespe Condor Sanctuary and Hopper Mountain National Wildlife Refuge. A recently released immature condor was trapped for behavioral reasons within 0.5 km of this spillage. (Photo by A. Mee.)

committee. Unpublished report to the US Fish and Wildlife Service, California Condor Recovery Team.

RESPONSIVE MANAGEMENT. 2003. Hunters' knowledge of and attitudes towards threats to California Condors. Unpublished report, D.J. Case and Associates, Mishawaka, Indiana.

SNYDER, N. F. R., AND H. F. SNYDER. 1989. Biology and conservation of the California Condor. Current Ornithology 6:175–267.

SNYDER, N. F. R., AND H. A. SNYDER. 2000. The California Condor: A Saga of Natural History and Conservation. Academic Press, San Diego, CA.

U.S. FISH AND WILDLIFE SERVICE. 1996. Final rule. Endangered and threatened wildlife and plants: establishment of a nonessential experimental population of California condors in northern Arizona. Federal Register 61:54044–54060.

WIEMEYER, S. N., J. M. SCOTT, M. P. ANDERSON, P. H. BLOOM, AND C. J. STAFFORD. 1988. Environmental contaminants in California Condors. Journal of Wildlife Management 52:238–247.

WOODS, C. P., W. R. HEINRICH, S. C. FARRY, C. N. PARISH, S. A. H. OSBORN, AND T. J. CADE. 2007. Survival and reproduction of California Condors released in Arizona. Pages 57–78 *in* California Condors in the 21st Century (A. Mee and L. S. Hall, Eds.). Series in Ornithology, no. 2.

7

Reintroduction of California Condors into Their Historic Range: The Recovery Program in California

Jesse Grantham

ABSTRACT.—The California Condor (*Gymnogyps californianus*) has been under an intensive recovery effort for the past 25 years. Successful captive breeding has produced 350 individuals from 27 birds. The wild population stands at 113 condors distributed between three geographically isolated sites: Arizona, California and Baja California, Mexico. Releases began in California in 1992. To date 121 condors have been released at five different sites in California; of these 41 (35%) have died and 17 (14%) birds have been returned to captivity. Over time, mortality in the wild California flock has declined at least partly as a result of birds feeding on contaminant-free carcasses at provisioned sites, and mimicking established patterns of behavior exhibited by older birds. However, observed behavioral problems may be exacerbated by constant feeding at a single site. Causes of death in free-flying condors in California have been lead poisoning, power line collisions, starvation, gunshot wounds, cancer, and drowning. First breeding occurred in the wild in California in 2001, with 13 eggs laid up through 2005. Only one chick has successfully fledged. Nest failure has occurred at the egg stage (*n* = 4), and at the nestling stage (*n* = 8) between three and six months of age. Causes of chick mortality have included direct and indirect effects resulting from trash ingestion. Three wild condors taken into captivity in the 1980s were released after 12–19 years in the captive breeding program. Upon release all three returned to their original ranges and resumed their historical movements. Shooting, ingestion of microtrash, contaminants in food, poor nest success and breeding effort, nutritional issues resulting from single sources of food, and innate tameness are management issues that need to be addressed for this population. Although successful captive breeding efforts continue to provide birds for release to supplement the wild population, the re-establishment of a viable, self-sustaining population in California is most likely a long way into the future.

U.S. Fish and Wildlife Service, 2493 Portola Road, Suite A, Ventura, California 93003, USA. E-mail: jesse_grantham@fws.gov

The last California Condor (*Gymnogyps californianus*) was removed from the wild on 19 April 1987. Few bird species have reached this level of endangerment in the U.S. and the removal of all individuals of the remaining population from the wild, with the probability that none of the original wild birds would ever be released back into the wild, was a last-ditch measure to prevent imminent extinction (see Snyder and Snyder 2000). Little was known about the likelihood of success of captive breeding and reintroduction efforts where the original population was removed from the wild. It was an unprecedented move in endangered species recovery and created significant controversy (see Snyder and Snyder 2000) but as we now see quite clearly it was the only viable approach to halt the population decline, quickly increase numbers and preserve genetic variability.

In 1987 the total captive population stood at 27 individuals: 13 males and 14 females. Although eggs removed from the wild between 1983 and 1986 had been previously hatched artificially in captivity (Kuehler and Witman 1988), the first captive laid egg from wild trapped birds was produced in 1988 by a male captured from the wild on 25 June 1985 and a female captured on 7 August 1985 (Kuehler et al. 1991). This was a pair, newly formed in the wild in 1984, that had not previously bred and was the only intact pair taken into captivity from the wild. All subsequent pairs formed in captivity were derived from the surviving members of wild pairs where one mate was deceased, or were eggs, nestlings or immature birds taken from the wild between 1982 and 1986. Eventually all birds removed from the wild became breeders in captivity (Mace 2004).

Of the 27 individuals that were in the captive population in 1987, 14 were considered founders. Founders are individuals from the wild population from which all others in the captive and reintroduced population are descended (see Ralls and Ballou 2004). Six of these founders did not survive in the wild to become part of the captive breeding program but produced offspring in the wild that subsequently became members of the captive breeding program. Condors within the captive breeding population are managed with the aim of preserving genetic diversity by using pedigree analysis to calculate important genetic parameters including heterozygosity and mean kinship (Ralls and Ballou 2004). Of particular importance in the recovery and genetic management of small remnant populations often containing closely related individuals is the avoidance of the potential deleterious effects of inbreeding (see Keller and Waller 2002). One such effect identified in condors is expression of the lethal recessive chondrodystrophy allele (Ralls et al. 2000), which results in embryo or early chick death. Wild adults of breeding age first produced eggs in captivity from 24 to 113 months after removal from the wild (Fig.1). Gender did not appear to influence the time in captivity before first breeding. One female laid her first egg two years after capture, another female did not produce her

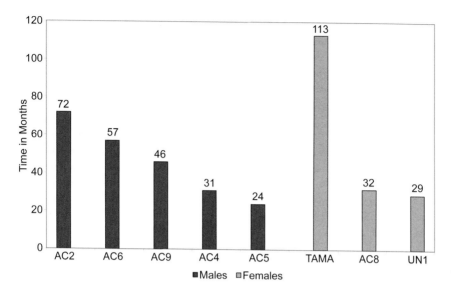

Fig. 1. Time spent in captivity before breeding by California Condors removed from the wild as adults.

first egg until 9.4 years after capture. One male failed to breed until six years after capture (Mace 2004). Failure to breed earlier by some adults in captivity appeared to be related to incompatibility between mates in some forced pairs. In most cases, this was addressed by repairing with a different adult (M. Mace pers. comm.).

REINTRODUCTION TO THE WILD

Releases.—In 1986 the California Condor Recovery Team (CCRT) established criteria for the potential release of any captive bred condors back into the wild. These included having a minimum of three actively breeding pairs in captivity, three chicks behaviorally suitable for release, and retaining at least five offspring from each breeding pair contributing to the release (Kiff et al.1996). Between 1988 and 1992, 18 condors were produced in captivity by the captive breeding programs at the Los Angeles Zoo and the San Diego Wild Animal Park. In 1992 there were 46 condors in the world population (Mace 2004). By 1991 several chicks met the CCRT criteria, and two were scheduled for release in early 1992. In preparation for logistical issues anticipated in the eventual release of California Condors, 13 female Andean Condors (*Vultur gryphus*) were released to the wild during 1988 and 1989 into the proposed condor release area in southern California (U.S. Fish and Wildlife Service and California Department of Fish and Game 1988). These birds served the purpose of maintaining and refining release site protocols, telemetry issues, and staff training in anticipation of planned releases of California Condors (Kiff et al. 1996).

The first releases of California Condors back into their historical range occurred on 14 January 1992, almost five years after the last condor had been removed from the wild. The first condors released were first generation offspring produced by founder individuals or offspring of founders removed from the wild as eggs or nestlings. Prior to release of California Condors all previously released Andean Condors were removed from the wild. Two new, inexperienced, immature female Andeans Condors unfamiliar with the range were then released with two juvenile California Condors aged 7.5 and 9.5 months (Mace 2004).

Between 1992 and 2005, 121 captive-reared California Condors were released into their historic range in California at five different release sites (Plate 3). These sites were the U.S. Forest Service's Sespe Condor Sanctuary and the U.S. Fish and Wildlife Service's (USFWS) Hopper Mountain National Wildlife Refuge (N.W.R.) in Ventura County; Lion Canyon on the Sierra Madre Ridge in Santa Barbara County; Castle Crags in San Luis Obispo County; the Big Sur area in Monterey County; and Pinnacles National Monument in San Benito County. In subsequent discussion of release sites Lion Canyon and Castle Crags were combined together as one site because of their close proximity to one another and an almost immediate interaction of released birds between the two sites. Use of these two release sites was discontinued in 2000.

Release sites were chosen based on criteria including historic use by condors, distance from human habitation, presence or absence of power lines, proximity of potential suitable nest sites, available tree roost sites, suitable flying conditions, land ownership issues, willing cooperators, and accessibility to biologists (USFWS unpubl. data). Success has varied widely among release sites. The Lion Canyon–Castle Crags locations have had the lowest success to date. Out of 39 birds released at these sites between 1995 and 2000, only 8 (21%) are still alive in the wild population. Of the three longest existing release sites in California (the discontinued Lion-Castle Crags sites, Hopper Mountain N.W.R., and Big Sur), the Big Sur release area has had the greatest success with 65% of the condors released at that location still flying free today.

As birds have become older and more experienced in the wild overall survival has apparently increased, with only seven mortalities in California since the fall–winter of 2003. However, increased survival has been attributed to older condors becoming more sedentary and keying in on permanent feeding sites while largely abandoning natural foraging behaviors (see Meretsky and Snyder 1992), rather than a reduction in the mortality factors which had brought the species close to extinction. Further, apart from the release of one male (studbook [SB] #6) from the historic wild population in

June 2005, no birds have been released in southern California since 2003. Higher mortality in the first few months after release has characterized releases in northern Arizona (Woods et al. this volume).

Generally condors move as a group with the members of the cohort in which they were released, or with condors previously released in the same area. Condors released at sites where there were existing older birds already present tended to adjust better to life in the wild than birds released in areas where there were no birds present (USFWS unpubl. data).

FIELD MANAGEMENT

Telemetry.—Radio-telemetry and tracking of nine condors in the remnant historical population in the 1980s revealed important information on movements (Meretsky and Snyder 1992) as well as being a critical management tool in recovering dead condors to determine causes of mortality (see Janssen et al. 1986, Wiemeyer et al. 1988). Today, all condors in reintroduced populations are fitted with patagial and/or tail mounted VHF transmitters, satellite transmitters and most recently, GPS satellite transmitters (PTTs) to facilitate location and determine range use and movements. Vehicles are equipped with omni-directional antennas that can detect the presence or absence of birds in an area, while field staff attempt to pinpoint locations using standard telemetry protocol (see Kenward 2000). Although condor recovery cooperators managing release populations (USFWS, Ventana Wilderness Society and the National Park Service in California, the Peregrine Fund in Arizona, and the Zoological Society of San Diego in Baja California) maintain and analyze telemetry location data independently, field staff communicate directly with each other when individual condors make significant movements between release sites or remain undetected for two or more days.

From 1992 through 2001 condors were monitored by field crews using both mobile and stationary tracking and conventional VHF telemetry only. As some birds in the population have become more sedentary in their movements mobile tracking has been relegated to responding to instances of birds perching on structures where flushing or hazing is required. Unless birds are fitted with satellite or GPS telemetry units and locations determined this way, little is currently known of a bird's exact whereabouts when it leaves an area where tracking personnel are located.

Provisioning.—Condors are provisioned with previously frozen stillborn dairy calves at all sites in California. The primary purpose of provisioning is to maintain condors on a dependable, easily accessible food source free from lead contamination (see Hall et al. this volume). These calves are retrieved from intensively operated feed-lot dairies located throughout the release areas. Heavy metal analysis of livers taken from dairy calves in 2002 revealed that a majority of animals had elevated copper and zinc levels (M. Fry unpubl. data). Newborn calves and fetuses often have higher liver copper concentrations than adults (Fry and Maurer 2003). The use of sewage sludge containing heavy metal residues as fertilizer for forage crops such as silage corn and bahia grass has become commonplace over the last decade and dairies are dependent on these crops as a food source. Fry and Maurer (2003) recommended the continual testing of dairy calves for heavy metals and, until the significance of elevated copper levels are known, the removal of calf livers before provisioning as food for condors. Whether there are any sub-clinical cumulative effects of heavy metal ingestion on adult or nestling condors needs further study.

In California, condors are fed at sites protected by an electric fence to thwart predators, such as black bears (*Ursus americanus*), coyotes (*Canis latrans*), mountain lions (*Felis concolor*), and bobcats (*Felis rufus*). Carcasses rarely last longer than one night at unprotected sites without losses to scavengers (USFWS unpubl. data). For this reason birds are fed repeatedly at the same one or two sites throughout the year. Evidence is beginning to emerge at Hopper Mountain N.W.R. that birds fed exclusively at the same site over a long period of time may lose their initiative to seek food elsewhere (USFWS unpubl. data.). Generally condors at Hopper Mountain N.W.R. now wait for the arrival of new carcasses rather than forage on their own for wild food. While this diminishes the probability of condors coming into contact with contaminated carcasses it has been shown to have a detrimental effect on the frequency at which some chicks are fed at some nests because of increased local competition, non-independent foraging by breeding pairs, and most particularly when management activities affect food availability (Mee et al this volume). At Hopper Mountain N.W.R. condors are generally fed on a three-day rotational schedule utilizing three calf carcasses for approximately 20–25 birds. Although condors are not trapped repeatedly for weighing, they are usually weighed once or twice a year at trappings for transmitter replacement. As of 2004 most bird weights were within the normal range of 40–46 kg (18–21 lbs) for free-flying condors, indicating that condors are obtaining sufficient food for the maintenance of body mass (USFWS unpubl. data). However as mentioned earlier, this feeding schedule may interfere with feeding rates for nestlings, and may be a contributing factor in chick health and/or mortality (Mee et al. this volume). In fact, the provisioning of food and how food is delivered may be a critical issue influencing all other behaviors.

LIMITING FACTORS IN THE REINTRODUCED POPULATION

Mortality.—The earliest releases in the program had the highest mortality but that high mortality has gradually diminished over time. Of the

121 captive-reared birds that have been released in California to date (2005), 43 (35%) have died or disappeared (Fig. 2). Of the 15 birds that disappeared with no trace, 12 (85%) vanished during the fall and winter months. The deaths of three condors that died of lead poisoning in the 1980s and that were recovered in January, March and April suggested that their initial exposure may have occurred during the traditional fall and winter hunting seasons (Bloom et al 1989, Pattee et al. 1990).

Lead poisoning was the leading cause of mortality of condors recovered in the 1980s (Janssen et al. 1986, Wiemeyer et al. 1988). Of the four birds that were recovered three were identified as having died of lead toxicosis. Two birds had small lead fragments in their digestive tracts (see Plate 2); the third bird had elevated lead levels (Janssen et al. 1986). Since 1992 one bird has been confirmed to have died of lead poisoning in California, while two other deaths are strongly suspected to have been lead related due to elevated lead levels in bone and feather samples (Church 2005). The latter two individuals were recovered some time after death so blood-lead levels were unavailable. This is likely to be a minimum estimate of mortality due to lead poisoning as a number of birds that disappeared during hunting seasons were never recovered and may have succumbed to lead. In addition, 12 birds have been recovered but actual cause of death has not been determined due to the condition of the specimen (Risebrough 2004). Lead isotope analyses of bone and feather may as yet identify lead as the ultimate cause of mortality of some of these birds (R. Risebrough pers. comm.).

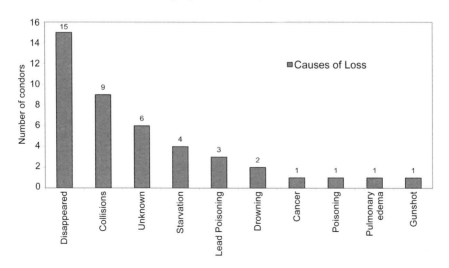

Fig. 2. Fate of 43 California Condors lost during releases in California between 1992 and 2005.

Behavior of released condors.—As of 1 January 2005, 17 (14%) birds had been permanently returned to captivity for behavioral reasons, such as continually approaching humans while showing little or no fear, and attraction to human structures. Their destructive habits included shredding campsites by entering tents and pulling apart sleeping bags and other paraphernalia; perching on houses and buildings and pulling apart roofing materials, TV antennas and associated wiring and weather stripping; perching on porch railings, and in some cases entering buildings; approaching and perching on vehicles and forcibly removing windshield wipers, rubber gaskets, hoses, and antennas; and approaching and accepting food from humans. As alarming as this is, it is difficult to attribute any condor deaths directly to this behavior, although mortalities of some wild hatched nestlings in southern California due to the ingestion of trash items brought to nests by parents may be an indirect result of attraction to humans and human-altered environments. The basis for such inappropriate and atypical species behavior, particularly among adults, has been the subject of some controversy (see Meretsky et al. 2000). Nestlings in the captive breeding program are either raised by their parents, or hand-reared using puppets as surrogate parents. Thus it has been suggested that parent-reared condors may be more likely to exhibit more species-typical behavior than puppet-reared condors, showing little or no attraction to humans, and thus possibly having a lower risk of mortality resulting from avoidance of human activity and structures, such as powerlines (Meretsky et al. 2000, Snyder and Snyder 2000). However, evidence to date suggests that all condors in the release program have participated in this behavior regardless of rearing techniques in captivity (USFWS unpubl. data). Two strategies have been used to discourage birds from participating in behaviors deemed detrimental. Hazing is an activity directed at a bird by humans in an attempt to discourage a behavior, and aversion training is making an undesirable activity or behavior unpleasant without direct human interaction. In general, hazing has had little measurable effect on the propensity of condors to engage in inappropriate behavior in California, despite hundreds of man-hours invested in such efforts (USFWS unpubl. data). Conversely, aversion training has appeared to have been effective in discouraging birds from landing on power poles, a frequent problem in the first years of condor releases prior to the installation of electrified mock powerpoles in pre-release facilities.

The historic literature and observations by biologists in the 1980s revealed interactions with humans where condors were closely approached, or condors landed on human structures. In most cases these encounters were with recently fledged or immature condors (Dyer 1935, Smith and Easton 1964, Borneman and Ogden 1981, C. Koford unpubl. data, USFWS unpubl. data). Observations of captive-reared released birds suggest they are attracted to activity associated with the presence of humans. As birds mature they have generally shown less interest in keeping up their attraction to human activity and human structures, although some birds have continued to show little or no wariness of humans (USFWS unpubl. data). For example, flushing and hazing over the past three years at a communications tower location has had no apparent effect on condor behavior or attraction to this site (Plate 4). The problem is accentuated by the fact that the condors perch high up on the towers where they are difficult to flush. Compounding the problem is that consistent hazing is nearly impossible since the birds vary their visits to individual sites daily (USFWS unpubl. data) and most hazing is retroactive rather than proactive, since birds have already landed and spent time on structures before being discovered and hazed.

An important conservation consideration is the degree to which we accept condors visiting and using human structures versus what should be the most desirable long term objective—the recovery of a fully functioning, viable population of condors with a range of species-typical behaviors that are likely to increase, rather than diminish, survivorship in the wild. If we accept condors visiting and sitting on human structures (Plate 5), then we must accept what comes along with that, including a potential lack of wariness toward humans, as well as increased contact with trash associated with human activity and the likelihood of detrimental effects on condor chick survivorship through trash ingestion (see Mee et al. this volume).

Ingestion of foreign, man-made material (trash) has reached epidemic proportions in the southern California population where breeders have brought trash items to nests and regurgitated them along with food for nestlings (see Mee et al. this volume). Condor parents have ingested anything from rags to bolts, washers, nuts, plastic, glass, chunks of PVC pipe, bottle-caps, spent 22 caliber ammunition shells, and pieces of copper wire. However, trash ingestion also appears to be widespread in some populations of Old and New World vulture species other than condors (see Mundy and Ledger 1976, Iñigo Elías 1987, Ferro 2000, Benson et al. 2004). A number of hypotheses have been proposed to explain trash ingestion by vultures including birds seeking bone as a source of calcium, as an aid in digestion, and picking up trash by mistake (see Mundy and Ledger 1976, Richardson et al. 1986). Certainly the urge to pick up objects in the environment and ingest them has not proven to be fatal in the past evolution of these species. However, it is likely that the items searched for and mistakenly consumed by vultures such as condors, whether as a calcium source or for its food value would have had little negative impact prior to the advent of modern-day trash such as plastics, glass shards, and toxic metal items. With regard to calcium, condors have been offered bone chips at carcasses, but it has not been determined if these are sought after by condors. Observers at feeding sites where bone chips are provided report that few birds have been documented ingesting bone fragments (USFWS unpubl. data). However, condors leave feeding sites where bone fragments are present to fly 40 km to an area of high human activity where they may land on the ground and ingest trash items. Indigestible items, such as trash, consumed by free-flying birds are likely to be regurgitated at roost sites, so digestive systems can essentially be purged. However, trash acquired by cave bound nestlings during feeding by parents (parents almost always regurgitate directly to nestlings) are either retained by nestlings or, if regurgitated onto the floor of the nest, may be subsequently re-ingested as they search through the substrate. To date, trash ingestion by nestlings is the primary cause of nest failure in the southern California breeding population (Mee et al. this volume).

RECOVERY: TOWARDS VIABLE POPULATIONS

Breeding.—First breeding in the wild in California took place in 2001 with two separate nesting attempts, one by a pair, and the second by a trio composed of two females and a male. Both attempts failed. In total, between 2001 and 2005, 13 eggs were laid by seven pairs. Five chicks have died in the nest. Of those that did not die in the nest, one was taken into captivity and later euthanized due to a perforated intestine, one was taken into captivity because of trash impaction, one fell from its nest and broke a wing and is temporarily being held in captivity, and one chick successfully fledged (Mee et al. this volume).

Movements.—Because captive-reared immature condors were released into an environment with no existing wild population with which to integrate, individuals in early releases were not influenced by individuals with already established movement patterns, but instead had to develop their own patterns without the benefit of cultural learning. Condors moved freely throughout their historic range visiting many of the historic roosting sites and foraging grounds. For a far-wide ranging species, which is naturally curious and basically fearless, condors have great potential to become involved in any number of interactions with humans.

Movements between release sites began with a few pioneering condors discovering birds at other release sites. The most noteworthy movements have been a condor released in San Luis Obispo County near the Carrizo Plain in 1997 (SB #130) that traveled 360 km northwest to Monterey County where it encountered birds from the central California population and remained for several days. Several central California released condors traveled 360 km south to join up with birds from the southern California release population for the first time in 2000. These exploratory encounters and subsequent interactions established a pattern of movements between the two release sites that still exists today (USFWS unpubl. data)

Of most interest is that over time condors from the southern California population have largely confined their movements to within 50–60 km of the Sespe Condor Sanctuary, whereas condors from the central California population regularly travel the 360 km distance between the Big Sur and the Sespe release areas. In general it appears that a number of central California birds move south to the Sespe in the spring where they may remain throughout the summer, and return north to the Big Sur area in the fall where they remain throughout the winter. This movement was most pronounced during the years 2002–2004 when much of the central California population spent extended periods in southern California. In 2005 there were fewer movements of older birds greater than six years old to southern California, while the younger birds from the Big Sur population continued this apparently seasonal movement pattern.

Fidelity to release sites appears to be strong in most populations. Thus, release sites may function as natal areas for released condors. Although condors range widely during their immature years (1–4 years old), there appears to be a tendency among males to restrict their movements in late winter and spring as they approach breeding age, presumably an effort to establish breeding "territories." There are exceptions to the apparent fidelity of most individuals in release populations to their release sites. For example, the Lion Canyon release site (1995–2000) that experienced the highest number of birds released ($n = 39$) but had the lowest success rate (21% still in the wild) has essentially been abandoned by condors even though suitable nest sites, foraging areas, and roosting sites are close by. In addition two females released at Big Sur have abandoned their natal release site for the Sespe area 360 km to the south where they have paired and bred with southern California males. Thus, although there has been some integration of condors between release sites, early indications suggest that most birds, particularly males, show strong fidelity to their release site, particularly as they approach breeding age (USFWS unpubl. data). Greater dispersal by females from their natal area is well documented from many bird species (Greenwood 1980). However, patterns of dispersal in reintroduced condor populations are likely to be confounded, at least partially, by food provision at or near release (natal) areas, which has also likely promoted higher levels of sociality than documented in historical populations (see Koford 1953, Snyder and Snyder 2000).

Release of original wild birds.—Eight adult condors were removed from the wild between September 1985 and the spring of 1987 to establish the captive breeding program. These eight condors were experienced birds with a complete knowledge of the species' range (Meretsky and Snyder 1992, USFWS unpubl. data). As such these individuals were the thin thread that connected the condors surviving from the Pleistocene to the present. Today five of these original wild birds survive, four in captivity and one in the wild. Criteria for the release of these condors back into the wild were based on their genetic distinctiveness, representation within the captive population (Ralls and Ballou 2004), and their physiological condition.

Since 2000 three wild-bred condors (AC2, AC8, AC9) with extensive radio telemetry data from the 1980s (Meretsky and Snyder 1992), have been reintroduced back into their former range in southern California. Two of these condors (AC2 and AC8) were no longer viable breeders in captivity, and the third (AC9) was already genetically well represented in the captive flock. Further, the latter was not considered a genetic founder (see Ralls and Ballou 2004). Upon release these condors immediately resumed their historic patterns of habitat and range use. These releases presented an opportunity to evaluate the role of wild birds, temporarily held in captivity as breeders, and then released at a later date into a captive reared population to act as mentors, and to contribute to the reestablishment of a viable breeding population in the wild.

The first condor to be released, adult condor eight (AC8), a female, was removed from the wild for the captive breeding program on 8 June 1986. She was released 14 years later on 4 April 2000 into her former breeding range in the Sespe Condor Sanctuary. The presence of an ovarian cyst discovered in 1999 while in captivity would have prevented her from producing fertile eggs in captivity (P. Ensley pers. comm.). During the portion of her lifetime in the wild when she was identified as a breeder (1980–1986) and in captivity (1986–2000) AC8 produced 20 eggs, 16 of which produced live chicks (Mace 2004). Seven days after release AC8 departed the Sespe Sanctuary alone, and traveled 190 km north into the southern Sierra Nevada in northern Kern County to one of her favored foraging areas last used 14 years earlier. For the next two years AC8 moved back and forth between the northern Kern County foraging grounds and the Sespe Sanctuary, exactly replicating the movements she exhibited when she was in the wild in the 1980s. As well as could be determined, AC8 traveled independently during those foraging trips (USFWS unpubl. data). During her visits back to the Sespe Sanctuary she tended to be a loner, rarely socializing with other condors in the southern California population. During her time in the wild AC8 showed little interest in humans and flushed quickly when approached despite having been in close proximity to humans every day for 14 years while in captivity. In the fall of 2002 she experienced a near-fatal lead poisoning event (365 µg dL^{-1} blood-lead) that required trapping and emergency chelation at the Los Angeles Zoo (see Hall et al. this volume). After a successful recovery she was released back into the wild on 23 December 2002. Sadly, AC8 was shot and killed by a hunter on Tejon Ranch, Kern County, on 13 February 2003. When killed she was a minimum of 30 years old.

Two adult males from the historic condor population were also released back into the wild. AC9 spent 15 years in captivity and produced 14 offspring during that time (Mace 2004). He was captured on 17 April 1987 as a seven year old, and released 15 years later on 1 May 2002. Since his release AC9 reared two chicks in the wild, although both were removed to captivity, one having fallen from the nest where it sustained a broken wing. Both chicks underwent surgery to remove large quantities of trash. In contrast to AC8, AC9's movements throughout his former range have been less extensive, and have tended to emulate those of the captive reared released birds. However, AC9 reclaimed his former breeding territory, nesting in 2005 just a few meters from the site of his breeding attempt in the wild in 1986 when paired with AC8, his only previous mate in the wild.

The second male, AC2, was released on 22 June 2005 after 19 years in captivity (Plate 6). This male was captured on 13 December 1986 as an adult of at least 16 years of age and released at approximately 37–40 years of age at Bittercreek National Wildlife Refuge (N.W.R.), the same location where he was captured in 1986. During his lifetime AC2 produced, with his various mates both in the wild and in captivity, 19 fertile eggs, at least 7 in the wild and 12 in captivity. Within minutes of release back into his historic foraging range, AC2 began making his way toward his former nesting territory in the Santa Barbara backcountry. After 19 years in captivity this condor showed no lapse of memory of his former range. Of particular interest is that he was released in an area where no other condors were present, so was not influenced by their movements or behaviors. Further, AC2 showed no interest in approaching humans. Comparison of this bird's movements in the 1980s (see Meretsky and Snyder 1992) with his movements following release showed no change in pattern (USFWS unpubl. data). Unfortunately AC2 was found dead on Bittercreek N.W.R. on 27 September 2005, 95 days after release at this location. The cause of his death remains undetermined.

Preliminary findings from these re-released adult condors strongly suggest that individual California Condors can be temporarily removed from the wild, placed in captive breeding programs, and then be returned to the wild sometimes many years later to serve as guide birds, mentors, or simply to supplement the wild population. This has important implications for other endangered species programs. Currently four original wild condors remain in captivity because of their importance in maintaining adequate genetic representation in captive and free-flying populations. If the threats of lead poisoning could be addressed and ameliorated these four birds might serve a critical role again in the wild where their extensive species-typical behavioral repertoires and proven foraging "knowledge" and ability, acquired from other historical condors and honed over many years in the wild, may be invaluable.

As of November 2005 there are 273 condors in the world population. Fifty-six are flying free in California within their historical range. The challenges that lie ahead for the recovery of this species are tremendous. We have saved the species, but can the species reclaim its place in southern California by establishing viable, self-sustaining breeding populations? This could well be the most serious question facing us in the remainder of this decade. The California Condor remains one of the most critically endangered birds in North America and the world (BirdLife International 2000). Its present and future survival requires creative, innovative, intuitive research and management. Scientific knowledge remains the key. Anything less and there will be no recovery.

ACKNOWLEDGMENTS

I am especially grateful to Dr. Allan Mee and Dr. Linnea Hall for their most constructive helpful comments on earlier drafts of this manuscript. The USFWS acknowledges the participation and support of many agencies, organizations, and individuals involved in the reintroduction efforts for the California Condor in California. Federal agencies supporting the efforts have been the U.S. Forest Service, Bureau of Land Management, California Fish and Game Department, and the National Park Service. The Zoological Society of San Diego, Los Angeles Zoo, the Peregrine Fund, and Oregon Zoo deserve special mention for captive breeding efforts that have produced quality birds for release. The Ventana Wilderness Society, a private non-profit organization, has been directly involved in condor reintroductions, managing the Big Sur release population in central California. Individual participants in the form of seasonal interns and volunteers that were directly involved are too numerous to mention but deserve recognition in many cases for their heroic efforts. Individuals deserving special mention are: Greg Austin, Chris Barr, Joe Burnett, Dave Clendenen, Steve Kirkland, Mark Hall, Jan Hamber, Jessica Koning, Dave Ledig, Rebecca Leonard, Allan Mee, Curt Mykut, Robert Mesta, Bruce Palmer, Richard Posey, Jim Peterson, Anthony Prieto, Kelly Sorenson, Mike Stockton, Dan Tappe, Nick Todd, Mike Wallace, and Marc Weitzel.

LITERATURE CITED

BENSON, P. C., I. PLUG, AND J. C. DOBBS. 2004. An analysis of bones and other materials collected by Cape Vultures at the Kransberg and Blouberg colonies, Limpopo Province, South Africa. Ostrich 75:118–132.

BIRDLIFE INTERNATIONAL. 2000. Threatened Birds of the World. BirdLife International, Cambridge, U.K.

Bloom, P. H., J. M. Scott, O. H. Pattee, and M. R. Smith. 1989. Lead contamination of golden eagles (*Aquila chrysaetos*) within the range of the California condor (*Gymnogyps californianus*). Pages 481–482 *in* Raptors in the Modern World. (B.-U. Meyburg and R. D. Chancellor, Eds.). World Working Group on Birds of Prey, London.

Borneman, J. C., and J. C. Ogden. 1981. Condor Anecdotes. Pg. 4. Condor Field Notes. California Condor Research Center.

Church, M. 2005. Sources of lead exposure in California Condors. M.S. thesis, University of California, Santa Cruz, CA.

Dyer, E. I. 1935. Meeting the California Condor on it's own ground. Condor 37: 5–11.

Ferro, M. 2000. Consumption of metal artefacts by Eurasian Griffons at Gamla Nature Reserve, Israel. Vulture News 43:46–48.

Fry, D. M., and J. R. Maurer. 2003. Assessment of lead contamination sources exposing California Condors. Final Report to the California Department of Fish and Game, Sacramento.

Greenwood, P. J. 1980. Mating systems, philopatry and dispersal in birds and mammals. Animal Behaviour 28:1140–1162.

Hall, M., J. Grantham, R. Posey, and A. Mee. 2007. Lead exposure among reintroduced California Condors in southern California. Pages 139–162 *in* California Condors in the 21st Century (A. Mee and L. S. Hall, Eds.). Series in Ornithology, no. 2.

Iñigo Elías, E. E. 1987. Feeding habits and ingestion of synthetic products in a Black Vulture population from Chiapas, Mexico. Acta Zoologica Mexicana 22: 1–15.

Janssen, D. L., J. E. Oosterhuis, J. L. Allen, M. P. Anderson, D. G. Kelts, and S. N. Wiemeyer. 1986. Lead poisoning in free ranging California condors. Journal of the American Veterinary Medical Association 189:1115–1117.

Keller, L. F., and D. M. Waller. 2002. Inbreeding effects in wild populations. Trends in Ecology and Evolution 17:230–241.

Kenward, R. E. 2000. A Manual for Wildlife Radio Tagging. Academic Press, San Diego, CA.

Kiff, L. F., R. I. Mesta, and M. P. Wallace. 1996. Recovery Plan for the California Condor. U.S. Fish and Wildlife Service, Portland, Oregon.

Koford, C. B. 1953. The California Condor. National Audubon Research Report 4: 1–154.

Kuehler, C. M., and P. N. Witman. 1988. Artificial incubation of California Condor *Gymnogyps californianus* eggs removed from the wild. Zoo Biology 7:123–132.

Kuehler, C. M., D. J. Sterner, D. S. Jones, R. L. Usnik, and S. Kasielke. 1991. Report on captive hatches of California Condors (*Gymnogyps californianus*): 1983–1990. Zoo Biology 10:65–68.

Mace, M. L. 2004. California Condor (*Gymnogyps californainus*) International Studbook. Zoological Society of San Diego, San Diego Wild Animal Park, Escondido, CA.

Mee, A., J. A. Hamber, and J. Sinclair. 2007. Low nest success in a reintroduced population of California Condors. Pages 163–184 *in* California Condors in the 21st Century (A. Mee and L. S. Hall, Eds.). Series in Ornithology, no. 2.

Meretsky, V. J., and N. F. R. Snyder. 1992. Range use and movements of California Condors. Condor 94:313–335.

Meretsky, V. J., N. F. R. Snyder, S. R. Beissinger, D. A. Clendenen, and J. W. Wiley. 2000. Demography of the California Condor: implications for reestablishment. Conservation Biology 14:957–967.

Mundy, P. J., and J. A. Ledger. 1976. Griffon vultures, carnivores and bones. South African Journal of Science 72:106–110.

Pattee, O. H., P. H. Bloom, J. M. Scott, and M. R. Smith. 1990. Lead hazards within the range of the California Condor. Condor 92:931–937.

Ralls, K., and J. D. Ballou. 2004. Genetic status and management of California Condors. Condor 106:215–228.

Ralls, K., J. D. Ballou, B. A. Rideout, and R. Frankham. 2000. Genetic management of chondrodystrophy in California Condors. Animal Conservation 3:145–153.

Richardson, P. R. K., P. J. Mundy, and I. Plug. 1986. Bone crushing carnivores and their significance to osteodystrophy in Griffon Vulture nestlings. Journal of Zoology (London) 210:23–43.

Risebrough, R. 2004. Protocols for the disposition of carcasses of California Condors. Unpublished report to California Condor Recovery Team.

Smith, D., and R. Easton. 1964. California Condor: Vanishing American. McNally and Loftin, Charlotte, NC.

Snyder, N. F. R., and H. A. Snyder. 2000. The California Condor: A Saga of Natural History and Conservation. Academic Press, San Diego, CA.

U.S. Fish and Wildlife Service and California Department of Fish and Game 1988. Experimental Release of Andean Condors in Ventura County, California. Final Joint Environmental Assessment and Environmental Impact Report. U.S. Fish and Wildlife Service, Portland, Oregon.

Wiemeyer, S. N., J. M. Scott, M. P. Anderson, P. H. Bloom, and C. J. Stafford. 1988. Environmental contaminants in California Condors. Journal of Wildlife Management 52:238–247.

Woods, C. P., W. R. Heinrich, C. N. Parish, S. C. Farry, and T. J. Cade. 2007. Survival and reproduction of California Condors released in Arizona. Pages 57–78 in California Condors in the 21st Century (A. Mee and L. S. Hall, Eds.). Series in Ornithology, no. 2.

8

Lead Exposure among Reintroduced California Condors in Southern California

Mark Hall,[1,3] *Jesse Grantham,*[1] *Richard Posey,*[1] *and Allan Mee*[2]

ABSTRACT.—Lead toxicity, perhaps the principal factor in the decline of the recent historic population of California Condors (*Gymnogyps californianus*) is still prevalent today. Ingestion of this contaminant, principally via bullet fragments and shotgun pellets in hunter-shot carcasses and gut-piles, poses a serious threat to the re-establishment of condor populations. Beginning in 1992, condors were released annually in southern California and lead exposure was assessed by blood sampling and analysis. Our data-set consisted of 214 samples from 44 individual condors, all but four samples of which were collected between 1997 and 2004. Ninety-five samples (44.4%) had blood-lead levels above background (>20 μg dL^{-1}), 18 (8.4%) were clinically affected (60–99 μg dL^{-1}), and 7 (3.3%) were in the acute toxicity range (>100 μg dL^{-1}). Of 44 individual condors, 34 (77.3%) had blood-lead levels above background, 14 (31.8%) were clinically affected and six (13.6%) had levels indicative of acute toxicity at least once during the sampling period. Twenty-three individuals (52.3%) were exposed to lead on multiple (2–7) occasions. Lead levels differed significantly between years and were related to a switch of release and provisioning sites between the Sierra Madre Mountains (1997–2000) and Hopper Mountain National Wildlife Refuge (2001–2004). Lead levels differed significantly between age-classes with exposure being highest among sub-adults (years 4–5). Blood-lead levels were significantly higher during the months of the deer-hunting season (31.8 vs. 22.4 μg dL^{-1}). Since releases began, three documented deaths have resulted from lead toxicity. Eight condors with chronic or acute lead levels have been chelated to prevent mortality and one condor was chelated twice in two consecutive years. Assuming that without treatment some of these would have been mortalities, lead poisoning was the

[1]*U.S. Fish and Wildlife Service, Hopper Mountain National Wildlife Refuge, 2493 Portola Road, Suite A, Ventura, California 93003, USA.*
[2]*CRES, Zoological Society of San Diego, 15600 San Pasqual Valley Road, Escondido, California 92027, USA.*
[3]*E-mail: mark_hall@fws.gov*

most significant limiting factor for free-flying condors in the southern California population. Removing the lead threat and replacing lead ammunition with alternative, safe ammunition remains an urgent priority for condor reestablishment.

First documented as a mortality factor in the remnant California Condor (*Gymnogyps californianus*) population in 1984, lead poisoning was determined to be the leading cause of known condor mortality when three of the remaining 16 birds in the wild died of lead poisoning and four others disappeared without being recovered (Snyder and Snyder 1989, 2000). This near-catastrophic increase in mortality led to the removal of the last remaining condors from the wild to form a captive breeding population along with birds previously removed from the wild as eggs and nestlings (see Snyder and Snyder 2000). The main pathway for lead exposure in condors, as scavengers that feed exclusively on carrion, is the ingestion of lead fragments in hunter-shot carcasses or gut piles left in the field (Janssen et al. 1986, Wiemeyer et al. 1988, Fry and Maurer 2003, Hunt et al 2006 this volume). Secondary lead exposure and poisoning have also been widely documented in raptors, principally among the large Nearctic and Palearctic eagles, where scavenged or wounded animals form a large part of the diet (e.g., Redig et al. 1980, Craig et al. 1990, Iwata et al. 2000). Within the present condor range in California, exposure to lead was identified in 36% of Golden Eagles (*Aquila chrysaetos*) sampled in the 1980s, with highest levels occurring during the fall-winter months when hunting was prevalent (Pattee et al. 1990). Condors may be even more vulnerable to lead poisoning and mortality because condors do not appear to cast pellets as frequently as eagles (see Pattee et al. 1981), presumably due to the paucity of hair and fur ingested during feeding on primarily large-bodied mammals. Further, condors may retain large lead fragments within the gizzard and intestines for several days without expelling them from the body, thus facilitating prolonged exposure, although the vast majority of bullet fragments are very small in mass and may be relatively quickly absorbed into the bloodstream (Hunt et al. 2006). Evidence from the northern Arizona population suggests that several condors succumbed to lead poisoning following the ingestion and retention of shotgun pellets within the gut for up to five weeks before death (see Hunt et al., Woods et al. this volume).

During the 1980s, very few blood samples were available from California Condors that could give a comprehensive picture of lead exposure in the remnant wild population. (see Wiemeyer et al. 1988). Since 1992, condors have been reintroduced into the wild in southern California in an effort to reestablish viable populations. More recent releases have taken place in central California in the Ventana Wilderness, Monterey County (1997–present), and at Pinnacles National Monument, San Benito County (2003–present). Evaluation and mitigation of lead exposure to reduce condor mortalities has been a major goal of the recovery effort (Kiff et al. 1996). Therefore, individual condors have been sampled at least once a year to assess levels of lead exposure. Further, condors in all reintroduced populations in California and Arizona are provisioned continuously with a source of lead-free food (stillborn dairy calves) to reduce potential exposure to lead. Despite this ongoing effort, lead has continued to be a persistent and pervasive contaminant for reintroduced condors resulting in several mortalities (Meretsky et al. 2000, Woods et al. this volume) and numerous emergency chelations to prevent mortality (see Parish et al. this volume).

Here, we examine the history and pattern of lead exposure in a population of reintroduced condors in southern California. Lead exposure might be expected to be random in its spatial and temporal occurrence in a population of independently foraging and highly mobile scavengers capable of covering much of the entire species' range in a single day (see Meretsky and Snyder 1992), and where the source of exposure is a widespread environmental factor such as wind-borne pollutants. However, accumulating evidence from several independent studies points to a close association between lead exposure and fall hunting seasons (Pattee et al. 1990, Fry and Maurer 2003, Hunt et al. this volume). Moreover, condors are highly social and gregarious at feeding sites (Koford 1953, Snyder and Snyder 2000), and the discovery of carrion by individual birds is probably non-independent (see also Prior and Weatherhead 1991, Buckley 1996), since condors use activity associated with the presence of Common Ravens (*Corvus corax*), Turkey Vultures (*Cathartes aura*), Golden Eagles and other condors to locate and assess potential feeding locations (A. Mee unpubl. data). In addition, condors exhibit delayed maturation with birds assuming full adult coloration by six years of age and most adults initiating breeding by seven (Snyder and Schmitt 2002). Thus, there may also be age differences in mobility if birds become progressively mobile and exploratory with age after initial release, until breeding activity and nest attendance restrict movement. To address these possibilities, we asked the following questions: (1) Has the overall level of lead exposure changed over the study period (1992–2004)? (2) Does lead exposure vary with age or release location? And (3), is lead exposure greater during the fall hunting season?

METHODS

Study site and population.—We investigated lead exposure in condors released into the wild in southern California since 1992. Releases have taken place at the Sespe Condor Sanctuary and Hopper Mountain National Wildlife Refuge (NWR), Ventura Co. (1992, 2000–2003); Lion Canyon, Santa Barbara Co. (1993–1999); and Castle Crags, San Luis Obispo Co. (1996) (Fig. 1). No releases took place in 2004 and 2005 other

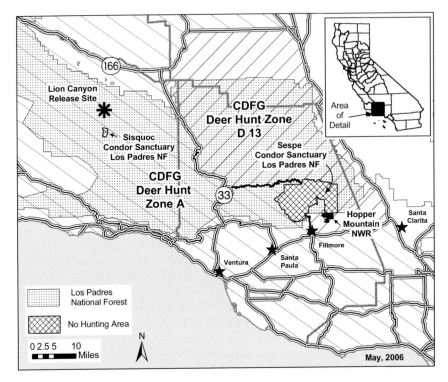

Fig. 1. California Condor release and provisioning sites in southern California (1992–2004). Boundaries show deer hunting zones in Ventura, Santa Barbara, Kern, and San Luis Obispo counties. Deer hunting season in Zone A extended from: 9–31 July (Archery), 13 August–25 September (General season); Zone D13: 3–25 September (Archery), 8 October–6 November (General season). We considered the "hunting season" to be 10 August–30 November to account for sampling during a 20 day post-hunting period when (1) lead-contaminated food may have still been available and because (2) elevated blood-lead during this period may reflect exposure prior to the end of the season (depuration period for blood-lead).

than the reintroduction of a male (AC2) in 2005 from the remnant wild population. The population of reintroduced condors in southern California increased from seven in 1992 to 23 in 2002 but declined to 21 by the end of 2004. Since 2000, the "resident" southern California population has been occasionally temporarily augmented by an influx of condors from release populations in central California. However, two females released in central California have become permanent residents in southern California since 2002, where they have been recruited into the breeding population. Beginning in 2001, reintroduced condors have initiated breeding in southern California and the first wild-bred condor fledged successfully in 2004 (but see Mee et al. this volume).

Throughout the study period, condor management in southern California has focused on attempting to maintain the release population on food sources free of lead contamination in an effort to reduce exposure to lead and, consequently, to increase survivorship. Condors released at Lion Canyon were provisioned at feeding sites in the Sierra Madre Mountains, Santa Barbara Co., between 1993 and 2000 (Fig. 1). Between 1999 and 2000 they were also provisioned periodically at Bitter Creek NWR, Kern Co., about 34 km from the Lion Canyon release site. A temporary release site at Castle Crags, San Luis Obispo Co., was destroyed by fire in 1996. Condors provisioned at the Castle Crags area subsequently relocated to Lion Canyon. Condors released in the Hopper Mountain–Sespe Condor Sanctuary area were provisioned with food at several sites adjacent to release areas between 1992–1993 and 2000–2002, but more recently (2003–2005) almost exclusively on Hopper Mountain NWR (Fig. 1).

Almost all provisioned food has consisted of stillborn dairy calves and more recently, a small quantity of domestic rabbits (*Oryctolagus cuniculus*) and rats (*Rattus norvegicus*). Food was provided, usually on a three-day cycle, at permanent or semi-permanent sites. These sites were monitored on days food was provided to identify individuals and determine their feeding status by recording the extent of time at carcass sites and estimating crop size. Feeding data were collected by observers hidden in blinds (10–200 m) or at some distance (>300 m) from feeding sites using a high-powered (20–60×) telescope. All condors were individually identifiable by having unique, numbered patagial tags composed of the last one or two digits of their studbook (SB) number (Mace 2005). In addition, all condors were fitted with at least one conventional VHF radio-transmitter attached to the patagium (Wallace et al. 1994), or mounted on the tail attached to a central retrix. Some condors (six by 2005) were also fitted with patagial mounted satellite transmitters (PTTs). One female released in central California and currently breeding in southern California was fitted with a GPS satellite transmitter.

Trapping, sampling and lead analysis.—Periodic trapping has been used as a management tool by the USFWS since the first reintroductions in 1992. Condors were retrapped and blood samples taken to determine lead levels at two sites: the Sierra Madre Mountains (1997–2001), and Hopper Mountain NWR (2001–2005). In addition to blood sampling, condors were weighed and transmitters and patagial tags were replaced when necessary. Condors were trapped in 6 m × 3 m × 2 m walk-in traps capable of capturing all birds in the population at any one time, although, in all cases, only a proportion of the population was ever trapped (Plate 13). Individual condors were captured inside the walk-in trap using a long-handled hoop net. During blood sampling and routine transmitter application, condors were subdued by at least two people to allow all operations to proceed safely and reduce handling time before re-release (Plate 14).

Intravenous blood samples were taken from the medial-tarsal vein using 19-gauge, ¾-inch, sterile heparinized needles and storage tubes. Two 0.5-cc samples of blood were taken from each individual. One sample was used for immediate analysis at the field site to determine the lead level of birds prior to release; the second sample was stored in ice on site and subsequently sent for laboratory analysis (Antech Diagnostics, Irvine, California). Apart from providing a reference against which field lead values could be compared, laboratory analyses also provided data on other heavy metals, thus giving a more complete picture of the health status of individual condors. Although there was a strong linear relationship between field and laboratory lead values ($F = 382.77$, $n = 135$, $P < 0.001$, $R^2 = 0.742$), field lead values consistently underestimated lead exposure relative to laboratory values by, on average, 30% (see also Parish et al. this volume). However, on-site lead analysis was the most important tool in deciding the immediate management action required by identifying individuals showing elevated levels of blood-lead prior to release.

To analyze blood-lead levels in the field, 50 µL of whole blood was transferred from each sample to a vial containing a treatment reagent consisting of 250 µL of a dilute hydrochloric acid solution in water (0.1 mol L^{-1}). Complete mixing of the blood and reagent occurred when the solution turned brown. A 50-µL sample was pippetted onto a sensor strip and inserted into a portable blood-lead analyzer (LeadCare Blood Lead Testing System, ESA Inc., Chelmsford, Massachusetts). After a period of 180 seconds, a digital display revealed lead values between zero and 65 µg dL^{-1}. Lead levels above the upper limit of 65 µg dL^{-1} registered as "high" on the digital display. Condors registering in the upper levels of exposure (>40 µg dL^{-1}) were usually held temporarily at the field site and retested two days later to determine if the lead levels were increasing or decreasing. Prior to August 2000, when use of the portable analyzer was instigated, blood lead levels were determined by laboratory analysis only. Thus, a lag time of five to six days would occur before receiving lab results. This necessitated the retrapping of condors with chronic or acute lead levels where possible and their return to temporary captivity for chelation treatment. After August 2000, condors registering as "high" on the portable analyzer were usually transported immediately to Los Angeles Zoo for emergency chelation therapy, a series of pectoral muscle injections of calcium edatate designed to purge lead from the body. In this treatment, lead displaces the calcium forming a stable chelate that is then excreted by the kidneys. About 50% of Ca-Pb chelate is excreted in the first hour following the commencement of chelation and over 95% is excreted within 24 hours (Peregrine Fund unpubl. data). In addition, affected condors were radiographed to determine if any lead fragments were still present in the digestive or intestinal tracts and, thus, likely to present problems of re-exposure to lead once chelation ended. However, radiography is less likely to reveal the often numerous tiny particles of lead associated with bullet fragmentation in unretrieved animals or gut piles (see Hunt et al. 2006) and which may account for much of the lead consumed by condors.

Data analysis.—We classified blood lead exposure levels using the criteria employed in previous studies (e.g., Pattee et al. 1990, Kramer and Redig 1997, Fry and Maurer 2003). Thus, background levels of lead were considered to be less than 20 µg dL^{-1} (<0.2 ppm) and were indicative of birds not having elevated levels of lead. Condors showing elevated blood lead levels (>20 µg dL^{-1}) were considered either as exposed (20–59 µg dL^{-1}), clinically affected (60–99 µg dL^{-1}) or exhibiting acute toxicity (>100 µg dL^{-1}). Although almost all condors (41 of 44) in this analysis were sampled more than once (range 1–14), we considered samples from the same individual as independent if they occurred more than 20 days apart, which was the mean depuration rate of lead in blood plus one standard deviation (13.3 ± 6.5 days) of condors as calculated by Fry and Maurer (2003). Thus, from a total of 222 samples, we excluded eight repeat samples from the same individuals falling within the 20 day time period as they were likely to be replicates of the same exposure event. In each case we used the first sample in the analyses regardless of whether the lead level was higher or lower. However, in most cases (six of eight) the first sample was higher. To allow comparison between years and sites, we used only lab lead values in this analysis as this method was available for most samples in all years and the values were considered likely to be more accurate than values derived from the field tester. However, a small number of samples had field tester derived lead values only ($n = 9$). For completeness, we included these samples with the lab-derived samples by calculating the overall difference between field and lab lead values (means of 14.7 vs. 21.1 µg dL^{-1} respectively) for all samples with both values ($n = 128$) and extrapolating as follows: $Pb_{lab} = Pb_{field}*1.435$ (correction factor). Mean blood lead levels were largely identical whether the full data-set ($n = 214$) was used (mean ± SD = 27.1 ± 35.6 µg) or the reduced data-set consisting of lead levels from lab values only (mean = 27.5 ± 36.2 µg, $n = 205$).

In summary, our baseline data-set consisted of 214 samples from 44 individuals. Sample sizes varied in some analyses where outliers that may have disproportionately influenced the data were removed to determine the effect on the parameters being tested and the robustness of our results. However, we included these outliers in all tests unless stated because such samples were important to describing the variation in blood lead levels. Very few blood samples were taken in the early years of the study (three in 1992 and one in 1994) and none were obtained in 1993,

1995 and 1996. Samples from 1992 and 1994 were omitted from some analyses, because of small sample size, where comparisons between years were made.

In order to investigate the potential effect of condor age, site and season on lead exposure, we broke these variables down into a number of categories. We classified condors according to the following age categories: immature (<4 years old), sub-adult (4–5 years) and adult (6+ years), because, apart from one reintroduced historical female, the exact age of all condors was known, and these age classes were morphologically distinct. Immatures have a basically all-dark head due to short down feathers and dark skin color on head and neck; sub-adults retain some sparse dark feathering on the head and neck but have developed some adult skin coloration; adults are largely free of feathering apart from the distinctive "saddle" on the forecrown and in front of the eyes (see Snyder and Schmitt 2002).

The variable "site" was defined as the location at which condors were trapped, either the Sierra Madre Mountains or Hopper Mountain NWR. Condors were trapped at the Sierra Madre Mountain site from 25 January 1997 until 31 January 2001, and at Hopper Mountain NWR from 1 March 2001 to 2 December 2004. "Season" was defined as either a hunting or non-hunting season based on the peak period of hunting activity within the condor range in southern California. Firearm seasons for mule deer (*Odocoileus hemianus*) and black bear (*Ursus americanus*) extend from approximately 10 August to 10 November each year for the hunting zones surrounding the Hopper and Sierra Madre sites (Fig. 1). The unrestricted season for feral pigs and "varmints" including coyotes (*Canis latrans*), presents a year-round source of potential lead exposure to condors, especially where carcasses are left in the field. However, in this analysis we considered the hunting season as corresponding to the deer hunting season only since hunter-shot deer appear to be the most likely source of much of the lead exposure for condors in southern California (USFWS unpubl. data). Further, we extended the "hunting season" to 30 November (20 days after the deer season closed) to allow for lead depuration in birds that may have consumed lead on or before 10 November but were sampled later that month.

We used the SPSS statistical package, Version 11.0 (Norusis 2000) for all analyses. Lead data were not normally distributed because the majority of the samples were skewed toward zero (overall mean = 27.1 μg dL^{-1} ± SD 35.6, n = 214). Therefore, we used non-parametric tests throughout: Mann-Whitney U-test (M-W), Kruskall-Wallis Analyses of Variance (K-W ANOVA), Spearman's rank correlations (r_s). All tests were two-tailed and significance was set at P = 0.05. Yates correction was applied to tests for differences between frequencies where there was only one degree of freedom.

RESULTS

Of the 214 samples in this analysis, 95 samples (44.4%) had blood-lead levels elevated above background (>20 µg dL⁻¹), 18 samples (8.4%) were in the clinically affected range (60–99 µg dL⁻¹), and seven (3.3%) samples were in the acute toxicity range (>100 µg dL⁻¹). Of 44 individuals sampled, 34 (77.3%) had blood lead levels above background, 14 (31.8%) were in the clinically affected range, and six (13.6%) had levels indicative of acute toxicity at least once during the sampling period. Twenty-three individuals, 52.3% of the sample population, had levels indicative of lead exposure on multiple occasions (2–7).

Year and site variation.—In this analysis, we omitted the few samples (n = 4) collected from the early years of condor releases (1992–1996). Blood-lead levels differed significantly between years (K-W ANOVA, χ² = 42.22, df = 7, P < 0.001; see Fig. 2), tending to be higher in the earlier part of the sampling period (1997–2000: mean = 38.46 ± SD 51.84, n = 76) and to decline in the latter part of the sampling period (2001–2004: mean = 19.22 ± SD 15.81, n = 134). Although removal of five extremely high outlying values over 150 µg dL⁻¹ (three in 1998 and one in 1997 and 2000) reduced the mean blood-lead values for these years (15.0, 38.0, and 40.5 µg dL⁻¹ in 1997, 1998, and 2000, respectively), blood-lead levels

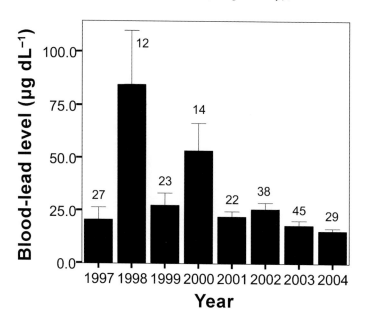

Fig. 2. Yearly variation in blood-lead levels of California Condors in southern California between 1997 and 2004 (n = 210).

remained significantly different between years (χ^2 = 35.61, df = 7, P < 0.001). This difference in lead levels between periods (1997–2000 and 2001–2004) coincided with a switch in trapping location from the Sierra Madre Mountains to Hopper Mountain in 2001. Although lead levels differed significantly between sites (M-W, Z = 2.204, P = 0.028, n = 76, 134), sampling effort also differed between sites (χ^2 = 6.13, df = 1, P < 0.01), with more sampling during the hunting season at the Sierra Madre Mountains (60.5% of samples) than at Hopper Mountain NWR (43.3% of samples). To test whether bias in sampling effort might explain the difference between sites, we compared samples from both sites collected during the hunting season only. Hunting season blood-lead levels were higher at the Sierra Madre Mountains than at Hopper Mountain NWR (mean = 43.86 µg dL^{-1} vs. 20.24 µg dL^{-1}), and this difference was significant (Z = 3.715, 58, P < 0.001, n = 46).

  Age and sex differences.—There was a significant difference in the blood-lead levels of condors of different age classes (χ^2 = 21.49, df = 2, P < 0.001), with sub-adults having higher levels than older condors (Fig. 3). We further examined this difference between age classes by determining

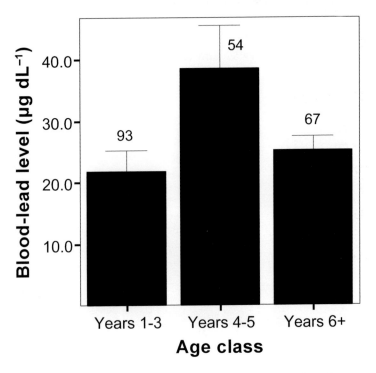

Fig. 3. Mean lead exposure (±SE) in different age-classes of condors in southern California (1997–2004). Years 1–3 were classed as immatures; years 4–5 were classed as sub-adults; and years 6+ were classed as adults.

the "exposure" periods of condors: the number of months and years condors were free-flying in the wild after their initial release but excluding any period spent in captivity, temporary or otherwise. There was a significant, albeit weak positive relationship between lead levels and the number of months spent in the wild after release (exposure months) ($r_s = 0.261$, $P < 0.001$, $n = 214$). Removal of outliers had no effect on the strength of this relationship ($r_s = 0.294$, $P < 0.001$, $n = 209$). Thus, we used exposure period (months or years) rather than age as the dependent variable in these tests because two condors in the sample population were reintroduced birds from the historical population, and thus there was a 15-year gap in the data set (Fig. 4). These were a 26 year old male (AC9) released in 2002 and a female of unknown age but believed to be at least 30 years old (AC8) when released in 2000. However, there was an almost perfect linear relationship between age and exposure months ($r_s = 0.991$, $P < 0.001$, $n = 209$) or exposure years ($r_s = 0.980$, $P < 0.001$, $n = 208$) when only condors

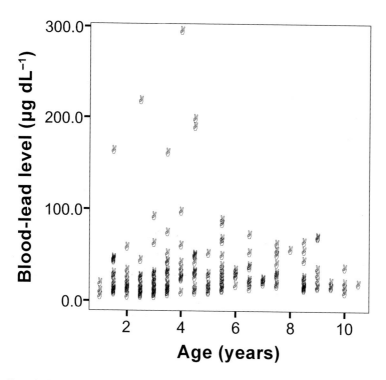

Fig. 4. Distribution of blood-lead samples in relation to age of condors in southern California. All released condors sampled during the study period were between 1–10 years old except for two birds reintroduced from the original historical population (excluded here).

between 1–10 years were considered. Thus, exposure period was a valid surrogate for age in this analysis.

Mean blood lead levels increased after the second year post-release and spiked in year four before declining again in year five (Fig. 5). This suggests that the significant difference in lead levels between age classes was largely a function of condors becoming more exposed to lead during their fourth year post-release. A second, smaller, spike in blood-lead levels occurred among condors that were free flying for eight years (Fig. 5). Mean lead levels of male (26.75 μg dL^{-1} ± SD 39.68, n = 94) and female (27.38 μg dL^{-1} ± SD 32.30, n = 120) condors were almost identical. Further, there was no significant difference in the proportion of blood-lead samples of male (33.0%) and female (45.0%) condors that were exposed to lead (χ^2 = 2.601, df = 1, P > 0.05).

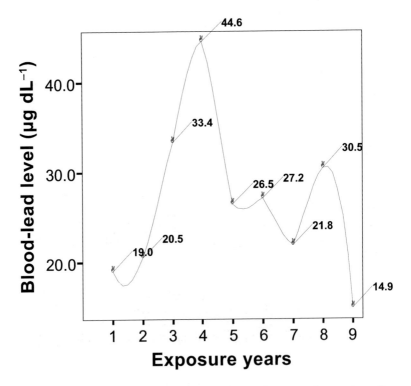

Fig. 5. Variation in mean blood-lead levels in relation to the number of exposure years, the period of years in which individuals were free-flying and therefore potentially exposed to lead. Periods during which an individual may have been temporarily held in captivity were excluded. Thus, Year 1 was defined as days 1–365 post-release during which an individual was free-flying, Year 2 was days 366–730, etc.

Hunting vs. non-hunting season.—Most variation in blood lead levels in condors occurred during the months of the deer hunting season in southern California, but also in June, prior to the start of the deer hunting season (Fig. 6). However, there was a noticeable lack of sampling effort in most months prior to the deer-hunting season with only 20 samples between January and May and a single sample in July. There was a significant difference in blood lead levels between hunting vs. non-hunting seasons ($Z = 2.344$, $P = 0.019$, $n = 107$) with higher lead levels during the hunting season (Table 1, Fig. 6). However, although more birds were exposed (>20 µg dL^{-1}) to lead during the hunting seasons (Table 1), there was no difference in the frequency of exposure between seasons ($\chi^2 = 2.92$, df = 1, $P > 0.05$).

Mortality and near-mortality.—Since releases of condors in southern California began in 1992, 34 (48.5%) of 66 birds released to the wild have died (to November 2005). Of 18 condors for which the cause of mortality was determined, three (16.6%) birds are now believed to have died from

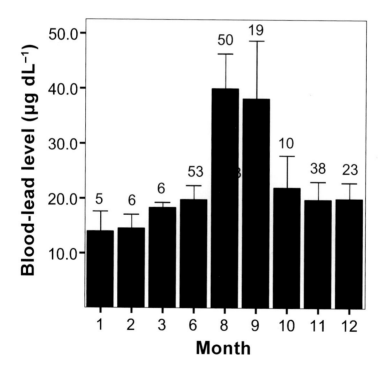

Fig. 6. Monthly variation in blood-lead levels of California Condors sampled in southern California between 1992 and 2004. Data from three months were excluded because sample sizes were inadequate ($n = 1$ in April and July, $n = 2$ in May). Bars represent mean + 1 SE. Numbers on bars represent sample size for each month.

Table 1. Blood lead levels of California Condors ($n = 107$) sampled during the non-hunting (1 December–9 August) and hunting seasons (10 August–31 November).

Season	Blood lead level ($\mu g\ dL^{-1}$)		No. exposed [a] (% of total)
	Mean ± SD	Range	
Non-hunting season	22.4 ± 32.0	0–291.4	41 (38.3)
Hunting season	31.8 ± 38.5	0–160.0	54 (50.5)

[a] Number of condors with blood-lead levels >20 $\mu g\ dL^{-1}$.

the effects of lead poisoning (Table 2). One condor (SB #132) was recovered dead near Castle Crags on 31 January 2001 and was subsequently found to have a high concentration of lead in its liver (Table 2). Another condor (SB #181) was trapped on 8 August 2000 and subsequently found to have acute blood lead levels (214.0 $\mu g\ dL^{-1}$). Chelation began on 8 August and the bird was re-released on 17 August when blood lead levels had dropped to what was considered safe (36.0 $\mu g\ dL^{-1}$). Forty-five days later SB #181 was recovered dead but the cause of death was undetermined at necropsy. However, subsequent stable isotope analysis of material from this condor, although not consistent with signatures of ammunition sources measured, strongly suggested an anomalous elevated lead source, such as as a yet unidentified ammunition type (Church 2005).

In addition to birds dying from lead poisoning, eight birds underwent emergency chelation to lower blood lead levels and prevent mortality (one bird was chelated twice). For example, AC8 was trapped on 11 November 2002 with a blood lead level of 101 $\mu g\ dL^{-1}$ and was subsequently chelated at the Los Angeles Zoo. During that time her blood lead levels spiked at 399 $\mu g\ dL^{-1}$ (not included in analyses as only the first lead exposure sample from any single exposure event was used). Despite surviving this acute lead poisoning and intensive emergency chelation over a period of two weeks, and being subsequently re-released to the wild at Hopper Mountain NWR on 24 Dec 2002, AC8 was shot on Tejon Ranch, Kern Co., on 8 February 2003. If, assuming that birds subject to chelation with lead levels over 180 $\mu g\ dL^{-1}$ had died without such intervention, then lead toxicity (32% of 22 determined deaths) would have been the single most important limiting factor in the free-flying population (excluding wild-bred nestling condors) (Table 3). We also considered the possibility that lead toxicity might have long-term sub-clinical effects that might decrease survivorship. Regardless of the ultimate mortality factor, condors that died during the study period tended to have higher blood lead levels throughout their lifetime than condors that survived (mean of 44.3 vs. 20.2 $\mu g\ dL^{-1}$, $n = 12$ dead and 23 living individuals, respectively). Although this difference was not statistically significant ($Z = 1.668$, $P = 0.095$), this was likely due to the low power of this test to detect a difference resulting from small sample size. Several

Table 2. Fate of 13 California Condors released in southern California (1992–2005). Indicated are the lead exposure and chelation history of birds still alive or subsequently dying from lead poisoning, or unrecovered in the wild.

Studbook no.	Release date	Age at death (years)	Max. blood-lead (μg dL^{-1})	Days to death [a]	Chelation date	Date of death	Ultimate cause of death
12	4/04/2000	35+	410.0	47	14/11/2002	08/02/2003	Shot
64	14/01/1992		160.0			Alive[b]	
98	8/02/1995		194.6		10/09/1998	Alive[c]	
102	8/02/1995	6.5	68.0	45		24/09/2000	Unknown
105	8/02/1995	6.0	291.4	820	4/05/1998	30/07/2000	Unrecovered
106	29/08/1995	6.0	64.1	200		19/02/2000	Unrecovered
107	29/08/1995		65.0		12/06/2003	Alive[c]	
111	29/08/1995		186.2		10/09/1998	Alive[c]	
113	29/08/1995	5.5	75.6	841	12/09/1997	29/12/1999	Unrecovered
130	13/02/1996	4.5	56.2	379	12/09/1997	2/10/1999	Unrecovered
132	19/11/1996	4.8	88.2d	546		31/01/2001	Lead poisoning
175	24/03/1999	1.5	18.2	104		15/11/1999	Lead poisoning
181	24/03/1999	2.5	214.0	54	8/08/2000	1/10/2000	Lead poisoning

[a] Days to death from previous maximum documented lead exposure.
[b] Alive in captivity.
[c] Alive in wild.
[d] Hepatic lead levels at necropsy = 26.4 ppm (2,600 μg dL^{-1}).

Table 3. Mortality factors among California Condors released in southern California between 1992 and 2005 (mortalities among wild-hatched nestlings not included here).

Mortality factors	n	Age Class 1–3	Age Class 4–5	Age Class 6+	% Total
Lead poisoning	3 [a] (7) [b]	2	1		8.8 [a] (19.4) [b]
Powerline collisions	6	6			17.6
Predation	1	1			2.9
Starvation	2	2			5.9
Drowning	2	2			5.9
Shooting	2	1		1	5.9
Ethylene glycol	1	1			2.9
Cancer	1	1			2.9
Unknown [c]	4	1		3	11.8
Missing [d]	12	6	4	2	35.3
Total	34	23	5	6	

[a] Mortalities due to lead poisoning only.
[b] Mortalities of condors likely to have died without chelation (>160 µg dL^{-1}) combined. Percentage in parentheses under Total (7 out of 36 birds) based on total of 34 birds plus two with blood-lead >160 µg dL^{-1} that survived after chelation (#98 and #111). Two other condors likely to have died without chelation subsequently died from shooting (#12) or were never recovered (#105).
[c] Cause of death undetermined at necropsy.
[d] Disappeared, subsequently unrecovered in the wild, presumed dead.

birds with a history of elevated blood lead levels that died in the wild after release were either never recovered or the cause of death was undetermined (Table 2). However, some birds experiencing acute toxicity recovered following emergency chelation (Table 2).

DISCUSSION

In this study, we found lead exposure to be widespread and pervasive among California Condors released in southern California. Almost half of all samples revealed blood-lead levels elevated above background. Further, some three-quarters of all condors were exposed to lead at some stage in their life. Even more worrying, half of all condors sampled exhibited lead toxicity on multiple occasions. While relatively few deaths (3) have, as yet, been definitively attributed to lead toxicity in southern California, this is likely to be an underestimate of the lethal effects of lead because many condors were never recovered or, in several cases, the cause of death was undetermined (e.g., Table 3; also see Table 4 in Fry and Maurer 2003). Thus, apart from the immediate effects of lead toxicity, birds experiencing chronic or acute levels of poisoning may become inactive, stop eating or digesting food and eventually starve to death (Pattee et al. 1981, Hohman et al. 1990). In a study to mimic the effects of lead in California condors, Pattee (unpubl. data) dosed captive Andean Condors (*Vultur gryphus*) with lead shot. The high-dose birds began showing clinical signs of lead poisoning on days 21–28 after dosing, including droopy wings, lethargy and depression, all of which increased until euthanization was employed to prevent further debilitating effects. Interestingly, low-dose Andean Condors (*n* = 2) lost almost as much of their body weight (21–27%) as high-dose condors (28–33%). Such debilitated birds are likely to be more vulnerable to predation or other mortality factors than unaffected birds. Thus, although the ultimate cause of death may be a factor other than lead toxicity, chronic or acute lead exposure may be the underlying causal factor of some mortalities not primarily assigned to lead.

To date, the long-term sub-lethal effects of lead toxicity have not been accounted for in any analysis of mortality factors in the literature for California Condors. Sub-lethal effects have been well documented in many animal taxa, especially humans, and include neurological damage and behavioral impairment (Hunter and Woebster 1980, Otto and Fox 1993, Burger and Gochfield 1997), chronic kidney disease (Brewster and Perazella 2004), and reproductive impairment including reduced fecundity and sterility (Foster et al. 1996). These effects may act to decrease survivorship, for example elevated lead levels may increase the risk of powerline collision by decreasing maneuverability (O' Halloran et al. 1989, Kelly and Kelly 2005). Apart from the effects of chronic or acute lead toxicity, the long-term effects of repeated exposure to low levels of lead in condors is not known but may affect survivorship (but see Rosen 1995, and Burger and Gochfield 2000, for effects in humans and gulls, respectively). In humans, blood-lead levels between 10 and 20 μg dL^{-1} have been shown to impact the central nervous system causing delayed development, diminished intelligence, and altered behavior in young children (Landrigan and Todd 1994).

Year and site variation.–Mean blood lead levels appeared to decline in the latter part of the study period (2001–2004) coinciding with a switch in release and food-provisioning sites from the Sierra Madre Mountains to Hopper Mountain NWR. Comparison of both sites during the hunting season revealed higher lead levels at the Sierra Madre Mountains, possibly associated with greater hunting pressure at this site. Hunting is currently allowed on a small area of land adjacent to Hopper Mountain NWR and the Sespe Condor Sanctuary, although both sites are closed to most public access and hunting. In contrast, all land in the Sierra Madre Mountains is open to hunting except the 485.6 ha Sisquoc Condor Sanctuary, although most hunting probably occurs in the vicinity of forest roads. Deer kill statistics verify that, between 1995 and 2004, mean annual buck kills were 51.2% higher in Santa Barbara County than in Ventura County (California Department of Fish and Game unpubl. data). Observational evidence also suggests that condors in southern California have become more heavily dependent on provisioned, lead-free food in the Hopper area, particularly in the last two years (USFWS unpubl. data). Therefore, a reduction in the foraging range of condors in this population may also partially explain the difference in lead exposure between sites. Although telemetry data exist for the population over the entire study period, these data have not been collected in a rigorous, quantifiable manner to allow comparison between sites. Satellite telemetry probably represents the best solution to obtaining unbiased, quantifiable data on range use and for modeling the effects of changes in management (e.g., provisioning at single vs. multiple sites) on foraging patterns and, consequently, changes in lead exposure.

Age and sex differences.—We found no differences in levels of exposure between the sexes. Interestingly, however, the data revealed a peak in lead levels in condors that had been free-flying for four years after their initial release. This corresponded to condors in their sub-adult phase, between four and six years of age. If all condors were equally mobile in all years and lead was randomly distributed in the environment, we would expect no differences among age classes. However, there may be an underlying biological explanation for this apparent difference in lead levels among classes. Newly released condors are normally faithful to the immediate environs of the release area for some time before gradually extending their range use (USFWS unpubl. data). Adult condors likewise may be restricted somewhat in their movements by parental care duties during breeding attempts, and the need to remain in close proximity to mates and nest sites during the months preceding nesting attempts (Mee et al. 2004). In contrast, sub-adult condors are likely to have developed more extensive foraging abilities and skills than younger birds, but without the restrictions of parental care or mate-guarding. For example, a particularly striking example of the propensity for sub-adult condors to engage in extensive "exploratory" movements occurred in 1999. Prior to this, immature condors released since 1995 had shown strong fidelity to their release site in the Sierra Madre Mountains, perhaps reinforced by the availability of proffered carcasses. This pattern was interrupted in November 1999 when four five-year old female condors (SBs #106, #108, #111, and #112) discovered a new foraging and roost area near Hopper Mountain NWR, approximately 76 km to the southeast of the Sierra Madre Mountains site (Fig. 1). This initial movement by these sub-adult condors would eventually precipitate the relocation and establishment of the entire southern California population to the Hopper–Sespe Condor Sanctuary area.

Another possible factor explaining higher lead levels in sub-adults condors may be priority of access to food as determined by social rank in condors (see also Donázar et al. 1999). Sub-adult condors are usually dominant over younger immatures at carcasses (USFWS unpubl. data). Thus, even if sub-adults and immatures arrive at carcasses together, dominant sub-adult birds are more likely to have priority at the onset of feeding. Since the majority of lead fragments remaining in hunter-shot carcasses are located in the area of the entry wound (see Hunt et al. 2006), and condors initially access meat at intact carcasses through orifices such as the mouth and rectal area (Koford 1953, USFWS unpubl. data), those birds having priority at feeding sites may be most vulnerable to accumulating lead fragments.

Hunting vs. non-hunting seasons.—During this study, we found more elevated lead levels in condors during the hunting season than during the non-hunting season. Further, a higher proportion of condors was exposed to lead during the hunting season although the difference between seasons was not significant. Higher lead levels during the hunting season have also been documented in several raptor species (Pain et al. 1997) and in California Condors (Fry and Maurer 2003, Parish et al. this volume). However, sampling effort of condors in southern California was very unevenly distributed throughout the year (see Fig. 8), with June ($n = 53$) accounting for half (49.5%) of all samples during the non-hunting season. Several condors were also exposed to lead in June (38% of 53 samples >20 µg dL^{-1}). The frequency of lead exposure in June, and other months during the "non-hunting" season, indicates that condors acquired lead throughout the year, although to a lesser extent than during the deer-hunting season. It is likely that condors feeding on depredated or hunter-killed wild pigs (*Sus scrofa*), coyotes, and to a lesser extent, California ground squirrels (*Spermophilus beecheyi*) and black-tailed jack rabbits (*Lepus californicus*), may explain most of this exposure pattern. All these species are hunted year-round in condor range with pigs (17,249 animals per year) and coyotes (10,816 animals per year) accounting for a large part of the biomass of wild food available to condors outside the deer-hunting season (see Fry and Maurer 2003). For example, the range use patterns of one condor, AC8 (SB #12), the last female of the historical wild population trapped into captivity in 1986, suggest that her lead poisoning in November 2002 may have resulted from her scavenging the remains of pigs shot on Tejon Ranch in southern Kern County. Based on satellite telemetry data since her release in 2000, AC8 spent much of her time foraging on the Tejon Ranch and in the southern Sierra Nevada Mountains. In the months immediately preceding her poisoning, AC8 moved between Tejon and Hopper Mountain NWR (USFWS unpubl. data). Although her satellite transmitter failed in October 2002, visual observations at Hopper on 1, 10 and 11 November suggested that AC8 was probably on the Tejon Ranch in the intervening days prior to her trapping on 11 November (USFWS unpubl. data).

Mortality and near-mortality.—Mortalities of condors released in southern California since 1992 have been many and various (Table 3). However, lead poisoning currently likely remains as serious a mortality factor for condors as it posed for the historical wild population (Janssen et al. 1986, Wiemeyer et al. 1988, Snyder and Snyder 2000). Although only three condors have been conclusively identified as victims of lead poisoning in the southern California population, at least four other potential mortalities were likely averted by emergency chelation. Since such intervention should strictly be defined as a "failure" in any calculation of survivorship, regardless of whether death was prevented or not, lead poisoning would thus technically account for seven "deaths" (see Table 3). In such an analysis, lead was the single most important mortality factor among condors where the cause of death was determined (Table 3). Moreover, the number of unrecovered condors that went missing during the fall-winter months suggests that some may have been additional lead related mortalities. Recent analyses of lead isotope ratios in blood, feather, and tissue samples have revealed lead concentrations and isotope signatures consistent with lead-based ammunition for many condors (Church 2005).

Conclusions.—We found exposure to lead to be pervasive among condors in southern California. Due to its outright effects on mortality and also its unquantified sub-clinical effects on condor health, behavior and, ultimately, on survivorship, we believe lead toxicity currently poses the biggest challenge to the reestablishment of viable condor populations (see also Parish et al., Woods et al. this volume). That lead poisoning has not taken a greater, direct toll on the condor population in southern California is attributable to highly invasive, emergency chelation directly countering mortality, and the high level of dependency of condors on lead-free food at provisioning sites. The apparent success of both of these labor-intensive methods should not, however, be a panacea for addressing the threat of lead poisoning. Instead, every effort needs to be directed at reducing the sources and causes of lead toxicity rather than addressing the symptoms. Alternative, field-tested, and safe sources of ammunition exist and are becoming more widely available (see Fry and Maurer 2003, Sullivan et al. this volume). While availability and price have often been touted as drawbacks to switching to alternatives, hunters generally are more concerned with ballistics. Price comparisons now reveal non-lead alternatives are only slightly more expensive than lead ammunition. While voluntary measures to eliminate lead ammunition from within the range of the condor are preferred, they are probably unrealistic. Regulations in the state of California restricting the use of lead ammunition in the range of this species should be considered, with the long term goal of eliminating this highly toxic metal from all ammunition within the state. The California Fish and Game Commission oversees hunting regulations in the state and would be responsible for approving restrictions. Although problems remain with availability and price, these are likely to improve with demand, as well as acceptability and popularity among hunters. Conservation measures including the provision of free, lead-safe alternatives in exchange for lead ammunition should be instigated by the state regulatory agency, California Department of Fish and Game, in condor range. Hunter education on the threat of lead to condors, as well as to the environment and to human health, as implemented recently through phone surveys, leafleting and local meetings is also likely to be beneficial (Byrne 2005). However, we feel that these measures alone are unlikely to lead to viable, self-sustaining populations, which are the long-term goal of the California Condor Recovery Program. Only complete removal of the lead threat from the condor range is likely to achieve this objective.

ACKNOWLEDGMENTS

Numerous people have assisted the condor program in southern California since the first birds were released in 1992. Special thanks go to USFWS staff that directly supervised or participated in condor monitoring, blood sampling and, less happily, the retrieval of condors suffering mortality in the wild. These include: Greg Austin, Chris Barr, Mike Barth, David Clendenen, Mike Stockton, Tessa Smith, and Dan Tappe. Invaluable assistance and expertise during trapping was provided by the condor keepers and vets at Los Angeles Zoo especially Mike Clark, Chandra David, Marti Jenkins, Debbie Sears, Cynthia Stringfield, Jeanette Tonnies, and Jana Wynn.

Many volunteers and cooperators assisted with condor trapping, sampling and monitoring over the years, especially Jan Hamber, Anthony Prieto, and Nick Todd. Other USFWS staff, interns and volunteers critical to the success of the monitoring program have been: G. Baluss, C. Barba, S. Beck, C. Beestman, J. Behrens, S. Bell, J. Brandt, A. Brown, G. Brown, R. Burns, M. Cacciapaglia, J. Caldwell, E. Campbell, M. Concepcion, N. Collier, S. Davidson, T. Davidson, B. Davy, M. Dominguez, E. Drake, G. Druliner, D. Drummond, M. Ennis, P. Ensley, B. Fahey, S. Farry, N. Favreau, T. Fonzo, A. Giese, J. Gibson, C. Grantham, V. Griego, J. Guenther, D. Guillot, J. Govan, J. Gonzalez, L. Greer, Z. Hambleton, S. Hanisch, S. Heath, D. Hernandez, R. Hilgris, J. Hoffman, J. Janowicz, S. Junker, S. Kirkland, P. Kleeman, K. Kontio, E. Kristofik, M. Lavelle, D. Laye, D. Ledig, J. Lysoby, J. Madison, M. Maxcy, J. McCloskey, R. Mesta, K. Milliken, E. Miranda, A. Molnar, J. Moran, M. Newheiser, C. Newton, R. Nichols, D. Nonne, B. Palmer, J. Parker, D. Pearl, D. Pedersen, H. Pedersen, J. Pelayo, D. Peterson, L. Pilkington, I. Plascencia, J. Pleasant, V. Poulter, P. K. Robbins, M. Ruane, S. Scherbinski, R. Schrag, B. Shewmaker, J. Sinclair, T. Stansbury, J. Sweet, J. Szamos, S. Treanor, K. Wakelee, L. Walcutt, M. Wallace, E. Weingert, C. West, M. Weitzel, T. Williams, K. Wain, B. Wood, C. Woodard, L. Woolaver and J. Zuba.

Literature Cited

Buckley, N. J. 1996. Food finding and the influence of information, local enhancement, and communal roosting on foraging success of North American vultures. Auk 113:473–488.

Burger, J., and M. Gochfield. 1997. Lead and neurobehavioral development in gulls: a model for understanding effects in the laboratory and the field. Neurotoxicology 18:495–506.

Burger, J., and M. Gochfield. 2000. Effects of lead on birds (Laridae): a review of laboratory and field studies. Journal of Toxicology and Environmental Health Part B: Critical Reviews 3:59–78.

Brewster, U. C., and M. A. Perazella. 2004. A review of chronic lead intoxication: an unrecognized cause of chronic kidney disease. American Journal of the Medical Sciences 327:341–347.

Byrne, R. L. 2005. Communicating with hunters and ranchers to reduce lead available to California Condors. Wildlife Management Institute. Report to California Department of Fish and Game, Sacramento, California.

Church, M. 2005. Sources of lead exposure in California Condors. M.S. thesis, University of California, Santa Cruz, CA.

Craig, T. H., J. W. Connelly, E. H. Craig, and T. L. Parker. 1990. Lead concentrations in Golden and Bald eagles. Wilson Bulletin 102:130–133.

Donázar, J. A., A. Travaini, O. Ceballos, A. Rodríguez, M. Delibes, and F. Hiraldo. 1999. Effects of sex-associated competitive asymmetries on foraging group structure and despotic distribution in Andean Condors. Behavioral Ecology and Sociobiology 45:55–65.

Foster, W. G., A. McMahon, and D. C. Rice. 1996. Sperm chromatin structure is altered in cynomolgus monkeys with environmentally relevant blood lead levels. Toxicology and Industrial Health 12:723–735.

Fry, D. M., and J. R. Maurer. 2003. Assessment of lead contamination sources exposing California Condors. Final Report to the California Department of Fish and Game, Sacramento.

Hohman, W. L., R. D. Pritchert, R. M. Pace III, D. W. Woolington, and R. Helm. 1990. Influence of ingested lead on body mass of wintering Canvasbacks. Journal of Wildlife Management 54:211–215.

Hunt, W. G., W. Burnham, C. N. Parish, K. Burnham, B. Mutch, and J. L. Oaks. 2006. Bullet fragments in deer remains: implications for lead exposure in scavengers. Wildlife Society Bulletin 34:168–171.

Hunt, W. G., C. N. Parish, S. C. Farry, T. G. Lord, and R. Sieg. 2007. Movements of introduced California Condors in Arizona in relation to lead exposure. Pages 79–96 in California Condors in the 21st Century (A. Mee and L. S. Hall, Eds.). Series in Ornithology, no. 2.

Hunter, B., and G. Wobeser. 1980. Encephalopathy and peripheral neuropathy in lead poisoned mallard ducks. Avian Diseases 24:169–178.

Iwata, H., M. Watanabe, E.-Y. Kim, R. Gotoh, G. Yasunaga, S. Tanabe, Y. Masuda, and S. Fujita. 2000. Contamination by chlorinated hydrocarbons and lead in Steller's Sea Eagle and White-tailed Sea Eagle from Hokkaido, Japan. Pages 91–106 in First Symposium on Steller's and White-tailed Sea Eagles in East Asia (M. Ueta and M. McGrady, Eds.). Wild Bird Society of Japan, Tokyo.

Janssen, D. L., J. E. Oosterhuis, J. L. Allen, M. P. Anderson, D. G. Kelts, and S. N. Wiemeyer. 1986. Lead poisoning in free-ranging California Condors. Journal of the American Veterinary Medical Association 189:1115–1117.

Kelly, A., and S. Kelly. 2005. Are Mute Swans with elevated blood lead levels more likely to collide with overhead power lines? Waterbirds 28:331–334.

Kiff, L. F., R. I. Mesta, and M. P. Wallace. 1996. Recovery Plan for the California Condor. U.S. Fish and Wildlife Service, Portland, Oregon.

Koford, C. B. 1953. The California Condor. National Audubon Research Report 4: 1–154.

Kramer, J. L., and P. T. Redig. 1997. Sixteen years of lead poisoning in eagles, 1980–95: an epizootiologic view. Journal of Raptor Research 31:327–332.

Landrigan, P. J., and A. C. Todd. 1994. Lead poisoning. Western Journal of Medicine 161:153–159.

Mace, M. E. 2005. California Condor (Gymnogyps californianus) International Studbook. Zoological Society of San Diego, San Diego Wild Animal Park, Escondido, California.

Mee, A., G. Austin, M. Barth, C. Beestman, T. Smith, and M. Wallace. 2004. Courtship behaviour in reintroduced California Condors: evidence for extra-pair copulations and female mate guarding. Pages 75–82 in Proceedings of VI World Conference on Birds of Prey and Owls (R. D. Chancellor and B.-U. Meyburg, Eds.). World Working Group on Birds of Prey and Owls/MME-Birdlife, Hungary.

Mee, A., J. A Hamber, and J. Sinclair. 2007. Low nest success in a reintroduced population of California Condors. Pages 163–184 in California Condors in the 21st Century (A. Mee and L. S. Hall, Eds.). Series in Ornithology, no. 2.

Meretsky, V. J., and N. F. R. Snyder. 1992. Range use and movements of California Condors. Condor 94:313–335.

Meretsky, V. J., N. F. R. Snyder, S. R. Beissinger, D. A. Clendenen, and J. W. Wiley. 2000. Demography of the California Condor: implications for reestablishment. Conservation Biology 14:957–967.

Norusis, M. J. 2000. SPSS 10.0 Guide to Data Analysis. SPSS Inc., Chicago.

O'Halloran, J., A. A. Myers, and P. F. Duggan. 1989. Some sub-lethal effects of lead on Mute Swan Cygnus olor. Journal of Zoology (London) 218:627–632.

Otto, D. A., and D. A. Fox. 1993. Auditory and visual dysfunction following lead exposure. Neurotoxicology 14:191–207.

Pain, D. J., C. Bavoux, and G. Burneleau. 1997. Seasonal blood lead concentrations in marsh harriers Circus aeruginosus from Charente-Maritime, France: Relationship with the hunting season. Biological Conservation 81:1–7.

Parish, C. N., W. R. Heinrich, and W. G. Hunt. 2007. Lead exposure, diagnosis, and treatment in California Condors released in Arizona. Pages 97–108 in California Condors in the 21st Century (A. Mee and L. S. Hall, Eds.). Series in Ornithology, no. 2.

Pattee, O. H., P. H. Bloom, J. M. Scott, and M. R. Smith. 1990. Lead hazards within the range of the California Condor. Condor 92:931–937.

Pattee, O. H., S. N. Wiemeyer, B. M. Mulhern, L. Sileo, and J. W. Carpenter. 1981. Experimental lead shot poisoning in Bald Eagles. Journal of Wildlife Management 45:806–810.

PRIOR, K. A., AND P. J. WEATHERHEAD. 1991. Competition at the carcass: opportunities for social foraging by Turkey Vultures in southern Ontario. Canadian Journal of Zoology 69:1550–1556.

REDIG, P. T., C. M. STOWE, D. M. BARNES, AND T. D. ARENT. 1980. Lead toxicosis in raptors. Journal of the American Veterinarian Medical Association 177:941–943.

ROSEN, J. F. 1995. Adverse health effects of lead at low exposure levels: trends in the management of childhood lead poisoning. Toxicology 97:11–17.

SNYDER, N. F. R., AND N. J. SCHMITT. 2002. California Condor (*Gymnogyps californianus*). *In* Birds of North America, no. 610 (A. Poole and F. Gill, Eds.). The Birds of North America, Inc., Philadelphia, PA.

SNYDER, N. F. R., AND H. SNYDER. 1989. Biology and conservation of the California Condor. Current Ornithology 6:175–267.

SNYDER, N. F. R., AND H. A. SNYDER. 2000. The California Condor: A Saga of Natural History and Conservation. Academic Press, San Diego, CA.

SULLIVAN, K., R. SIEG, AND C. PARISH. 2007. Arizona's efforts to reduce lead exposure in California Condors. Pages 109–122 *in* California Condors in the 21st Century (A. Mee and L. S. Hall, Eds.). Series in Ornithology, no. 2.

WALLACE, M. P., M. FULLER, AND J. WILEY. 1994. Patagial transmitters for large vultures and condors. Pages 381–387 *in* Raptor Conservation Today: Proceedings of the IV World Conference on Birds of Prey and Owls (B.-U. Meyburg and R. D. Chancellor, Eds.). World Working Group for Birds of Prey. Pica Press, Shipman, VA.

WIEMEYER, S. N., J. M. SCOTT, M. P. ANDERSON, P. H. BLOOM, AND C. J. STAFFORD. 1988. Environmental contaminants in California Condors. Journal of Wildlife Management 52:238–247.

WOODS, C. P., W. R. HEINRICH, S. C. FARRY, C. N. PARISH, S. A. H. OSBORN, AND T. J. CADE. 2007. Survival and reproduction of California Condors released in Arizona. Pages 57–78 *in* California Condors in the 21st Century (A. Mee and L. S. Hall, Eds.). Series in Ornithology, no. 2.

9

Low Nest Success in a Reintroduced Population of California Condors

Allan Mee,[1,3] *Janet A. Hamber,*[2] *and Jennie Sinclair*[1]

ABSTRACT.—The primary goal in the recovery of any formerly extirpated taxa is the establishment of a viable, self-sustaining breeding population. Reintroduced populations of the endangered California Condor (*Gymnogyps californianus*) began breeding in southern California and northern Arizona in 2001. Here, we studied breeding condors in southern California from 2002–2005 to determine nest success and identify limiting factors for nesting condors. Although hatching success (66.7%) was comparable to the historic wild population of the 1980s, fledging success was extremely low (8.3%). Of 10 chicks hatched in the wild since 2001, only one survived to fledge successfully. All post-hatching mortality since 2002 occurred in the mid to late nestling phase. In two cases, heavy metal toxicosis and complications due to the ingestion of foreign material, principally man-made trash, were the cause of death. All but one chick handled since 2002 held such trash (≤193.5 g). On average, feeding rates were similar to those at historic nests but were more variable. Most nests had lower feeding rates and more prolonged periods of food deprivation than historical nests. Our data suggest that management, principally provisioning at single sites, has significantly altered foraging behavior with detrimental effects on chick survivorship. Whether trash ingestion is related to calcium or other nutritional requirements needs urgent investigation. As a priority, we recommend determining the timing of bone mineralization, and capacity for pellet formation and regurgitation, of nestlings in captivity. In the wild, we recommend the removal of problem birds, closing or cleaning up trash sites and, most importantly, altering current management to reduce dependence on single provisioning sites to promote the development of more natural foraging patterns. However, this is likely to come at a cost of increased exposure to lead contamination. Removal of the threat of lead poisoning would allow more flexible and scientifically driven management of condor populations.

[1]*CRES, Zoological Society of San Diego, 15600 San Pasqual Valley Road, Escondido, California 92027, USA.*
[2]*Santa Barbara Museum of Natural History, 2559 Puesta del Sol, Santa Barbara, California 93105, USA.*
[3]*E-mail: allan.mee@ireland.com*

Apart from preventing extinction, the primary long-term goal in the recovery of any endangered taxa is the establishment of viable, self-sustaining breeding populations in the wild, usually within the species' historical range (Scott and Carpenter 1987, Kleiman et al. 1994). Without the establishment of such populations a species cannot be considered functionally secure from extinction regardless of population size, because such a population can only be maintained either by immigration or augmentation with individuals from an artificially maintained source population. Criteria for assessing the success of a reintroduction necessitate the long-term monitoring of demographic parameters such as population growth, survival, and recruitment rates (see Sarrazin and Barbault 1996, Sarrazin and Legendre 2000). However, in long-lived species with low reproductive rates and delayed maturation, it may be several years after initial releases before reliable empirical data emerge. Therefore, a first step in assessing the viability of breeding populations is an accurate measure of breeding success and productivity. Further, many recovery programs involve intensive, hands-on management to mitigate the effects of factors limiting species recovery (e.g., Jones et al. 1995, Biggins et al. 1998, Ellis et al. 2000). Therefore, it is also important to evaluate the effect of management strategies themselves on the recovery of the reintroduced population.

With the recent initiation of breeding by reintroduced California Condors (*Gymnogyps californianus*), we had the opportunity to carry out intensive studies of nesting condors to determine nest success and identify potential limiting factors for the re-establishment of viable breeding populations in the wild. Previous studies of the recent historic population found no apparent deficiencies in either breeding effort or nest success (Snyder and Hamber 1985, Snyder and Snyder 1989). Instead, the major limiting factor and apparent cause of the catastrophic decline to near extinction of the condor population was high adult mortality primarily due to lead poisoning (Snyder and Snyder 1989, 2000; Snyder this volume). However, the intensive research conducted at nests in the 1980s provides an excellent baseline against which current breeding effort and nest success can be evaluated (see Snyder and Hamber 1985, Snyder and Snyder 2000, Snyder and Schmitt 2002).

The California Condor is one of the most critically endangered birds in the world with a current population, as of 1 January 2006, of 275 birds including 128 free-flying and 147 captive individuals (J. Grantham in litt.). Reintroduction to the wild began in southern California (1992), and subsequently in northern Arizona (1996), central California (1997) and most recently, Baja California, Mexico (2002). The first breeding attempts occurred in 2001 in southern California and northern Arizona with the first successful fledging in the wild in 2003 in northern Arizona. Here, we evaluate the measure most critical to attaining the goal of viable self-sustaining breeding populations in the wild—nest success—and ask what the data tell us about the likelihood of reaching that goal after five years of reproduction in the wild. Further, we consider the effects of current management of the southern California condor population on nest success.

METHODS

Study area and population.—We studied condors nesting in the Los Padres National Forest, southern California, between 2002 and 2005. All condor nesting attempts occurred in the Transverse Ranges and were most often characterized by steep-sided canyons dominated by xeric chaparral vegetation communities (Plate 15) similar to those described for the historic southern California condor population (see Koford 1953, Snyder and Snyder 2000). During the study period the resident condor population in southern California varied between 18 (2003) and 24 birds (2005). Although the number of condors in southern California may be augmented at any one time by a temporary influx of birds from the central California population, the two "populations" have remained largely discrete. However, during the study period two females released in central California took up permanent residence in southern California and commenced breeding in 2004. To date, no southern California released birds have dispersed to join other populations. Likewise, no central California released males have paired or attempted to breed in southern California.

All adult condors were individually identifiable by having patagial tags with a unique number and color combination. Patagial numbers were derived from the last two digits of an individual's studbook number (SB), a number given to all condors for individual identification and population management (Mace 2005). In addition, all adults were fitted with at least one conventional VHF radio-transmitter attached to the patagium (Wallace et al. 1994) or mounted on the tail attached to a central retrix. Some breeders were also fitted with solar-powered satellite transmitters (PTTs) attached to their patagia. One female released in central California and now breeding in southern California was fitted with a GPS satellite transmitter.

General methods.—To assess nest success we monitored breeding pairs throughout the year from the pre-breeding courtship phase through egg-laying, incubation, and brood care until the nesting attempt either failed or succeeded in fledging a chick. Prior to egg-laying, pairs typically engage in two to three months of courtship involving extended pair or tandem flights, mate grooming and roosting, wing-out courtship displays, mounting and eventually copulation (Koford 1953, Snyder and Snyder 2000, Mee et al. 2004). Pairs may also inspect a number of potential nest sites during this period but especially in the weeks prior to egg-laying. We monitored pairs closely to locate nests, and determine the timing of egg-laying and onset of incubation. Following egg-laying, we observed nests to determine attendance patterns, hatching, and subsequent brood care. Nests were occasionally visited to check egg fertility ($n = 3$), to carry out health checks on nestlings ($n = 3$), and to sift nest cave substrates to recover eggshell fragments and identify faunal and non-faunal material brought to nests by condors ($n = 8$). Parental care in condors is one of the most extreme of any bird species including 53 to 60 days of incubation and up to six months or more of brood care prior to fledging (Snyder and Schmitt 2002). Parental care also extends for several months post-fledging so that pairs successfully rearing a chick in one year may skip breeding the next presumably because of the demands of care (Snyder and Hamber 1985). By studying pairs throughout the breeding season we could assess parental effort at nests and identify factors that may be limiting breeding effort and nest success in the study population.

Nest success.—We considered nest success as having two components: hatching and fledging success. We defined hatching success as the proportion of nests that successfully hatched a chick, and fledging success as the proportion of nests that successfully fledged a chick. Fledging is somewhat arbitrary in condors as chicks may leave nests without flying in some cases. Here, we define fledging as the day on which a chick took its first sustained flight. This is a more conservative measure of fledging but is less ambiguous than a chick simply leaving a nest and not returning since some such events may result from a fall from the nest. In most bird species, estimates of nest success are calculated using the Mayfield method (Mayfield 1961, 1975) as failed and active nests do not have an equal probability of being found. In this study, all nests were located and the fate of nesting attempts known. Therefore, we were able to calculate a precise measure of nest success. However, we also calculated Mayfield estimates of nest success to gauge the accuracy of this method in estimating future nest success when it is likely that some nests may fail before they are located. In these calculations, the incubation and nestling period was defined as 58 and 180 days respectively. Where nests failed, eggs or nestlings were sent to the Pathology Department, San Diego Zoo, for analysis and necropsy. Results from necropsies are presented here in brief, courtesy of Dr. B. Rideout. Live chicks were removed from three nests for health reasons and transported to Los Angeles Zoo. Information relating to these chicks is presented courtesy of Dr. S. Klause and M. Clark.

Nest observations.—Observers monitored nests during daylight hours from concealed locations at a distance (mean = 488 m, range = 80–1,000 m) from nests so as to minimize any potential disturbance to breeding adults or nestlings. Nest observers timed the start and end of observation periods and recorded the following data: identity of attending adult if any; activity;

location in nest or at nearby roost; time off and on the egg (incubation) or nestling (brooding); time away from (off-duty) and at (attending) nests; chick feeding and chick activity. Individual feeding bouts were timed when possible. For comparison with historical data, we defined all feeding bouts occurring within the same 15-min period as a single feeding session (see Snyder and Snyder 2000, Snyder and Schmitt 2002). Therefore, we defined the feeding rate as the number of feeding sessions per hour. Observer effort at nine nests studied during the nestling phase between 2002 and 2005 totaled 5,278 h (mean = 586 h, range = 219–1,308). Nests with too few hours of observation in any one period were excluded from analysis of feeding rates.

We used the SPSS 11.0 statistical package (SPSS, Chicago, Illinois) for data analysis. All tests were two-tailed and results were considered significant if $P < 0.05$. Proportional data were arcsine transformed before parametric tests were performed.

RESULTS

Nest success.—Thirteen eggs have been laid in the wild in southern California since breeding began in 2001, of which eight hatched successfully in nests (Table 1). Two eggs were laid in one nest in 2001 and attended by two females and a single male. Both eggs were removed from the wild because of erratic incubation behavior and egg-neglect; one egg subsequently hatched in captivity. A viable captive-laid egg placed in this nest hatched. However, the chick was found dead soon after the hatch,

Table 1. Productivity of reintroduced California Condors in southern California, 2001–2005. Number of eggs hatched and chicks fledged refers to unmanipulated wild-laid eggs only (see footnotes).

Year	No. pairs	No. pairs breeding	No. eggs laid	No. eggs hatched	No. chicks fledged
2001	2 [a]	2	3	0 [b]	0 [c]
2002	3	3	3	3	0
2003	3	1	1	1	0
2004	3	3	3	3	1
2005	4	3	3	1 [d]	0

[a] Includes one pair, and one polygynous trio (two females laying single eggs in the same nest cave).

[b] Two wild-laid eggs removed, one hatched in captivity; other inviable; replaced with zoo-laid egg that subsequently hatched in wild; chick died within two days of hatch.

[c] Chick (SB #262) fledged in captivity from wild-laid egg; released to wild in southern California in 2002.

[d] Second egg hatched in wild following switch of live egg from San Diego Wild Animal Park with inviable, wild-laid egg (not included here).

apparently having been killed by one of the condor trio (USFWS unpubl. data). An egg that failed to hatch in the wild in 2005 was also replaced with a captive-laid egg and subsequently hatched successfully. However, between 2001 and 2005, only a single chick survived to fledge successfully in the wild, the first wild fledged chick in California in 22 years.

Hatching success in the current southern California reintroduced population compared reasonably well with that documented from the historic condor population and from Old World Vultures (Table 2). All eggs laid between 2002 and 2004 ($n = 7$) hatched successfully, but two out of three pairs failed to hatch eggs laid in the wild in 2005. In contrast, fledging success has been extremely poor to date compared to the historical condor population and to other vulture species (Table 2). Mayfield estimates were a reasonably good indicator of actual hatching success but seriously overestimated fledging success because most nests were discovered soon after egg-laying (Table 2).

Nestling mortality.—During the study period (2002–2005), all but one chick died or was removed from the wild during the mid to late nestling phase (Table 3). Of these, five died in or near nests and three were removed

Table 2. Nest success of historic and reintroduced condors in California (CA) and comparison with estimates of nest success in some Old World vultures.

Species	Years	n	Nest success (%)	
			Hatching	Fledging
California Condor				
Historical CA pop.[a]	1980–86	17	56.3	41–47
Reintroduced CA pop.	2001–05	12	66.7[b]	8.3[c]
Old World Vultures				
Eurasian Griffon[d]				
(*Gyps fulvus*)	1982–92	3–33	57.2	87.1[e]
Cinereous Vulture[f]				
(*Aegypius monachus*)	1996–03	44	25–90	43.3
Cape Vulture[g]				
(*Gyps coprotheres*)	1992–99	477	–	56.9
Cape Vulture[g]	1992–99	1,108	–	38.8

[a] Snyder and Snyder (2000).

[b] Only unmanipulated wild laid eggs included in this analysis (thus eggs hatched in wild in 2001, 2005 from captive-laid eggs are excluded and nests counted as failures). One wild-laid egg removed from nest in 2001 and hatched in captivity counted as a failure. Daily nest survival (DNS) = 0.9954, Nest success$_{hatch}$ = 76.1%.

[c] DNS$_{fledge}$ = 0.9935, Nest success$_{fledge}$ = 30.9%. Overall DNS = 0.9940, Nest success$_{egg+brood}$ = 23.9%.

[d] Sarrazin et al. (1996).

[e] Percentage of nestlings hatching that subsequently fledged.

[f] Terrase et al. (2004).

[g] Borello and Borello (2002).

Table 3. Outcome of breeding attempts and cause of failure at condor nests in California (2001–2005).

Year	Pair	Eggs laid	Eggs hatched	Nestling ID (SB#)	Outcome	Cause of failure
2001	SC1 [a]	2	–	–	Egg-switch	Wild-laid eggs removed, one hatched LAZ; captive-laid egg hatched in wild, failed
	SC2	1	0	–	Fail	Unknown [b]
2002	SC1 [c]	1	1	271	Died 5½ months	Undetermined, elev. Cu
	SC3	1	1	285	Died 4 months	Trash, zinc toxicosis
	SC2	1	1	288	Died 4½ months	Visceral gout, elev. Cu [d]
2003	SC4	1	1	308	Died 4½ months	Trash; pneumonia, elev. Cu [e]
2004	SC5 [f]	1	1	326	Fledged	Still in wild
	SC6	1	1	328	Fell from nest	Broken wing, trash [g]
	SC4	1	1	333	Died 4 months	Undetermined; trash, elev. Cu
2005	SC6	1	– [h]	370	Egg-switch	Removed from nest, trash [h]
	SC4	1	1	386	Died 3 months	WNV; aspergillosis, trash [i]
	SC7 [j]	1	0	–	Fail	Egg predated

[a] SC1 "pair" composed of trio: male SB #100, and females SB #108, SB #111.

[b] Nest not visited until early 2003, large eggshell fragments found; egg broken accidentally during incubation?

[c] Female SB #111 trapped prior to breeding to break up 2001 trio.

[d] Chick likely to have died from dehydration.

[e] Removed from wild at 125 days; trash regurgitated, also removed by surgery; poor development; respiratory problems including bacterial infection, lesions on gut wall; euthanized at LAZ.

[f] New pair composed of male SB #107 (formerly SC2), now repaired with new mate, female SB #161.

[g] Fell from nest at 117–121 days, removed to LAZ; trash items removed by surgery including 35 bottle-tops.

[h] Incubated three weeks past estimated hatch date; dead egg replaced with live egg on 21 April, hatched 22–23 April; chick removed from nest at 118 days, surgery at LAZ removed 204 g of trash.

[i] Chick removed from nest at 98 days; died during removal; necropsy revealed West Nile Virus combined with fungal infection; large number of trash items removed (B. Rideout et al. unpubl data).

[j] New pair composed of male SB #08 (formerly SC3), now repaired with new mate, female SB #216.

from nests for health reasons (Plate 16). One was subsequently euthanized and two are recovering following surgery to remove ingested foreign material (hereafter called trash) at Los Angeles Zoo. Causes of nest failure during the nestling phase have been various (Table 3). However, seven out of eight chicks examined between 2002 and 2005 held quantities of trash (Plate 17). In the most extreme case, one surviving chick removed from the wild in 2004 held 222.5 g of foreign material, 193.5 g of which were trash items. Necropsy of the six chicks that died revealed that in two cases death resulted directly from ingesting trash; one (SB #285) died from acute zinc toxicosis resulting from the ingestion of metallic objects; another (SB #308) was euthanized following surgery to remove trash and the development of chronic respiratory aspergillosis. Cause of death in a third chick (SB #333) was undetermined but the presence of numerous trash items was the most significant post-mortem finding. One chick (SB #288) probably died of dehydration as a result of food deprivation over a period of at least 6–8 days (Table 3). A chick (SB #386) that died during recovery from a nest in 2005 was subsequently diagnosed as having succumbed to West Nile Virus, the first documented California Condor fatality to this disease (B. Rideout unpubl. data). Interestingly, most dead chicks examined to date have exhibited elevated levels of copper in liver samples, although the significance of this finding is unknown. In two cases where the cause of death of nestlings was undetermined (SB #271, SB #333), elevated hepatic copper was the only noteworthy finding: 531 ppm and 341 ppm, dry weight, respectively (B. Rideout unpubl. data).

Food delivery at nests.—We investigated whether the frequency of food delivery to nests might influence nest success by comparing feeding rates at nests of reintroduced condors with those from the historical population during a period (1980–1984) when nest success and chick survivorship were thought to be normal. Mean feeding rates of reintroduced pairs averaged across all nests were similar to that of condors in the historic population but showed greater variability (Plate 18). Feeding rates typically declined at reintroduced and historic condor nests after the first month of brood care. However, at all reintroduced condor nests feeding rates were lower than the average for historic nests in the first few weeks after hatching (Table 4 and Plate 18). Further, at some reintroduced condor nests, pairs delivered food at lower rates than at historical condor nests over prolonged periods (e.g., SC4 pair in 2005; see Table 4). Although feeding rates at two nests during the mid to late nestling phase were lower than that recorded for any nest in the historic population of the 1980s (Table 5), there was no overall difference in feeding rates between the populations ($t = 0.132$, $n = 5$, $P = 0.89$).

Effects of management.—Another useful measure of chick feeding frequency is the proportion of days on which feeding occurs. Currently,

Table 4. Feeding rates at nests hatching chicks in southern California (2002–2005).

Pair [a]	Feeding rate (events h⁻¹) by week after hatch						Mean ± SD
	1–4	5–8	9–12	13–16	17–20	21–24	
2002							
So. Cal 1	0.392	0.151	0.098	0.060	nd [b]	nd [b]	0.176 ± 0.149
2003							
So. Cal 4	0.127	0.079	0.115	0.111	0.098	– [c]	0.106 ± 0.018
2004							
So. Cal 5	0.207	0.226	0.109	0.156	0.157	0.133	0.161 ± 0.041
So. Cal 6	0.340	0.266	0.098	0.133	– [d]		0.209 ± 0.113
2005							
So. Cal 4	0.319	0.131	0.073	– [e]			0.174 ± 0.129

1980–86 (n = 5): mean = 0.50 h⁻¹ in week 1 after hatch [f]
1980–86 (n = 5): range = 0.09–0.12 h⁻¹ in week 10–25 after hatch [f]

[a] Only pairs hatching chicks with comprehensive data for each time period are presented here.
[b] No data (nd) for this period; chick died day 171–174 (week 25).
[c] Chick removed from nest on day 223 (week 14) for health reasons, subsequently euthanized at LAZ.
[d] Chick fell from nest on day 117–121 (week 19–20), removed to LAZ.
[e] Chick died during removal from nest on day 98 (week 14).
[f] Snyder and Snyder (2000).

Table 5. Chick-feeding at reintroduced and historic condor nests during the mid-late nestling phase.

Year	Pair	Weeks 10–25 post-hatch	
		Feeding rate (events h⁻¹)	Non-food days (%)
2002	So. Cal 1	0.073	46.2
2003	So. Cal 4	0.109	29.7
2004	So. Cal 5	0.143	35.1
2004	So. Cal 6	0.109	40.9
2005	So. Cal 6	0.065	62.5
	Mean ± SD = 0.099 ± 0.031		42.9

1980–84 (n = 5): Mean ± SD = 0.102 ± 0.012 [a]   14–30 [b]
Range = 0.09–0.12 [b]

[a] Mean feeding rate for historical nests derived from data presented in Snyder and Snyder (2000).
[b] Snyder and Snyder (2000).

reintroduced condor parents obtain a large proportion of their food from provisioned sites designed to maintain birds on food free of lead contamination. Thus, because chicks may be fed disproportionately on days on which food is available at provisioned sites but not on other days, nestlings may be exposed to periods of food deprivation. In contrast to the historic condor population, chicks at reintroduced condor nests experienced a significantly higher proportion of days on which no food was delivered ($t = 3.06, n = 5, P = 0.016$). Only one pair (SC4) from the reintroduced population showed an overlap with the historic population, but this was with the nest with the highest proportion of non-food days in that population (see Table 5). Importantly, the pair with the highest feeding rate (SC5 in 2004) and a lower proportion of non-food days than all but one other pair was the only one to successfully fledge a chick during the study period (Table 5).

Unlike the historical population, extended periods of food deprivation at reintroduced condor nests were not infrequent. Such periods were usually related to poor weather and loss of provisioned food to mammalian scavengers such as black bears (*Ursus americanus*), and coyotes (*Canis lantrans*). However, management also directly influenced feeding rates and the proportion of non-food days at some nests (Table 6). For example, at one nest in 2004, a trapping event resulted in a sharp drop in the trapping and post-trapping feeding rate (10–25 June: 0.086 feeds h^{-1}) and a high number of consecutive non-feeding days compared to the immediate pre-trapping period (1–9 June: 0.242 feeds h^{-1}). Thus, even routine events may have a profound effect on food delivery to nests in managed populations. In contrast, extended periods of food deprivation were largely unknown at historical nests (see Snyder and Snyder 2000, Snyder and Schmitt 2002).

Discussion

Nest success.—In this study, we documented a very low level of nest success in the southern California condor population, principally due to high nestling mortality and removal of debilitated chicks from the wild at the mid to late nestling stage (Plate 19). Trash ingestion was identified as the primary cause of death of at least two chicks, and the presence of trash in all but one chick handled to date indicates the pervasiveness and deleterious effects of this material. Whether trash ingestion by condors has had sub-lethal effects that have contributed to other nest failures is unknown, although at least one surviving chick (SB #370) was severely debilitated by ingested trash and would likely have died without emergency surgery to remove trash items (A. Mee unpubl. data). From a purely physiological viewpoint, however, it seems likely that the accumulation of a large quantity of foreign material, either trash or naturally occurring, in both the crops and stomachs of condor chicks may impede normal food processing and reduce nutrient intake (see also Huin and Croxall 1996, Liitschwager and Middleton 2003, Pierce et al. 2004, for effects of trash on seabirds). If this persists over an extended period, the result may be reduced growth rates, retarded development and, ultimately, death. Poor nutrition and retarded development are also likely to increase the risks of developing secondary infections perhaps due to compromised immune systems (B. Rideout pers. comm.).

The lethal or sub-lethal effects of elevated levels of some heavy metals in liver samples of dead condor chicks also poses serious questions. While the diagnosis is apparently straightforward in one case (zinc toxicosis associated with the ingestion of metallic trash; Table 3), the significance of elevated hepatic copper in particular is concerning and requires study. Elevated hepatic copper was previously documented in several dead immature and adult condors (Wiemeyer et al. 1983, Risebrough et al. 2001), and condors appear to have a greater propensity to accumulate copper in their livers than other smaller-bodied cathartid vultures (Risebrough et al. 2001). Preliminary investigations suggest that condors obtain most or all of their copper from food (Fry and Maurer 2003). An analysis of liver samples from food (stillborn calf carcasses) at provisioned feeding sites found variable but elevated copper in all samples (M. Fry unpubl. data). Previous studies have shown that copper occurs at relatively elevated levels in the livers of fetal and newly born mammals compared to that of adults (see Fry and Maurer 2003). Heavy dependence on stillborn calves from intensively reared cattle as a primary food source for condors is likely therefore to underlie hepatic copper accumulation in nestlings. Until further research defines reference levels for copper in condors and provides a definitive answer on the effects, if any, of copper on condors, it seems prudent to avoid over-dependence on this single food source. This could be addressed by provisioning where possible with free-ranging, adult mammals free of lead contamination. Further, the livers of all stillborn calves provided to condors should be removed, at least while condors are still in the nestling phase, to minimize any potential negative effects on the nestlings.

Food delivery at nests.—Current studies at nests of reintroduced condors show that behavioral patterns and levels of parental care at most nests were similar to those found in the historical wild population (A. Mee unpubl. data). However, we also documented lower than expected feeding rates at some nests and a higher proportion of non-feeding days than reported from the historic population. For example, in 605 observation days at five intensively studied nests in the 1980s, consecutive non-food days were recorded only on 13 occasions (Snyder and Snyder 2000, Snyder and Schmitt 2002). Further, only on one occasion did a chick go three full days without food. In contrast, periods of food deprivation were more common at reintroduced condor nests from 2001 to 2005. This was usually a period of two days following feeding (condors were normally provided with food on a three day

cycle as part of routine management) but sometimes extended to at least
five days without parents delivering food to nests (Table 6). While any one
period of food deprivation may not be critical, repeated short bouts of such
deprivation over some weeks or months are likely to be debilitating. For
example, periods of food deprivation were related to a greater propensity in
Cape Vulture (*Gyps coprotheres*) nestlings to ingest foreign material, nest
material, and human artifacts (Dobbs and Benson 1984).

Counterintuitively then perhaps, it appears that efforts to provision
condors in southern California with a predictable food source free of lead
contamination may pose serious risks for chicks. A number of factors may
be driving this: (1) condors have become more heavily dependent on provisioned food with little documentation of adults feeding away from the main
provisioning site during breeding attempts (Plate 20). Simultaneous observations at nests and at feeding sites confirm breeding adults routinely leaving
feeding sites and returning directly to nests to feed chicks. At 12 km from
the provisioning area, even the most distant nest-feeding site commute may

Table 6. Effect of a trapping event on feeding frequency at one condor nest (SC6)
in 2004. Missing days are days on which there were no observations.

Date	Chick age (days)	No. feeds		Comments
		#21 (♂)	#192 (♀)	
1–9 June	51–59	12	5	No observations: June 5–7
10 June	60	0	0	Start trapping, food in trap:
11 June	61	0	0	June 10–12, 15–17
12 June	62	1	1	
13–14 June	63–64	–	–	No observations
15 June	65	0	0	
16 June	66	2	1	Pair at nest with "mystery" crops [a]
17 June	67	1	2	End trapping attempt
18–21 June	68–71	–	–	No observations
22 June	72	0	0	
23 June	73	0	0	
24 June	74	0	0	
25 June	75	0	1	
26–28 June	76–78	–	–	No observations
29 June	79	0	0	
30 June	80	0	0	
1 July	81	0	0	
2 July	82	0	0	

[a] Both adults arrive at nest with food not obtained at the provisioned site (Hopper Mountain
NWR); satellite data revealed that female #192 had traveled some 160 km N into southern
San Luis Obispo Co. over previous day, the only documented large-scale movement by this
condor throughout the breeding season.

take just a matter of minutes (A. Mee unpubl. data). Although, under normal circumstances, this should be beneficial to chick provisioning, the greater dependency on accessing such food places condors at greater risk when food becomes temporarily unavailable (e.g., through loss to other scavengers; during trapping events, etc.). (2) The nature of provisioning at single sites where food location and availability are entirely predictable, especially where nests are only a few kilometers away, results in breeding pairs returning to nests to feed chicks on the same day, often within hours or minutes of each other. In many cases this leads to the later arriving adult either not going to the nest at all, visiting the nest but not feeding the perhaps already satiated chick, or feeding the chick only briefly. In contrast, wild pairs in the historic population largely foraged independently of each other over a much greater area (mostly up to 50–70 km but occasionally up to 150–180 km away from active nests), typically in the foothills of the Central Valley, for food that was usually less predictable in time and space (see Meretsky and Snyder 1992). Thus, the return of adults to nests to feed chicks was probably independent of their mates. Therefore, consideration of feeding rates alone may not adequately reflect the quality of food delivery to chicks. Although we did not directly compare the biomass of food delivered to chicks at reintroduced and historic nests, it is likely that food not only reached chicks at historic nests more dispersed in time but also in greater quantity. A comparative analysis of data collected at historic and reintroduced condor nests could examine this hypothesis. (3) Freed from the need to forage extensively to find food as did birds in the historical population, reintroduced condors now have time to explore and indulge in social activities on days when food is not available, such as landing on human structures and searching out or incidentally picking up trash that appears to be all pervasive in the environment.

Trash ingestion by condors.—Evidence of organisms faced with a human-altered environment where previously adaptive cues are now maladaptive is increasing (see review in Schlaepfer et al. 2002). Thus, organisms may become trapped by their evolutionary responses to cues and suffer reduced survival or reproduction. Condors in early releases commonly landed on utility powerpoles where historically, birds would have found safe perches on trees or cliffs (see Snyder and Snyder 2000). Following aversion training at captive facilities using electrified mock powerpoles, condors avoided such perches when subsequently released into the wild (USFWS unpubl. data). If trash ingestion also fits this model, what then is the cue that elicits this behavior and can we possibly alter either the cue, the response, or the environment to reduce or eliminate effects on chick survivorship and nest success? So far the evidence is equivocal on whether the cue is related to a need to supplement calcium in the diet (i.e., condors mistaking white plastic or ceramic items for bone) or if it is simply a hard-wired behavior unrelated to calcium needs that is maladaptive in the present day environment of southern California. Meat is a poor source of calcium (Mundy and Ledger 1976, Tabaka et al. 1996) and condors may search for bone especially during periods when calcium demands are likely to be higher, such as during egg formation and the peak period of nestling feather development (3–5 months). In the remnant historic condor population, trash items such as plastic and glass were found at 12% of nests (Collins et al. 2000). However, in comparison to the reintroduced population, the quantity and size of these items were much smaller and no reproductive problems were encountered (Mee et al. in press). Many of the items recently brought to nests in the study population would be hard to ascribe to birds searching for a source of calcium, and bone-like items made up only a small part of all trash (15%) recovered from nests and chicks (Mee et al. in press). Efforts to supplement condors with bone chips at feeding sites in 2003–2005 have had no apparent effect on the propensity of parents to provision nestlings with trash items. However, whether condors require and search for supplemental calcium in the form of bone has not been rigorously tested. In the southern California population, provision of bone chips and small mammal carcasses at feeding sites has been erratic at best and the quantity provided (e.g., up to three rabbits [*Oryctolagus cuniculus*] and several rats [*Rattus norvegicus*] at a feeding) has probably been too small to impact the target breeding pairs. Not only do breeding condors compete with other condors in the population, but Golden Eagles (*Aquila chrysaetos*) and Common Ravens (*Corvus corax*) also usually arrive first at most carcasses (A. Mee unpubl. data), and thus may preferentially consume much of these smaller and easier to access carcasses. Further, Golden Eagles are dominant at carcasses and often exclude condors entirely from access to food until having fed and left the site (A. Mee unpubl. data).

Trash ingestion by condors might also indicate a need to supplement energetic and nutritional requirements. Thus, bone itself may be sought not just to supply calcium needs but as an alternative food source high in energy, for example, 15% greater than meat in the case of the bone consumed by the Bearded Vulture (*Gypaetus barbatus*), an obligate bone-eating scavenger (Brown and Plug 1990). Even taking into account the lower digestive efficiency of consuming bone rather than meat (Barton and Houston 1994), bone may be especially important when meat is unavailable or limited (Benson et al. 2004). Further, the current diet of condor nestlings in southern California is almost exclusively derived from one food source, stillborn dairy calves. This diet may be sufficient to meet the daily body maintenance requirements of free-flying condors, however, egg-laying females, breeders attending and feeding nestlings, and nestlings themselves are likely to have higher qualitative nutritional requirements that may not be met by a single food source (see for example Nisbet 1973, Parker and Holm 1990, Alisauskas and Ankney 1994). The energetic and nutritional value of food items of raptors and carrion-dependent vultures may vary greatly, and the adequacy of different food sources partly depends on the digestive efficiency of the predator or scavenger (Barton and Houston 1993). Thus, for example, meat with a high fat content is energetically more valuable than meat that is low in fat but high in protein (Barton and Houston 1993). Poor nutrition may result in reduced breeding effort with some pairs failing to breed in some years (Monaghan et al. 1989, Phillips et al. 1996).

In contrast to the extremely low fledging success of condors in southern California, all nestlings hatched to date in northern Arizona have fledged successfully (see Woods et al. this volume). No nestlings have suffered from crop impaction or heavy metal toxicosis resulting from ingesting trash, although one recently fledged juvenile had to be retrapped and underwent surgery to remove a large quantity of naturally occurring material (e.g., sticks, rocks) from its crop (C. Parish pers. comm.). Further, while trash items have been documented at some nests, the level of trash appears to be much lower than in southern California. This may reflect the relatively more pristine environment of northern Arizona or a lower propensity of condors in Arizona to bring trash to nests. Although the type of provisioned food is the same between sites (stillborn calves), condors in Arizona commonly exploit a wide variety of natural food sources throughout the greater Grand Canyon area (see Hunt et al. this volume), so much so that some condors spend months at a time away from the release and provisioning sites (S. Osborn pers. comm.). Further, some nests are located up to 80 km from the provisioned site, in contrast to the close proximity of nests and provisioning sites (1.5–12 km) in southern California. Thus, regardless of the source of their food, breeding pairs in Arizona often have to forage extensively to obtain food for nestlings. These breeding birds thus probably have little time available to search for trash items that are also less prevalent in the environment. Moreover, the lack of dependence of breeding Arizona condors on provisioned food may have benefited nestling development by providing a more balanced and nutritious diet.

So what are the prospects for attaining viable breeding populations in the wild in southern California when nest failure is so high, particularly due to the pervasive effects of trash on chick survivorship? There would appear to be two ways in which condors can escape from a scenario that would otherwise lead to population extinction without continued "artificial" recruitment of birds from captive-breeding facilities: natural selection or experienced-based learning (Schlaepfer et al. 2002). Because of the extreme generation times of condors and a host of ongoing mortality factors (see Snyder this volume), condor populations in southern California will likely become inviable or go extinct if left to natural selection alone. Indeed a trait selecting against trash ingestion might be slow to evolve if the acceptance threshold of condors is broad and there is a low level of discrimination between what might have been the original cue, bone fragments, and the novel cue, in this case trash (Schlaepfer et al. 2002). However, as has been shown in the case of power pole aversion, experience-based learning plays an important role in the behavioral development of condors. Thus, an option to be seriously considered before initiating new releases in southern California is to start with naive birds in a favorable environment where the original cue can be reinforced prior to release to promote behavior that is adaptive. In this regard, captive breeding facilities would be the ideal locations to test aversive techniques and reinforcement prior to release. A first effort at investigating the utility of aversion training for condors is being initiated at the San Diego Wild Animal Park in 2006 using electrified wires attached to trash items commonly ingested by condors (M. Mace pers. comm.).

Because cultural transmission is likely to be a strong force in a long-lived, social or semi-social species, the influence of birds already in the wild will probably have a large effect on the success or failure of attempts to condition birds prior to release (see Sarrazin et al. 1994, 1996). Recent evidence suggests that even re-released wild-bred condors from the historic population occasionally engage in behavior initiated by captive bred condors released to the wild. For example, on one occasion AC8 (SB #12), the last female trapped and brought into captivity from the wild in 1986 and released back to the wild in 2000, was observed landing on an active oil-pad near Hopper Mountain NWR in 2002 at a time when almost all the southern California population was visiting oil-pads on a daily basis (A. Mee pers. obs). Condors landing on oil-pads perched on structures and vehicles, and engaged in social "play," picking up and pulling on man-made material. However, AC8 was never observed engaging in such behavior. Likewise, male AC9 (SB #21), the last condor trapped and brought into captivity from the wild in 1987 and released in 2002, was recently documented visiting a site in the San Gabriel Mountains frequented by most of the southern California population where condors regularly land on human structures such as communications towers. Although only previously observed landing and roosting on trees at this site, in 2005 AC9 was seen to land on a vehicle with several other condors (USFWS unpubl. data). This location is also believed to be the principal site where condors have picked up trash items in recent times (2002–2005). To our knowledge, apart from during nest visits (e.g., Finley 1906, Koford 1953), adults in the historic population never closely interacted with humans or landed on human structures, although there was at least one instance of an immature condor landing in a populated area (see Smith and Easton 1964) and a few cases of immature condors landing near humans or allowing humans to closely approach them (Condor Information System archive, Santa Barbara

Museum of Natural History, California). While immature condors appear to be inherently curious about their environment, the consistency with which reintroduced condors in the southern California population land on human structures, and approach or allow close approach by humans, is on a much greater scale than previously documented. Most recently, the only wild fledged condor of the southern California reintroduced population was also documented visiting the San Gabriel site and regularly landing on human structures. Without the influence of cultural transmission in the population, we believe it extremely unlikely than any of these wild-reared condors would have shown this behavior. Ironically, one of the main reasons for re-releasing adult, wild birds from the historic population back into the southern California population was the potential benefit such birds might have on the existing reintroduced population.

   Conclusions and recommendations.—In summary, extremely low nest success in the southern California condor population, principally due to high chick mortality, has reached crisis proportions and threatens the long-term re-establishment of viable breeding populations in the region. Almost all post-hatching nest failure has been in the mid to late nestling phase while the single most important factor determining nest failure at this stage is trash ingestion by chicks. Behavioral observations suggest that management itself, principally provisioning the population at a single predictable site largely with a single food type, has significantly altered the population's foraging behavior so that most birds are largely dependent on provisioned food. This has resulted in detrimental effects on feeding rates and a higher proportion of non-food days at some nests, so that chicks suffer longer period of food-deprivation than experienced in the historic population. Whether trash ingestion is related to calcium or other nutritional requirements is yet to be determined. The hypothesis that condors ingest trash in a now maladaptive search for alternative food sources needs immediate investigation.

   As a matter of some urgency we suggest methods to test these ideas in both the captive and wild environment. In captivity: (1) test aversive conditioning techniques with naive, pre-release condors; (2) test calcium requirements and rate and timing of skeletal mineralization of chicks by instigating nutritional trials (D. Houston pers comm.); (3) determine whether chicks have the capacity to cast pellets including trash items by testing on Andean Condor (*Vultur gryphus*) surrogates. In the wild: (1) identify and remove "problem" birds either temporarily (subject to the outcome of aversive conditioning in captivity) or permanently; (2) clean up sites frequented by condors and, where possible, close such sites to vehicular access; (3) alter current management practices by providing food at multiple sites to encourage more natural foraging patterns and less dependence on single site food subsidy; (4) improve the quantity and quality of data collection at nests by employing full-time biologists and volunteers dedicated and trained to closely monitor condor reproduction throughout the breeding attempt; (5) identify nutritional deficiencies, if any, in the current condor diet and provision with alternative sources of lead-free food; (6) provide bone fragments directly to nests during the breeding effort; and (7) determine the significance of elevated copper and other heavy metals in the condor diet, particularly their impact on chick health and development.

Altering the current foraging patterns of reintroduced condors is contrary to recommendations to reduce condor mortality from lead poisoning by feeding at single sites (see Meretsky et al. 2000). However, most mortality in southern California in recent years has been chick mortality prior to fledging. Thus, it appears that management of condors is faced with a paradox: reduce the detrimental effects of provisioning at a single site by encouraging natural foraging patterns and experience higher mortality of free-flying birds, or reduce lead mortality by provisioning at a single site and suffer detrimental effects on chick survivorship. This paradox in unlikely to be solved until lead is removed from the condor range. Thus, removal of the threat of lead poisoning would allow more flexible and scientifically driven management of condor populations. We consider it extremely unlikely that a viable, self-sustaining breeding population can be established in southern California without addressing this all-pervasive limiting factor. Therefore, we support and encourage legislation to remove the threat of lead from the condor range in southern California as a prerequisite to attaining this central goal of the recovery effort.

ACKNOWLEDGMENTS

Many people contributed to the intensive effort to find, monitor and occasionally enter condor nests in southern California. Several thousand hours of nest data at 10 nests (2002–2005) were collected by many observers apart from the authors including: G. Austin, C. Barba, M. Barth, C. Beestman, J. Brandt, M. Cacciapaglia, J. Caldwell, E. Campbell, M. Dominguez, L. Drake, G. Druliner, P. Ensley, K.Fairclough, T. Fonzo, M. Hall, Z. Hambleton, R. Hilgris, S. Junker, K. Kontio, M. Lavelle, J. Lysoby, R. Nichols, D. Nonne, J. Parker, D. Pedersen, R. Posey, A, Prieto, N. Sandberg, S. Schierbinski, B. Shewmaker, T. Smith, T. Stansbury, M. Stockton, J. Szamos, D. Tappe, N. Todd, E. Weingert, C. West and L. Woolaver. Thanks go to the people who helped carry out nest visits as well as the unenviable task of retrieving dead or debilitated nestlings, especially Greg Austin (USFWS) and Mike Clark (LAZ). Drs. Cynthia Stringfield, Leah Greer (LAZ) and Jeff Zuba (SDWAP) provided expertise during health checks of nestlings in the wild. Dr. Bruce Rideout and pathologists at the San Diego

Zoo, especially Rebecca Papendick and April Gorow, carried out necropsies on nestlings. Dr. Steve Klause (LAZ) carried out emergency surgery to remove trash items as well as repairing a broken wing in one nestling. The condor facility keepers at LAZ, especially Mike Clark, Chandra David, Marti Jenkins and Debbie Sears, deserve huge credit for their constant care for condor nestlings (two to date) undergoing rehabilitation. A.M. thanks the Zoological Society of San Diego for their financial support over the past five years. J.H.'s more than 30 years of involvement and dedication to the survival and conservation of California Condors has been supported by SBNHM and the U.S. Fish and Wildlife Service (USFWS). J.S. was funded initially by USFWS (Apr-Sept 2004) to monitor nests, and later (October–January 2005), by the Zoological Society of San Diego through a grant from the Offield Foundation.

LITERATURE CITED

ALISAUSKAS, R. T., AND D. ANKNEY. 1994. Nutrition of breeding female Ruddy Ducks: the role of nutrient reserves. Condor 96:878–897.

BARTON, N. W. H., AND D. C. HOUSTON. 1993. A comparison of digestive efficiency in birds of prey. Ibis 135:363–371.

BARTON, N. W. H., AND D. C. HOUSTON. 1994. Morphological adaptation of the digestive tract in relation to feeding ecology of raptors. Journal of Zoology (London) 232:133–150.

BENSON, P. C., I. PLUG, AND J. C. DOBBS. 2004. An analysis of bones and other materials collected by Cape Vultures at the Kransberg and Blouberg colonies, Limpopo Province, South Africa. Ostrich 75:118–132.

BIGGINS, D. E., J. L. GODBEY, L. R. HANEBURY, B. LUCE, P. E. MARINARI, M. R. MATCHETT, AND A. VARGAS. 1998. The effect of rearing methods on survival of reintroduced black-footed ferrets. Journal of Wildlife Management 62:643–653.

BORELLO, W. D., AND R. M. BORELLO. 2002. The breeding status and colony dynamics of Cape Vulture *Gyps coprotheres* in Botswana. Bird Conservation International 12:79–97.

BROWN, C. J., AND I. PLUG. 1990. Food choice and diet of the Bearded Vulture *Gypaetus barbatus* in southern Africa. South African Journal of Zoology 25:169–177.

COLLINS, P. W., N. F. R. SNYDER, AND S. D. EMSLIE. 2000. Faunal remains in California Condor nest caves. Condor 102:222–227.

DOBBS, J. C., AND P. C. BENSON. 1984. Behavioral and metabolic responses to food deprivation in the Cape Vulture. Pages 211–214 *in* Proceedings of the 2nd Symposium on African Predatory Birds (J. M. Mandelsohn and C. W. Sapsford, Eds.). Natal Bird Club, Durban.

ELLIS, D. H., G. F. GEE, S. G. HEREFORD, G. H. OLSEN, T. D. CHISOLM, J. M. NICOLICH, K. A. SULLIVAN, N. J. THOMAS, M. NAGENDRAN, AND J. S. HATFIELD. 2000. Post-release survival of hand-reared and parent-reared Mississippi Sandhill Cranes. Condor 102:104–112.

FINLEY, W. L. 1906. Life history of the California Condor I. Finding a condor's nest. Condor 8:135–142.

FRY, D. M., AND J. R. MAURER. 2003. Assessment of lead contamination sources exposing California Condors. Final Report to California Department of Fish and Game, Sacramento.

HUIN, N., AND J. P. CROXALL. 1996. Fishing gear, oil and marine debris associated with seabirds at Bird Island, South Georgia, during 1993/1994. Marine Ornithology 24:19–22.

HUNT, W. G., C. N. PARISH, S. C. FARRY, T. G. LORD, AND R. SIEG. 2007. Movements of introduced California Condors in Arizona in relation to lead exposure. Pages 79–96 in California Condors in the 21st Century (A. Mee and L. S. Hall, Eds.). Series in Ornithology, no. 2.

JONES, C. G., W. HECK, R. E. LEWIS, Y. MUNGROO, G. SLADE, AND T. CADE. 1995. The restoration of the Mauritius Kestrel Falco punctatus. Ibis 137(Suppl. 1):S173–S180.

KLEIMAN, D. G., M. R. STANLEY PRICE, AND B. B. BECK. 1994. Criteria for reintroductions. Pages 288-303 in Creative Conservation: Interactive Management of Wild and Captive Animals (P. J. S. Olney, G. M. Mace, and A. T. C. Feistner, Eds.). Chapman & Hall, London, U.K.

KOFORD, C. B. 1953. The California Condor. National Audubon Research Report 4: 1–154.

LIITSCHWAGER, D., AND S. MIDDLETON. 2003. Hawaii's other kingdom. National Geographic, October, 70–88.

MACE, M. E. 2005. California Condor (Gymnogyps californianus) International Studbook. Zoological Society of San Diego, San Diego Wild Animal Park, Escondido, California.

MAYFIELD, H. 1961. Nest success calculated from exposure. Wilson Bulletin 73: 255–261.

MAYFIELD, H. 1975. Suggestions for calculating nest success. Wilson Bulletin 87: 456–466.

MEE, A., G. AUSTIN, M. BARTH, C. BEESTMAN, T. SMITH, AND M. WALLACE. 2004. Courtship behaviour in reintroduced California Condors: evidence for extra-pair copulations and female mate guarding. Pages 75–82 in Raptors Worldwide: Proceedings of VI World Conference on Birds of Prey and Owls (R. D. Chancellor and B.-U. Meyburg, Eds.). World Working Group on Birds of Prey and Owls/MME-Birdlife, Hungary.

MEE, A., B. A. RIDEOUT, J. A. HAMBER, J. N. TODD, G. AUSTIN, M. CLARK, AND M. P. WALLACE. 2007. Junk ingestion and nestling mortality in a reintroduced population of California Condors Gymnogyps californianus. Bird Conservation International 17:1–13.

MERETSKY, V. J., AND N. F. R. SNYDER. 1992. Range use and movements of California Condors. Condor 94:313–335.

MERETSKY, V. J., N. F. R. SNYDER, S. R. BEISSENGER, D. A. CLENDENEN, AND J. W. WILEY. 2000. Demography of the California Condor: implications for reestablishment. Conservation Biology 14:957–967.

MONAGHAN, P., J. D. UTTLEY, M. D. BURNS, C. THAINE AND J. BLACKWOOD. 1989. The relationship between food supply, reproductive effort and breeding success in Arctic Terns Sterna paradisaea. Journal of Animal Ecology 58:261–274.

Mundy, P. J., and J. A. Ledger. 1976. Griffon vultures, carnivores and bones. South African Journal of Science 72:106–110.

Nisbet, I. C. T. 1973. Courtship feeding, egg size and breeding success in Common Terns. Nature 241:141–142.

Parker, H., and H. Holm. 1990. Patterns of nutrient and energy expenditure in female Common Eiders nesting in the high Arctic. Auk 107:660–668.

Phillips, R. A., R. W. G. Caldow, and R. W. Furness. 1996. The influence of food availability on the breeding effort and reproductive success of Arctic Skuas *Stercorarius parasiticus*. Ibis 138:410–419.

Pierce, K. E., R. J. Harris, L. S. Larned, and M. A. Pokras. 2004. Obstruction and starvation associated with plastic ingestion in a Northern Gannet *Morus bassanus* and a Greater Shearwater *Puffinus gravis*. Marine Ornithology 32: 187–189.

Risebrough, R. W., R. Valencia, D. Clendenen, A. Z. Mason, P. H. Bloom, M. P. Wallace, and R. Mesta. 2001. Absence of demonstrable toxicity to Turkey Vultures, *Cathartes aura*, of copper and tungsten-tin-bismuth-composite pellets. Final Report to US Fish and Wildlife Service, California Condor Recovery Program, Ventura, CA, under Contract 14-48-0001-95822. The Bodega Bay Institute, Berkeley, CA. 14 pp.

Sarrazin, F., C. Bagnolini, J. L. Pinna, E. Danchin, and J. Clobert. 1994. High survival estimates of Griffon Vultures (*Gyps fulvus fulvus*) in a reintroduced population. Auk 111:853–862.

Sarrazin, F., C. Bagnolini, J. L. Pinna, E. Danchin, and J. Clobert. 1996. Breeding biology during establishment of a reintroduced Griffon Vulture *Gyps fulvus* population. Ibis 138:315–325.

Sarrazin, F., and R. Barbault. 1996. Reintroduction: challenges and lessons for basic ecology. Trends in Ecology and Evolution 11:474–478.

Sarrazin, F., and S. Legendre. 2000. Demographic approach to releasing adults versus young in reintroductions. Conservation Biology 14:488–500.

Schlaepfer, M. A., M. C. Runge, and P. W. Sherman. 2002. Ecological and evolutionary traps. Trends in Ecology and Evolution 17:474–480.

Scott, J. M., and J. W. Carpenter. 1987. Release of captive-reared or translocated endangered birds: what do we need to know? Auk 104:544–545.

Smith, D., and R. Easton. 1964. California Condor: Vanishing American. McNally and Loftin, Charlotte, NC.

Snyder, N. F. R. 2007. Limiting factors for wild California Condors. Pages 9–34 *in* California Condors in the 21st Century (A. Mee and L. S. Hall, Eds.). Series in Ornithology, no. 2.

Snyder, N. F. R., and J. A. Hamber. 1985. Replacement clutching and annual nesting of California Condors. Condor 87:374–378.

Snyder, N. F. R., and N. J. Schmitt. 2002. California Condor (*Gymnogyps californianus*). *In* Birds of North America, no. 610 (A. Poole and F. Gill, Eds.). The Birds of North America, Inc., Philadelphia, PA.

Snyder, N. F. R., and H. Snyder. 1989. Biology and conservation of the California Condor. Current Ornithology 6:175–267.

Snyder, N. F. R., and H. A. Snyder. 2000. The California Condor: A Saga of Natural History and Conservation. Academic Press, San Diego, CA.

TABAKA, C. S., D. E. ULREY, J. G. SIKARSKIE, S. R. DeBAR, AND P. K. KU. 1996. Diet, cast composition, energy and nutrient intake of Red-tailed Hawks (*Buteo jamaicensis*), Great-horned Owls (*Bubo virginianus*), and Turkey Vultures (*Cathartes aura*). Journal of Zoo and Wildlife Medicine 27:187–196.

WALLACE, M. P., M. FULLER, AND J. WILEY. 1994. Patagial transmitters for large vultures and condors. Pages 381–387 *in* Raptor Conservation Today: Proceedings of the IV World Conference on Birds of Prey and Owls (B.-U. Meyburg and R. D. Chancellor, Eds.). World Working Group for Birds of Prey. Pica Press, Shipman, VA.

WIEMEYER, S. N., A. KRYNITSKY, AND S. R. WILBUR. 1983. Environmental contaminants in tissues, foods, and feces of California condors. Pages 427–439 *in* Vulture Biology and Management (S. R. Wilbur and J. A. Jackson, Eds.). University of California Press, Berkeley.

WOODS, C. P., W. R. HEINRICH, S. C. FARRY, C. N. PARISH, S. A. H. OSBORN, AND T. J. CADE. 2007. Survival and reproduction of California Condors released in Arizona. Pages 57–78 *in* California Condors in the 21st Century (A. Mee and L. S. Hall, Eds.). Series in Ornithology, no. 2.

10

Lead Concentrations in the Blood of Big Sur California Condors

Kelly J. Sorenson[1] and L. Joseph Burnett

ABSTRACT.—Lead poisoning in California Condors (Gymnogyps californianus) was first documented in the 1980s and continues to be a major threat to the recovery of the species. We collected 126 independent blood samples from 33 free-flying individuals in Big Sur, Monterey County, California, between 1998 and 2006. Twenty-seven samples (21.4%) were above background (>20 µg dL⁻¹), four (3.2%) were clinically affected (60–99 µg dL⁻¹), and two (1.6%) were indicative of acute toxicity (≥100 µg dL⁻¹). Twenty-one individuals of the total exposed (64%) were exposed at least once and nine (27%) were exposed on two or more occasions. We found significant differences among calendar years, the number of years condors were in the wild, and month. Most notably, we found the months of September and October to be significantly higher than any other times of the year, most likely due to condors feeding on hunter-killed deer during the fall deer-hunting season. One condor from the Big Sur population died due to lead poisoning in southern California and two additional birds were treated for acute poisoning to prevent mortality. We also found that blood-lead levels increased significantly after one year in the wild. The threat of lead exposure in Big Sur appears to be less severe than in Arizona and southern California. Nonetheless all condors in the wild are at risk of lead poisoning.

Lead toxicity has long been recognized for its detrimental effects on the health of avian species. Mortality from lead poisoning has been extensively documented in both waterfowl and raptors (Locke and Thomas 1996, Kramer and Redig 1997, Fisher et al. 2006). During the late 1970s and early 1980s the endangered California Condor (*Gymnogyps californianus*) was significantly impacted by lead toxicity (Janssen et al. 1986, Weimeyer et al. 1988, Pattee et al. 1990). Data collected on the wild population

[1]Ventana Wildlife Society, 19045 Portola Drive, Suite F-1, Salinas, California 93908, USA. E-mail: kellysorenson@ventanaws.org

from 1981–1986 confirmed three California Condor deaths caused by lead poisoning (Janssen et al. 1986). The precipitous historic condor population decline continued into the '80s, prompting the U.S. Fish and Wildlife Service (USFWS) to remove eggs and nestlings from the wild and to trap the remaining wild condors to initiate a captive breeding program (Snyder and Snyder 1989, 2000). In 1987 the last free-flying condor was captured from the wild bringing the captive population to 27 individuals. Successful captive breeding efforts doubled the population within a few years (Kuehler and Witman 1988) and in 1992 the first captive-born condors were released into the wild in southern California (Snyder and Snyder 2000). By January 2006, 128 condors were free-flying in the wild following releases in California and Arizona, USA, and Baja California, Mexico.

The recovery goal set for California Condors is to establish at least two self-sustaining wild populations of 150 condors (Kiff et al. 1996). Ventana Wildlife Society, in cooperation with the USFWS, began releasing condors in Big Sur, Monterey County, California, in 1997. In 2003, a cooperative release effort between Ventana Wildlife Society and the National Park Service began at Pinnacles National Monument, San Benito County, approximately 45 km east of the Big Sur release site. By January 2006 the condor population in California stood at 57 individuals, including 37 in central California (28 in Big Sur and 13 at Pinnacles National Monument) and 20 in southern California.

California Condors forage exclusively on carrion (Koford 1953) and are known to ingest lead residues and fragments from carcasses shot with ammunition (Janssen et al. 1986, Weimeyer et al. 1986, Hunt et al. 2006). Although the timing of deer hunting seasons vary between release areas, condors in both Arizona and southern California have significantly higher blood-lead levels during those months (see Hall et al., Hunt et al. this volume). Lead poisoning accounted for six confirmed and two suspected deaths in Arizona from 1996 to 2005 and is the leading known cause of mortality in that population (Woods et al. this volume). In southern California a total of three condors have died from lead poisoning between 1992 and 2005, presenting a major limiting factor in recovery efforts in that region (see Hall et al. this volume). Given the extent of lead exposure in the recent historic and reintroduced populations, blood sampling for this toxin was initiated for Big Sur condors in 1998. The purpose of this present study is to determine whether wild condors in Big Sur have experienced any lead exposure events since releases began, and if so, to analyze exposure patterns.

METHODS

Study site.—The condor release site used for this project was located in Big Sur, Monterey County, California, on the western slope of the Santa

Lucia Mountains, 1 km east of the Pacific coastline, at an elevation of 818 m. The release pen (Fig. 1) consisted of an observation blind and a large netted aviary, 7.8 m wide × 14.1 m long × 9.4 m high. Captive breeding facilities in southern California (Los Angeles Zoo and San Diego Wild Animal Park) annually transferred condors at 3–9 months of age to the release site from 1997 to 2006. After arriving at the field site, condors were held in the release pen for a minimum acclimation period of 90 days. Young condors spent a majority of their acclimation period in the aviary portion of the release pen. The aviary contained natural perching, pool, perch scales, and a mock power-pole that was utilized for behavioral aversion training to counter potential landing on utilities following release (Snyder and Snyder 2000). An adult condor was placed temporarily in the aviary as a mentor to young release candidates (see Clark et al. this volume). Inside the aviary condors were primarily fed small to large-sized carcasses consisting of stillborn calves (*Bos taurus*), domestic rabbits (*Oryclolagus cuniculus*), and rats (*Rattus norvegicus*).

The first supplemental feeding station for condors post-release was established in a large grassy area adjacent to the release pen. In the first two years of releases, five additional supplemental feeding stations were

Fig. 1. Big Sur condor release pen with double-door trap visible on left (door open), Monterey County, California. Photo by Joe Burnett.

established north of the release site in suitable open grassland habitat at 800–1,200 m elevation. Food was randomly moved between the stations to promote food searching and to provide a non-lead food source for the birds. The principal foods provided at feeding stations were domestic rats, rabbits, and calves; secondary food items included black-tailed deer (*Odocoileus hemionus californicus*), feral pig (*Sus scrofa*), tule elk (*Cervus nannodes*), and domestic sheep (*Ovis aries*). We observed condors feeding at each station, as well as at non-proffered food sites (wild food), to record individual use and establish feeding histories.

Prior to release condors were fitted with patagially mounted VHF transmitters (Biotrack, Wareham, Dorset, United Kingdom), or PTT GPS satellite transmitters (Microwave Telemetry Inc.), to track post-release movements and to determine mortality causes. Individually unique wing-tags showing each condor's studbook number (see Mace 2006) were attached in conjunction with transmitters for visual verification in the field.

Trapping and lead sampling.—Recapturing condors for lead testing and routine transmitter replacements began in 1998 using a "walk-in" trap. We attempted to capture each bird at least once per year. The walk-in trap, 5 m^2 × 1.9 m in height, was made of chain-link fence with a netted roof. The trap was baited prior to a capture event to encourage condors to enter in and out. The trap door was closed using a rope pulley operated from an observation blind. A second trapping method was instituted in 1999 by adding a double-door trap system (Fig. 1) to the release pen's aviary. The double-door trap, 2 m^3, enabled biologists to capture individuals without handling and to hold them until processing. Doors were opened and closed using cable pulleys operated from inside the release pen's observation blind. The same baiting strategy was used in both types of walk-in trap.

In both trapping scenarios the handling and sampling of condors were the same. Condors were individually captured using a hand net and each bird was restrained by three people. An additional person collected an intravenous 3.0 mL blood sample from the medial-tarsal vein using a 21-ga. needle and heparinized storage tubes. On-site lead analysis was conducted on blood using a portable lead analyzer (Lead Care Blood Lead Testing System, ESA Inc., Chelmsford, Massachusetts) capable of measuring lead levels from 0 to 65 mg dL^{-1}. A 1.5 mL vial of blood was stored on ice and subsequently sent for laboratory analysis (Louisiana Animal Disease Diagnostic Laboratory, Baton Rouge, Louisiana). In most, but not all cases, a pre-release blood sample was collected. Pre-release blood samples collected at captive breeding facilities were submitted to the California Animal Health and Food Safety Lab system in Davis, California, IDEXX Veterinary Services or Antech Laboratories. We grouped the blood-lead results using the convention of Redig (1984) converted to µg dL^{-1}: <20 = background; 20 to 59 = exposed; 60 to 99 = clinically affected; ≥ 100 = acute toxicity.

Statistical analyses.—Fry and Maurer (2003) calculated the depuration rate of lead in condor blood to be 13.3 ± 6.5 days. In our analyses, we considered blood samples from the same individual as independent if they occurred more than 20 days apart. We tested for normality using the Kolmogorov-Smirnov One Sample Test and found that the data were not normally distributed, and therefore all tests used were nonparametric. We compared blood-lead results by calendar year, month, season, sex, and the number of years a condor was in the wild using Kruskal-Wallis One-Way Analyses of Variance (ANOVAs), and Mann-Whitney U-tests where appropriate. In addition, we used linear regression analysis (after natural log data transformations) to determine the relationship between blood-lead levels, years in the wild, and calendar year. We used Wilcoxon Signed-Rank tests to compare pre- and post-release samples within and after one year in the wild. Given the use of several different labs, we determined the least common denominator among all the lab's lower detection limit (3 µg dL^{-1}) and adjusted upwards all blood-lead values that were reported below this value so as to avoid artificial results. Only blood samples collected prior to individuals' first documented visits to southern California were used to determine lead exposure in Big Sur. We compared the blood-lead values between the portable lead analyzer and the laboratory result using a Wilcoxon Signed-Rank test as well as a linear regression analysis. However, only lab values for blood-lead were used in our analyses.

Results

Lead exposure.—A total of 126 independent blood-lead samples from 33 free-flying condors was collected between May 1998 and June 2006, during which time Ventana Wildlife Society biologists released 42 condors to the wild in Big Sur. Of the 126 samples, 69 were tested in the lab as well as measured using the field tester. Although there was a strong relationship between field and lead values ($R^2 = 0.744, P < 0.001$), lab values were on average 21% higher. Thus, only the lab results ($n = 126$) were used for the remaining analyses. Of the 126 post-release blood-lead samples, 33 (26.2%) were indicative of exposure (including six that showed clinical effects or acute poisoning events), and 93 (73.8%) were background. Total post-release blood-lead concentrations ranged from as low as 2.0 µg dL^{-1} to as high as 170.0 µg dL^{-1}. Twenty-one (64%) of free-flying individuals sampled were exposed at least once and nine (27%) were exposed on two or more occasions. The ratio of birds sampled relative to those in the wild varied from 38% (in 2004) to 100% (in 2000), while the percentage of birds exposed ranged from 0% to 50% (Fig. 2). We found no difference in blood-lead values between the sexes ($U = 1,752.0, P = 0.393$).

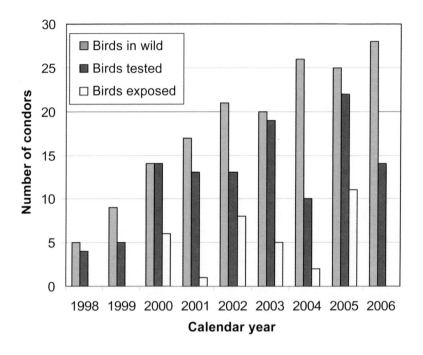

Fig. 2. Number of condors in the wild, blood-lead tested and exposed by calendar year. Five condors in 1998 were released on 12 December 1997. Note: in 2006, results were based on samples through June and not for the full calendar year.

Yearly variation.—We found significant variation in blood-lead levels among calendar years (F = 22.01, P = 0.005, n = 126). Yearly mean blood-lead levels ranged from 3.3 μg dL^{-1} to 29.7 μg dL^{-1} (Table 1), with 2005 being the worst year. Blood-lead levels also differed depending on the number of years a condor was in the wild (F = 31.15, P < 0.001), where levels were generally higher after the first year in the wild (Table 2). Mean lead values were highest during condors' sixth and eighth years in the wild (Table 2). We also found a significant difference among months of the year (F = 35.661, P < 0.001). Concerned that we were obtaining skewed results due to the inclusion of the two highest blood-lead values (100 and 170 μg dL^{-1}), we excluded these data and ran the same tests; however variation among calendar years (n = 124, F = 20.70, P = 0.008), years in the wild (F = 29.57, P = 0.001), and month (F = 40.33, P < 0.001) remained significant. We compared the variation among six, two-month periods (Table 3) and found a significant difference in blood lead levels (F = 29.35, P < 0.001), with the September–October period showing the highest levels (mean = 30.4 ± SD 19.5, n = 31).

Table 1. Yearly variation in blood-lead levels (μg dL^{-1}) of California Condors at Big Sur, California, 1998–2006.

Year	n	Mean blood-level	Min	Max	SD
1998	4	3.3	2	6	1.9
1999	5	8.8	3	17	6.7
2000	14	20.1	2	62	20.1
2001	18	10.1	2	37	8.5
2002	20	21.0	5	80	21.0
2003	19	22.0	2	100	24.3
2004	10	11.7	2	29	8.6
2005	22	29.7	3	170	36.3
2006[a]	14	7.9	2	19	5.1

[a] Data analysis includes results up to June 2006.

Table 2. Variation in blood-lead levels (μg dL^{-1}) of California Condors at Big Sur, California, by the number of years condors were in the wild between 1998 and 2006.

Year(s) in wild	n	Mean blood-lead levels	Min	Max	SD
1	18	5.6	2	46	10.5
2	36	14.4	2	38	11.5
3	18	26.1	3	80	22.1
4	14	21.3	2	100	24.4
5	19	17.2	5	61	14.0
6	11	29.1	4	170	48.4
7	4	16.8	4	42	17.3
8	4	29.8	8	76	31.8
9	2	9.5	5	14	6.4

Table 3. Bi-monthly variation in blood-lead levels (μg dL^{-1}) of California Condors in Big Sur, California, 1998–2006.

Months	n	Mean blood-lead levels	Min	Max	SD
January–February	3	8.0	4	15	6.1
March–April	11	9.9	3	22	5.8
May–June	38	14.7	2	100	19.4
July–August	23	9.4	2	38	8.4
September–October	31	30.4	3	80	19.5
Nov–December	20	19.5	2	170	36.2

Movements and post-release exposure.— Of the 33 birds sampled during this study, 21 condors (64%) released in Big Sur made at least one visit to southern California whereas 8 (24%) had not yet made the trip by June 2006; 3 (9%) were removed from the population; and 1 (3%) died prior

to making a first trip. One bird remained in the Big Sur area for nearly
four years and has yet to visit southern California. Of those that did visit
southern California they did so for the first time an average of nearly two
years after release (mean ± SD = 1.9 ± 0.55). Of the 33 total individuals
sampled, blood was sampled in 25 prior to their initial release. Of those
that were sampled before their initial release, 16 condors were also sampled
before visiting southern California and within one year in the wild, and 13
(many of the same individuals) were also sampled after one year in the
wild. Therefore, 29 post-release samples were tested versus 25 pre-release
samples. We found no difference between pre-release blood-lead samples
and those collected within one year of release in Big Sur ($Z = -0.911$, $P =$
0.362, $n = 16$). However, blood-lead samples of free-flying Big Sur condors
after one year in the wild were significantly higher than pre-release values
($Z = 2.090$, $P = 0.037$, $n = 13$).

We documented Big Sur condors feeding routinely at the supplemental
feeding stations as well as at sites where non-proffered food items were
found by condors. Between March 1999 and June 2006, we documented
condors feeding on 26 non-proffered food items in Big Sur, including
20 (76.9%) California sea lions (*Zalophus californianus californianus*),
3 (11.5%) black-tailed deer, and single (3.8%) tule elk, gray whale
(*Eschrichitus robustus*), and domestic cattle.

Discussion

Our study found that 26% (33 of 126) of the blood samples for
California Condors released between 1998 and 2006 in Big Sur showed
exposure to lead above background levels. Of these samples, condors were
clinically or acutely affected in six cases. Blood-lead levels in condors in
September and October were significantly higher than in all the remaining
months combined. Also, blood-lead samples of free-flying Big Sur condors
after one year in the wild were significantly higher than their pre-release
values, indicating that Big Sur condors are experiencing lead exposure
similarly to all of the other populations of recovered condors (e.g., Parish
et al. this volume, Hall et al. this volume).

Although the overall threat of lead exposure to condors in Big Sur
(26% above background) was less than that documented in southern
California (44%; Hall et al. this volume) and Arizona (40%; Parish et al.
this volume), it is still very significant, indicating that ingestion of lead
by condors is occurring at an alarming rate. In Big Sur, no deaths of condors specifically due to lead ingestion occurred during the present study.
However, one Big Sur condor died in June 2003 of severe visceral gout
complicated by lead poisoning in southern California. In addition, 2 acute
lead poisoning events were recorded in Big Sur condors, whereas there were

6 such acute exposures in southern California (Hall et al. this volume) and 25 in northern Arizona (Parish et al. this volume). However, it should be noted that southern California and northern Arizona sampled more birds (214 and 437 samples from 44 and 50 birds respectively) up to the end of 2005 (Hall et al., Parish et al. this volume).

The majority of hunter-shot deer occur in August and September within the coast ranges where Big Sur is located (Fry and Maurer 2003), which may explain why blood-lead levels in condors in September and October were significantly higher than in all the remaining months combined. As has been shown in other, recent condor studies (e.g., Hall et al., Hunt et al., Parish et al. this volume), fall lead exposure events seem to be tied to the deer hunting season, since whole deer carcasses or lead-contaminated gut piles left in the field in mid- to late August are commonly eaten by scavengers such as condors. Lead exposure due to ingestion of bullet fragments or lead shot in carrion has also been widely reported for scavenging raptors where poisoning events often closely track the hunting seasons for food sources of these species (see review in Fisher et al. 2006).

The most likely explanation for why blood-lead levels in Big Sur are less severe than those in the other reintroduced populations, is the unique marine influence and a strong preference among Big Sur condors for sea lion carrion, which accounted for nearly 77% of their non-proffered diet during our study. In roughly the same time period, 78 cases of deer foraging were documented in Arizona (Hunt et al. this volume) whereas we only found three such cases. Nevertheless, Big Sur condors overlap in range with southern California birds and all individuals in California are at risk of exposure to lead poisoning, some of which can be fatal.

Replacement of lead ammunition with non-toxic ammunition must be a top priority for the California Condor Recovery Program. Arizona Department of Game and Fish implemented a non-lead coupon program for deer hunters in 2005, during which they provided hunters the opportunity to receive non-lead ammunition free of charge. Of those hunters that used non-lead ammunition, 93% stated that it performed as good or better than lead, and 72% would recommend its use to other hunters (Sullivan et al. this volume). While a prohibition on the use of lead ammunition in California would be the most direct way to address the issue, we are concerned that enforcement would prove to be challenging due to difficulties differentiating between lead and non-lead bullets and a current lack of law enforcement personnel in the field. Given the positive results of the Arizona coupon program, we recommend that a similar effort—coupled with a prohibition—be implemented within the range of the condor in California, particularly if voluntary efforts alone do not solve the problem.

SORENSON AND BURNETT

ACKNOWLEDGMENTS

We thank the veterinary staff at the Zoological Society of San Diego and the Los Angeles Zoo for blood sampling of condors prior to their transport to the field. Condor capture and blood sampling assistance in Big Sur was provided by Jessica Koning, Eric Stover, Marylise Levefre, Shay Hillary, Curt Mykut, and Sayre Flannagan. We thank Michael Murray DVM, for his unwavering veterinary support. We want to especially thank Sal and Ada Lucido for their long time dedication and making the Big Sur release site a reality.

LITERATURE CITED

CLARK, M., M. WALLACE, AND C. DAVID. 2007. Rearing California Condors for release using a modified puppet-rearing technique. Pages 213–226 in California Condors in the 21st Century (A. Mee and L. S. Hall, Eds.). Series in Ornithology, no. 2.

FISHER, I. J., D. J. PAIN, AND V. G. THOMAS. 2006. A review of lead poisoning from ammunition sources in terrestrial birds. Biological Conservation 131:421–432.

FRY, D. M., AND J. R. MAURER. 2003. Assessment of lead contamination sources exposing California Condors. Final Report to the California Department of Fish and Game, Sacramento.

HALL, M., J. GRANTHAM, R. POSEY, AND A. MEE. 2007. Lead exposure among reintroduced California Condors in southern California. Pages 139–162 in California Condors in the 21st Century (A. Mee and L. S. Hall, Eds.). Series in Ornithology, no. 2.

HUNT, W. G., W. BURNHAM, C. N. PARISH, K. K. BURNHAM, B. MUTCH, AND J. L. OAKS. 2006. Bullet fragments in deer remains: implications for lead exposure in avian scavengers. Wildlife Society Bulletin 34:167–170.

HUNT, W. G., C. N. PARISH, S. C. FARRY, T. G. LORD, AND R. SIEG. 2007. Movements of introduced California Condors in Arizona in relation to lead exposure. Pages 79–96 in California Condors in the 21st Century (A. Mee and L. S. Hall, Eds.). Series in Ornithology, no. 2.

JANSSEN, D. L., J. E. OOSTERHUIS, J. L. ALLEN, M. P. ANDERSON, D. G. KELTS, AND S. N. WIEMEYER. 1986. Lead poisoning in free-ranging California condors. Journal of the American Veterinary Medical Association 189:1115–1117.

KIFF, L. F., R. I. MESTA, AND M. P. WALLACE. 1996.Recovery Plan for the California Condor . U.S. Fish and Wildlife Service, Portland, Oregon.

KOFORD, C. B. 1953. The California Condor. National Audubon Research Report 4: 1–154.

KRAMER, J. L., AND P. T. REDIG. 1997. Sixteen years of lead poisoning in eagles, 1980–95: an epizootiologic view. Journal of Raptor Research 31:327–332.

KUEHLER, C. M., AND P. N. WITMAN. 1988. Artificial incubation of California Condor Gymnogyps californianus eggs removed from the wild. Zoo Biology 7:123–132.

LOCKE, L. N., AND N. J. THOMAS. 1996. Lead poisoning of waterfowl and raptors. Pages 108–117 in Noninfectious Diseases of Wildlife, 2nd edition (A. Fairbrother, L. N. Locke and G. L. Huff, Eds.). Iowa State University Press, Ames, Iowa.

MACE, M. E. 2006. California Condor (*Gymnogyps californianus*) International Studbook. Zoological Society of San Diego, San Diego Wild Animal Park, Escondido, CA.

PARISH, C. N., W. R. HEINRICH, AND W. G. HUNT. 2007. Lead exposure, diagnosis, and treatment in California Condors released in Arizona. Pages 97–108 *in* California Condors in the 21st Century (A. Mee and L. S. Hall, Eds.). Series in Ornithology, no. 2.

PATTEE, O. H., P. H. BLOOM, J. M. SCOTT, AND M. R. SMITH. 1990. Lead hazards within the range of the California Condor. Condor 92:931–937.

SNYDER, N. F. R., AND H. SNYDER. 1989. Biology and conservation of the California Condor. Current Ornithology 6:175–267.

SNYDER, N. F. R., AND H. A. SNYDER. 2000. The California Condor: A Saga of Natural History and Conservation. Academic Press, San Diego, CA.

SULLIVAN, K., R. SIEG, AND C. PARISH. 2007. Arizona's efforts to reduce lead exposure in California Condors. Pages 109–122 *in* California Condors in the 21st Century (A. Mee and L. S. Hall, Eds.). Series in Ornithology, no. 2.

WOODS, C. P., W. R. HEINRICH, S. C. FARRY, C. N. PARISH, S. A. H. OSBORN, AND T. J. CADE. 2007. Survival and reproduction of California Condors released in Arizona. Pages 57–78 *in* California Condors in the 21st Century (A. Mee and L. S. Hall, Eds.). Series in Ornithology, no. 2.

WIEMEYER, S. N., R. M. JUREK, AND J. R. MOORE. 1986. Environmental contaminants in surrogates, foods, and feces of California Condors (*Gymnogyps californianus*). Environmental Monitoring and Assessment 6:91–111.

WIEMEYER, S. N., J. M. SCOTT, M. P. ANDERSON, P. H. BLOOM, AND C. J. STAFFORD. 1988. Environmental contaminants in California Condors. Journal of Wildlife Management 52:238–247.

11

A Quantitative Assessment of the California Condor Mentoring Program

Anna T. Bukowinski,[1,3] *Fred B. Bercovitch,*[1]
Allison C. Alberts,[1] *Mike P. Wallace,*[1]
Michael E. Mace,[2] *and Sergio Ancona*[1]

ABSTRACT.—The California Condor (*Gymnogyps californianus*) mentoring program was developed in order to address the concern that young puppet-reared condors exhibited unacceptable levels of maladaptive behavior when released to the wild. The purpose of our study was to quantitatively assess the efficacy of this mentoring program. We collected behavioral data in 2004 and 2005 on a cohort of young condors living with an adult mentor. Data collection occurred in two contexts: while the cohort was housed at the San Diego Wild Animal Park prior to their transfer to the release site; and at the release site in the Sierra de San Pedro Mártir National Park in Baja California, Mexico, where they were placed with a new adult mentor. We found that the social relationships established early in life were retained in the pre-release pen, and that the dominance hierarchy among peers remained consistent across contexts. The dominance hierarchy based upon social interactions differed from the hierarchy based upon feeding order. At the field site, the lowest ranking bird, who was also the one interacting least with the other birds, was the last to emerge from the pre-release pen and remained solitary after release. Although our sample size was limited, our results indicated that systematic assessment of social behavior prior to release can serve as a good predictor of initial post-release activity. Ultimately, pre-release behavioral assessment may also be useful in predicting the long-term success and survival of release candidates.

[1]*Conservation and Research for Endangered Species, Zoological Society of San Diego, 15600 San Pasqual Valley Road, Escondido, California 92027, USA.*
[2]*San Diego Wild Animal Park, Zoological Society of San Diego, 15500 San Pasqual Valley Road, Escondido, California 92027, USA.*
[3]*E-mail: abukowinski@sandiegozoo.org*

California Condors (*Gymnogyps californianus*) are monogamous, solitary breeders, but, similar to other scavenging birds, they often congregate in large groups to feed at carcasses (Koford 1953; Snyder and Snyder 1989, 2000), where priority of access to food appears to be at least partly determined by social rank. These complex social dynamics require development of appropriate social behaviors. California Condors typically attain breeding age at around five to six years old, so they have a period of several years to refine social and foraging skills (Snyder and Snyder 2000, Wallace 2000). Young condors learn their survival skills, including appropriate social behaviors, through interactions with other condors (Wallace 2000, Alagona 2004). In the wild, young condors learn these skills primarily from their parents, during a relatively long period of dependence ranging from 12 to 18 months (Snyder and Snyder 2000).

Since the mid-1980s, captive breeding and, more recently, the release of juvenile condors have been employed to reestablish condor populations in the wild (Snyder and Snyder 1989, Kiff et al. 1996). In order to increase productivity in captivity, breeding pairs are often double-clutched, with the first clutch of eggs removed from the parents for artificial incubation (Kuehler and Witman 1988, Kiff et al. 1996). Chicks that hatch from artificially incubated eggs are then puppet-reared according to methods developed using Andean Condors (*Vultur gryphus*) as a surrogate species (Bruning 1983, Wallace and Temple 1987a). Although this method has been successful for one of the program's goals (i.e. increasing the number of chicks produced), it has introduced some problems into the release program in the form of high rates of maladaptive behavior exhibited by the puppet-reared birds (Meretsky et al. 2000, 2001; Snyder and Snyder 2000). In early release years, birds that were puppet-reared in captivity lacked parental role models to guide their social development. Instead, the young condors were socialized together in small groups from 30 days of age until post-fledging release (at six months of age or older), with emphasis on maintaining visual and auditory isolation from humans (Wallace 1991). When these birds were released, they often did not have the social skills necessary to integrate into the condor social structure (Cade et al. 2004). In addition, they lacked wariness of humans (Meretsky et al. 2001).

Several studies have shown that hand-rearing animals for release can lead to behavioral deficiencies, including: abnormal reproductive behavior (Hutchins et al. 1995, Curio 1998, Myers et al. 1988); impaired parental behavior (Hutchins et al. 1995, Curio 1998); lack of predator recognition and avoidance (Brakhage 1953, Hill and Robertson 1988, Snyder et al. 1994); tameness (Curio 1998); and compromised social competence (Meder 1989, Martin 2005). These behavioral deficiencies can lead to reduced survival of hand-reared versus parent-reared animals when released to the wild (Brakhage 1953, Hill and Robertson 1988, Snyder et al. 1994).

Solutions to these problems can involve a variety of strategies, including puppet-rearing (Bruning 1983, Valutis and Marzluff 1999), costume-rearing (Horwich 1989, Ellis et al. 2000), foster or surrogate-rearing (Ellis et al. 1977, Biggins 1998), and group-rearing with conspecifics (Ellis et al. 1977, Biggins 1998). These strategies have been used individually and in combination. All of these methods have been shown to alleviate the above behavioral problems and improve survival after release (Ellis et al. 1977, 2000; Horwich 1989; Biggins et al. 1998; Valutis and Marzluff 1999).

In recent years, puppet-rearing protocols have been modified in an attempt to raise condors that are better prepared for integration in the wild (Clark et al. this volume). All chicks are initially reared alone, rather than with other nestlings. Also, to emulate parental treatment of chicks, condor caretakers are assertive in their treatment of chicks with the hand-puppet, encouraging chicks to become more submissive. At 30 days old each chick is moved into a facility that allows visual access to mature condors (Clark et al. this volume). In addition, mentoring programs have been implemented at captive breeding facilities located at the San Diego Wild Animal Park, the Los Angeles Zoo, the Peregrine Fund's World Center for Birds of Prey, and the Oregon Zoo. The premise of the mentoring program is that a cohort of immature birds will have a greater likelihood of integrating with a wild population if they have developed proper social skills under the tutelage of an adult bird (Cohn 1999, Alagona 2004). Once chicks fledge at around five to six months of age, they are transferred to a large outdoor pen and housed with an adult condor, which serves as a mentor, and with other fledglings of similar age. The young condors remain in this social environment for 6–12 months prior to release. With the mentor's guidance, they are expected to learn how to interact and integrate socially with other individuals, as well as acquire other appropriate social behaviors (Clark et al. this volume).

The first field studies of California Condors began in the 1930s (see Robinson 1939, 1940; Koford 1953), followed by more recent systematic efforts beginning in the 1950s (see Snyder and Snyder 1989, 2000 for a review of previous research). Despite the considerable amount of information these studies contributed, quantitative data are still lacking about the social behavior and social structure of California Condors. This makes it difficult to evaluate the efficacy of the current mentoring program, because specific information is not available about the behaviors that might be indicative of juvenile readiness for release into the wild. The current study was initiated with the intention of providing the type of information that makes these evaluations possible.

For this study, we collected systematic data on a cohort of four puppet-reared young condors destined for release to the wild. Data were collected at both their rearing site at the San Diego Wild Animal Park, and their release site in the Sierra de San Pedro Mártir National Park, Baja California, Mexico. A different adult condor served as a mentor to the birds at each site. We collected behavioral data aimed at the following specific goals: (1) to describe the social dynamics among the cohort and their mentor, and how they varied with time and context; (2) to determine the hierarchical structure of the group, including the rank of each individual; (3) to identify specific patterns of behavior for use in evaluating individuals' prospects for success in the wild; and (4) to evaluate the potential of these techniques as a tool for increasing the probability of future successful reintroduction of condors to the wild.

METHODS

Study population.—Subjects for this study were four puppet-reared juvenile condors hatched at the San Diego Wild Animal Park (SDWAP) in 2004, and two adult female condors that served as mentors, one at the SDWAP and one at the release site in Baja California. All individual condors are assigned unique identification numbers (studbook numbers) as a primary tool in genetic and conservation management of the captive and release populations (e.g., see Ralls and Ballou 2004, Mace 2005). Studbook (SB) numbers of our study subjects and other individual details are provided in Table 1.

Each chick was reared in total isolation from humans, with all feeding and handling performed with a puppet that closely resembled an adult condor (Wallace 1994, Snyder and Snyder 2000). The SDWAP mentor was hatched and puppet-reared at the Los Angeles Zoo (LAZ) in 1996

Table 1. California Condor mentoring study subjects.

Studbook number	Sex	Hatch date	Pre-transfer wt (kg)[a]	Fledge date[b]	Transfer date[c]	Release date[d]
Juveniles						
321	F	19 Mar 2004	8.0	24 Aug 2004	4 Apr 2005	22 Jul 2005
322	F	24 Mar 2004	8.2	2 Sept 2004	4 Apr 2005	22 Jul 2005
323	M	29 Mar 2004	8.6	9 Sept 2004	4 Apr 2005	22 Jul 2005
325	M	5 Apr 2004	8.5	16 Sept 2004	4 Apr 2005	22 Jul 2005
Wild Animal Park mentor						
141	F	28 Apr 1996	N/A	N/A	N/A	N/A
Release site mentor						
64	F	8 Apr 1991	N/A	N/A	N/A	N/A

[a] Weight recorded during examination prior to transfer to the release site.

[b] Date juvenile introduced into pen with SDWAP mentor.

[c] Date juveniles transferred to pre-release pen in the Sierra de San Pedro Mártir National Park.

[d] Date juveniles released into the wild in the Sierra de San Pedro Mártir National Park.

and transferred to the SDWAP later that year. The release site mentor was hatched and puppet-reared at the LAZ in 1991. This female was originally released in January 1992 in southern California, but was returned to captivity in April 1994 due to concerns about her long-term survival in the wild. She has been housed at the release site in Baja California since 2002 (Mace 2005).

Rearing site.—During data collection at the SDWAP, the juveniles and their mentor were housed in a semi-natural outdoor enclosure situated on a hillside in an off-exhibit area on the northeast side of the SDWAP. The enclosure consisted of a single large flight pen, with three adjacent smaller holding pens along the west side (Condor Release Pens [CRPs] 1, 2, and 3 from south to north), and a blind at the north end. A single nest cave was attached to each of the three CRPs. The large flight pen measured 30.5 m × 12.2 m with height ranging from 4.6 m to 7.6 m. The flight pen was equipped with three artificial perching trees, a pool for water, and a utility pole wired to deliver a mild electric charge for aversion training. This technique was designed to discourage condors from landing on utility poles after their release to the wild. The CRPs each measured 6.1 m × 12.2 m, with height ranging from 2.1 m to 5.5 m. Each CRP was also equipped with two perching poles and a pool for water. Condor Release Pen 3 was also equipped with a chute through which food could be dropped.

The condor chicks were initially housed at the Condor Conservation Breeding Facility at the SDWAP. Once the nestlings were old enough to feed themselves (at approximately 30 days old), they were transferred to individual nest boxes where they each had visual contact with an adult condor. As the young condors reached fledging age, they were introduced individually into CRP3 with the adult condor that would serve as their mentor (SB #141). When all four fledglings had been introduced and acclimated, the group was given access to the larger flight pen. The door between the two pens remained open to allow the birds access to the holding pen where food was delivered through the chute. The condors were provided with food four days a week, between 0800 and 1400 hours, and fasted on three nonconsecutive days of the week. Their diet consisted of rabbits, rats, trout, beef spleens, and carnivore meat diet.

Release site.—At about one year old, the four juveniles were transferred, on 4 April 2005, to their release site located in the Sierra de San Pedro Mártir National Park in northern Baja California, Mexico. Upon transfer, the juveniles were housed in a pre-release pen with their new mentor (SB #64). The pre-release pen measured 18.3 m × 18.3 m × 9.1 m high. A blind was located on the southern side of the pen. The four juveniles were later released into the wild as a group on 22 July 2005. At the release site food was provided opportunistically, usually two or three times in any given two-week period. Food items included parts and carcasses of goats, cows and dogs.

Data collection.—Data at the SDWAP were collected using both video and live observations. The blind situated at the northern end of the flight pen was equipped with three one-way glass windows, two looking into the flight pen, and one looking into CRP3. The blind was also equipped with a digital video camera, a digital video recorder, and a DVD burner. Video recording took place on days that the birds were supplied with fresh food. The camera was aimed through the window into CRP3, where the food was dropped. Recording was started immediately after the food was offered. The video was later transferred to DVD for behavioral sampling and coding. Live observations were conducted from inside the blind on one or two fasting days each week.

During both video and live observations, we conducted 15-min focal animal samples (Altmann 1974). Focal order was rotated independently for feeding and fasting days. Each 15-min sample was divided into 30-s intervals. Behavioral data were collected using instantaneous, all-occurrence, and one/zero scoring (Altmann 1974). We recorded behaviors in four categories: proximity of the subjects to each other, feeding behavior, affiliative behavior, and dominance-related behavior (Table 2). In order to evaluate the utility of feeding ranks for estimating dominance hierarchy, we also recorded the order in which the individuals fed each day fresh food was provided. All data at the release site were recorded during live focal animal observations. While the condors were housed in the pre-release pen, observations were conducted from inside the blind, three days a week, four times each day (two morning and two afternoon sessions, each lasting 15 min). All other data collection methods were the same as described above.

Data analysis.—Raw data were converted to rates (number of events observed per 15 min) and proportions of intervals during which a behavior was observed. From these, we calculated mean rates and proportions for interactions for each dyad at each study site. Samples in which the focal animal was in view for less than 10 min were excluded from calculations. Data analyses were based on approximately 27 h of observation at the SDWAP and approximately 109 h of observation at the release site. Further, the proportion of observation time was distributed equally across subjects.

Mean rates and proportions were used to construct sociograms for different types of interactions between the dyads. A sociogram is a diagram depicting patterns of interactions between individuals in a group. Relative rates and percentages are represented by arrows between the individuals, the thicker the arrow, the more frequent or prevalent the interaction. Double-headed arrows depict mutual behaviors, while single-headed arrows depict directional behaviors, with the arrow pointing from the actor to the recipient. We constructed sociograms for proximity, affiliative behavior, and dominance interactions for each of the sites. Affiliative activities included physical contact, preening, and mutual play, while dominance interactions were based on both displacements and avoidance (see Table 2). The mean rate of interactions in which an individual was dominant was the sum of the mean rate of displacements by that individual plus the mean rate at which that individual was avoided. In the sociograms, the arrow pointing away from the individual reflects the rate of interactions in which that individual was dominant. We also used the dominance measures (displacements plus avoidance) to conduct a hierarchy analysis. We performed a matrix analysis to test for a linear hierarchy among the juveniles and their mentor at each of the sites. These analyses were performed in Microsoft EXCEL X for Mac, using MATMAN 1.0 (Noldus Information Technology 1998).

To analyze feeding order, a bird that was first to feed was given a rank of 1, second to feed was 2, etc. Feeding order data were included only if at least four of the five birds were observed feeding. We performed a Friedman test to determine whether or not feeding ranks differed between the birds at either site. For a significant Friedman test, in order to determine where differences existed we performed post-hoc multiple comparisons according to the method described in Conover (1980). Friedman tests were performed using STATVIEW 5.0.1, and multiple comparisons were performed in EXCEL.

RESULTS

Proximity.—The percentage of time spent in proximity was greatest among juveniles #321, #322, and #325 at the SDWAP (Plate 21). This pattern of interactions persisted at the release site. Juvenile #323 spent relatively little time in proximity to other birds at either site. The SDWAP mentor also spent relatively little time in proximity to the other birds at the SDWAP. The release site mentor, on the other hand, spent much more time in proximity to juveniles #321, #322, and #325, but still very little time in proximity to juvenile #323.

Affiliative behavior.—Affiliative behavior was most prevalent among juveniles #321, #322, and #325 at the SDWAP (Plate 22). This association decreased at the release site, but the relative prevalence remained highest between juveniles #321 and #322 and between juveniles #321 and #325. Juvenile #323 spent relatively little time engaged in affiliative behavior at both sites, and his involvement in such interactions decreased in frequency from the SDWAP to the release site. The SDWAP mentor was not observed engaging in any affiliative behavior with the juveniles, and the release site mentor spent relatively little time engaging in such behaviors.

Dominance.—For the dominance sociograms, the directions of the interactions are more meaningful than the rates (Plate 23). For example, although rates of interaction in which the SDWAP mentor was dominant

Table 2. Operational definitions and scoring methods for California Condor mentoring study behaviors.

Behavior	Operational definition	Scoring method
Proximity		
Near	Bird within 4.5 m of focal bird	Instantaneous
Distant	No other bird within 4.5 m of focal bird	Instantaneous
Feeding		
Feeds with others	Birds within 4.5 m of focal bird while it feeds	Instantaneous
Feeds alone	Focal bird feeding alone (i.e., no other bird within 4.5 m while it feeds)	Instantaneous
Feeding order	Order in which each bird feeds	N/A
Affiliative Behaviors		
Preen	Bird preens, nibbles or rubs another with head, beak or neck, or wing tags	One/zero
Physical contact	Two birds lie, sit or stand while touching; birds may twine necks around each other	One/zero
Mutual play with object	Two birds manipulate or play with same object or food item at same time	One/zero
Dominance Behaviors		
Displace	Bird takes over another's perch, food, play object, preening partner, or other resource	All-occurrence
Avoid	Bird A abandons its perch, food, play object, preening partner, or other resource, as a result of bird B's behavior directed toward bird A	All-occurrence

were clearly much greater than those for the release site mentor, both mentors were always dominant in these interactions. Juvenile #325 was dominant to juveniles #321, #322, and #323 at both sites, and subordinate to both mentors. Juvenile #321 was dominant to juvenile #323 at both sites and subordinate to juvenile #325 and the mentor at both sites. The relationship between juveniles #321 and #322 was somewhat bi-directional at the SDWAP, although the rate of interactions in which juvenile #321 was dominant was lower than the rate of interactions in which juvenile #322 was dominant. At the release site, juvenile #322 was always dominant to juvenile #321. Juvenile #322 was also dominant to juvenile #323 at both sites, and subordinate to juvenile #325 and the mentor at both sites. Juvenile #323 was always subordinate to all of the other birds at both of the sites.

Hierarchy and feeding order.—The dominance relationships determined by focal sampling support the results of the hierarchy analysis (Plate 23). Landau's linearity index, h', had a value of 1.0, indicating a perfect linear hierarchy, for both of the sites. This value was statistically significant for both sites ($\chi^2 = 84$, df = 60, $P < 0.025$). The linear order, identical at both of the sites, from most to least dominant, was: (1) mentor, (2) juvenile #325, (3) juvenile #322, (4) juvenile #321, (5) juvenile #323.

Feeding rank differed significantly at both sites (SDWAP: $\chi^2 = 46.0$, df = 4, $P < 0.001$; release site: $\chi^2 = 30.7$, df = 4, $P < 0.001$). Multiple comparisons revealed that the birds fell into distinct feeding rank groups at each of the sites. Feeding ranks between birds in the same rank group could not be statistically differentiated. At the SDWAP, there were three rank groups, which were, from first to last to feed: (1) mentor; (2) juvenile #322; and (3) juveniles #321, #323, and #325. At the release site there were two rank groups, which were, from first to last to feed: (1) juveniles #321, #322, and #325; and (2) mentor and juvenile #323.

Post-release observations.—The four juveniles were released from captivity on 22 July 2005. Juveniles #321, #322, and #325 left the release pen 2 h after the door was opened, while juvenile #323 did not leave until 4.5 h later. After leaving the pen, juveniles #321, #322, and #325 stayed together, and were soon seen feeding together. Juvenile #323, on the other hand, flew away from the others and remained alone. Eleven days after the release, juvenile #323 approached some of the field crew, after which he was recaptured and returned to captivity.

DISCUSSION

Our results suggested a relationship between social dynamics among young condors in captivity and their initial success following release into the wild. However, it is important to keep in mind that our sample size was limited to one cohort and collection of data for additional cohorts will be necessary to confirm our findings.

The pre-release data revealed several significant patterns of association among the four juveniles and each of their two mentors. Juveniles #321, #322, and #325 formed a socially bonded group, as was reflected by the large amount of time spent in proximity to one another, and by their relatively high rates of affiliative interactions. These patterns were observed at both the SDWAP and the Baja California release site. Juvenile #323 was always a peripheral member of the group. He spent very little time in proximity to any other bird and rarely engaged in affiliative behavior.

The two mentors exhibited quite different patterns of behavior and interaction with the juveniles. The SDWAP mentor spent little time in proximity to any of the juveniles and never engaged in affiliative interactions with any of them. The release site mentor, on the other hand, spent much more time in proximity to some of the juveniles, and engaged in limited affiliative behavior.

Among Andean Condors a dominance hierarchy is established according to age and sex, with adults being the most dominant, followed by subadults, then juveniles. Within an age class, males are typically dominant to females (Donázar and Feijóo 2002). Unpublished data suggest that a similar age-related structure exists among California Condors (A. Mee unpubl. data). However, there is one key difference between Andean Condors and California Condors that could influence the hierarchical structure of each species: among Andean Condors, males and females are sexually dimorphic, with males being significantly larger than females, whereas there is no apparent sexual dimorphism in California Condors (Houston 1994). This difference could specifically be played out in the ranking of males versus females among California Condors since body size is a trait that is commonly reflected in a social hierarchy (Searcy 1979, Robinson-Wolrath and Owens 2003).

We found that a perfect linear hierarchy was established among the four juveniles and their mentor at the SDWAP, and was maintained with the new mentor after their transfer to the release site. The mentor, the oldest and largest bird at both sites, was the most dominant individual. The most dominant juvenile, #325, was a male, while the second and third ranking juveniles, #322 and #321, respectively, were both females. However, the least dominant juvenile, #323, was a male. In fact, juvenile #323 was older than juvenile #325 by one week, was introduced into the cohort a week earlier than juvenile #325, and was slightly heavier than juvenile #325 (Table 1). On the other hand, both of the females, #322 and #321, were the oldest, but also the lightest birds in the group (Table 1). It is unclear what factors played a role in determining the relative ranks of the four juveniles. Sex and size could explain the ranks of juveniles #325,

#322, and #321, however they would not explain the rank of juvenile #323. Behavioral characteristics could also play a role in determining social rank such that certain birds are more behaviorally inclined to be dominant or higher-ranking than other birds. Finally, we must consider the possibility that juvenile #323 was the lowest ranking bird because he suffered from some behavioral deficiencies. Further studies will be necessary to elucidate specifically what factors play a role in determining the hierarchical structure among California Condors.

As scavengers, condors, as well as other vultures, often congregate at carcasses to feed. Because carcasses are a spatially and temporally ephemeral and unpredictable food source, this can induce a high degree of interspecific and intraspecific competition (Wallace and Temple 1987b, Houston 1988, Donázar et al. 1999). Hierarchical social structures, which are typical of vulture species, serve to reduce this competition (Koenig 1976, Wallace and Temple 1987b). We looked at the order in which the individual condors fed to determine if this feeding order reflected the social hierarchy based on dominance interactions, as described above. We found that feeding order within the cohort differed between the SDWAP and the release site but did not reflect the social hierarchy at either site. At the SDWAP, the mentor, who was the most dominant bird in the group, was on average the first to feed, but among the rest of the individuals there was no correlation between social rank and feeding order. Additionally, the social hierarchy at both sites was found to be perfectly linear, whereas feeding order was not linear at either site; rather, individuals fell into distinct feeding rank groups. Several factors may help explain these findings including hunger level, individual food preferences, the nature of food distribution at feeding sites (i.e., several small carcasses and pieces rather than a single large carcass), variability in food availability, and group size. Additional factors that would play a role primarily in a non-captive setting include perceived predation risk and order of arrival at the food source. A final possible explanation for our findings could simply be that feeding order does not reflect social dominance within a condor group. For instance, Koenig (1976) found that in some Old World vulture species hunger level determines the hierarchy at a given carcass. While there have been some primate studies that have shown that feeding order is a reliable measure of social rank, these studies differed in how they defined that order, or in the nature of the food resource (Richards 1974). Other studies have indicated that priority of access to resources, such as food, is a better indicator of dominance, where priority does not necessarily correspond to order of access (Drews 1993). Regardless of the reason for our findings, we believe that, at least in captivity, feeding order may not be an appropriate measure for determining the social hierarchy of a group. The extent to which feeding order at a carcass among wild birds indicates their social dominance based upon non-feeding interactions remains to be determined.

Post-release observations were consistent with what we observed in captivity: the socially bonded birds, juveniles #321, #322, and #325, remained together, while the peripheral bird, juvenile #323, separated from the group. The solitary behavior of juvenile #323 may explain this bird's attraction to humans and subsequent recapture. Why this juvenile's behavior differed so greatly from that of the other juveniles is unknown. These behavioral patterns may have had some intrinsic cause, or they may have been influenced by unknown events that occurred early in this bird's life. Additionally, we must acknowledge the possibility that his behavioral pattern was merely a reflection of his subordinate status in the group. However, it is interesting to note that he did exhibit some unusual behavior early after formation of the cohort. Days after the last juvenile was introduced into the group, the door between CRP3 and the large flight pen was opened to allow the birds access into the larger pen. Juveniles #321, #322, and #325 moved into the larger pen within 48 h; juvenile #323, however, did not leave the small pen for approximately two weeks. Again, additional data should clarify whether these behavioral patterns reflected the subordinate status of an individual, or if they were truly aberrant. Depending on the ultimate findings, extra efforts may be necessary to monitor specific birds after their release based upon relative social inadequacies. Alternatively, such birds could be retained in captivity if their behavior were considered to pose a risk to themselves (e.g., from predation or malnutrition) or to other released birds (e.g., by introducing inappropriate behaviors into an otherwise appropriately behaving group).

The results of this study indicate that systematic collection of behavioral data on juvenile condors in captivity can likely yield some predictions about their post-release success and behavior in the wild. The potential for identifying birds that are not ready for release could have multiple benefits for the condor recovery effort, including savings in time and money. These benefits provide strong grounds for continuing this study.

Acknowledgments

We would like to express our gratitude to the many individuals and organizations that have helped make this study possible: the Condor staff at the SDWAP: Don Sterner, Tom Levites, Ron Webb, Sheila Murphy, and Beth Hoffower; Baja field biologists: Juan Vargas and Catalina Porras; Sierra de San Pedro Mártir National Park; Ejido Bramadero; the Virginia Friedhofer Charitable Trust, which provided the funding for this study; and to Allan Mee and Linnea Hall for their constructive comments on this manuscript.

Literature Cited

Alagona, P. S. 2004. "Biography of a feathered pig": the California Condor conservation controversy. Journal of the History of Biology 37:557–583.

Altmann, J. A. 1974. Observational study of behaviour: sampling methods. Behaviour 49:227–267.

Biggins, D. E., J. L. Godbey, L. R. Hanebury, B. Luce, P. E. Marinari, M. R. Matchett, and A. Vargas. 1998. The effect of rearing methods on survival of reintroduced black-footed ferrets. Journal of Wildlife Management 62:643–653.

Brakhage, G. K. 1953. Migration and mortality of ducks hand-reared and wild-trapped at Delta, Manitoba. Journal of Wildlife Management 17:465–477.

Bruning, D. 1983. Breeding condors in captivity for release into the wild. Zoo Biology 2:245–252.

Cade, T. J., S. A. H. Osborn, W. G. Hunt, and C. P. Woods. 2004. Commentary on released California Condors Gymnogyps californianus in Arizona. Pages 11–25 in Raptors Worldwide: Proceedings of VI World Conference on Birds of Prey and Owls (R. D. Chancellor and B.-U. Meyburg, Eds.). World Working Group on Birds of Prey and Owls/MME-Birdlife, Hungary.

Clark, M., M. Wallace, and C. David. 2007. Rearing California Condors for release using a modified puppet-rearing technique. Pages 213–226 in California Condors in the 21st Century (A. Mee and L. S. Hall, Eds.). Series in Ornithology, no. 2.

Cohn, J. P. 1999. Saving the California Condor. BioScience 49:864–868.

Conover, W. J. 1980. Practical Nonparametric Statistics, 2nd edition. John Wiley & Sons, New York.

Curio, E. 1998. Behavior as a tool for management intervention in birds. Pages 163–187 in Behavioral Ecology and Conservation Biology (T. M. Caro, Ed.). Oxford University Press, New York.

Donázar, J. A., and J. E. Feijóo. 2002. Social structure of Andean Condor roosts: influence of sex, age, and season. Condor 104:832–837.

Donázar, J. A., A. Travaini, O. Ceballos, A. Rodríguez, M. Delibes, and F. Hiraldo. 1999. Effects of sex-associated competitive asymmetries on foraging group structure and despotic distribution in Andean Condors. Behavioral Ecology and Sociobiology 45:55–65.

Drews, C. 1993. The concept and definition of dominance in animal behavior. Behaviour 125:283–313.

Ellis, D. H., S. J. Dobrott, and J. G. Goodwin, Jr. 1977. Reintroduction techniques for Masked Bobwhites. Pages 345–354 in Endangered Birds: Management Techniques for Preserving Threatened Species (S. A. Temple, Ed.). University of Wisconson Press, Madison.

Ellis, D. H., G. F. Gee, S. G. Hereford, G. H. Olsen, T. D. Chisolm, J. M. Nicolich, K. A. Sullivan, N. J. Thomas, M. Nagendran, and J. S. Hatfield. 2000. Post-release survival of hand-reared and parent-reared Mississippi Sandhill Cranes. Condor 102:104–112.

Hill, D., and P. Robertson. 1988. Breeding success of wild and hand-reared ring-necked pheasants. Journal of Wildlife Management 53:446–450.

Horwich, R. H. 1989. Use of surrogate parental models and age periods in a successful release of hand-reared sandhill cranes. Zoo Biology 8:379–390.

Houston, D. C. 1988. Competition for food between Neotropical vultures in forest. Ibis 130:402–417.

Houston, D. C. 1994. Family Cathartidae (New World Vultures). Pages 24–41 *in* Handbook of the Birds of the World, vol 2: New World Vultures to Guineafowl (J. del Hoyo, A. Elliott, and J. Sargatal, Eds.). Lynx Ediciones, Barcelona, Spain.

Hutchins, M., C. Sheppard, A. M. Lyles, and G. Casadei. 1995. Behavioral consideration in the captive management, propagation, and reintroduction of endangered birds. Pages 263–298 *in* Conservation of Endangered Species in Captivity: An Interdisciplinary Approach (E. F. Gibbons, B. S. Durrant, and J. Demarest, Eds.). State University of New York Press, Albany.

Kiff, L. F., R. I. Mesta, and M. P. Wallace. 1996. Recovery Plan for the California Condor. U.S. Fish and Wildlife Service, Portland, Oregon.

Koenig, C. 1976. Interspecific and intraspecific competition for food in Old World vultures. Journal für Ornithologie 117:297–316.

Koford, C. B. 1953. The California Condor. National Audubon Research Report 4: 1–154.

Kuehler, C. M., and P. N. Witman. 1988. Artificial incubation of California Condor *Gymnogyps californianus* eggs removed from the wild. Zoo Biology 7:123–132.

Mace, M. E. 2005. California Condor (*Gymnogyps californianus*) International Studbook. Zoological Society of San Diego, San Diego Wild Animal Park, Escondido, California.

Martin, J. E. 2005. The effects of rearing conditions on grooming and play behaviour in captive chimpanzees. Animal Welfare 14:125–133.

Meder, A. 1989. Effects of hand-rearing on the behavioral development of infant and juvenile gorillas (*Gorilla gorilla gorilla*). Developmental Psychobiology 22:357–376.

Meretsky, V. J., N. F. R. Snyder, S. R. Beissinger, D. A. Clenenden, and J. W. Wiley. 2000. Demography of the California Condor: implications for reestablishment. Conservation Biology 14:957–967.

Meretsky, V. J., N. F. R. Snyder, S. R. Beissinger, D. A. Clendenen, and J. W. Wiley. 2001. Quantity versus quality in California Condor reintroduction: reply to Beres and Starfield. Conservation Biology 15:1449–1451.

Myers, S., J. R. Millam, T. E. Roudybush, and C. R. Grau. 1988. Reproductive success of hand-reared vs. parent-reared cockatiels (*Nymphicus hollandicus*). Auk 105:536–542.

Noldus Information Technology. 1998. MatMan, reference manual, Version 1.0. Wageningen, The Netherlands.

Ralls, K., and J. D. Ballou. 2004. Genetic status and management of California Condors. Condor 106:215–228.

Richards, S. M. 1974. The concept of dominance and methods of assessment. Animal Behaviour 22:914–930.

Robinson, C. S. 1939. Observations and notes on the California Condor from data collected on Los Padres National Forest. U.S. Forest Service, Santa Barbara, California.

Robinson, C. S. 1940. Notes on the California Condor, collected on Los Padres National Forest, California. U.S. Forest Service, Santa Barbara, California.

ROBINSON-WOLRATH, S. I., AND I. P. F. OWENS. 2003. Large size in an island-dwelling bird: intraspecific competition and the dominance hypothesis. Journal of Evolutionary Biology 16:1106–1114.

SEARCY, W. A. 1979. Morphological correlates of dominance in captive male Red-winged Blackbirds. Condor 81:417–420.

SNYDER, N. F. R., S. E. KOENIG, J. KOSCHMANN, H. A. SNYDER, AND T. B. JOHNSON. 1994. Thick-billed parrot releases in Arizona. Condor 96:845–862.

SNYDER, N. F. R., AND H. A. SNYDER. 1989. Biology and conservation of the California Condor. Current Ornithology 6:175–267.

SNYDER, N. F. R., AND H. A. SNYDER. 2000. The California Condor: A Saga of Natural History and Conservation. Academic Press, San Diego, CA.

VALUTIS, L. L., AND J. M. MARZLUFF. 1999. The appropriateness of puppet-rearing birds for reintroduction. Conservation Biology 13:584–591.

WALLACE, M. P. 1991. Methods and strategies for releasing California condors to the wild. Pages 121–128 in American Association of Zoological Parks and Aquariums Annual Conference Proceedings, Wheeling, WV.

WALLACE, M. P. 1994. Control of behavioral development in the context of reintroduction programs for birds. Zoo Biology 13:491–499.

WALLACE, M. P. 2000. Retaining natural behaviour in captivity for re-introduction programmes. Pages 300–314 in Behaviour and Conservation (L. M. Gosling and W. J. Sutherland, Eds.). Cambridge University Press, Cambridge, United Kingdom.

WALLACE, M. P., AND S. A. TEMPLE. 1987a. Releasing captive-reared Andean Condors to the wild. Journal of Wildlife Management 51:541–550.

WALLACE, M. P., AND S. A. TEMPLE. 1987b. Competitive interactions within and between species in a guild of avian scavengers. Auk 104:290–295.

12

Rearing California Condors for Release Using a Modified Puppet-rearing Technique

Michael Clark,[1,3] *Michael Wallace,*[2]
and Chandra David[1]

ABSTRACT.—Because of the highly endangered status of the California Condor (*Gymnogyps californianus*), captive production of eggs was artificially increased four to six times over that seen in the wild by removing eggs and inducing female condors to lay one to two more than their usual single egg per season. From 1983 to 1990, all chicks that hatched from these eggs were hand reared by keepers using human isolation techniques that included socializing the chicks with a condor-like hand puppet. Starting in 1991, however, "puppet-reared" nestlings were also reared and placed in small nestling groups. Although effects of rearing method (puppet vs. parent-reared) did not appear to be significantly different for young condors, young birds released from captive parents who raised their own chicks for three to six months appeared to be better adjusted socially and initially approached people less often than puppet-reared chicks. This observation led us to modify puppet-rearing techniques beginning in 2000 to mimic more closely the social experience of parent-reared chicks. Modifications included nestlings reared singly instead of in cohorts; less traumatic handling during necessary zoo procedures; reduced but more assertive and realistic use of rearing puppets; the use of mentors in fledging pens; food restriction to induce better feeding responses; reduced moves during the nestling phase; greater isolation from humans throughout the captive phase; and more chick-oriented determination of readiness for transfer to release sites. Preliminary findings from the various modifications to the social environment of puppet-reared chicks are discussed, and although results are encouraging, the sample size is small. Only long-term post-release observations will indicate whether behavioral improvements seen in this exercise quate to permanent behavioral improvements in released, wild condors.

Los Angeles Zoo, 5333 Zoo Drive, Los Angeles, California 90027, USA.
Conservation and Research for Endangered Species Zoological Society of San Diego, 15600 San Pasqual Valley Road, Escondido, California 92027, USA.
Address correspondence to this author. E-mail: slipjoneser@yahoo.com

214   CLARK, WALLACE, AND DAVID

California Condors (*Gymnogyps californianus*) have one of the lowest
reproductive rates and longest periods of parental care of any bird species,
laying a single egg and providing some eight months of pre-fledging egg
and brood care (Snyder and Schmitt 2002). However, in the wild condors
have the ability to lay replacement eggs if the first egg is lost early in the
laying period to predation or breakage (Harrison and Kiff 1980, Snyder
and Hamber 1985). Because of the highly endangered status of California
Condors in the wild, biologists used the knowledge of their laying abilities
to justify the removal of wild eggs to encourage pairs to lay second eggs
and to help kick start a captive breeding program (see Snyder and Snyder
2000). Following the removal of the last birds from the wild in 1987, the
future recovery of the species lay largely in the hands of captive breeding
facilities, located initially at the Los Angeles Zoo and the San Diego Wild
Animal Park in California, but subsequently at the World Center for Birds
of Prey (1993) in Boise, Idaho, and most recently (2003) at the Oregon Zoo
in Portland, Oregon.

Captive reproduction, essentially multi-clutching of breeding pairs by
removal of first eggs to induce replacement eggs, has been highly successful
in increasing productivity of birds, providing many more young for potential reintroduction to the wild than would otherwise be possible (Kuehler
et al. 1991). Initially, because of the relative inexperience of most captive
condor pairs, all eggs were removed and incubated artificially (Kuehler and
Witman 1988). All chicks that hatched from these eggs between 1983 and
1990 were hand reared by keepers using human isolation techniques that
included socializing the chicks with a condor-like hand puppet. However,
starting in 1991, "puppet-reared" nestlings were placed in pairs or trios and
reared as small nestling groups. These groups were gradually introduced to
each other during the six-month nestling period until 5–10 member cohorts
were formed for release to the wild. This rearing system worked well for
Andean Condors (*Vultur gryphus*) in South America where release candidates were set free to integrate into existing natural populations (Wallace
and Temple 1987a). However, in California and Arizona the first released
California Condors did not have the benefit of an existing wild population
to impose social rules and teach condor foraging traditions since the entire
wild population was removed for captive breeding in 1987 (Snyder and
Snyder 2000). In the wild the natural curiosity of unchaperoned juvenile
condors, especially when dehydrated or food stressed, led some individuals to seek out novel stimuli including, at times, human contact (U.S. Fish
and Wildlife Service [USFWS] unpubl. data). Although effects of rearing
method (i.e. puppet vs. parent-reared) did not appear to significantly influence survivorship in the wild (see Woods et al. this volume), young released
from captive parents who raised their own chicks for three to six months
appeared to be better adjusted socially and initially approached people

less often than puppet-reared chicks (M. Wallace or M. Clark pers. obs.). While these differences were sometimes overstated by critics of the program (see for example Meretsky et al. 2000), parent-reared birds tended to be more shy in novel situations and focused more on the social activities of other condors than did the puppet-reared birds. This observation led us to experimentally modify puppet-rearing techniques to mimic more closely the social experience of parent-reared chicks. Here, we describe the various modifications made to the social environment of puppet-reared chicks and also describe the preliminary results of these modifications.

Methods and Results

Background to study.—In the wild, the single condor nestling leads a rather solitary existence for a social species. Only in about the first 4–6 weeks of its six month-long nestling phase does the chick receive a high degree of parental interaction with nearly constant brooding from one or the other parent (Koford 1953, Snyder and Snyder 2000). During the last few months of the nestling period the chick is left alone for increasing periods, occasionally not seeing either parent for several days at a time (Snyder and Snyder 2000). Nest visits in these latter months of the nestling phase may be for brief periods of food delivery to chicks, with parents later sitting off at a distance from the nest cave, and spending relatively little time interacting with the young (Snyder and Snyder 2000). Even in captivity where parent condors have no need for foraging and could have unlimited time with their chicks, we observed less social contact during the latter months of the nestling phase than expected (M. Wallace and M. Clark unpubl. data). Hand-reared chicks of the original puppet-rearing program were brought up in a social environment very different from chicks in the wild or parent-reared birds in captivity. From 1990 to 2000 we placed groups of 2–10 chicks together during the six-month nestling phase. While this achieved good group cohesiveness within a cohort during the first days and weeks after release to the wild (which was crucial to our management of the birds during this critical period), it also appeared to create an abnormally intensive social environment too early in each chick's behavioral ontogeny. Thus, an intense hierarchy rapidly formed with some birds exhibiting over-confidence while others seemed overly repressed by the group, further complicating their transition to life in the wild (M. Wallace and M. Clark unpubl. data). In this study we attempted to define the salient differences in rearing conditions between parent- and puppet-reared chicks, and to make specific changes in the rearing technique in hopes of obtaining more positive behavioral results that at least matched those seen in parent-reared condors after release. By carefully observing chick behavior when we entered a pen to trap birds, and also their reactions when they first entered pens, we were able to note differences such as increased shyness toward novel situations and objects by individuals, hoping that these behaviors might later be expressed as a greater wariness of people and less curiosity about human-made objects and structures. We also hoped for fewer "social outcasts" within the hierarchy of the release group. These were released condors that failed to integrate within the release population, particularly lacking social skills at feeding sites where they tended to remain aloof from the group and feed only when other condors had left the site (M. Wallace and M. Clark pers. obs). To achieve these results, we made several modifications to the original puppet rearing procedure.

Nestlings reared singly.—The most appropriate modification to the puppet-rearing method was to rear chicks as individuals isolated from other chicks rather than in groups. The logic behind grouping the chicks in the original method was to promote group cohesiveness after release to the wild. Although this was accomplished, the resulting unnaturally intense social environment often created overly confident Alpha individuals in the hierarchy and non-group participants at the lower end of the hierarchy at the time of release (M. Wallace and M. Clark unpubl. data). In anticipation of greater production early in the program a $13 \times 7 \times 3$ m horse barn was installed at the Los Angeles Zoo and modified to accommodate individuals and groups of condors. By remotely sliding doors measuring 2.5×2.5 m, stalls holding one or two young condor nestlings could be enlarged to double or triple the size at the appropriate time, enabling nestlings in those rooms to socialize with neighboring birds. As many as 10 young condors were introduced to one another at one time before being transferred to the large open aviary where they would be staged before being transferred to release sites (Fig. 1) To evaluate different rearing techniques, in 1999 we changed the above technique to that of providing nestlings with individual nest boxes and with no chance of seeing other nestling condors during the first five months of that ontological phase. To provide socialization similar to what a parent-reared chick might experience, however, one-way glass observation ports allowed us to feed and "socialize" each chick using a hand-puppet as was done in the older group-rearing method. In addition, a chick could look through the wire mesh into the large flight pen, $33 \times 17 \times 17$ m, where it would eventually "fledge" at five months old (Fig. 2). As other chicks in adjacent nest boxes came of age they would be allowed to "fledge" into the same pen. In this aviary older juveniles and adults provided a constant visual demonstration of an active condor social hierarchy without the potential detrimental side effects of a chick's premature participation.

Less traumatic handling of chicks.—While physical restraint of a nestling by a keeper is unnatural and appears to be quite traumatic for all age groups, it is necessary for captive husbandry during management such as

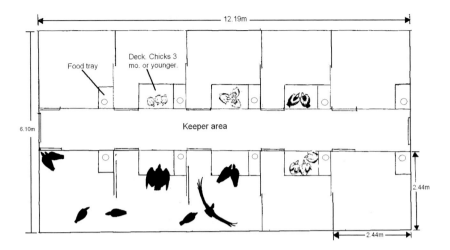

Fig. 1. Condor chick "barn" employed prior to the instigation of the modi-fied rearing method. Up to 10 condor chicks could be introduced to each other by removing sliding doors between stalls. Chicks were reared here prior to transfer to a large aviary at the Los Angeles Zoo.

weighing, cleaning the nest box and medical checks. However, hand-reared chicks regularly restrained can become desensitized and may possibly asso-ciate the experience positively such as with a puppet and food. Near the latter part of the nestling stage, chicks were restrained for physical exams and ID tagging. During these episodes they inevitably saw humans during the catching and restraining process. We feared that some level of habitua-tion might be occurring during the restraining procedure since some of the young birds often became calm and accepting of the situation. To evaluate the effects of handling, in 1999 we changed our restraining activities to avoid potential habituation by condor nestlings. In this modification we conditioned each nestling to allow a black cloth hood to be placed over its head holding it in place with an elastic collar during the chick's regular interactions with the puppet. With the palm facing up, the chick was taught to step up and balance on the keeper's hand (Plate 24). Since the chick is unable to see with the hood on, the keeper could now enter the rearing area and carry the nestling out without breaching human isolation. It could be transported from one room or building to another and management per-formed such as weighing, beak filing, or medical treatment including the taking of blood. During transport the unrestrained chick continued to wing beg as well as to vocalize normally during handling, indicating to us a lack of stress. After each management operation was completed the chick was returned to its nest box and the hood removed by another keeper using the puppet through the port (Fig. 2).

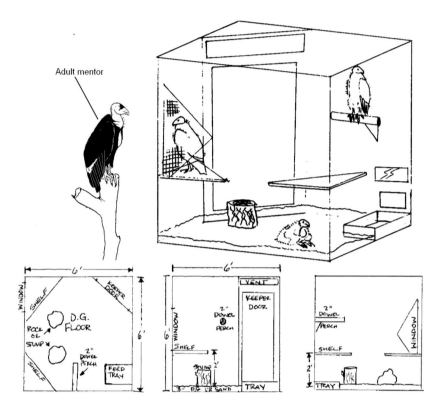

Fig. 2. Condor chick rearing chamber employed using the new modified rear-ing method. Single chicks were held in individual chambers up to five months old without being exposed to other chicks (figure shows perches available to chicks). Chicks were fed and socialized through a port (lower right) using a hand-puppet resembling an adult condor. Chicks were also exposed to an adult mentor visible through a wire-mesh screen (on right).

Reduced but more assertive and realistic puppet use.—During the first years of the captive-breeding program only the original puppet-rearing method was used to rear chicks for release, but after we observed pairs raising their own chicks we noticed a dramatic difference between puppet and parent-reared chick behavior toward the real parents. Although three to four month old puppet-reared nestlings would literally attack the pup-pet in the group-reared setting during feeding bouts, parent-reared chicks of the same age were much more tentative, acting almost frightened of the parent. Some parent-reared chicks consistently threatened and struck in apparent fear when the parents arrived and as the adults approached, the chicks sometimes showed conflicting responses of submissive wing-begging posture alternating with hissing defensive strikes (M. Wallace and M. Clark unpubl. data). However, real parents did not tolerate abusive behavior by nestlings and reprimands were quick and severe, but not damaging. Similar interactions between parents and nestlings have been documented at condor nests in the wild (Koford 1953, Snyder and Schmitt 2002, A. Mee unpubl. data). Wing-begging by parent-reared chicks was just as enthusiastic and exuberant as with hand-reared chicks, but body positioning was exaggeratedly low to the substrate and actual body contact was rare. In the original method, by not reprimanding "unruly" chick behavior as the parents did to their chicks during feeding bouts, we had inadvertently reinforced bad behavior that could encourage inappropriate behavior once condor young were in the wild. By mimicking real parent behaviors and postures with the puppet, we could solicit more appropriate behavioral attitudes from chicks and then reward them with food, as did parents. We learned that with careful puppet use during the first interactions with chicks, more normal behaviors were easily maintained throughout the period of nest box use.

Use of mentors.—Condors, like other members of the family Cathartidae, are highly gregarious, exhibiting a social hierarchy determined by an individual's personal status within the group. A condor's status is based on a number of parameters such as age, sex, body weight and experience with other group members (Wallace and Temple 1987b, Bukowinski et al. this volume). Beginning in 1991 and continuing for the first several years of the reintroduction phase of the condor program, all release candidates were sent as newly hatched chicks to the rearing facility at the Los Angeles Zoo and prepared for release. We first experimented using older birds as mentors in the condor program at the Los Angeles Zoo in 1995 with the assumption that social contact with older birds should be positive. Condor nestlings reared in groups in zoos naturally formed a social hierarchy but one without the benefit of any adult influence.

In an attempt to more closely duplicate the positive influence parents and other adults have on younger condors, we used older condors as mentors in the large pens young condors fledged into. We attempted to create a non-intimidating environment where a chick could develop confidence in its surroundings based on a predictable daily routine. When we first considered modifying the rearing method, we believed that a pair of breeding adults would likely be the best role models because that arrangement would be most similar to what was experienced by parent-reared chicks. However, we found breeding pairs to be extremely territorial in their living space. Fledging chicks into the flight cage of a breeding pair that was not their own was a risky option because of potential harm to the chick. In parent-reared situations in captivity we observed that the female of a pair tended to become less tolerant of her own fledged chick in the flight cage, eventually competing with it for resources. In contrast, males were

very accommodating toward their own chicks and rarely competed with
them for food or perching spots. Instead the male of a pair would chase
the adult female as she tried to displace a chick from perches, take food
away from, or otherwise antagonize it. Chicks usually roosted at night with
adult males within the first few weeks after fledging. Males did not allow
females to displace chicks from roosts, forcing females to roost elsewhere.
Occasionally captive male condors allowed their chicks to displace them
from perches as well as shared food with them. Rarely did we observe male
parents show antagonistic behavior toward their chicks, in contrast to
females, until chicks were much older and more independent.

Adult males proved to be almost as accommodating towards fledgling
hand-reared chicks as they were toward chicks of their own. In our experience males were not aggressive toward puppet-reared fledglings introduced
into their pens, often giving them a wide berth. This allowed fledglings
to explore their new living spaces without being intimidated, similar to
interactions between fledglings with their own parents. After at least two
months, older aged birds and adult females were added to the group to give
chicks more experience with group dynamics and to enable them to find
their place (at the bottom) within the social hierarchy.

Careful food restriction to induce better feeding response.—In the
original method chicks were served more food than they could eat consistently and much food was wasted (M. Wallace and M. Clark unpubl. data).
Rarely did we observe puppet-reared chicks fill their crops to full capacity
as did parent-reared chicks in captivity and in the wild. In addition, those
birds low in social status often became intimidated by group-feeding sessions, yet since they relied on a group setting to feed, they often lost body
weight before they had sufficient confidence to join in the feeding sessions.
Low body weight combined with a low social rank within a group seemed
to be a setting for behavioral problems that could carry over into the field
after release. To address these problems, in 2000 we began using a strategy of mild hunger to teach each chick in the new rearing method to take
fuller crops during feedings. Hunger was also used to encourage young, at
an early age, to eat an adult diet—to tear up whole mice, rats and rabbits
on their own. We wanted them to maintain better body weights by feeding
self-sufficiently, regardless of what their position in the hierarchy would be
when they integrated into a group after fledging.

Reduced moves during nestling phase.—We were concerned that chicks
reared under the original method experienced too many changes in their
environment during rearing. Thus, under the modified technique, implemented in 2000, we reduced those moves. Whereas parent-reared chicks
fledged in the same place they hatched, puppet-reared chicks were originally
moved from place to place as facility needs dictated and depending on the
stage a chick was in, or to allow socialization of chicks with other condors of

the same age. Getting the chicks comfortable with changes made management easier. In the modified method, we reduced the amount of change in a chick's environment and attempted to create a predicable routine that they could rely on. For example, we moved them outside to the rearing chamber where they could see adult role models as soon as they could thermoregulate on their own at 4–5 weeks old. Once there, chicks were not moved again until they fledged into the pen about four months later.

Greater human isolation throughout the captive phase.—In the original method, we maintained condor chicks in visual isolation from human contact during the six-month nestling period to avoiding human imprinting, human food associations and tameness (Lorenz 1935, Wallace and Temple 1983). Although the original method, in general, achieved this there were husbandry and medical situations that sometimes compromised isolation. Under the original method, chicks were also exposed to humans during aversive training experiments where several people in the flight cage hazed the whole release cohort until all were captured and placed into kennels. This aversion training was an attempt at providing the fledglings an amount of negative training with people in order to instill a degree of wariness prior to their release. The results of this were mixed and aversive hazing was dropped from the program. Under the modified method, which was implemented in 2000, there were no breaches in isolation unless there was an emergency. During such emergencies when birds were exposed to humans, we made great efforts to do such work as needed at night when the birds were roosting. In addition, if chicks observed people (exposure was sometimes unavoidable), the birds were not fed for two days or more after the exposure in an attempt to diffuse any positive associations with humans.

Determining the readiness of each individual before translocation to release site.—Previously, the scheduling of translocations from the Los Angeles or San Diego Zoos to a release site was based more on convenient management of groups and field site schedules and less on a consideration of how each individual condor chick was functioning within a cohort. Under the modified method, started in 2000, we only shipped a cohort out when all birds were successfully functioning both individually and as a group. Lower status birds were the most likely to be returned to captivity for failing to adapt in the wild due to behavioral problems or for health reasons. Under the modified method, each bird was evaluated for its readiness for release using several parameters such as body weight as indicated by the perch scale in each pen; affiliation with the cohort; and degree of confidence in moving about a pen and interacting with both dominant and subordinate birds (see also Bukowinski et al. this volume). Release candidates that did not appear ready for transfer to the field were held back to be socialized with the cohort produced the following year. These birds would invariably be at the top of the hierarchy of the next cohort because of greater age and experience

(M. Clark pers. obs.). Also, if one of the birds was injured or observed acting aberrantly, they would be separated from the cohort so as not to adversely influence the group. Such birds were included for release with a cohort in a later season, depending on the severity of the behavior.

Discussion

In order to increase survivorship and overall success in release programs of a variety of species greater emphasis has been placed on improving rearing methods (Biggins et al 1998, Valutis and Marzluff 1999, Van Heezik et al. 1999, Brightsmith et al. 2005, Mathews et al. 2005). With condors reared using the modified method we tried to improve their behavior in captivity in hopes that it might improve subsequent behavior and survivorship in the wild, as well as reducing the intense level of care and resources necessary for managing unwary condors. In contrast to behaviors seen in previous groups of chicks after they were fledged into the large aviary at the Los Angeles Zoo, we documented that birds prepared using the modified methods described above spent less time on the ground, and preferred to perch on the higher perches in the pen than those reared using the original method. Chicks fledged under the original rearing methods were all allowed access to the flight cage at the same time. They initially spent the majority of their time during the day on the ground exploring the floor of the cage with each other, potentially maladaptive behavior likely to increase predation risk in the wild, and which often continued for some period of time after release to the wild. For these chicks, perching on safer natural snags in the pen seemed awkward. Using the modified methods, however, chicks were fledged singly, usually a few weeks apart. They were more confident at gaining perches that the mentor frequented and could be seen confidently using these perches within minutes or hours after fledging.

Chicks reared using the original methods explored the flight pen after fledging and returned to the rearing chamber at night to roost. This often continued for several weeks before they gradually began roosting outside in the flight cage. In contrast, chicks produced by the modified method sometimes spent the first few nights out in the flight cage roosting on high snags usually at some distance from the mentor. Within a few days they typically returned to the nest box for several more days, not seeming to recognize that the wire barrier to the open door was still removed, and that they could move freely. These chicks moved tentatively between the two environments (nest box and flight cage), exhibiting behavior more similar to parent-reared chicks than to puppet-reared birds reared using the original group-fledging method.

A group behavior described by condor keepers as "dog piling," where two or more chicks lie on their sternums in physical contact with other condors to sleep, rest, or mutually preen, was a behavior regularly seen in groups of hand-reared chicks in the rearing chamber. Under the original rearing methods, we commonly observed this behavior after chicks fledged into the flight pen and even after release to the wild. The birds seemed to be focused only on each other and not on the environment around them. Under the modified methods described in this paper, this behavior was rarely observed. Instead, the infrequent close contact between chicks was much more tentative, and episodes such as allopreening would often abruptly terminate with a participant moving cautiously away from the other bird.

Further, condors raised using the new method also played less. Under the original methods, chicks spent greater amounts of time exploring objects on the ground after fledging into the large pen. Their behaviors were generally relaxed and incautious. For example, when one bird interacted with a stick or feather of interest it typically initiated long bouts of group play with little notice of the environment beyond its immediate activity. Chicks reared under the modified methods, however, seemed immediately cautious when on the ground after fledging and, as mentioned above, spent more time up on perches. When on the ground they walked hurriedly from one place to the other with head movements quick and high with the neck ruff up, signifying concern and caution. When exploring objects on the ground or eating, these chicks appeared vigilant because they frequently raised their heads to survey their environment in a nervous manner.

Condor chicks reared under the modified methods reacted behaviorally more like parent-reared condors during and after wing-tagging operations than chicks reared under original methods. For identification purposes we placed a numbered tag on one wing of the chicks several weeks prior to their fledging into the large flight pen at about four and a half months of age. Under the original group-rearing method, chicks hardly seemed to notice the addition of vinyl tags attached to them. We speculated that this was the result of their more stimulating environment and a greater acceptance of change. In contrast, about 60% of the time chicks reared in the more socially isolated environment of the modified rearing method reacted adversely to the wing-tags, hissing and biting at the tags and, in attempting to retreat from them, becoming further upset by their inability to escape. They initially struck at the tag, sometimes flipping over on their backs in attempts to rid themselves of the tags. Using the old rearing method this was almost never observed but was observed frequently when tagging parent-reared chicks.

Conclusions

The purpose of this study was to improve overall post-release behaviors of young condors. We applied specific modifications based on a comparison of puppet-reared and parent-reared chick behaviors observed during our experience of rearing condors at the Los Angeles Zoo and their success or failure after release to the wild. Overall, the chicks produced using the modified methods behaved more similarly to captive, parent-reared birds than did the chicks produced using the original methods involving group-rearing. Chicks raised with modified methods integrated more cautiously into their surroundings when fledging into the large zoo pen, and focused initially more on the adult behavior and actions of mentors than on interactions of the other chicks. Zoo staff placed greater emphasis on the overall socialization of individual condor chicks rather than groups of chicks, with more time and care given to birds showing difficulty integrating with the group. Concomitant with qualitative changes in socialization, release candidates reared using the new methods were kept markedly longer in stable social situations before their transfer to the field, with captive periods up to two years versus four to ten months under the original method. A consistent difference exhibited by fledglings in this study was their intense negative reaction to the presence of people in the pen at the time of transfer to field release sites. So dramatic was their negative reaction, to humans, for example, that they often risked severe injury as they crashed into the chain-link wire mesh at the end of the large pen when trying to avoid trapping, without regard to their own safety. As a result, it was necessary to encourage them to feed in a smaller $2 \times 3 \times 3$ m high chamber for several days where they could be trapped and extracted safely at the time of transfer.

Ultimately, the definitive test for the positive changes we observed will occur after the release of young condors to the wild. While the results presented here are encouraging, the sample size is still small with only 11 birds reared under the modified methods and released to the wild thus far. Only long-term post-release observations will indicate whether behavioral improvements seen in this exercise equate to permanent behavioral improvements and, possibly increased survivorship, in released, wild condors.

Acknowledgments

This work could not have been done without the support of the Los Angeles Zoo. Support in many forms came from individuals like Susie Kasielke, Mike Maxcy, Michlin Hines, Debbie Sears, Cynthia Stringfield, Bruce Palmer, and Joe Burnett. Los Angeles Zoo Director, Warren Thomas, gave invaluable support to the zoo condor program at various levels. Several condor eggs and young chicks came from the San Diego Zoo's Wild Animal Park and the Peregrine Fund breeding facilities in Boise, Idaho. We also thank the California Condor Recovery Team for continued support.

LITERATURE CITED

BIGGINS, D. E., J. L. GOODBEY, L. R. HANABURY, B. LUCE, P. E. MARINARI, M. R. MATCHETT, AND A. VARGAS. 1998. The effect of rearing methods on survival of reintroduced black-footed ferrets. Journal of Wildlife Management 62:643–653.

BRIGHTSMITH, D., J. HILBURN, A. CAMPO, J. BOYD, M. FRISIUS, R. FRISIUS, D. JANIK, AND F. GUILLEN. 2004. The use of hand-raised psittacines for reintroduction: a case study of scarlet macaws (*Ara macao*) in Peru and Costa Rica. Biological Conservation 121:465–472.

BUKOWINSKI, A. T., F. B. BERCOVITCH, A. C. ALBERTS, M. P. WALLACE, M. E. MACE, AND S. ANCONA. 2007. A quantitative assessment of the California Condor mentoring program. Pages 197–212 *in* California Condors in the 21st Century (A. Mee and L. S. Hall, Eds.). Series in Ornithology, no. 2.

HARRISON, E. N., AND L. F. KIFF. 1980. Apparent replacement clutch laid by wild California Condor. Condor 82:351–352.

KOFORD, C. B. 1953. The California Condor. National Audubon Research Report 4:1–154.

KUEHLER, C. M., D. J. STERNER, D. S. JONES, R. L. USNIK, AND S. KASIELKE. 1991. Report on captive hatches of California Condors (*Gymnogyps californianus*): 1983–1990. Zoo Biology 10:65–68.

KUEHLER, C. M., AND P. N. WITMAN. 1988. Artificial incubation of the California Condor *Gymnogyps californianus* eggs removed from the wild. Zoo Biology 7:123-132.

LORENZ, K. Z. 1935. Der kumpan in der umwelt des vogels. Journal für Ornithologie 83:137–213:289–413.

MATHEWS, F., M. ORROS, G. MCLAREN, M. GELLING, AND R. FOSTER. 2005. Keeping fit on the ark: assessing the suitability of captive-bred animals for release. Biological Conservation 121:569–577.

MERETSKY, V. J., N. R. F. SNYDER, S. R. BEISSINGER, D. A. CLENDENEN, AND J. WILEY. 2000. Demography of the California Condor: implications for reestablishment. Conservation Biology 14:957–967.

SNYDER, N. F. R., AND J. A. HAMBER. 1985. Replacement-clutching and annual nesting of California Condors. Condor 85:374–378.

SNYDER, N. F. R., AND H. A. SNYDER. 2000. The California Condor: A Saga of Natural History and Conservation. Academic Press, San Diego, CA.

SNYDER, N. F. R., AND N. J. SCHMITT. 2002. California Condor (*Gymnogyps californianus*). *In* Birds of North America, no. 610 (A. Poole and F. Gill, Eds.). The Birds of North America, Inc., Philadelphia, PA.

VALUTIS, L. L., AND J. M. MARZLUFF. 1999. The appropriateness of puppet-rearing birds for reintroduction. Conservation Biology 13:584–591.

VAN HEEZIK, Y., P. J. SEDDON, AND R. F. MALONEY. 1999. Helping reintroduced houbara bustards avoid predation: effective anti-predator training and the predictive value of pre release behavior. Animal Conservation 2:155–162.

WALLACE, M. P. 1994. Control of behavioral development in the context of reintroduction programs for birds. Zoo Biology 13:491–499.

WALLACE, M. P., AND S. A. TEMPLE. 1983. An evaluation of techniques for releasing hand-reared vultures to the wild. Pages 400–423 *in* Vulture Biology and

226   CLARK, WALLACE, AND DAVID

43
Management (S. R. Wilbur and J. A. Jackson, Eds.). University of California Press, Berkeley.

WALLACE, M. P., AND S. A. TEMPLE. 1987a. Releasing captive-reared Andean Condors to the wild. Journal of Wildlife Management 51:541–550.

WALLACE, M. P., AND S. A. TEMPLE. 1987b. Competitive interactions within and between species in a guild of avian scavengers. Auk 104:290–295.

WOODS, C. P., W. R. HEINRICH, C. N. PARISH, S. C. FARRY, AND T. J. CADE. 2007. Survival and reproduction of California Condors released in Arizona. Pages 57–78 in California Condors in the 21st Century (A. Mee and L. S. Hall, Eds.). Series in Ornithology, no. 2.

13

Release of Puppet-reared California Condors in Baja California, Mexico: Evaluation of a Modified Rearing Technique

Michael P. Wallace,[1,3] *Michael Clark,*[2] *Juan Vargas,*[1]
and Maria Catalina Porras[1]

ABSTRACT.—The California Condor (*Gymnogyps californianus*) Recovery Plan calls for re-establishing condors in as much of the original range of this endangered species as feasibly possible. Releasing condors in the Sierra San Pedro Mártir region of Northern Baja California, Mexico, in the southern portion of the species' former range, afforded an opportunity to evaluate the effects of modifications to the puppet rearing technique. Differences observed between parent-reared and puppet-reared condors led to modifications to improve puppet-rearing results in captivity. Since the growing Baja population would remain isolated from condor populations released in California for several years, we took the opportunity to release only condors puppet-reared using the modified technique. Preliminary results with 11 free flying condors over a three-year period indicated that the changes in socialization made during the rearing and release process may have a positive effect on the behavior of released condors. Condors in Baja appeared to exhibit activities more restricted to remote areas and a wariness of people as they expanded their ranges.

California Condors (*Gymnogyps californianus*) are a highly social *K*-selected species that exhibit a low rate of reproduction and an extended parent-young dependency period (Koford 1953, Pianka 1970, Snyder and Hamber 1985). Social and feeding traditions in condors are passed on to

[1]*Conservation and Research for Endangered Species, Zoological Society of San Diego, 15600 San Pasqual Valley Road, Escondido, California 92027, USA.*
[2]*Los Angeles Zoo 6400 Griffith Park Boulevard, Los Angeles, California 90027, USA.*
[3]*E-mail: mwallace@sandiegozoo.org*

young by parents during the post-fledging dependence period and through interactions and integration with the local population over several years, as opposed to more solitary birds of prey (Wallace and Temple 1988). However, with the capture and removal of all remaining condors from the wild in the 1980s (Snyder and Snyder 2000), opportunities for young condors to acquire these extensive traditions were temporarily disrupted. Beginning in 1992 in southern California, reintroductions have attempted to recreate condor foraging traditions by releasing captive bred juveniles to the wild.

Techniques to prepare captive-reared condors for release to the wild were initially based on Black Vulture (*Coragyps atratus*) and Turkey Vulture (*Cathartes aura*) experiments in Florida and Andean Condor (*Vultur gryphus*) release experiments in Peru (Wallace and Temple 1983, 1987). Andean Condors released in Peru and others released in Colombia (Lieberman et al. 1993) and Argentina (Jácome 2005) integrated reasonably well into existing populations but complications arose when using the same method to release California Condors into their previous habitat where no parent population existed (Wallace 1991).

Over the last 25 years, California Condors destined for release to the wild have been reared using two techniques: (1) parent-rearing, where captive pairs rear their own young, or (2) puppet-rearing, in which young birds are "reared" by realistic puppets resembling adults and subsequently fledge into social groups consisting of peers of the same season before release to the wild (see Clark et al. this volume). Parent-reared condors were raised in captivity by their own or surrogate parents for some, if not all, of their six-month nestling phase before release to the wild in groups mixed with puppet-reared birds. Production of parent-reared young is lower than puppet-reared young as the single egg clutch and the potential for mate compatibility problems among forced pairs in captivity increases the risk of nest failure (see Hartt et al. 1994). In contrast, removal of eggs laid by condors in captivity for artificial incubation has increased productivity by multi-clutching (Kuehler and Witman 1988), while puppet-rearing young from these additional eggs may decrease risks to chicks posed by pair incompatibility (D. Sterner, M. Clark pers. comm.). Puppets have been employed in various captive rearing programs (Wallace 1994, Valutis and Marzluff 1999) to avoid malimprinting in release candidates (Lorenz 1981). Although survivorship was not significantly different between released puppet and parent-reared condors in northern Arizona (Woods et al. this volume), condors reared by their parents in captivity and subsequently released into the wild in California tended to exhibit more species-typical behavior, showing less interest in the activities of people and human built structures after release (U.S. Fish and Wildlife Service unpubl. data).

Because naive condors are influenced socially and behaviorally when released into an established population regardless of rearing technique, it is difficult to ascertain the effects of changes in rearing methods since birds released at all three sites in the United States (southern and central California, northern Arizona) are composed of puppet and parent-reared condors. However, by releasing only puppet-reared condors in the isolated region of the Sierra San Pedro Mártir, Baja California, Mexico, we hoped to examine the influence of modifications to the original puppet-rearing method without the influence of a condor population with established behaviors. Thus, this study serves as the field evaluation for condors released using the modified puppet-rearing technique described by Clark et al. (this volume).

Methods

General methods.—We released 11 California Condors that were reared using the modified rearing program developed at the Los Angeles Zoo (LAZ). For release candidates in this study, we evaluated a modified puppet-rearing technique that in general paid more attention to the social experience of each individual in an effort to duplicate key features in the rearing environment of either wild or captive parent-reared condors (Clark et. al. this volume). Using standard radio-tracking techniques (Kenward 2000) and new GPS–satellite transmitters, we released condors in Baja raised under these new conditions to determine if they indeed focused more appropriately on the social dynamics of other released condors and less on the activities of people and human-made structures as they expanded their range.

Captive management.—In this study we released and evaluated 10 condors over the study period. Most were reared at the LAZ (Table 1) incorporating changes to previous puppet-rearing methodologies (see Clark et al. this volume). Four of the chicks were hatched and reared for less than one month at other facilities. Prior to one month chicks of both methods were treated similarly regardless of the rearing institution. None of the changes made under the new method took place until after one month when the chicks could thermoregulate on their own and could be moved to the modified chambers. Briefly, the changes in methodology were: greater attention to human isolation throughout the captive phase, reduced moves during the nestling phase; reduced but more assertive and realistic puppet use; nestlings reared singly and not in groups; nestlings could observe older condors from the security of an artificial nest cave–box; less traumatic handling of chicks during health checks and tagging; and, finally, integration of chicks at fledging age into an older established social group or with a single adult mentor for a period of months prior to transfer to the field (see Clark et al. this volume for details).

WALLACE ET AL.

Table 1. California Condors reared under the new rearing technique at captive breeding facilities, 2000–2005, and released in Baja California, Mexico (2002–2005). Captive breeding facilities were the Los Angeles Zoo (LAZ), San Diego Wild Animal Park (WAP), and the Peregrine Fund's World Center for Birds of Prey (TPF).

Year	Studbook	Sex	Date hatched	Source of egg	Date transferred to Baja
2000	217	F	3 Apr 00	LAZ	12 Aug 02
	218	F	5 Apr 00	LAZ	12 Aug 02
	220	F	10 Apr 00	LAZ	12 Aug 02
2001	259[b]	M	26 May 01	TPF	12 Aug 02
	261[c]	M	7 June 01	TPF	12 Aug 02
2002	269	M	6 Apr 02	LAZ	4 Dec 03
	279[d]	M	28 Apr 02	WAP	4 Dec 03
	284	F	7 May 02	LAZ	4 Dec 03
2003	315[e]	M	19 May 03	WAP	4 Sep 04
	320[g]	M	24 Jun 03	LAZ	4 Sep 04

[a] Moved to LAZ on 22 June 2000, held for extra year in captivity; died in the release pen on 23 December 2003 before release to the wild.
[b] Chick moved to LAZ on 24 June 2001.
[c] Moved to LAZ on 24 June 2001.
[d] Moved to LAZ on 23 May 2002; missing December 2004, presumed dead.
[e] Moved to LAZ on 12 June 2003.
[f] Lead poisoned, not released.
[g] Egg moved to LAZ from TPF on 3 June 2003.

Release area and management.—For transport from the captive facility to the release area each of the condors was placed in a visually enclosed, large, plastic dog kennel and, in groups of three or four, flown by small plane from Burbank Airport, California, to the Meling Ranch, Baja California, Mexico, an air strip within a one hour drive of the release site. In the spring and summer of 2002, the condor release site was selected and constructed in the Sierra San Pedro Mártir, Baja California Norte, Mexico. Situated in a forest of large Jeffery pines (*Pinus jefferyi*) and facing west atop a ridge at 666 m in elevation, thermals and onshore winds off the distant (75 km) Pacific Ocean afforded adequate lift for inexperienced, newly released birds (Plate 25). The release facility location and design helped with pre- and post-release management of the birds by maintaining the high degree of human–bird isolation that was initiated at LAZ. The main aviary, larger than typical release pens, afforded management features that maximized isolation between biologists and the birds being managed. Original condor release pens were relatively small with the intent that the birds would be contained for only one or two weeks before release. Once the condors were released, they were not encouraged or expected to return to it and only when new birds were brought in for release was it used again. The

Baja release–holding pen was similar but more extensive than the flight-pen design at another release location, the Big Sur release site in central California operated by the Ventana Wilderness Society (M. Wallace pers. obs.), with more space and comfort, enabling us to continuously maintain captive birds in the field for extended periods of time if necessary.

The main holding–release enclosure measured 20 × 20 × 10 m high and was built by suspending nylon netting over a steel cable attached 10 m high, encircling six trees and extending down to a 1.5-m chain-link perimeter fence, where it was secured in the ground with concrete). A 5 × 3 × 3 m blind with one-way viewing ports was attached to the structure and could be approached and entered without observation by condors inside the pen. If released condors were in the area of the pen, approach and entry to the blind was done at night. Even though food and water delivery to the pen was accomplished using visual barriers, it was always done at night to further guarantee the condors would not associate noise or movement with people and food. The perimeter pine trees that served as supports for the nylon net were trimmed so specific branches provided natural perches inside the enclosure. Paths and openings were made through meter high manzanita (*Arctostaphylos pungens*) vegetation to allow movement of the birds on the ground but to encourage them to seek higher perches. A 1 × 1 × 0.3 m deep pool was constructed with rocks and concrete in the center of the pen that could be filled and drained remotely. A weighing scale fashioned in the form of a perch was placed with the dial positioned so it could be read from inside the blind through small ports of one-way glass.

A sliding door between the large enclosure and an adjacent smaller chamber (7 × 7 × 3 m high) could be surreptitiously remotely operated from the attached blind. A second remotely operated door on the opposite side of the small pen led to the outside. Food delivered to either pen through ports under the blind allowed us to influence where the birds fed and, by managing the food position and doors carefully, groups or even single birds could be isolated in either pen or released to the wild. Likewise, attracted to the food and feeding birds inside, previously-released birds could be encouraged to enter the smaller chamber for food and then moved to join the birds in the larger pen without stress or even much notice by the trapped birds. At a later time, new transmitters could be fitted or routine health checks performed without the birds negatively associating the trapping event with the management. Except for emergencies, all handling of the condors in the aviary was done after dark. Managing the release and trapping of the birds in this way reduced the stress on both birds and biologists but more importantly eliminated the danger of habituation that may occur by regularly handling condors in the daytime.

Both in captivity and after release, condors were fed portions of ungulate carcasses such as horse (*Equus caballus*), goat (*Capra hircus*), burro

(*Equus asinus*) and cow (*Bos taurus*). At the release site, young and/or mature animals were either purchased from local ranchers and killed using a standard slaughterhouse methods or retrieved from local sources after death due to disease, trauma, or old age. A portion of a carcass sufficient in size for one person to carry (25–30 kg) was delivered to the large or small pen at night. Each condor was provided with about 0.5 kg of meat per day on average. Food delivery was made every three to five days depending on the need as determined by daily observations of the birds. Water was available *ad libitum* both inside the pen during captivity and outside the pen after their release.

    Release management.—Although conventional VHF radio-transmitters, placed on each wing of the condor, were our primary means of tracking the birds' daily movements (Kenward 2000), we also relied on highly accurate GPS transmitters linked to the ARGOS satellite system. These lightweight (45 g) GPS–satellite transmitters (Microwave Telemetry Inc., Columbia, Maryland) are capable of taking 15 position readings (hits) daily that are uploaded every three days to ARGOS satellites. These latitude and longitude positions were received via email from ARGOS, and were then plotted on Global Information System (GIS) based maps using ARCVIEW software (ESRI, Redlands, California). GPS satellites also recorded the altitude and speed of condors, allowing us to plot roost (determined by nighttime hits with a speed of 0) and potential feeding locations (i.e., determined by hits of multiple birds in the same daytime location with a speed of 0). These data have the potential to allow us to determine more accurately range and habitat use by condors, and are especially useful in documenting condor use of "wild" food sources away from provisioning sites (see also Hunt et al. this volume).

    The large aviary with its isolated, natural setting was used for acclimating new birds over the months before release or used for housing retrapped birds for extended periods of time. Because the aviary was set back in the shelter of pines from the best flying conditions at the cliff 0.4 km to the west, only experienced birds that knew the area well were released from the main facility. When birds were to be released for the first time they were transported at night to a smaller 7 × 7 × 3 m pen near the cliff edge. During the two to four weeks in the small pen prior to release, they could observe avian and mammalian scavengers, including previously released condors, feeding at nearby sites provisioned at night by biologists.

    After a release, we managed the feeding so that previously released condors fed near the pen, encouraging newly released birds to also feed and roost in the immediate area. Before a release, food in the form of large animal parts was placed in three areas within 100 m of the release pen. Carrion was secured with a chain embedded in the rock to prevent removal by the larger nighttime scavengers such as coyotes (*Canis latrans*) and pumas (*Felis concolor*). Water was provided in a large tub placed near the release pen and replenished when food was delivered. From this "home base" of food, water and safety, condors gradually made exploratory flights in different directions as they perfected their flying skills over the first few months. As the birds became more proficient flyers the food was placed at greater distances in order to give them more options to feed at different sites and to occupy their time with other activities. Ultimately, food was placed at specific sites several kilometers apart in order to encourage a more naturalistic foraging pattern, similar to that described for the historic wild condor population (e.g., Koford 1953, Meretsky and Snyder 1992).

Behavioral assessment.—Because it was becoming obvious that mentors were playing an important role in giving social structure to release candidates in captivity at LAZ (see Clark et al. this volume), in 1997 the authors recommended that the Ventana Wilderness Society use an older captive condor as a mentor in their field pen while their young condor release candidates acclimated to an area prior to release. Since then, mentors have been used at all release-site holding pens in California. From the onset of the project in Baja in 2002, we used adult female condor "Xewe," (studbook [SB] #64), as a mentor (Mace 2005). During the study period (2002–present), she remained captive in the large aviary, associating with the release candidates prior to their initial release to the wild and subsequently during periods spent in captivity following recapture (see Results).

Most Cathartid vultures are highly social and many species exhibit near linear dominance hierarchies that play an important role in the social organization of the species (Wallace and Temple 1987; see also Bukowinski et al. this volume). An individual condor is likely to benefit when participating socially with a flock by acquiring knowledge such as locations of roosting places, water holes, feeding areas and types of food. In addition, foraging for carcasses may be more efficient when individuals associate with conspecifics during foraging flights and at overnight roosts (see Buckley 1996). Condors are keenly aware of the social status of other birds in a group based on earlier interactions between individuals. A dominant individual has priority access to resources such as food and water, favorite roosting spots and when mature, possibly mates and territory and knowing one's social place within the flock, conflict can be minimized. Overt fighting is usually only seen between birds close in social status where their ranking may be ambiguous (Wallace and Temple 1987). One of the factors condor field managers have associated with a higher risk of failure in the early acclimation period just weeks after release is low social rank (Bukowinski et al. this volume). To asses an individual's status we noted the outcomes of its interactions with other birds over resources such as a favored perch, or food or play items, by indicating the winner of these challenges. By scoring large numbers of these encounters over time a pattern of dominance emerged within groups. The main questions of interest to us in this study were whether hierarchy changed dramatically over time after release, and whether correlations could be made between condors' social status and their success at adapting to the wild.

RESULTS

Post-release behavior.—The first release of three birds on 10 October 2002 was aborted after two weeks because of interference from Golden Eagles (*Aquila chrysaetos*) and impending winter weather. All the condors were recaptured without incident and maintained in captivity though the winter in the large pen. In April 2003, releases were continued from the new smaller pen (7 × 5 × 2 m) near the cliffs. Each release group was staged for a brief, three-week acclimation period within the small pen before release. Although we observed several altercations between condors and Golden Eagles in winter, it appeared that the territorial activities of the local Red-tailed Hawks (*Buteo jacmaicensis*) and Common Ravens (*Corvus corax*) in spring and summer may have acted as a sufficient deterrent to Golden Eagle intrusion into the release area (M. Wallace and J. Vargas pers. obser.). We observed minimal interference from eagles during subsequent releases at this time of year. In the hierarchy that formed in each of their respective release groups, condors SB #217, #284, and #320 were the most subordinate (Table 2) and as each group merged with the previously released population these subordinate individuals maintained low status until another (younger) group was released. At that time they appeared to immediately gain a higher status than the younger newcomers. While each of these subordinate birds typically remained aloof from other condors after the release of their group, often feeding alone and earlier in the day than the higher status birds, they gradually became more integrated into the group, and within one month were routinely feeding and flying short distances with other condors in the wild. Released condor flights gradually became more extensive and birds were increasingly more likely to roost overnight on cliffs several kilometers away from the release site (Plate 26). While not common during these early stages of release, some of the released condors fed on carrion other than that provided at or near the release site. However, the released condors' apparent inability to consistently find such wild food on excursions away from the release site, the presence of other condors and a reliable source of food at the release area, probably enhanced the attraction of the release area to these wild-ranging condors and encouraged their return on a regular basis.

Table 2. Release (Rel.), recapture (Cap.) history, and number of days in the wild for California Condors released in Baja California, Mexico (10 October 2002–1 September 2005).

Stud-book #	2002		2003		2004		2005	Days free-flying	Days free-flying (%)
	Rel.	Capt.	Rel.	Capt.	Rel.	Capt.	Rel.		
217			25 May	15 Feb	25 May	5 Dec	7 Apr	607	73
218	10 Oct	22 Oct	23 July	13 Jan	25 May	5 Dec	16 May	489	40
220			25 May	15 Feb	25 May	3 Dec	5 Apr	607	73
259	10 Oct	24 Oct	23 July	15 Feb	25 May	6 Oct	7 Apr	503	42
261	10 Oct	27 Oct	25 May	13 Feb	25 May	3 Dec	5 Apr	622	75
284					31 Jul	9 Dec	5 Apr	280	71
269					31 Jul	6 Oct	5 Apr	216	54
279					31 Jul[a]			116	100
315							16 May	108	100
320							16 May	108	100

[a] Disappeared; last contact with #279 on 4 Dec 2004.

Very soon after the oldest, most experienced birds began using new areas, the most recently released condors also began frequenting these sites, eventually returning on their own to the release site. By June 2005, the month during which flying conditions were best, radio-telemetry and GPS satellite data indicated that released condors had ranged 400 km north and south of the release site along the Sierra San Pedro Mártir and Juarez ranges (Plate 26). During winter months, characterized by the worst flying conditions with shorter days and weaker thermals, released condors typically did not range much beyond the release site and adjacent feeding areas, as well as favorite canyons 15 km east on the Sierra San Pedro Mártir escarpments overlooking the San Felipe Desert (Plate 27).

Condor mortality.—Three condors were lost or removed from the release program during the study period: SB #225, #279, and #319. Male condor SB #225 was killed by a bobcat overnight on 23 December 2003 in the small section of the release pen where it was recovering from a wing injury. One confirmed case of lead poisoning occurred to male condor SB #319 after ingesting burro meat fed inside the release pen on 7 October 2004, which was unknowingly contaminated with lead. Multiple blood tests revealed #319's lead levels to be 736 μg dL^{-1}; far higher than previously documented cases of lead exposure at U.S. release sites (see Hall et al., Parish et al. this volume). Chelation treatment was given and the bird physically recovered although, to date, #319 remains un-releasable because of behavioral problems. Whether the daily handling over several weeks during chelation treatment at the San Diego Zoo's Wild Animal Park had a negative effect or whether neurological damage occurred due to the high lead levels was unknown. However, this condor was behaviorally compromised rendering him unlikely to succeed in the wild at this point in time.

Another section of the same lead-tainted burro was placed at an outside site and fed upon by free-flying condors, including condor SB #279. Concurrent with the lead poisoning of #319, condor #279 began exhibiting atypical behavior, including flying off in various directions and not returning. Although it was successfully tracked on several occasions, using radio-telemetry and visual sightings, over a two-month period between 12 October and 4 December 2004, it was never recovered and is presumed dead. Whether #279 also suffered from sub-lethal levels of lead poisoning that altered its behavior and compromised its survivorship remains open to question.

Non-proffered feeding.—Our data were based on the cumulative number of days spent in the wild (3,583 days) by 11 condors between October 2002 and September 2005 (see Table 2). The older, more experienced birds (SB #217, #218, #220, #259, and #261) each spent over one year in the wild over a three year period and their use of non-proffered carcasses was indicated in three ways: they were directly observed feeding on non-proffered carcasses, were seen returning from multi-day excursions with full crops and, on occasion, GPS tracking data indicated that feeding probably took place away from the proffered feeding sites. Based on these data, we estimated that such non-proffered food constituted 2–5% of all documented feeding events. It was likely that the activity of other diurnal scavengers such as Turkey Vultures, Common Ravens, Golden Eagles and coyotes attracted the condors' attention to non-proffered carcasses of mule deer (*Odocoileus hemionus*), bighorn sheep (*Ovis canadensis*), cows, horses, and burros that died in the Sierra San Pedro Mártir and surrounding area. Compared to reintroduction sites in the U.S., the rate of integration into the environment by the young birds and their use of non-proffered carcasses appeared similar (C. Parish and G. Austin pers. comm.), but much lower than the non-proffered carcass use recorded for most condors in the longer established northern Arizona population (Hunt et al. this volume).

Response to humans.—As released condors gradually ranged farther from the release area during exploratory flights they had many opportunities to see, approach and investigate people or human structures in the environment. During this study, there were one to five biologists in the field on a daily basis. While concerted effort was made to stay hidden from the birds and significant time was spent in blinds, the free-ranging condors were often aware of the presence of humans as the biologists moved between observation points (OP) on the ground. However, at no time during the study period did any of the released condors approach our field biologists when they were discovered in the environment (e.g., by condors overflying an OP). Moreover, condors would typically flush away if they were accidentally approached by biologists. The field camp, only two kilometers from the release pen, consisted of two mobile homes, campers and tents which, although painted in a camouflaged pattern, were often in view when the birds gained altitude. However, although the birds obviously noticed our activities while flying overhead, they never came to investigate the camp or ever appeared to alter their flight path because of human activity.

A dramatic example of the behavior of released condors in the presence of humans occurred within a few months after the release of the first three birds in 2003 (see Table 2). On 4 July, a wild fire broke out within a few kilometers of the release site and burned for two weeks causing us to evacuate the captive birds from the site while the fire raged throughout the area. Although the three released birds escaped the flames and often used the huge plumes of smoke as they would thermals to gain altitude, several hundred, often brightly clothed fire fighters descended upon the area of the release site. However, despite intense human activity levels, the three condors kept a distance and no incidents of their approaching humans were reported.

Another potential site for released condors to interact with humans was the National Observatory (Universidad Nacional Autonoma de México), the only permanent occupied building in the area, located on the highest peaks of the Sierra San Pedro Mártir National Park. The facility is situated at 3,150 m along the highest ridge of the range, directly uphill at a distance of 30 km from the release site. Consisting of several buildings and continuously housing 15 to 30 researchers and workers throughout the year, it offered an enticing attraction to any curious condor. As released condors became better flyers they naturally explored these higher elevations. We accurately predicted that as flying experience increased, released condors would move in the direction of the observatory area. The very first documented flights by condors to the observatory area were of birds flying at altitudes of 1,000 m or more over the observatory buildings as they explored the Sierra peaks. Following this a weekly pattern of high-altitude flights ensued, with no evidence of any contact between observatory personnel and condors until mid-2004, when condors were observed roosting in the area's tall pines along with Turkey Vultures. Unfortunately, at this time Turkey Vultures, Common Ravens and coyotes were visiting the observatory's dump site, a pit among the trees, and feeding on garbage left in the open within 500 m of some of the observatory buildings. Within days of the first observation of the condors in the area, some condors were seen on the ground at the dump by observatory personnel apparently attracted to the activities of the other scavengers. Frightening the birds with loud noises, and launching pinecones in their direction, was only temporarily effective. Observatory personnel cooperated by covering the original dump with soil and creating a scavenger-proof system at a new site. Without the attraction of other avian and mammalian scavengers, condors discontinued their interest in the area. However, they continued to occasionally roost in tall pine trees about a kilometer from the observatory buildings.

In 2005, reports by local people in the small township of Valle de la Trinidad some 80 km to the north of the release site suggested that condors were occasionally utilizing that area. Thus, we made a concerted effort to educate the public in the area by providing pamphlets, posters and giving talks to the community schools and to the Kiliwa people (Native Americans) in the area. As indicated by interviews with local people, we know of only seven occasions when it was likely that the local inhabitants observed condors, often describing them as huge "tagged" birds. In all cases, the condors were perched or flying at a distance. These observations corresponded to the GPS data collected from the five oldest release birds, showing that they often flew in this area at high altitude, or that they roosted in the area on distant, uninhabited cliffs. We presumed that the condors were attracted to the large flocks of Turkey Vultures that used this lowland ranching area, particularly during winter. Observations suggested that Turkey Vultures virtually abandon the higher altitudes in winter, presumably due to the difficulty of obtaining sufficient carrion.

Discussion

Curiosity plays an important role in the life of scavengers. Condors must continually investigate the activity of other species if they are to be consistently successful at foraging. For example, California Condors appear to monitor the activity of smaller avian scavengers to help in locating food sources in a manner similar to that suggested for King Vultures (*Sarcohamphus papa*) in Neotropical forests (Houston 1988). When it comes to humans, however, ideally a condor in the release program should be at least neutral, if not negative, toward the sight of people in the post-release period. Yet some condors previously released at sites in California and Arizona as part of the ongoing condor recovery program were notably curious toward humans and their structures to a degree that could have jeopardized their survivorship (Meretsky et al. 2000). Typically these were condors that appeared to be low in the social hierarchy of their release cohorts, as observed by zookeepers prior to release (M. Clark and D. Sterner pers. comm.). Further, their tame behavior often attracted the attention of other condors and acted as a negative influence on less human-oriented birds.

The most practical and meaningful way to assess whether changes in the puppet rearing technique (see Clark et al. this volume) resulted in beneficial behavioral changes in the wild was to closely follow the released condors and document their reactions when exposed to situations that might induce "bad" or maladaptive behavior (see Snyder and Snyder 2000, Cade et al. 2004). Based on our initial evaluations, we believe that released condors at the Baja site were exposed to a similar degree of situations that might lead to human–condor interactions relative to those experienced by condors released in California and Arizona. Yet, the condors released in Baja have shown a marked difference in maintaining a lack of interest in human activities and artificial structures to date, relative to the interest in human activities and structures shown by condors in both the southern California population (e.g., see Mee et al. this volume) and the Arizona population (Cade et al. 2004). Further, other than the release pen itself, we know of no instances of the birds released in Baja landing on any man made structures.

We recognize that the social rank is an important behavioral parameter for understanding intraspecific relationships in condors and other vulture species (Donázar et al. 1999, Bukowinski et al. this volume), and appears to plays some role in how well an individual adjusts to the wild after being released. Based on the casual observations of various released groups in Arizona and California (S. Farry and S. Osborn in Arizona; G. Austin, J. Burnett, and D. Clendenen in California, pers comm.), we would have predicted the most subordinate condors in a release group to do less well than

240 WALLACE ET AL.

higher status birds. However, in this study, low ranking birds did remarkably well. While the most subordinate birds of various release groups, SB #217, #284, and #320, were less social and more conservative in their movements and interactions in the beginning, they never showed tameness and eventually increased in status, integrating well into the overall release population.

This study was unable to determine which adjustments to the modified rearing method described by Clark et al. (this volume) played the most important role in producing socially well-adjusted birds that are not inclined to investigate the activities of people. While these refinements to the puppet rearing technique are initially encouraging, the method needs to be tested rigorously over a longer period of time with more condors, and with controls, to validate our findings to date.

ACKNOWLEDGMENTS

In Mexico, support, collaboration, and funding came from The National Institute of Ecology (INE), the Mexican Department of Natural Resources (SEMARNAP), National Park Service (CONANP), the Center for Higher Learning in Science and Education (CICESE); the non-government organizations Terra Peninsular and Pro Natura; the University of Baja (UNAM); local ranchers especially Ejido Bramadero, and CONABIO, a government–private funding agency. In the United States we worked with the U.S. Fish and Wildlife Service, the Santa Barbara Zoo, the Peregrine Fund and volunteer pilots James Lemke, Greg George, Phil Benham and Mike Essery, who offered their time and planes to help the project. Thanks to Joe Burnett for the discussions on the pen–trap. Also, Exequiel Ezcurra, Allison Alberts, Horacio de la Cueva, Alejandro Inojosa Eduardo Peters and Elvia de la Cruz, whose assistance and support made the study possible.

LITERATURE CITED

BUCKLEY, N. J. 1996. Food finding and the influence of information, local enhancement, and communal roosting on foraging success of North American vultures. Auk 113:473–488.
BUKOWINSKI, A. T., F. B. BERCOVITCH, A. C. ALBERTS, M. P. WALLACE, M. E. MACE, AND S. ANCONA. 2007. A quantitative assessment of the California Condor mentoring program. Pages 197–212 in California Condors in the 21st Century (A. Mee and L. S. Hall, Eds.). Series in Ornithology, no. 2.
CADE, T. J., S. A. H. OSBORN, W. G. HUNT, AND C. P. WOODS. 2004. Commentary on released California Condors Gymnogyps californianus in Arizona. Pages 11–25 in Raptors Worldwide: Proceedings of VI World Conference on Birds of Prey and Owls (R. D. Chancellor and B.-U. Meyburg, Eds.). World Working Group on Birds of Prey and Owls/MME-Birdlife, Hungary.

CLARK, M., M. WALLACE, AND C. DAVID. 2007. Rearing California Condors for release using a modified puppet-rearing technique. Pages 213–226 *in* California Condors in the 21st Century (A. Mee and L. S. Hall, Eds.). Series in Ornithology, no. 2.

DONÁZAR, J. A., A. TRAVAINI, O. CEBALLOS, A. RODRÍGUEZ, M. DELIBES, AND F. HIRALDO. 1999. Effects of sex-associated competitive asymmetries on foraging group structure and despotic distribution in Andean Condors. Behavioral Ecology and Sociobiology 45:55–65.

HARTT, E.W., N. C. HARVEY, A. J. LEETE, AND K. PRESTON. 1994. Effects of age at pairing on reproduction in captive California Condors (*Gymnogyps californianus*). Zoo Biology 13:3–11.

HOUSTON, D. C. 1988. Competition for food between Neotropical vultures in forest. Ibis 130:402–417.

HUNT, W. G., C. N. PARISH, S. C. FARRY, T. G. LORD, AND R. SIEG. 2007. Movements of introduced California Condors in Arizona in relation to lead exposure. Pages 79–96 *in* California Condors in the 21st Century (A. Mee and L. S. Hall, Eds.). Series in Ornithology, no. 2.

JÁCOME, N. L. 2005. Programa binacional de conservación del Cóndor Andino Chile y Argentina. Registro Sudamericano del Cóndor Andino Jardín Zoológico de la Ciudad de Buenos Aires, República de la India 3000 (1425) Buenos Aires, Argentina.

KENWARD, R. E. 2000. A Manual for Wildlife Radio Tagging. Academic Press, San Diego, CA

KOFORD, C. B. 1953. The California Condor. National Audubon Research Report 4: 1–154.

KUEHLER, C. M., AND P. N. WITMAN. 1988. Artificial incubation of California Condor *Gymnogyps californianus* eggs removed from the wild. Zoo Biology 7:123–132.

LIEBERMAN, A., J. V. RODRIGUEZ, J. M. PAEZ, AND J. WILEY. 1993. The reintroduction of the Andean Condor into Colombia, South America: 1989–1991. Oryx 27:83–90.

LORENZ, K. Z. 1981. The Formations of Ethology: The Principal Ideas and Discoveries in Animal Behavior. Simon and Schuster, New York.

MACE, M. E. 2005. California Condor (*Gymnogyps californianus*) International Studbook. Zoological Society of San Diego, San Diego Wild Animal Park, Escondido, California.

MERETSKY, V. J., AND N. F. R. SNYDER. 1992. Range use and movements of California Condors. Condor 94:313–335.

MERETSKY, V. J., N. F. R. SNYDER, S. R. BEISSINGER, D. A. CLENDENEN, AND J. W. WILEY. 2000. Demography of the California Condor: implications for reestablishment. Conservation Biology 14:957–967.

PIANKA, E. R. 1970. On r and K selection. American Naturalist 104:592–597.

SNYDER, N. F. R., AND J. A. HAMBER. 1985. Replacement clutching and annual nesting of California Condors. Condor 87:374–378.

VALUTIS, L. L., AND J. M. MARZLUFF. 1999. The appropriateness of puppet-rearing birds for reintroduction. Conservation Biology 13:584–591.

WALLACE, M. P. 1991. Methods and strategies for releasing California condors to the wild. Pages 121–128 *in* American Association of Zoological Parks and Aquariums Annual Conference Proceedings, Wheeling, West Virginia.

WALLACE, M. P. 1994. Control of behavioral development in the context of reintroduction programs for birds. Zoo Biology 13:491–499.

WALLACE, M. P., AND S. A. TEMPLE. 1983. An evaluation of techniques for releasing hand-reared vultures to the wild. Pages 400–423 *in* Vulture Biology and Management (S. R. Wilbur and J. A. Jackson, Eds.). University of California Press, Berkeley.

WALLACE, M. P., AND S. A. TEMPLE. 1987. Competitive interactions within and between species in a guild of avian scavengers. Auk 104:290–295.

WALLACE, M. P., AND S. A. TEMPLE. 1988. A comparison between raptor and vultures hacking techniques. Pages 75–81 *in* Proceedings of the International Symposium on Raptor Reintroduction (D. K. Garcelon and G. W. Roemer, Eds.). Institute for Wildlife Studies, Arcata, California.

WOODS, C. P., W. R. HEINRICH, S. C. FARRY, C. N. PARISH, S. A. H. OSBORNE, AND T. J. CADE. 2007. Survival and reproduction of California Condors released in Arizona. Pages 57–78 *in* California Condors in the 21st Century (A. Mee and L. S. Hall, Eds.). Series in Ornithology, no. 2.

14

California Condors in the 21st Century—Conservation Problems and Solutions

Allan Mee,[1,3] *and Noel F. R. Snyder*[2]

ABSTRACT.—Releases of captives to re-establish the critically endangered California Condor (*Gymnogyps californianus*) in the wild were begun in 1992 and continue at present in southern and central California, northern Arizona, and Baja California, Mexico. However, most of the problems leading to the historic population decline in the wild still operate today and threaten the success of recovery efforts. We review the major conservation problems facing condor populations in the wild: achieving adequate survival rates, adequate reproduction, and normal behavior. We also consider the impacts of land-use changes and development of condor habitat. Lead poisoning, utility line collisions and electrocutions, shooting, and predation have been the most serious problems affecting survival rates. Poor nest success rates and depressed breeding effort hinder the establishment of viable breeding populations especially in southern California. Human-oriented behavior of release birds still persists in populations while effects of management (especially food subsidy) to reduce exposure to lead have grossly altered foraging behavior in some populations. Establishing viable, self-sustaining populations must be the overriding goal of the condor recovery program. Achieving this goal requires that these problems are corrected by innovative and flexible research and management. Critical to this effort will be the elimination of lead in the condor's range, the re-establishment of research-driven management, conservation goals such as time limits for the establishment of populations, testing new rearing and release methods, and independent review of progress.

CRES, Zoological Society of San Diego, 15600 San Pasqual Valley Road, Escondido, California 92027, USA.
P.O. Box 16426, Portal, Arizona 85632, USA.
E-mail: allan.mee@ireland.com

The long campaign to save the endangered California Condor (*Gymnogyps californianus*) from extinction had its primary origins in studies of the species in the 1930s–1940s (Robinson 1939, 1940; Koford 1953). These early efforts were followed by a succession of intensive research and conservation efforts in the 1960s, 1970s, and 1980s (Miller et al. 1965; Sibley 1968, 1969; Wilbur 1978; Snyder and Snyder 2000, 2005) and culminated in the ongoing captive-breeding and reintroduction programs initiated in the late 1980s and 1990s (see Grantham, Snyder this volume). Together, these various efforts constitute one of the most engrossing and instructive chapters in endangered species conservation. The condor as a taxonomic entity is no longer in imminent danger of departing the planet, thanks in large part to the tireless efforts of many dedicated field and zoo biologists and conservationists. But, despite the apparent safety of the species in terms of immediate conservation status, most of the problems that contributed to the species' decline to near extinction still persist, and the species is still far from full recovery in the wild (Plate 28). Moreover, new problems not documented for the historic population have emerged to threaten the re-establishment of viable wild populations.

Most of the major limiting factors for California Condor populations in the 21st century are addressed in this volume, including lead poisoning (Hall et al., Hunt et al., Parish et al., Snyder, Sorenson and Burnett, Sullivan et al., Woods et al.), high nestling mortality (Mee et al.), and, to some extent, persistent behavioral problems (Snyder, Mee et al.). Other studies included in this volume have focused on genetic variability in the post-bottleneck condor population (Adams and Villablanca), effects of changes in rearing methods on puppet-reared chicks in captivity (Clark et al.), pre-release mentoring (Bukowinski et al.), and releases to the wild in Baja California, Mexico (Wallace et al.). As detailed in these studies, certain problems that were important in early condor releases appear to have declined in recent years. For example, the propensity of released condors to land on powerpoles has been reduced by aversion training using electrified mock powerpoles at captive and pre-release facilities. However, collisions with utility lines still occur at a modest frequency, and other problems have increased in severity and remain as major challenges yet to be satisfactorily addressed.

Here, we review the major immediate conservation problems still faced by California Condors and consider potential solutions to these problems, recognizing that it is possible, and even likely, that some additional stresses not addressed here may emerge to threaten condor populations in the future. For example, the effects of global climate change on populations, communities, and ecosystems could be catastrophic (e.g., Visser et al. 1998, Buse et al. 1999, Inouye et al. 2000), but the future importance of these effects for condor populations is presently unknown and beyond the scope of this review. The immediate conservation problems faced by condors can perhaps best be broken down into the problems relating to the three primary goals of any faunal recovery program: (1) achieving adequate survival rates in the wild, (2) achieving adequate reproduction in the wild, and (3) achieving normal behavior in the wild. While all three goals are essential to full success, and all are inextricably linked with one another, it is useful to separate them in terms of the solutions needed. Our plan of presentation is to discuss major immediate problems in decreasing order of priority for each of the major goals. In the final sections we also consider habitat deterioration threats affecting releases and give major recommendations for the future.

ACHIEVING ADEQUATE SURVIVAL RATES

Lead poisoning.—Lead poisoning was first documented as a major threat to California Condors in the mid 1980s (Janssen et al. 1986, Wiemeyer et al. 1988), although absence of earlier documentation was almost surely due to a failure to look for this contaminant in early necropsies. Lead contamination remains the most serious impediment to condor recovery today (see Hall et al., Hunt et al., Parish et al., Snyder, Sorenson and Burnett, Sullivan et al., Woods et al. this volume). Lead poisoning was not the only factor leading to the demise of the historic condor population (Snyder this volume), and it was not a major issue during the first years of releases when birds were mostly dependent on clean food subsidy, but it has again emerged as the major mortality threat to birds in the wild and perhaps the principal factor precluding full success of reintroduction efforts. Lead poisoning due to ingestion of ammunition fragments in carcasses and gut piles of hunted animals is not a problem limited to the California Condor (see Wiemeyer et al. 1988, Craig et al. 1990, Pattee et al. 1990, Harmata and Restani 1995, Kramer and Redig 1997). It is, however, an especially severe problem for obligate scavengers such as the condor, and its full correction appears to be essential, especially in view of the continued existence of other significant threats to wild condors that may be much more difficult to correct.

Although more released condors have died from other mortality factors than lead poisoning, this comparison is fundamentally misleading because of the many birds rescued from lead poisoning by intensive management, involving regular trapping and blood-sampling of birds, and emergency chelation therapy for heavily contaminated birds (see Hall et al., Parish et al., Sorenson and Burnett this volume). If the 39 condors (77 chelations) saved to date by emergency chelation are regarded as potential mortalities averted, lead poisoning becomes far and away the most serious mortality threat to released populations (see Snyder this volume). Furthermore, all released populations are still at least partially dependent on subsidies of clean food, and cases of lead poisoning would undoubtedly be even much more frequent if subsidy were abandoned.

Lead poisoning has been a particularly prominent problem for released condors in northern Arizona where it has paralleled the development of desirable wide-ranging foraging patterns, along with the birds' discovery of plentiful food supplies during the hunting season on the nearby Kaibab Plateau (Hunt et al. this volume). In contrast, the reduction in frequency of lead poisoning seen in southern California released birds in recent years has almost surely been due to greatly increased dependence of this population on clean food subsidy (Hall et al. this volume). Unfortunately, the many problems associated with food subsidy (Mee et al. this volume) clearly indicate that this remedy does not represent a satisfactory long-term solution to the lead problem or a desirable long-term practice in the conservation of the species. Similarly, endless intensive efforts to detoxify poisoned condors through chelation therapy are clearly an unacceptable long-term solution to the problem of lead ingestion.

Although releases in central California and Baja California have not experienced major lead-poisoning problems, these problems are almost sure to develop for any free-ranging condor population in regions where shooting of wildlife occurs (i.e., virtually everywhere except within no-hunting reserves, none of which today is large enough to encompass a viable condor population). Chamberlain et al. (2005) suggested that marine mammal carcasses represent an alternative food supply that could provide protection from lead contamination to released condors, but this conclusion must be questioned because of long-term data indicating shooting as a frequent cause of death in California's marine mammals (Goldstein et al. 1999). Further, marine mammals constitute a highly questionable food supply because of their continuing high organochlorine contaminant loads, especially PCBs (see Le Boeuf and Bonnell 1971, Le Boeuf et al. 2002, Ylitalo et al. 2005), the butyltins in marine food chains (Kannan et al. 1998), and domoic acid contamination resulting from diatom blooms (Scholin et al. 2000). Recent reproductive failures of reintroduced Bald Eagles (*Haliaeetus leucocephalus*) on Santa Catalina Island, California, have evidently been due primarily to contamination with organochlorines originating in marine foods (Garcelon 1997, Sharpe and Dooley 2001), and concerns have been raised regarding the viability of various marine mammal populations at the top of food chains because of contamination with a variety of environmental pollutants (Ross et al. 1996, Kannan et al. 1998, Ylitalo et al. 2005). Thus, encouraging the California Condor to become an additional link in severely contaminated marine food chains carries major risks.

Solutions.—As long as lead contamination of carcasses in the wild persists, it appears that wild condor populations cannot be sustained without continued releases and intensive and expensive management (chelations and food subsidy) to mitigate the effects of chronic poisoning. Removing lead from the condor's range appears to be an essential step in achieving truly self-sustaining wild populations. Research has clearly indicated that the primary exposure pathway for condors and other vultures and raptors is through the ingestion of lead fragments in carrion or prey items killed or wounded by hunters and other shooters (Fry and Maurer 2003; Church 2005; Hunt et al. this volume). Thus, the continuing use of lead ammunitions is the problem needing correction.

In theory, the problem could be solved by abolishing hunting and other shooting activities in the condors' range. However, no historic condor researchers and none of the contributors to this volume have advocated eliminating hunting and shooting in the range of the species, in part because of the tremendous political and enforcement difficulties posed by such a step. Also, hunting is a legitimate and basically positive activity for many residents of the region, and might, on balance, be a positive activity for condor conservation via increased food supplies, if lead ammunitions could be replaced by the non-toxic alternatives now becoming available.

Although resisted by certain elements of the hunting community, removing the lead threat through a switch to alternative ammunitions does not pose a basic threat to hunting activities. Instead, such a move offers significant health benefits to hunters and their families by helping avert the unavoidable ingestion of small, but nevertheless detrimental, amounts of lead prevalent in wild game killed with lead ammunitions (Hunt et al. 2006). The sublethal effects of lead ingestion on humans are well documented and severely debilitating (e.g., see Otto and Fox 1993, Rosen 1995, Brewster and Perazella 2004). The debate should not be about whether it is advisable to fully replace lead ammunitions with alternative non-toxic ammunitions, but about what is the best strategy to achieve this goal.

One strategy, already implemented in Arizona, is an aggressive program of education and incentives, including supplying hunters with free non-toxic ammunitions (Sullivan et al. this volume). We endorse these efforts strongly, but believe it is questionable how much reduction in lead contamination such efforts alone can achieve as long as lead ammunitions remain fully available. Especially in view of the substantial amount of poaching of game that still occurs in many parts of the condor's range, it is doubtful that more than part of the problem can be addressed by education efforts with responsible hunters. For this reason, we view the value of such efforts not so much as promising a full or adequate solution to the lead problem, but as a valuable initial step toward full removal of lead ammunitions from the market. Once hunters have a chance to become familiar with the use and advantages of non-toxic ammunitions, including their human-health advantages, it is doubtful that major opposition to a full phase-out of lead ammunitions would persist. Unfortunately, efforts comparable to the hunter education program in Arizona have yet to be formally initiated in California, despite endorsement of such efforts by the California Condor Recovery Team in 2001.

We believe that the goal should be no less than full removal of lead ammunitions nationwide, not to mention internationally, as the benefits would apply not only to condors but also to many other species and to human health in general. With only partial removal of lead ammunitions, overall mortality rates of condors may still remain too high for viable populations because of the persistence of other threats, including such problems as collisions and direct illegal shooting of condors, threats that are very difficult to reduce to zero, but cumulatively could still result in mortality rates too high for populations to persist (see Snyder this volume). Recognition of a goal of full removal of lead ammunitions in combination with public education about the health risks of continued use of lead ammunitions (see Otto and Fox 1993, Landrigan and Todd 1994, Brewster and Perazella 2004) are matters that deserve substantially increased emphasis in the future. To date, the state and federal agencies with authority over condor conservation have not endorsed full removal of lead ammunitions, but rather have called only for voluntary efforts to reduce their use. We consider it unlikely that this limited approach will be enough to achieve viable condor populations. Further, a reliance on the voluntary approach may delay the implementation of effective solutions unnecessarily, and will obligate the conservation program to conduct expensive and intensive efforts to monitor blood lead levels of released condors and to practice emergency chelations indefinitely.

Ultimately, the most straightforward and effective strategy to solve the lead problem may well be regulations mandating the use of safe alternatives and banning the use of lead ammunitions, as has been achieved for waterfowl hunting (U.S. Fish and Wildlife Service [USFWS] 1986). In 2005 a petition proposing a full conversion to non-toxic ammunitions in California was presented to the California Fish and Game Commission by the Center for Biological Diversity (CBD) and the Natural Resources Defence Council (NRDC). This petition was, however, refused. Efforts are now being made to introduce a lead ban via bills in the California Assembly, although these efforts have not yet received official support from the condor program. Other options, including legal remedies under the Endangered Species Act, may also be pursued by the CBD and NRDC. Thus, perhaps surprisingly, the primary impetus toward removing lead ammunitions from the environment has come from parties external to the condor program and has yet to be embraced by either the California Condor Recovery Team or the agencies directly involved in condor recovery.

Some condor program participants have expressed concerns that efforts to fully replace lead ammunitions with non-toxic alternatives could cause more harm than good due to a backlash from hunters directed against the condor and other endangered species. However, based on surveyed attitudes of individual hunters in Arizona and California (Sullivan et al. this volume.), we feel this position greatly exaggerates the potential for negative fallout. Alternative ammunitions with ballistic performance and killing power equal to or exceeding those of lead are now becoming increasingly available (e.g., see www.projectgutpile.org), while the cost differentials between lead and non-toxic ammunitions can be addressed in various ways to make a transition to non-toxic ammunitions desirable for hunters (as for example, in the Arizona program). Further, the new non-toxic ammunitions do not pose risks of damage to guns as were initially posed by steel shot in the conversion to non-toxic ammunitions for waterfowl hunting. Altogether, anticipating major resistance or backlash from hunters to a full conversion to non-toxic ammunitions appears unwarranted, especially if the switch is justified primarily on human health grounds. Also unwarranted is any unnecessary delay in achieving a full solution to the lead problem. With proper investments in education and publicity efforts, we firmly believe that a full conversion is practical in the near term. Maximal speed toward this goal would be highly beneficial, especially when all the costs of continuing the status quo are considered.

Compliance with the ban on the use of lead shot for waterfowl hunting has been high (90–98%), and use of non-toxic alternatives has become standard for this kind of hunting (Havera et al. 1994). Lead exposure and lead-poisoning mortality declined significantly in some duck species following the ban on lead shot in 1991 (Anderson et al. 2000, Samuel and Bowers 2000), although ingestion by waterfowl and other bird species of historic spent lead shot continues to be a problem that may persist for many years (Kendall et al. 1996, Schulz et al. 2002). The removal of all lead ammunitions from the market represents a logical sequel to the switch from lead to non-toxics for waterfowl hunting, a conversion that was achieved successfully in spite of much greater hurdles than are faced today with a comprehensive ban. With a comprehensive ban, once lead ammunitions disappear from the market, compliance and enforcement issues can be expected to disappear, along with a need for continued close monitoring and treatment of lead-poisoned condors.

Utility line collisions and electrocutions.—Utility line collisions and electrocutions are an important source of mortality for many bird species (Janss and Ferrer 1998), including raptors (e.g., Harmata et al. 1999, Krone et al. 2003) and Old World vultures (Mundy et al. 1992, Sarrazin et al. 1994). Likewise, utility line collisions have been an important source of mortality for reintroduced condors in California ($n = 9$), but less so in northern Arizona ($n = 1$) where utility lines are much less prevalent. Only three cases of collision-related deaths were documented in the historic wild condor population, although it is likely that other undocumented cases occurred (Snyder and Snyder 2000).

Early condor releases resulted in birds often using utility poles as perches (a tendency unknown in the historic wild population), and frequent utility line collisions may have resulted in part from this tendency. Aversion training at captive and pre-release facilities has apparently been success-ful in reducing this tendency, and most recent releases have been free of major collision problems. However, the problem resurfaced temporarily in the first release of condors at the Pinnacles National Monument, San Benito County, California, in 2003. These birds were eventually retrapped and held for further pre-release aversive training before re-release while some birds were transferred to northern-Arizona in 2005. No further such problems have been encounted in this release area.

Collisions with utility lines can result in instantaneous death or ter-minal injury from the impact of collision (Janss and Ferrer 1998) or from electrocution (Lesham 1985, Lehman 2001). Single strand utility lines may be a greater hazard than multiple strands because they may be less visible to condors or be situated in locations where condors are relatively likely to come into contact with them. In December 2004, a recently fledged condor chick was observed clipping a single-strand utility line apparently without harm within a few hundred meters of its nest in Grand Canyon National Park (J. Sinclair pers. comm.). More recently, the same juvenile condor was recovered injured with a broken wing in Arizona, possibly a victim of a col-lision of some sort. Flying in poor light conditions or in fog may be particu-larly hazardous for condors in areas with powerlines, but we have regularly observed birds flying in fog. More insidiously perhaps, birds with elevated lead levels resulting from ingestion of bullet fragments or lead shot may be especially likely to collide with powerlines (O'Halloran et al. 1989, Kelly and Kelly 2005), perhaps due to neurological impairment. To what extent lead poisoning contributes to powerline collisions and mortality in condors is unknown, but could be studied retrospectively and in the future by deter-mining lead levels in feather and bone samples of collision victims.

Solutions.—Pre-release aversive training of condors with dummy utility poles apparently reduces collision mortalities significantly and should be continued, although it cannot be expected to prevent all colli-sion mortalities. Aversion training has not resulted in condors avoiding all human structures, and instances are still seen of birds landing on build-ings, vehicles, and microwave towers. In addition to aversion training, the burying or retrofitting of utility lines with visual markers can be expected to significantly reduce collision rates (see Janss and Ferrer 1988, Ferrer and Hiraldo 1991) and should be seriously considered in all places where condors congregate or are found consistently over long periods (e.g., vicinity of nests). Moreover, condor releases should be avoided in areas where utility lines are present nearby and likely to be a source of mortality. While significant reductions in collision mortalities can be anticipated from the above actions, the expense and difficulties of implementing some of these actions are considerable, and at best they cannot be expected to completely remove the problem. Some level of collision mortalities will probably continue into the indefinite future, despite all remedial actions, although this should not be used as a justification to avoid corrective actions where they are especially relevant and affordable.

Shooting.—Historically, shooting was long considered to be the most important source of mortality for the condor (Miller et al. 1965, Wilbur 1978), although its importance relative to other mortality factors now appears to be more modest (Snyder this volume). Shooting for museum and private collections ceased in the early 20th century, and although wanton shootings continue to occur (five mortalities of released condors documented, three in Arizona and two in California, between 1999 and 2003; another bird wounded in southern California in fall 2005), it seems likely that the problem may have been considerably greater in the 19th and early 20th centuries. Nevertheless, it is reasonable to speculate that additional undocumented cases may have occurred in recent years, as 20 released condors overall have died without recovery and many of these (n = 12) went missing during the hunting season when risks of both shooting and lead poisoning were presumably at a maximum.

Solutions.—Investigations into the deaths of two condors, one in Arizona and one in California, have led to criminal prosecutions, although neither case resulted in the maximum sentence being imposed (i.e., incarceration). Neither case was prosecuted under the Endangered Species Act (ESA). In part, this was because the condor population in Arizona does not have full ESA protection. The other case, the shooting of AC8 in California in 2003, was prosecuted under the Migratory Bird Treaty Act as a case of mistaken identity for the protected but non-endangered Turkey Vulture (*Cathartes aura*). Apart from such prosecutions, public education efforts about condors and the bird's protected status are essential activities to minimize such threats. It seems likely, however, with the prevalence of firearms and the tendency of condors to key in on areas of high shooting activity because of increased availability of carrion (see Hunt et al. this volume), that shooting will continue to be an additional source of mortality for condors even with substantial education and enforcement efforts.

Predation.—Although predation is a natural part of the biology of virtually all species, extremely few cases of natural predation or attempted natural predation were documented for the historic wild condor population aside from predation on condor eggs by Common Ravens (*Corvus corax*).

During the 1980s, observed predation attempts by predators other than ravens were limited to one case of attempted but unsuccessful predation on a nestling condor by a black bear (*Ursus americanus*), two unsuccessful predation attempts on nestling condors by Golden Eagles (*Aquila chrysaetos*), and one apparently serious but unsuccessful predation attempt on a recent fledgling condor by a Golden Eagle (Snyder and Snyder 1991, 2000). Chronic problems with raven predation during the 1980s were addressed in part by shooting the ravens threatening two condor nests and by quick removal of condor eggs from the wild for artificial incubation. Plans to investigate the potential for deterring ravens from egg predation by taste-aversion conditioning were developed but never implemented before the last of the historic birds were taken captive. No specific management efforts were ever implemented against the predation threats represented by black bears and Golden Eagles.

In contrast, predation on reintroduced populations of condors by coyotes (*Canis latrans*), bobcats (*Lynx rufus*), and Golden Eagles has been quantitatively conspicuous during condor releases to the wild, with the loss of 11 birds since 1997 (eight in Arizona, one in southern California and two in Baja California). In addition, there has been one documented loss of a condor egg to ravens during release efforts in southern California (see Mee et al. this volume). In part, the substantial frequency of coyote predation events ($n = 6$) appears to have been a result of recently released condors roosting in locations easily accessible to predators instead of using safer sites on vertical cliffs or trees, a tendency resulting perhaps from the absence of parent birds to guide the behavior of the released birds. An absence of parental guardians may also have predisposed captive-reared birds to eagle predation. However, captive-reared individuals, even when parent-reared, are often more naïve in many aspects of their responses to predators than are wild-reared individuals because of the difficulty in providing fully appropriate environments for behavioral development in captivity (see Miller et a. 1990, Biggens et al. 1998, van Heezik et al. 1999, Stoinski et al. 2003). Predation susceptibility during releases of other species has been related to both physical and behavioral attributes of released birds (Snyder et al. 1994, van Heezik et al. 1999), pre-release training and acclimation to predators and release sites (Ellis et al. 1978, Griffin et al. 2000, White et al. 2005), as well as to characteristics of the release sites, including the presence or absence of introduced predators (e.g., Cade and Jones 1993, Priddel and Wheeler 1994).

Solutions.—Potentially the most effective way to reduce predation on released birds would be to limit releases of captive-reared birds to releases of parent-reared birds accompanied by their parents, especially if their parents might be fully experienced in dealing with natural predators. Unfortunately, the opportunities for such releases are very limited.

However, to the extent that new recruits to the wild populations in the future may increasingly be youngsters that are parent-reared in the wild, one would predict that such problems could diminish over time.

At the Arizona release site, where elevated tree perches for roosting are largely absent, a policy has been implemented of closely monitoring newly released condors and making sure that they do not remain perched on the ground and vulnerable to predators overnight. This policy appears to have had some beneficial effect in reducing predation events. In addition, the recent predation loss of condor #267 in southern California suggests that susceptibility to predation may depend importantly on the health status of newly released birds. In this case the condor involved was evidently nutritionally stressed at the time of the event, and may have been especially vulnerable as a result. A policy of providing released birds with multiple and diverse feeding stations might reduce competition with other condors and potential predators such as Golden Eagles and minimize chances of birds failing to obtain enough food to maintain body condition and ability to avoid predation. Intensive, regular food provisioning of condors at a small number of closely located feeding sites has undoubtedly exacerbated the frequency of condor-predator interactions in all release areas. Apart from coyotes and Golden Eagles, mountain lions (*Felis concolor*), bobcats, and black bears have all been documented at condor provisioning sites. In southern California in 2002, frequent losses of condor food to black bears and frequent encounters between condors and other potential predators resulted in the establishment of two "permanent" sites protected by electric fencing to exclude mammalian predators. Losses of food and interactions with mammalian predators have since declined substantially. Similar protected feeding sites have been established at central California release areas, although interspecific competition for food, especially feral pigs, has remained seasonally problematic at the Big Sur release site in central California.

In view of the frequency of raven predation on condor eggs in the historic population, the continued high populations of ravens in release areas, and the recent case of raven predation documented in southern California, we also recommend reviving efforts to evaluate the effectiveness of taste-aversion conditioning in reducing threats of ravens to condor eggs (see discussion in Snyder and Snyder 2000). Potentially, such methodology could substantially reduce such threats at very low cost. Why raven predation on eggs appears so far to have been much less frequent in released populations than in the historic wild population is presently unclear, but merits study. Conceivably, it could relate to a recent absence of condors from their historic range (especially in Arizona) and an unfamiliarity of many contemporary resident ravens with condors and their egg-laying habits. Raven problems could potentially increase over time, if the current low frequency of interactions between the two species rises to the historic levels known for southern California.

In the near term, it appears that predation from all sources may represent a continued moderate threat to release efforts, and to what extent this threat can be reduced remains unclear. Since a variety of factors may be contributing to predation rates, there may be no single route for achieving a significant reduction in this problem. The goal should be one of achieving condor populations that are capable of existing in natural communities including a full complement of natural predators, and to this end we see no merit in general control programs to reduce or eliminate predator populations in release regions either in the short or long term. In most cases, benefits from predator removal could be expected to be temporary and local at best, judging from results in other control programs. The emphasis instead should be on efforts to improve the avoidance responses of condors to predators and to reduce the attractions of predators to condors by whatever effective and practical means can be devised.

Other sources of mortality.—Free-flying reintroduced condors have died from a variety of miscellaneous causes, including ingestion of ethylene glycol (Murnane et al. 1995) and drowning (Snyder and Snyder 2000). Three condors were never relocated following an intense fire that burned much of the Hopper Mountain National Wildlife Refuge, Ventura County, California, in 2003 (USFWS unpubl. data), and almost certainly perished in the fire. In addition, deaths of historical condors resulted from cyanide poisoning at a coyote trap (Snyder and Snyder 2000) and strychnine poisoning at predator baits (Miller et al. 1965). At the present time, there is no evidence that these sources of mortality constitute more than relatively low-level threats for reintroduced populations in the United States. However, strychnine is still widely used in ranching areas in Baja California, where condor reintroductions began in 2002 (J. Vargas verbally), and could become a significant problem there if condors begin to forage more widely in lowland areas distant from the release site in the Parque Nacional Sierra San Pedro Mártir. In addition, it is important to recognize that condor deaths from predator-poisoning incidents may sometimes be concealed by the parties doing the poisoning (see Snyder and Snyder 2000). The absence of recent documented incidents of such poisonings does not represent rigorous evidence that such mortalities are not still occurring, especially in view of the substantial number of condors that have not been recovered after death during the release program.

One further stress that has only just emerged as a mortality factor for condors is West Nile Virus. One wild-hatched nestling perished from this disease in southern California in 2005 (B. Rideout unpubl. data), the first documented death among released condors. The future impact of this disease on condor populations is difficult to predict at this stage but effects of the virus on other avian species, particularly raptors, have been on a low to moderate scale despite its prevalence in many species and some populations (Stout et al. 2005).

Solutions.—Presumably little can be done to prevent most miscellaneous causes of mortality because of their unpredictability in location and cause. The expense of attempting to correct most low-level threats may not justify the effort. Occasional losses of birds to fires can be expected to continue, especially in nesting areas. This threat was probably a relatively small one for the dispersed historic population, judging from the absence of confirmed mortalities to fire in the historical record (see Wilbur 1978, Snyder and Snyder 2000). However, the concentration of most or all of the individuals of a population in a single area, as has been the case in southern California over the last few years, apparently places condors at greater risk to large-scale, unpredictable events such as fire. Such risks appear to be inherent in a policy that maintains a heavy dependency of the birds on provisioned, lead-free food at a single site (e.g., Hopper Mountain NWR), but efforts to disperse the birds more widely would of course increase the risks of lead poisoning. Thus, the continuing failure to achieve a proper solution to the lead problem carries a variety of penalties.

Predator poisoning campaigns were probably a major source of condor mortalities historically, but whether any cases of such mortalities are continuing to occur is undocumented. To what extent more stringent regulation of predator poisoning might be needed is unknown. As indicated above, if such problems develop in the Baja California release, corrective actions may become necessary. In addition, prior to the documented nestling mortality in California in 2005, all captive and released condors, apart from wild-hatched nestlings, were vaccinated against West Nile Virus. Examination of antibody titers in captive-raised nestlings has suggested that nestlings gain temporary immunity to the virus from their vaccinated mothers for the first 2–3 months after hatching (C. Stringfield pers. comm.) and thus, such protection appears to be time dependent (i.e., passive immunity passed on from female to chick via the egg wears off over time as the chick grows). It is now likely that in the near term all wild-hatched chicks in California will be vaccinated during the nestling stage (1–2 months old) to ensure more lasting immunity. However, reliance on such intensive efforts may prove problematic on a long-term basis.

ACHIEVING ADEQUATE REPRODUCTION

Nest success.—The recent historic condor population exhibited a nest success rate of about 40–50% according to data from Koford (1953), Sibley (1968), and Snyder and Snyder (2000), and this rate appears to lie within the expected range for solitary vultures in other studies (Mundy 1982,

Jackson 1983, Mundy et al. 1992). Assuming achievement of this rate of success in releases, and assuming that 50–80% of adults might breed in any year (the rate documented in the 1980s), population stability would require no more than a 10% annual mortality rate (Meretsky et al. 2000). These parameters offer reasonable goals to be achieved in the release program, but are obviously interrelated so that exceeding goals in one aspect could allow deficiencies in others, within limits. In any event, overall nest success in releases has not yet equaled levels recorded in the historic population. In the two release populations showing breeding activity so far, nest success has been especially poor in southern California, where only 8% of eggs laid have resulted in fledged young (Mee et al. this volume). Results have been much better in northern Arizona where all nestlings hatched have fledged to date and 46% of known eggs have resulted in wild fledglings (Woods et al. this volume).

In northern Arizona, all known nest failures ($n = 6$) have occurred during incubation, apparently due to a combination of infertility, egg breakage during early nest attempts, and disruptions caused by multi-mate pairings. Detrimental effects of multi-mate pairings have been reduced by trapping one, or occasionally two, individuals in the pre-nesting phase and holding them long enough to allow a pair to nest and hatch eggs without interference. Nest success in Arizona has come close to fitting the scenarios required for population stability proposed by Meretsky et al. (2000), assuming survival rates and levels of breeding effort might also reach or exceed target levels in the long run. However, it is worth noting that no cases of nest failure due to egg predation by ravens have yet appeared in the Arizona population, despite presence of ravens in the nesting region. Should ravens in the region develop an interest in condor eggs comparable to that documented in the historic California population, nest success could decline significantly without intervention.

Most nest failures in southern California releases have occurred during the nestling stage, with only a single successful wild fledgling to date (Mee et al. this volume). Almost all nests and nestlings have been found to contain quantities of foreign material, principally man-made trash items, and trash ingestion has resulted in the death or removal of three nestlings. Thus, nest success in this population has been far lower than even the most pessimistic viable scenario proposed by Meretsky et al. (2000). Unfortunately, despite the critical importance of data collection at nests to record attendance patterns, feeding rates, the status of chicks, and predation attempts, no priority has been given to nest monitoring in southern California, resulting in an overall decline in nest site coverage over the last two years (2005–2006). Moreover, no experiments have so far been conducted with captives in an effort to gain a comprehensive understanding of the causes and cures for excessive trash ingestion.

Solutions.—In southern California, the most important proximate problem depressing nest success has been the feeding of trash to chicks. Why adult condors ingest and feed trash items to their chicks is as yet unresolved, but the offering of some increased calcium supplies at provisioning sites has not resulted in any obvious reduction in the tendency, suggesting it may not be a misdirected search for calcium sources as suggested by Snyder and Snyder (2000). However, it appears that the increased supplies of calcium at feeding sites in southern California were not provided systematically enough to afford condors adequate time or opportunity to use them to any significant degree (see Mee et al. this volume). For example, no calcium was provided in most years (2002–2004) prior to or during egg-laying when female condors may seek additional sources of calcium for egg formation.

Conceivably the problem could also be related to the current absence in the southern Californian population of the more typical wide-ranging foraging behavior of this species (see Meretsky and Snyder 1992), which has resulted from the condors' dependence on food provided at a single, predictable feeding station. Thus, the time available to condors for non-essential activities, coupled with their attraction to areas of human activity where such trash is abundant and obvious, may promote their propensity to search for and ingest trash. The absence to date of problems with trash-ingestion in the wide-ranging northern Arizona population suggests that both time-budget considerations as well as site characteristics could be important. Thus, the difference between the two populations might relate mainly to different amounts of time spent foraging and to the relatively pristine environment of the greater Grand Canyon area, as opposed to any basic differences in the propensities of condors in California to ingest trash.

Whether anything effective can be done to reduce the trash ingestion problem in California is uncertain, in part because causes of the problem are not surely known. Presumably efforts could be made to convert the population to its former, wide-ranging foraging habit to see if this might reduce the problem to acceptable levels. However, this effort could also increase the birds' exposure to lead-contaminated carcasses, which is at best trading one problem for another. Nevertheless, if such an effort were to solve the trash ingestion problem, this would be important information to gain in understanding causes of the problem and in designing ultimately successful releases.

Experiments are needed to determine why condors ingest trash (e.g., for calcium, or to satisfy other nutritional needs), and whether such behavior is related to stages of the breeding cycle. Such experiments might be most easily accomplished in a captive setting, where variables can be controlled. The apparent limitation of mortality to nestlings is especially intriguing, and might conceivably relate to more regular and efficient pellet egestion in adults. Although this difference is not well documented, it could presumably be readily evaluated in studies of captives. Knowledge of the timing and rate of bone mineralization in nestlings also is critical to gaining an insight into their calcium requirements (D. Houston pers. comm.). Such a study would require regular handling of nestlings (to carry out radiographs, etc.) and would require precise, meticulous data collection and analysis by suitably qualified nutritionists. The use of Andean Condor (*Vultur gryphus*) nestlings as surrogates for California Condors would avoid the risks posed by repeated handling and habituation to humans. Until the results of such a study are available, bone fragments could be provided directly to nests during the nestling phase. This might have a twofold effect: (1) providing an alternative nutritional resource to adults and chicks other than trash, and (2) acting to "swamp" any trash items regurgitated onto the nest cave floor by adults or chicks, making it more likely that chicks pick up and ingest bone rather than re-ingest debilitating trash items.

Detailed studies of nests in the release population in southern California suggest that nestlings have been receiving more irregular feedings than did nestlings in the historic population, a feature that may relate to the timing of food availability at feeding stations, and ultimately may be influencing the trash ingestion behavior of adults (Mee et al. this volume). Experimental and observational efforts looking for correlations between regularity and spacing of feedings and frequency of trash ingestion would be of considerable value.

Breeding effort.—Breeding effort, defined as the percentage of birds six years old and older in egg-laying pairs, ranged from about 50% to 80% in the historic wild condor population of the 1980s (Snyder and Snyder 2000), a rate similar to the percentage of breeding adults known for various normally-reproducing large Old World vultures (see Mundy 1982, Mundy et al. 1992, Blanco et al. 1997). By comparison, breeding effort in all reintroduced condor populations combined has declined from 50% to 29% (mean of 38%) from the year of first breeding in the wild in 2001 to the present in 2005 (A. Mee unpubl. data). Reasons for this decline appear to be various, and whether or not the decline will continue into the future is very difficult to predict. Of perhaps special concern is the fact that no confirmed breeding has yet been seen in the releases in central California despite the presence of adult birds of both sexes in this population since 2003 (six males and six females in 2006). In Arizona, breeding effort has remained below historical levels in all years since 2001, with the exception of 2003 (50%). In 2004, breeding effort was the lowest to date with only 31% of adults attempting to breed. Likewise in southern California, breeding effort declined to a low of 20% in 2003 and remained at or near the low end of the recent historical range in 2004 (55%) and 2005 (46%). In summary, breeding effort through 2005 has been below historical levels in most years in southern California (46%), central California (0%), and Arizona (36%).

Lower than expected levels of breeding effort in populations can result from a variety of factors, including poor nutritional status of birds, multi-mate pairings, and factors relating to small population size such as locally skewed sex ratios, limited mate choice, and mate incompatibility. In southern California, breeding effort has apparently been depressed by pair break-ups and a female-biased operational sex ratio (A. Mee unpubl. data). Thus, in 2003 only a single newly formed pair bred following the break up of all three pairs breeding in 2002 (two divorces and one break-up due to the loss of a pair member). In 2005, all adult males, except for one six-year-old condor, were either breeding or paired, and thus, unavailable to any unpaired females. In addition, it is important to note that two of three breeding pairs in this population in 2004 and 2005 were made up of first-order relatives (father–daughter, and brother–sister). Chronic pairing of close relatives in release populations could pose potential problems from a genetic standpoint (Adams and Villablanca this volume), for example the expression of detrimental recessive traits such as the fatal chondrodystrophy gene. Although only two birds are known to be carriers, the average probability of being a carrier (18%, see Ralls et al. 2000, Ralls and Ballou 2004) is higher than would be expected in an outbred population.

Solutions.—To the extent that depressed breeding effort has been due primarily to small population size effects, such as biased sex ratios and limited mate choice, there are grounds to be hopeful that breeding effort may increase as a function of increased population size, providing a general justification for achieving "critical mass" in sizes of release populations. However, the low levels of breeding effort seen so far, in spite of steadily increasing numbers of adult-aged birds in the wild, runs basically counter to this expectation, and we have concerns in particular about additional potential problems with weak and abnormal pair bonds that may be resulting from various aspects of rearing techniques (see discussion under *Abnormal Breeding Behavior* section below). In the short term, translocation of non-reproductive adults from one isolated population to another (e.g., males from northern Arizona to southern California where there are several non-reproductive females) should be considered. To the extent that both depressed breeding effort and depressed breeding success may be resulting from abnormal behavior of released birds, the most important solution may be the development of release techniques that result in more natural and normal behaviors in wild populations, as is discussed below.

Correcting human-oriented behavior.—California Condors are clearly highly intelligent and social birds in which learning from parents and peers plays a prominent role in the development of their behavior. The historic norms of behavior in condors, as documented by Finley (1906), Koford (1953), and Snyder and Snyder (2000), did not include chronic close interactions with humans or attractions to humans or human structures. Although the historic wild birds were often quite approachable by humans at their nests, they showed no appreciable tendencies to come into civilized areas, to perch on buildings, utility poles, or vehicles, or to land near humans and approach them curiously (J. Hamber pers. comm., Condor Information Service archives). In most contexts they were simply aloof from humans and in some cases, such as around carcasses, they tended to be quite wary of human approach. Historic condors would sometimes fly in to circle overhead and inspect people intruding on their range, much as they also would circle close over groups of cattle and sheep (possibly in a search for dead and dying food sources), but such behavior was not known to result in the condors landing near people and approaching them on foot. Only one historic instance is known of a condor entering an urbanized area, an immature that perched on a rock wall in Arroyo Grande, San Luis Obispo County (Smith and Easton 1964), and historic interactions of condors with human structures in rural environments were limited to a few cases of immatures landing near or on remote fire lookouts likely adjacent to their nests of origin (J. Hamber pers. comm.).

    In contrast, excessive human-oriented behaviors have been chronic, though irregular, in released populations, with frequent perching on buildings, vehicles, and other human structures; frequent curious approach of humans; and occasional vandalism of human property, such as tents, sleeping bags, roofing shingles, and windshield wipers on cars (see Snyder and Snyder 2000). The tendencies to approach people have almost certainly been exacerbated by people offering food to birds coming close to them, a situation reminiscent of problems that were once rampant with overly tame and overfed bears in Yellowstone National Park.

    Between 1992 and 2005, 34% of all condors released in southern California were retrapped and removed either permanently or temporarily from the wild for behavioral reasons. Only five condors in this population have been retrapped for behavioral reasons since 2000. Of these, three were re-released after short periods in captivity at the field site, while two others were re-released in 2001 and 2005 after 15 and 24 months, respectively, in captivity. However, the lower numbers of birds trapped in more recent years should not necessarily be interpreted as an indication of improved behavior in the southern California population, but rather a shift in the birds' focus from areas of human habitation (e.g., Pine Mountain Club near Frazier Park) to industrial or recreational sites with high human activity (e.g., the San Gabriel Mountains). In 2002 and 2003, condors frequented oil pads within and just outside of Hopper Mountain NWR on an almost daily basis for a period of some months beginning in late January. During this time, most of the population landed or attempted to land on oil pads as well as on oilrigs and vehicles.

Beginning in 2002, condors in this release also began visiting a developed site in the San Gabriel Mountains 45 km southeast of the release area where they evidently interacted with recreational users (especially hang-gliding enthusiasts). Subsequently, condors have returned to the site regularly, sometimes on a daily basis, often landing on human structures. This is also the site where condors may be picking up most of the trash items brought to nests (see Mee et al. this volume). On occasion, the whole condor population may be present at this site, including birds from the central California release populations. Furthermore, in 2005, one of the re-released condors from the historic population (AC9) and the only wild-fledged condor of the southern California reintroduced population began to frequent the site (Mee et al. this volume).

Behavioral patterns in the northern Arizona releases have been similar to those in southern California, and condors have been observed in areas frequented by people, such as on the South Rim of the Grand Canyon. Here, efforts have been most intensive to chase condors away from developed areas, with apparently positive results in some birds. However, interactions between condors and humans have been especially difficult to monitor away from the South Rim, and condors in this population still approach humans, while humans still approach condors at sites within Grand Canyon National Park (A. Mee pers. obs.).

Unfortunately, unlike in Arizona, there has been no truly systematic approach to the problem of condor–human interactions in southern California, despite a large commitment of time, funds and manpower to hazing. Thus, without personnel constantly present at problem sites, hazing is only intermittent and inconsistent, and responses to misbehaving birds are usually reactive (e.g., USFWS personnel following-up on reports from the general public). Even when biologists are present, condors have often been allowed to land on human structures (e.g., communications towers, buildings) before being hazed, and sometimes they have even been allowed to remain on structures unmolested due to limited manpower or because landing on structures has been perceived to be the lesser of evils compared to landing on roadside pull-outs and potentially interacting directly with people. Regrettably, there again has been no systematic collection of data to determine which birds are the most persistent offenders, which birds land first on structures, and the effects, if any, of hazing.

Attempts to reduce human-oriented behaviors in releases have been focused primarily on educating passers-by not to feed or handle condors; aversive conditioning with electrified mock power poles pre- and post-release; and hazing birds from human use areas, often coupled with use of water-soaker guns, followed in some cases by retrapping birds with especially problematic behavior. But in spite of some success with these efforts, condors in most releases still exhibit tendencies to come into close proximity to people and structures many years after their releases.

Efforts have also been made to reduce human-orientation problems by improving pre-release experience of juvenile condors through parent rearing in zoos, and through rearing of birds in the presence of unrelated adult "mentor" birds (see Clarke et al. this volume). But although condors given such early experience have often exhibited improved aversion to humans before release, they have in almost all cases been released into populations of birds exhibiting behavioral problems and have soon adopted the maladaptive behavioral patterns already existing in the released populations (but see Wallace et al. this volume). Thus, the full potentials of most improved rearing regimes have not been adequately tested because the results have been confounded by interactions with poorly behaving birds. More recently, condors reared by puppets and later socialized with mentors have been released into the wild in a remote region of Baja California, Mexico, a region not inhabited by other released condors and nearly free of human structures and urban areas (Clark et al., Wallace et al. this volume). The success of this release remains to be seen, although to date the released condors apparently have not shown tendencies to seek out interactions with humans (Wallace et al. this volume).

Results were very different in experimental releases of Andean Condors to the wild in Peru, where captive-reared released birds, including hand-reared individuals, quickly adopted appropriate, aloof, species-typical behavior as they integrated into a healthy pre-existing wild population (Wallace and Temple 1987). Unfortunately, no such appropriately behaving wild population has been in existence in the U.S. or Mexico to channel the behavior of released condors into appropriate patterns. Although a number of condors from the historic wild population are still alive in captivity, releasing these birds as a group into the wild to serve as a nucleus of properly-behaving condors would have the obvious down-side that they could be expected to immediately readopt historic foraging patterns, rendering them susceptible to still-existing lead contamination problems. Three historic birds have been released as singletons in southern California in recent years (AC8, AC2, and AC9); two of these three birds died fairly quickly (3 and 35 months after release). AC8 was shot after barely surviving a case of lead poisoning, and AC2 died from as yet undetermined causes, while AC9 has recently shown a tendency to visit sites with high levels of human activity along with other birds in the population.

Unfortunately, the goal of obtaining full genetic representation of founding condors (Ralls and Ballou 2004), coupled with the current failure to remove the lead threat from the wild, has precluded a combined release of all historic, wild-experienced condors in captivity to form a critical mass of properly-behaving birds that could provide a "norm" of good behavior for other released birds. While efforts have been made to minimize the contact of pre-release birds with humans through the use of different rearing techniques (i.e., puppet-rearing, some parent-rearing, and more recently, mentoring of puppet-reared chicks by adult condors; Clarke et al. this volume), the release program has continued to rear condors in building-like structures, and the birds have not been completely isolated from human contact or the sights and sounds of human activity. As a consequence, it is perhaps not too surprising that many condors have shown strong attractions to humans and human structures on release, especially in the absence of opportunities for them to join a population of properly behaving condors. A reliance on artificial rearing techniques such as puppet-rearing and rearing young with "mentor" adults, rather than with their parents, has resulted in large part because of a commitment towards multi-clutching of birds to maximize reproductive rates in captivity. Neither puppet- nor mentor-rearing closely mimics the normal interactions of parents with young. These interactions are normally extensive in condors (Koford 1953, Snyder and Snyder 2000). However, in the rearing programs, adult mentors engage in relatively few interactions with the pre-release young placed with them, and do not, for example, feed or preen such birds as would parent condors (see Clark et al. this volume).

Multi-clutching has been invaluable from a demographic and genetic standpoint in rapidly increasing the size of the captive population (Kuehler and Witman 1988) and ensuring adequate representation of all founding family lines in succeeding generations (Ralls and Ballou 2004). However, multi-clutching entails a continuing commitment to non-parental rearing of a large fraction of young produced. With the substantial size of the present captive population (146 birds as of December 2005), and attention turning increasingly toward achieving proper behavior after releases, some observers (e.g., Meretsky et al. 2000) have called for a phase-out of routine multiple-clutching efforts, and a commitment to consistent parent-rearing in naturalistic enclosures set in field environments. In species with extended periods of parental care such as the condor (i.e., six months pre-fledging and about another six months post-fledging), depriving young birds of normal parental interactions may result in behavioral deficiencies that may later affect survival and reproduction in the wild (e.g., see Curio 1996, McLean 1997, McDougall et al. 2005).

Solutions.—To objectively evaluate the effects of improved rearing environments for pre-release birds on post-release behavior, condors will need to be released into wild environments where their behaviors cannot quickly be corrupted by misbehaving birds. However, because condors in southern California now have frequent contact with condors in central California, and may soon have contact with condors in Baja California, the opportunities to experiment with and improve behaviors of released birds may soon be lost in the whole region. In view of the many continuing problems with human-oriented behaviors of condors, it is regrettable that no attempts have been made as of yet to experiment with much more thoroughly naturalistic rearing and release methods, attempting to match what happens in the wild as closely as possible by using consistent parent-rearing in naturalistic field enclosures that have no close resemblance to rectangular human structures. Such methods, as well as avoiding all human contact with released birds where possible, housing breeding pairs in separate enclosures apart from other pairs, and allowing only parental contact with progeny through to the fledgling stage, were some of the principal recommendations developed at a 1994 USFWS workshop that was convened to design methods to counter behavioral problems that were becoming chronic in condor releases (Anonymous 1994). Work towards a more naturalistic rearing method for puppet reared young at the Los Angeles Zoo, prompted by apparent behavioral and developmental advantages of similar aged parent reared young, has demonstrated the potential benefits of replicating normal parental behavior as closely as possible (see Clark et al. this volume). Similarly, the most naturalistic parent reared methods possible, short of birds reared in nests in the wild, are likely to produce the best release candidates with a full behavioral repertoire acquired from their parents. Some preliminary evidence suggests that young that are somewhat retarded in acquiring behavioral skills in captivity are also likely to be those birds that become problematic on release to the wild, necessitating intensive monitoring and, often, returns to captivity (see Bukowinski et al., Wallace et al. this volume). Thus, it seems likely that young reared by their parents in settings mimicking natural situations would not only produce well adjusted young most likely to succeed in the wild but would also reduce the intensive monitoring and recapture efforts needed for problematic individuals documented in many previous release cohorts.

To create the most promising chance for achieving a naturally behaving population of condors, we also suggest that the historic, wild condors still alive in captivity should be released to form a nucleus of role-model condors for other released birds to emulate, and that all other birds released in the future be parent-reared in field enclosures closely resembling cliff caves. However, the lead contamination problems that precipitated bringing all condors into captivity in the 1980s still persist, making it likely that some or all historic wild birds would be lost to lead poisoning over time in such a combined release. Clearly the prospects for success in such a release hinge crucially on a full solution to the lead contamination problem, and the longer such a solution is delayed, the less likely it will be that a release utilizing the full behavioral potentials of the remaining historic captives will be possible before all such condors die of old age in captivity. We do not recommend the initiation of such a release until a full solution to the lead problem is achieved. The last condors from the historic wild population still in captivity represent an irreplaceable behavioral resource that simply should not be squandered.

In the near term, however, it makes sense to at least attempt releases in which birds are parent reared in as fully a naturalistic manner as possible to determine if this methodology can succeed in producing wild birds lacking significant attractions to humans and human structures even without properly behaving adults present in the wild as mentors. Absolutely crucial in such releases is the avoidance of physical and visual contact of released birds with humans or human structures prior to and immediately following release. Also crucial is that such releases be conducted in regions remote from civilization where contact between newly-released condors and condors from previous releases cannot occur, so that results from the use of new techniques can be evaluated properly. Also important is maximizing the numbers of parent-reared condors available for such releases. To this end parental pairs in naturalistic breeding efforts should not be multi-clutched, although they could receive fostered fertile eggs from other sources in the event they lay infertile eggs.

Correcting abnormal breeding behavior.—In addition to human-oriented behaviors, early releases have also been characterized by a number of problems related to pair formation and pair maintenance. Pairs in the historic wild population were very stable over time, with birds taking on new mates only when their former mates had died. Further, no instances were observed of groups larger than pairs attempting to nest (see Snyder and Snyder 2000). Yet, as discussed above, the releases in California and Arizona have yielded a number of instances of divorced pairs and of formation of multi-mate breeding groups (trios and one quartet). The exact causes of such apparently abnormal breeding results are speculative, and while they are often dismissed as just a result of inexperience, the absence of similar observations for the historic wild population suggests the existence of basic behavioral problems resulting from aspects of captive-rearing techniques.

We are particularly concerned about the possibility that abnormal breeding characteristics may be traced to (1) many birds failing to experience normal parent-chick interactions in development, and (2) the practice of grouping pre-release juveniles together in common cages prior to release. The free association of pre-fledging or recently fledged juvenile condors with other similarly aged juveniles does not normally occur in nature. However, in the current captive-breeding program, even when captive condors have been parent-reared or introduced to adult mentors after puppet-rearing (see Clark et al. this volume), they are usually placed in groups with other young condors prior to release. In nature, broods invariably consist of single chicks that associate only with their parents until some time after fledging. Hartt et al. (1994) have called attention to pairing problems in young condors reared together under captive conditions, potentially an example of the widespread Westermarck effect, an incest-avoidance mechanism (see Westermarck 1891, Harvey and Ralls 1986). Thus, rearing and release practices may inadvertently limit the options for "acceptable" pairings among released birds, potentially leading to weak pair bonds and frequent pair split-ups, and depressed breeding effort. Whether placing youngsters together in pre-release groups might also be an important cause of the odd multi-individual breeding groups seen in release populations and the lack of breeding activity seen in some wild birds has not been investigated, but these hypotheses deserve consideration.

   Solutions.—As of yet no releases have been attempted that have allowed pre-release fledglings to associate only with their parents to see if better socialized birds with enhanced breeding behavior might result. This strategy, if coupled with consistent rearing in naturalistic field enclosures, as suggested in the previous section, might produce birds with a close-to-full repertoire of normal interactions with parents and without those behaviors produced by exposure to other birds prior to the time fledglings normally begin to interact with other unrelated condors (see Clark et al. this volume). Although multi-mate pairings and frequent divorce may be partly a result of small population size and restricted mate choice, no such pairing anomalies were seen in the recent historical population despite its small population size (Snyder and Snyder 2000). Two potential homosexual pairs were seen in the historic population, possibly a result of sex ratio imbalance, but surviving members of both pairs later paired heterosexually and successfully, indicating no permanent, aberrant pairing problems (Snyder and Snyder 2000).

   Correcting abnormal foraging behavior.—In an effort to ensure adequate food for released condors and to minimize lead contamination in released birds, condors in all releases in California, Arizona, and Mexico have been provided with a food subsidy of clean carcasses, mostly stillborn calves obtained from dairies. Such carcasses have usually been offered at a small number of sites relatively close together, and have been readily used by the birds. Conversely, when carcasses are placed in unpredictable and increasingly widespread locations, they can promote normal foraging behavior in released condors, but the trade-off in doing so is an increased risk of lead contamination in birds discovering hunter-shot carcasses during searches for food. However, when carcasses are placed in predictable locations and at predictable intervals, this management strategy may result in release populations abandoning tendencies for normal wide-ranging foraging behavior, as has been seen in the southern California releases in recent years. As mentioned above, condors in this release population now spend very little of their time in wide-ranging foraging activities, in contrast to normal wild populations, and it is these same birds that have shown some of the worst problems with trash ingestion and human interactions, perhaps in part as a result of their having too much time to frequent civilized areas and engage in activities unrelated to basic biological needs.

Thus, food subsidy has been associated with several other problems, such as trash ingestion, that may be traced to birds not engaging in normal foraging activity. Predictability in the provisioning and frequency of food at condor "restaurants" also promotes an unusual degree of sociality among individuals that might otherwise forage more widely and more independently of other condors in the population (see Meretsky and Snyder 1992). Thus, it is not unusual for all condors in the southern California population to be present together at a single feeding site on a particular day (A. Mee unpubl. data), although this was never observed in the historic population. Ultimately, the goal of releases should be populations exhibiting normal foraging behavior, an activity that occupied a large fraction of the time budgets of historic wild condors (Plate 29).

Solutions.—Clearly, a failure to remove the lead-contamination problem has presented the release program with two unsatisfactory alternatives regarding foraging behavior: (1) either an emphasis on food subsidy which preempts normal foraging behavior and may be a major factor leading to a variety of other problems, or (2) an emphasis on getting condors off subsidy, which promotes normal foraging behavior but also leads to frequent lead poisoning. The way out of this paradox is clear, although challenging: first, solve the lead contamination problem effectively, and then work toward developing normal foraging behavior in released birds. Once condors are foraging normally, the behavioral problems associated with food subsidy and frequent handling of birds may decrease to a major extent.

Safeguarding Habitat in the Condor Range

Preserving critical habitat.—Fortunately, much of the present condor nesting range is located on publicly owned land, principally within National Forests in California; National Parks or Bureau of Land Management lands in northern Arizona; and the Parque Nacional Sierra San Pedro Mártir, Baja California Norte, Mexico. Much of the present foraging range of condors released in Arizona is also on publicly owned land, such as Grand Canyon National Park, the Kaibab National Forest, and to a lesser extent,

Zion National Park in southern Utah (see Hunt et al. this volume). Further, current land use patterns and human densities do not appear to negatively impact condors in Arizona and southern Utah. In contrast, the potential remaining foraging range of condors in southern California is primarily private land and the quality of these lands for condors has declined ever since European settlers arrived in the late 19th century. Loss of quality occurred first with the extirpation of native ungulate populations in the Central Valley, followed by conversion of many former grazing lands to agricultural crops, and then recently, with the greatly increased urbanization of many regions. Livestock grazing operations, formerly mostly sheep and later cattle, replaced wild carrion as the main source of condor food in the foothills of the Central Valley and other areas in the 19th century (Koford 1953, Miller et al. 1965, Wilbur 1978). However, recent years have seen a steadily continuing decline in the number of grazing operations and a steadily increasing loss of foraging habitat to housing developments.

Perhaps the most significant potential loss of prime foraging habitat is currently threatened by proposed future conversion of a substantial portion of the Tejon Ranch in the Tehachapi Mountains, Kern County, to housing development, despite its designation as critical habitat for condors. Apart from the direct effects of habitat loss on potential food supplies, further encroachment of humans on this pivotal foraging area offers many additional threats to condors, ranging from increased risk of shooting to collisions with powerlines. The Tehachapi Mountains are located on what was once the major flyway for condors moving between the coastal Transverse Ranges and the southern Sierra Nevada in the historic population (Meretsky and Snyder 1992). Thus, degradation of this area is an especially severe threat to reconstituting a viable wild population in California.

Solutions.—Conservation of foraging habitat in southern California is essential if a viable, self-sustaining condor population is eventually to be achieved and maintained in that region. Cumulative losses from habitat degradation and/or alteration, such as switching of land-use away from livestock grazing, will undoubtedly impact condors negatively in the long term, even if condor populations are currently far below the carrying capacity of available food resources. If the critical habitat designation is to mean anything, then the existing area designated as critical habitat should indeed be protected from development and degradation, and not compromised away through political expediency.

The acquisition of additional foraging habitat by public and private conservation organizations should be encouraged as a high priority. Likewise, the negotiation of management partnerships or agreements with private landowners (e.g., conservation easements) has the potential to help preserve adequate amounts of condor foraging habitat into the future. In particular, efforts to expand lands already under considerable protection in the Wind Wolves Preserve, the Bittercreek NWR, and the nearby Carrizo Plain National Monument, probably represent the best hope for the long-term maintenance and protection of a viable wild condor population in southern California. Management of the Tejon Ranch to maintain and promote the conservation value of this area for condors is a crucial component of this effort. Likewise, the long-term viability of condor populations in central California demands the development of strategic planning to maintain and expand protection for areas crucial as foraging habitat.

Controlling oil development.—The Sespe Sanctuary, a focal region for condor nesting by historic and released condors, has come under renewed threats from oil development, despite relatively meager oil reserves believed to exist in the region (<0.5% of the total annual output of the U.S.). Thus, oil from this region represents an apparently negligible contribution to meeting the country's energy needs and will likely do nothing of significance to reduce the dependence of the country on foreign oil sources, an argument widely invoked to support drilling in sensitive protected areas. Nevertheless, the U.S. Forest Service has recently identified 52,000 acres as areas of high oil and gas potential for expanded drilling in regions adjacent to the Sespe Sanctuary and Hopper Mountain NWR (USFS 2005). Indeed, one of the proposed new drilling areas encompasses the site of an active condor nest in 2005! The immediate consequences of drilling in the region can be expected to be increased human traffic leading to increased interactions between condors and people, drilling pads, and structures, and increased risks of collisions with utility lines. Oil pads are also frequently littered with trash and are suspected as the source of some of the trash items brought to condor nests and ingested by nestlings in recent years. Indeed, one pair that nested within 1 km of an active oil pad in 2004 may have been directly disturbed at the nest by extremely loud and constant noise from drilling over a period of 1–2 weeks (J. Hamber pers. obs). This pair rarely left the Hopper area during the chick phase but suffered repeated nest failure (2003, 2004, and 2005) with chicks ingesting large quantities of trash in all years (Mee et al. in press). Pollution of creeks in the southern California condor range due to leaks of oil from pipes and machinery also pose risks to condors drinking or bathing (Plate 30). On one occasion in 2002, a condor adult returning to a nest to brood and feed its chick had oil on its head, presumably obtained from a nearby-oil pad (A. Mee pers. obs).

Thus, ironically, despite the condor's status as a federally protected endangered species and the identification of the Hopper Mountain NWR as critical habitat for condors, this area and nearby lands are already some of the most industrially developed in the whole of the condor range, containing a high density of active oil pads and other infrastructure, as well as numerous roads and powerlines. Such developments seriously undermine the long-term compatibility and viability of such areas for condor populations. Despite this, condors continue to be released into this area, and the existing southern California population is maintained on food subsidy within 0.5 km of the nearest oil pad and roads carrying oil tankers and other oil-related equipment.

Solutions.—Further oil development should be tightly controlled and restricted to areas not normally frequented by nesting or foraging condors. Existing oil operations within or near protected areas should be required to remove all debris and maintain clean, trash-free sites as part of their licenses to operate, and compliance with such requirements should be comprehensively monitored. Although U.S. Forest Service and oil drilling operators in the Hopper Mountain NWR area have attempted to do this, maintaining sites free of all trash and other debris is difficult to achieve. The concentration of optimal nest sites in the Sespe region demands maximal efforts to maintain this region as a viable portion of the condor range.

Summary

The goal of achieving viable wild populations of condors exhibiting behaviors typical of historic condors has so far been elusive, despite many encouraging aspects of the condor recovery program. Captive breeding of condors has been highly successful, and threats of immediate extinction of the species have declined enormously. At least certain release populations have shown a strong tendency to occupy historic nesting regions and to initiate breeding activity, suggesting that viable wild populations may well be an attainable goal. Nevertheless, the behavioral problems of released birds and problems with lead poisoning in particular have so far defied adequate solution, while continued habitat loss and degradation threaten the long-term potential of conserving a population in southern California in particular. Results to date are particularly discouraging for the establishment of a viable population in southern California, given high mortality, very poorly behaving birds, and an almost total failure of released condors to successfully fledge young. Results as yet are too incomplete to analyze most aspects of the releases in central California and Baja California. Although mortality rates have been relatively low at both these sites, the former has yet to have any breeding attempts, and problems with lead contamination may well increase with time in both populations as has been seen in releases elsewhere. Relatively successful breeding in the northern Arizona released population gives hope that this region may ultimately support a viable population of condors, but released condors in this region have had special difficulties with lead poisoning and have exhibited much of the bad behavior typifying releases in California. These problems need full correction in all release locations.

Overall, we believe that despite the many problems outlined in this chapter, population recovery and viability of the California Condor in the wild is still possible, but probably will not occur unless the key problems outlined in this review are corrected. Of overriding importance is a full solution to the lead contamination problem, which not only promises unacceptable mortality rates into the distant future but chronic behavioral problems in condors due to the endless process of having to save them from contamination. These problems cannot be expected to go away spontaneously and demand timely and courageous corrective actions by all personnel and organizations involved in condor conservation.

Major Recommendations

1. Highest priority needs to be given to the removal of the lead threat from condor range, both to achieve adequate survival rates and to facilitate achievement of proper behavior in released birds. We believe that the most practical strategy for achieving this end is a complete replacement of lead ammunitions by non-toxic alternatives. Primary components of a campaign to remove this threat should emphasize education of the public regarding the risks to human health and to wildlife that are intrinsic to continued use of lead ammunitions, and regarding the benefits of alternative ammunitions, coupled with a campaign to rapidly phase out lead ammunitions through legal or legislative means that do not impose burdensome financial penalties on hunters.

2. There needs to be a revival of the premise that the condor release program is still primarily a "research" program, rather than a "management" program. To make this possible, the program would benefit substantially from addition of staff researchers highly qualified in interpretation of field data and design of experimental techniques, both in zoo and field contexts. Many of the ongoing problems in the program are still far from solution and would benefit from the initiation of well-designed experimental testing of alternative techniques that represent fundamentally new approaches. In our view, the most promising release techniques to solve ongoing behavioral problems have not yet been tested, although recommended by concerned parties for more than a decade. Ongoing releases should not be viewed as permanent programs, but as initial efforts to be fully replaced by better designed efforts when they do not yield satisfactory results.

3. Continued breeding failure and behavioral problems in southern California necessitate a review of the future of releases in this area. In the absence of major progress to correct problems, a time limit of perhaps three to five years should be set before existing birds in the wild are returned to captivity and fundamentally new release strategies instituted. A primary component of such new releases should be the testing of release

methods designed to mimic natural wild rearing as closely as possible, such as parent rearing, no or minimal contact of pre- and post-release birds with humans, avoidance of contact of pre-release birds with condors other than their parents, and avoidance of contact of pre- or post-release birds with obvious rectangular human structures or human activities. Absolutely essential for such testing is the siting of naturalistic rearing facilities far from zoo and city environments. Further, releases from rearing facilities must be conducted in regions where the birds cannot come into contact with condors released under other rearing regimes.

4. Assuming the lead contamination problem is solved in a timely fashion through termination of the use of lead ammunitions, strong consideration should be given to a combined release of the last survivors from the historic wild population to serve as a nucleus of birds with memories of proper foraging behavior and hopefully historic tendencies to avoid interactions with humans and human structures, much as was seen in the release of AC8. These birds could be released into their historic range and into an environment free of misbehaving condors, followed by introductions of additional condors resulting from naturalistic rearing techniques into the same population. Such a scenario may provide some possibility of establishing a viable population of condors in southern California. Most of the remaining birds from the historic population once had breeding sites in remote portions of the region, and other historically active nests distant from urban areas could make attractive sites for naturalistic breeding and release enclosures.

5. Other new initiatives that should be considered include:
   a. Identification of crucial areas where marking and burial of overhead utility wires could significantly reduce risks of collisions, and development of practical means to reduce these risks.
   b. Development of improved means to increase predator wariness of released condors.
   c. Testing of raven taste-aversion methodology to prevent egg predation on breeding wild condors.
   d. Experimentation to gain a better understanding of the causes and prevention of trash-ingestion in breeding condors and their nestlings.
   e. Enhanced protection of officially identified critical habitat, and development of protection for other key areas of foraging habitat in southern and central California.

6. To facilitate an evaluation of the full extent of continuing threats from lead-poisoning, predator-poisoning, shooting, and other factors, efforts to track movements of released condors through radio-telemetry must be expanded to significantly reduce the surprisingly large numbers of condors dying without recovery and to greatly reduce the numbers of birds recovered too long after death to allow comprehensive necropsy. The

removal and analysis of feather and bone material from all condors where the cause of death is not otherwise established at necropsy should become standard protocols. High-resolution analysis of growing feathers (see Fry and Maurer 2003), and stable-isotope analysis of feather and bone to determine the levels and source of heavy metal contamination, offer potentials for resolving causes of death in some cases. Continued and comprehensive tracking of sources of mortality in released birds is absolutely essential to the success of the program.

7. As a general strategy, progress toward major goals would likely be greatly enhanced through adoption of a policy of regular and rigorous outside review of all aspects of the release program by world-class ecologists, ethologists, and other experts who are completely independent of the condor program. Such an independent review has been instituted to identify critical problems affecting recovery of endangered species such as the Kakapo (*Strigops habroptilus*), resulting in a restructuring of that species' recovery program and the formation of a team to integrate research and management, overseen by an advisory panel of independent scientists and technical experts (Clout and Merton 1998). Independent review has served the condor program very well in the past (see Ricklefs 1978, Verner 1978) and can be expected to provide valuable guidance in the future.

ACKNOWLEDGMENTS

Many people have contributed significantly over the years to recovery efforts for the California Condor. Studies of the species biology vital to its conservation began in earnest with Carl Koford in the 1930s and 1940s, following by Alden Miller, Ian and Eben McMillen, Fred Sibley, John Borneman, and Sandford Wilbur in the 1960s and 1970s. Our greatest debt of gratitude goes to those who contributed much to field research and rescue efforts for the historical population in the 1980s including: V. Apanius, B. Barbour, P. Bloom, D. Clendenen, G. Falxa, J. Grantham, E. Johnson, J. and H. Hamber, L. Hecht, J. Ingram, S. Kimple, D. Ledig, V. Meretsky, J. Ogden, S. Pletschet, R. Ramey, L. Riopelle, B. Roberts, J. Schmitt, and H. Snyder. Others have contributed valuable and critical work in establishing and maintaining highly successful captive breeding populations including: M. Clark, C. Cox, M. Cunningham, C. David, M. Jenkins, S. Kasielkie, and D. Sears (Los Angeles Zoo); C. Kuehler, A. Kumamoto, T. Levites, D. Lindburg, M. Mace, A. Risser, D. Sterner, W. Toone, and M. Wallace (Zoological Society of San Diego); R. Townsend (World Center for Birds of Prey, Boise). Many highly skilled veterinarians provided critical medical care for condors in both captivity and in the wild, especially J. Allen, P. Ensley, B. Gonzales, D. Janssen, J. Oosterhuis, G. Kuehn, A. Shima, C. Stringfield, and J. Zuba. Pathologists at the San Diego Zoo performed numerous necropsies and played a critical role in determining the cause of death of condors, especially M. Anderson, R. Papendick, and B. Rideout. Still others have been involved in the reintroduction and re-establishment of populations in the wild including: G. Austin, M. Barth, D. Clendenen, J. Grantham, and M. Hall (southern California); J. Burnett, J. Koening, and K. Sorenson (central California); C. Porras, J. Vargas, and M. Wallace (Baja California, Mexico); S. Farry, T. Lord, C. Olson, S. Osborn, and C. Parish (northern Arizona). Ultimately, full success of the recovery effort and conservation of the species in the wild still lies ahead but much progress has been made, thanks to the tireless efforts of these people and many others.

LITERATURE CITED

ADAMS, M. S., AND F. X. VILLABLANCA. 2007. Consequences of a genetic bottleneck in California Condors: A mitochondrial DNA perspective. Pages 35–56 in California Condors in the 21st Century (A. Mee and L. S. Hall, Eds.). Series in Ornithology, no. 2.

ANDERSON, W. L., S. P. HAVERA, AND B. W. ZERCHER. 2000. Ingestion of lead and non-toxic shotgun pellets by ducks in the Mississippi Flyway. Journal of Wildlife Management 64:848–857.

ANONYMOUS. 1994. Ad-hoc meeting to address status of California Condors. Conservation Biology 8:942.

BIGGINS, D. E., J. L. GODBEY, L. R. HANEBURY, B. LUCE, P. E. MARINARI, M. R. MATCHETT, AND A. VARGAS. 1998. The effect of rearing methods on survival of reintroduced black-footed ferrets. Journal of Wildlife Management 62:643–653.

BLANCO, G., F. MARTÍNEZ, AND J. M. TRAVERSO. 1997. Pair bond and age distribution of breeding Griffon Vultures *Gyps fulvus* in relation to reproductive status and geographic area in Spain. Ibis 139:180–183.

BREWSTER, U. C., AND M. A. PERAZELLA. 2004. A review of chronic lead intoxication: an unrecognized cause of chronic kidney disease. American Journal of the Medical Sciences 327:341–347.

BUKOWINSKI, A. T., F. B. BERCOVITCH, A. C. ALBERTS, M. P. WALLACE, M. E. MACE, AND S. ANCONA. 2007. A quantitative assessment of the California Condor mentoring program. Pages 197–212 in California Condors in the 21st Century (A. Mee and L. S. Hall, Eds.). Series in Ornithology, no. 2.

BUSE, A., S. J. DURY, R. J. W. WOODBURN, C. M. PERRINS, AND J. E. G. GOOD. 1999. Effects of elevated temperature on multi-species interactions: the case of pedunculate oak, winter moths, and tits. Functional Ecology 13:74–82.

CADE, T. J., AND C. G. JONES. 1993. Progress in restoration of the Mauritius Kestrel. Conservation Biology 7:169–175.

CHAMBERLAIN, C. P., J. R. WALDBAUER, K. FOX-DOBBS, S. D. NEWSOME, P. L. KOCH, D. R. SMITH, M. E. CHURCH, S. D. CHAMBERLAIN, K. J. SORENSON, AND R. RISEBROUGH. 2005. Pleistocene to recent dietary shifts in California Condors. Proceedings of the National Academy of Sciences USA 102:16707–16711.

CHURCH, M. 2005. Sources of lead exposure in California Condors. M.S. thesis, University of California, Santa Cruz, CA.

CLARK, M., M. P. WALLACE, AND C. DAVID. 2007. Rearing California Condors for release using a modified puppet-rearing technique. Pages 213–226 in California Condors in the 21st Century (A. Mee and L. S. Hall, Eds.). Series in Ornithology, no. 2.

CLOUT, M. N., AND D. V. MERTON. 1998. Saving the Kakapo: the conservation of the world's most peculiar parrot. Bird Conservation International 8:281–296.

CRAIG, T. H., J. W. CONNELLY, E. H. CRAIG, AND T. L. PARKER. 1990. Lead concentrations in Golden and Bald eagles. Wilson Bulletin 102:130–133.

CURIO, E. 1996. Conservation needs ethology. Trends in Ecology and Evolution 11: 260–263.

ELLIS, D. H., S. J. DOBROTT, AND J. G. GOODWIN. 1978. Reintroduction techniques for Masked Bobwhites. Pages 345–354 in Endangered Birds: Management Techniques for Preserving Threatened Species (S. A. Temple, Ed.). University of Wisconsin Press, Madison.

FERRER, M., AND F. HIRALDO. 1991. Evaluation of management techniques for the Spanish Imperial Eagle. Wildlife Society Bulletin 19:436–442.

FINLEY, W. L. 1906. Life history of the California Condor I. Finding a condor's nest. Condor 8:135–142.

FRY, D. M., AND J. R. MAURER. 2003. Assessment of lead contamination sources exposing California Condors. Final Report to the California Department of Fish and Game, Sacramento.

GARCELON, D. K. 1997. Effects of organochlorine contaminants on bald eagle reproduction at Santa Catalina Island. Unpublished Report to U.S. Fish and Wildlife Service, Sacramento, California.

GOLDSTEIN, T., S. P. JOHNSON, A. V. PHILLIPS, K. D. HANNI, D. A. FAUQUIER, AND F. M. D. GULLAND. 1999. Human-related injuries observed in live stranded pinnipeds along the central California coast 1986–1998. Aquatic Mammals 25:43–51.

GRANTHAM, J. 2007. Reintroduction of California Condors into their historic range: the recovery program in California. Pages 123–138 in California Condors in the 21st Century (A. Mee and L. S. Hall, Eds.). Series in Ornithology, no. 2.

GRIFFIN, A. S., D. T. BLUMSTEIN, AND C. S. EVANS. 2000. Training captive-bred or translocated animals to avoid predators. Conservation Biology 14:1317–1326.

HALL, M., J. GRANTHAM, R. POSEY, AND A. MEE. 2007. Lead exposure among reintroduced California Condors in southern California. Pages 139–162 in California Condors in the 21st Century (A. Mee and L. S. Hall, Eds.). Series in Ornithology, no. 2.

HARMATA, A. R., G. J. MONTOPOLI, B. OAKLEAF, P. J. HARMATA, AND M. RESTANI. 1999. Movements and survival of bald eagles banded in the Greater Yellowstone Ecosystem. Journal of Wildlife Management 63:781–793.

HARMATA, A. R., AND M. RESTANI. 1985. Environmental contaminants and cholinesterase in blood of vernal migrant Bald and Golden Eagles in Montana. Intermountain Journal of Sciences 1:1–15.

HARTT, E. W., N. C. HARVEY, A. J. LEETE, AND K. PRESTON. 1994. Effects of age at pairing on reproduction in captive California Condors (*Gymnogyps californianus*). Zoo Biology 13:3–11.

HARVEY, P. H., AND K. RALLS. 1986. Do animals avoid incest? Nature 320:575–576.

HAVERA, S. P., C. S. HINE, AND M. M. GEORGI. 1994. Waterfowl hunter compliance with nontoxic shot regulations in Illinois. Wildlife Society Bulletin 22:454–460.

HUNT, W. G., W. BURNHAM, C. N. PARISH, K. BURNHAM, B. MUTCH, AND J. L. OAKS. 2006. Bullet fragments in deer remains: implications for lead exposure in scavengers. Wildlife Society Bulletin 34:168–171.

HUNT, W. G., C. N. PARISH, S. C. FARRY, AND T. G. LORD. 2007. Movements of introduced California Condors in Arizona in relation to lead exposure. Pages 79–96 in California Condors in the 21st Century (A. Mee and L. S. Hall, Eds.). Series in Ornithology, no. 2.

INOUYE, D. W., B. BARR, K. B. ARMITAGE, AND B. D. INOUYE. 2000. Climate change is affecting altitudinal migrants and hibernating species. Proceedings of the National Academy of Sciences USA 97:1630–1633.

JACKSON, J. A. 1983. Nesting phenology, nest site selection, and reproductive success of Black and Turkey Vultures. Pages 245–270 in Vulture Biology and Management (S. R. Wilbur and J. A. Jackson, Eds.). University of California Press, Berkeley.

JANSS, G. F. E., AND M. FERRER. 1998. Rate of bird collision with power lines: effects of conductor-marking and static wire-marking. Journal of Field Ornithology 69:8–17.

JANSSEN, D. L., J. E. OOSTERHUIS, J. L. ALLEN, M. P. ANDERSON, D. G. KELTS, AND S. N. WIEMEYER. 1986. Lead poisoning in free-ranging California Condors. Journal of the American Veterinary Medical Association 189:1115–1117.

KANNAN, K., K. S. GURUGE, N. J. THOMAS, S. TANABE, AND J. P. GIESY. 1998. Butylin residues in Southern Sea Otters (Enhydra lutris nereis) found dead along California coastal waters. Environmental Science and Technology 32: 1169–1175.

KELLY, A., AND S. KELLY. 2005. Are Mute Swans with elevated blood lead levels more likely to collide with overhead power lines? Waterbirds 28:331–334.

KENDALL, R. J., T. E. LACHER, C. BUNCK, B. DANIEL, C. DRIVER, C. E. GRUE, F. LEIGHTON, W. STANSLEY, P. G. WANTANABE, AND M. WHITWORTH. 1996. An ecological risk assessment of lead shot exposure in non-waterfowl avian species: upland game birds and raptors. Environmental Toxicology and Chemistry 15:4–20.

KOFORD, C. B. 1953. The California Condor. National Audubon Research Report 4: 1–154.

KRAMER, J. L., AND P. T. REDIG. 1997. Sixteen years of lead poisoning in eagles, 1980–95: an epizootiologic view. Journal of Raptor Research 31:327–332.

KRONE, O., T. LANGEMACH, P. SÖMMER, AND N. KENNTNER. 2003. Causes of mortality of white-tailed sea eagles from Germany. Pages 211–218 in Sea Eagle 2000 (B. Helander, M. Marquiss, and W. Bowerman, Eds.). Proceedings of the Swedish Society for Nature Conservation/SNF, Stockholm, Sweden.

KUEHLER, C. M., AND P. N. WITMAN. 1988. Artificial incubation of California Condor Gymnogyps californianus eggs removed from the wild. Zoo Biology 7:123–132.

LANDRIGAN, P. J., AND A. C. TODD. 1994. Lead poisoning. Western Journal of Medicine 161:153–159.

LE BOEUF, B. J., AND M. L. BONNELL. 1971. DDT in California sea lions. Nature 234: 108–110.

LE BOEUF, B. J., J. P. GIESY, K. KANNAN, N. KAJIWARA, S. TANABE, AND C. DEBIER. 2002. Organochlorine pesticides in California sea lions revisited. BMC Ecology 2:11.

LEHMAN, R. N. 2001. Raptor electrocution on power lines: current issues and outlook. Wildlife Society Bulletin 29:804–813.

LESHAM, Y. 1985. Griffon Vultures in Israel—electrocution and other reasons for a declining population. Vulture News 13:14–20.

McDOUGALL, P. T., D. RÉALE, D. SOL, AND S. M. READER. 2005. Wildlife conservation and animal temperament: causes and consequences of evolutionary change for captive, reintroduced, and wild populations. Animal Conservation 9:39-48.

McLEAN, I. G. 1997. Conservation and the ontogeny of behavior. Pages 132–156 *in* Behavioral Approaches to Conservation in the Wild (J. R. Clemmons and R. Buchholz, Eds.). Cambridge University Press, Cambridge, U.K.

MEE, A., J. A. HAMBER, AND J. SINCLAIR. 2007. Low nest success in a reintroduced population of California Condors. Pages 163–184 *in* California Condors in the 21st Century (A. Mee and L. S. Hall, Eds.). Series in Ornithology, no. 2.

MEE, A., B. A RIDEOUT, J. A. HAMBER, J. N. TODD, G. AUSTIN, M. CLARK, AND M. P. WALLACE. 2007. Junk ingestion and nestling mortality in a reintroduced population of California Condors *Gymnogyps californianus*. Bird Conservation International 17:1–13.

MERETSKY, V. J., AND N. F. R. SNYDER. 1992. Range use and movements of California condors. Condor 94:313–335.

MERETSKY, V. J., N. F. R. SNYDER, S. R. BEISSENGER, D. A. CLENDENEN, AND J. W. WILEY. 2000. Demography of the California Condor: implications for reestablishment. Conservation Biology 14:957–967.

MILLER, A. H., I. McMILLAN, AND E. McMILLAN. 1965. The current status and welfare of the California Condor. National Audubon Society Research Report 6:1–61.

MILLER, B., D. BIGGINS, C. WEMMER, R. POWELL, L. CALVO, L. HANEBURY, AND T. WHARTON. 1990. Development of survival skills in captive-raised Siberian polecats (*Mustela eversmanni*) II: predator avoidance. Journal of Ethology 8: 95–104.

MUNDY, P. J. 1982. The Comparative Biology of Southern African Vultures. Academic Press, London.

MUNDY, P., D. BUTCHART, J. LEDGER, AND S. PIPER. 1992. The Vultures of Africa. Academic Press, London.

MURNANE, R. D., G. MEERDINK, B. A. RIDEOUT, AND M. P. ANDERSON. 1995. Ethylene glycol toxicosis in a captive-bred released California condor (*Gymnogyps californianus*). Journal of Zoo and Wildlife Medicine 26:306–310.

O'HALLORAN, J., A. A. MYERS, AND P. F. DUGGAN. 1989. Some sub-lethal effects of lead on Mute Swans *Cygnus olor*. Journal of Zoology (London) 218:627–632.

OTTO, D. A., AND D. A. FOX. 1993. Auditory and visual dysfunction following lead exposure. Neurotoxicology 14:191–207.

PARISH, C. N., W. R. HEINRICH, AND W. G. HUNT. 2007. Lead exposure, diagnosis, and treatment in California Condors released in Arizona. Pages 97–108 *in* California Condors in the 21st Century (A. Mee and L. S. Hall, Eds.). Series in Ornithology, no. 2.

PATTEE, O. H., P. H. BLOOM, J. M. SCOTT, AND M. R. SMITH. 1990. Lead hazards within the range of the California Condor. Condor 92:931–937.

PRIDDEL, D., AND R. WHEELER. 1994. Mortality of captive-raised malleefowl, *Leipoa ocellata*, released into a mallee remnant within the wheat-belt of New South Wales. Wildlife Research 21:543–551.

RALLS, K., AND J. D. BALLOU. 2004. Genetic status and management of California Condors. Condor 106:215–228.

RALLS, K., J. D. BALLOU, B. A. RIDEOUT, AND R. FRANKHAM. 2000. Genetic management of chondrodystrophy in California Condors. Animal Conservation 3:145–153.

RICKLEFS, R. E. (ED.) 1978. Report of the advisory panel on the California Condor. National Audubon Society Conservation Report 6:1–27.

ROBINSON, C. S. 1939. Observations and notes on the Califiifornia Condor from data collected on Los Padres National Forest. U.S. Forest Service, Santa Barbara, California.

ROBINSON, C. S. 1940. Notes on the California Condor, collected on Los Padres National Forest, California. U.S. Forest Service, Santa Barbara, California.

ROSS, P., R. DE SWART, R. ADDISON, H. VAN LOVEREN, J. VOS, AND A. OSTERHAUS. 1996. Contaminant-induced immunotoxicity in harbour seals: wildlife at risk? Toxicology 112:157–169.

SAMUEL, M. D., AND E. F. BOWERS. 2000. Lead exposure in American Black Ducks after implementation of non-toxic shot. Journal of Wildlife Management 64:947–953.

SARRAZIN, F., C. BAGNOLINI, J. L. PINNA, E. DANCHIN, AND J. CLOBERT. 1994. High survival estimates of Griffon Vultures (*Gyps fulvus fulvus*) in a reintroduced population. Auk 111:853–862.

SCHOLIN, C. A., F. GULLAND, G. J. DOUCETTE, S. BENSON, M. BUSMAN, F. P. CHAVEZ, J. CORDARO, R. DELONG, A. DE VOGELAERE, J. HARVEY, M. HAULENA, K. LEFEBVRE, T. LIPSCOMB, S. LOSCUTOFF, L. J. LOWENSTINE, R. MARIN III, P. E. MILLER, W. A. MCLELLAN, P. D. R. MOELLER, C. L. POWELL, T. ROWLES, P. SILVAGNI, M. SILVER, T. SPRAKER, V. TRAINER, AND F. M. VAN DOLAH. 2000. Mortality of sea lions along the central California coast linked to a toxic diatom bloom. Nature 403:80–84.

SCHULZ, J. H., J. J. MILLSPAUGH, B. E. WASHBURN, G. R. WESTER, J. T. LANIGAN III, AND J. C. FRANSON. 2002. Spent-shot availability and ingestion on areas managed for mourning doves. Wildlife Society Bulletin 30:112–120.

SHARPE, P. B., AND J. DOOLEY. 2001. Restoration and management of Bald Eagles on Santa Catalina Island, California, 2001. Unpublished Report to U.S. Fish and Wildlife Service, Sacramento, California.

SIBLEY, F. C. 1968. The life history, ecology and management of the California Condor (*Gymnogyps californianus*). Annual Progress Report Project No. B-22. U.S. Fish and Wildlife Service, Patuxent, Maryland.

SIBLEY, F. C. 1969. Effects of the Sespe Creek Project on the California Condor. U.S. Fish and Wildlife Service, Laurel, Maryland.

SMITH, D., AND R. EASTON. 1964. California Condor, Vanishing American. McNally and Loftin, Charlotte, NC.

SNYDER, N. F. R. 2007. Limiting factors for wild California Condors. Pages 9–34 *in* California Condors in the 21st Century (A. Mee and L. S. Hall, Eds.). Series in Ornithology, no. 2.

SNYDER, N. F. R., S. E. KOENIG, J. KOSCHMANN, H. A. SNYDER, AND T. B. JOHNSON. 1994. Thick-billed parrot releases in Arizona. Condor 96:845–862.

SNYDER, N., AND H. SNYDER. 1991. Birds of Prey. Voyageur Press, Stillwater, Minnesota.

SNYDER, N. F. R., AND H. A. SNYDER. 2000. The California Condor: A Saga of Natural History and Conservation. Academic Press, San Diego, CA.

SNYDER, N. F. R., AND H. A. SNYDER. 2005. Introduction to the California Condor. California Natural History Guides, University of California Press, Berkeley.

SORENSON, K. J., AND L. J. BURNETT. 2007. Lead concentrations in the blood of Big Sur California Condors. Pages 185–195 in California Condors in the 21st Century (A. Mee and L. S. Hall, Eds.). Series in Ornithology, no. 2.

STOINSKI, T. S., B. B. BECK, M. A. BLOOMSMITH, AND T. L. MAPLE. 2003. A behavioral comparison of captive-born, reintroduced golden lion tamarins and their wild-born offspring. Behaviour 140:137–160.

STOUT, W. E., A. G. CASSINI, J. K. MECCE, J. M. PAPP, R. N. ROSENFIELD, AND K. D. REED. 2005. Serologic evidence of West Nile Virus infection in three wild raptor populations. Avian Diseases 49:371–375.

SULLIVAN, K., R. C. SIEG, AND C. PARISH. 2007. Arizona's efforts to reduce lead exposure in California Condors. Pages 109–122 in California Condors in the 21st Century (A. Mee and L. S. Hall, Eds.). Series in Ornithology, no. 2.

VAN HEEZIK, Y., P. J. SEDDON, AND R. F. MALONEY. 1999. Helping reintroduced houbara bustards avoid predation: effective anti-predator training and the predictive value of pre-release behaviour. Animal Conservation 2:155–163.

VERNER, J. 1978. California Condors: status of the recovery effort. General technical report PSW-28, U.S. Forest Service, Washington, D.C.

VISSER, M. E., A. J. VAN NOORDWIJK, J. M. TINBERGEN, AND C. M. LESSELLS. 1998. Warmer springs lead to mistimed reproduction in Great Tits (Parus major). Proceedings of the Royal Society of London, Series B 256:1867–1870.

WALLACE, M. P., M. CLARK, J. VARGAS, AND M. C. PORRAS. 2007. Release of puppet-reared California Condors in Baja California: Evaluation of a modified rearing technique. Pages 227–242 in California Condors in the 21st Century (A. Mee and L. S. Hall, Eds.). Series in Ornithology, no. 2.

WALLACE, M. P., AND S. A. TEMPLE. 1987. Competitive interactions within and between species in a guild of avian scavengers. Auk 104:290–295.

WESTERMARCK, E. A. 1891. The History of Human Marriage. MacMillan, London.

WHITE, T. A., JR., J. A. COLLAZO, AND F. J. VILELLA. 2005. Survival of captive-reared Puerto Rican Parrots released in the Caribbean National Forest. Condor 107: 424–432.

WIEMEYER, S. N., J. M. SCOTT, M. P. ANDERSON, P. H. BLOOM, AND C. J. STAFFORD. 1988. Environmental contaminants in California Condors. Journal of Wildlife Management 52:238–247.

WILBUR, S. R. 1978. The California Condor, 1966–1976: a look at its past and future. U.S. Department of the Interior, Fish and Wildlife Service, Washington, D.C.

WOODS, C. P., W. R. HEINRICH, S. C. FARRY, C. N. PARISH, S. A. H. OSBORN, AND T. J. CADE. 2006. Survival and reproduction of California Condors released in Arizona. Pages 57–78 in California Condors in the 21st Century (A. Mee and L. S. Hall, Eds.). Series in Ornithology, no. 2.

YLITALO, G. M., J. E. STEIN, T. HOM, L. L. JOHNSON, K. L. TILBURY, A. J. HALL, T. ROWLES, D. GREIG, L. J. LOWENSTINE, AND F. M. D. GULLAND. 2005. The role of organochlorines in cancer-associated mortality in California sea lions (Zalophus californianus). Marine Pollution Bulletin 50:30–39.